Cardinal

The Rise And Fall Of George Pell

Louise Milligan

EasyRead Large

Copyright Page from the Original Book

MELBOURNE UNIVERSITY PRESS
An imprint of Melbourne University Publishing Limited
Level 1, 715 Swanston Street, Carlton, Victoria 3053, Australia
mup-info@unimelb.edu.au; www.mup.com.au

First published 2017; reprinted with corrections 2017
Text © Louise Milligan, 2017
Design and typography © Melbourne University Publishing Limited, 2017

This book is copyright. Apart from any use permitted under the *Copyright Act 1968* and subsequent amendments, no part may be reproduced, stored in a retrieval system or transmitted by any means or process whatsoever without the prior written permission of the publishers.

Every attempt has been made to locate the copyright holders for material quoted in this book. Any person or organisation that may have been overlooked or misattributed may contact the publisher.

Thanks to Tim Minchin for permission to reproduce lyrics from 'Come Home (Cardinal Pell)' on pages 129 and 134; to Bill Callahan for permission to reproduce lyrics from 'Cold Blooded Old Times' on page 235; and to Dr Richard Sallie, for permission to reproduce his *Sydney Morning Herald* Letter to the Editor on page 132.

Text design and typesetting by Megan Ellis
Cover design by Philip Campbell Design
Printed in Australia by McPherson's Printing Group

National Library of Australia Cataloguing-in-Publications entry
    Milligan, Louise, author.
    Cardinal: the rise and fall of George Pell/Louise Milligan.

    9780522871340 (paperback)
    9780522871357 (ebook)

    Pell, George.
    Catholic Church—Australia—Bishops.
    Catholic Church—Australia.
    Cardinals—Australia.
    Bishops—Australia.
    Child sexual abuse by clergy—Australia.

If the content of this book brings up issues for readers, for help or information call:
Lifeline: 131 114
Broken Rites: (03) 9457 4999
beyondblue: 1300 224 636
Centres Against Sexual Assault: 1800 806 292

TABLE OF CONTENTS

AUTHOR'S NOTE	iii
1: THE KID	1
2: LORD HIGH EVERYTHING ELSE	9
3: THE AUXILIARY	43
4: THE FIXER	74
5: A TWEETER BEFORE TWITTER	105
6: TOWARDS HEALING?	126
7: BIG GEORGE	163
8: SOUTHWELL	182
9: EMINENCE	215
10: TWO COUNTRY COPS	248
11: ON DEFENCE OF THE INDEFENSIBLE	262
12: A SAD STORY THAT WASN'T OF MUCH INTEREST	295
13: EDENHOPE	323
14: MORTLAKE	344
15: ALL THE BISHOP OF BALLARAT'S MEN	369
16: DOUBT	410
17: OPERATION PLANGERE	444
18: DOVETON	469
19: THE BIRD	490
20: THE LAST DAYS OF ROME	521
21: EUREKA	539
22: AFTER 'THE GAME'	580
23: THE SURF CLUB	607
24: ON CREDIBILITY	630
25: BREEN	659
26: THE CHOIRBOYS	686
LIST OF PEOPLE	731

ACKNOWLEDGEMENTS	748
BACK COVER MATERIAL	750
Index	753

'This is in part a story of a notable Prince of the Church, a staunch defender of Vatican authority. It is also a heartbreaking tribute to the children abused within his circle, and both before and during his time of authority—knowledge of which he denies, as is his legal right. But above all, *Cardinal* introduces new evidence indicating that as engrossing as this account may be, George Pell's career has not yet taken its final direction.'

Tom Keneally

For my Dad, a fine man and a believer

AUTHOR'S NOTE

All references to the 'Royal Commission' indicate the Royal Commission into Institutional Responses to Child Abuse.

All references to the 'Victorian parliamentary inquiry' indicate the Inquiry into the Handling of Child Abuse by Religious and Other Organisations by the Victorian Parliament's Family and Community Development Committee.

1

THE KID

I first meet The Kid at a local RSL. An unprepossessing place, of mission-brown bricks, set back on a treeless lawn from a grimy street. Inside, it's lit with a green fluorescent glare. Grey carpet, slightly sticky red vinyl chairs, walls adorned with military crests, fighting guns and lists of the dead. A television blares sport in the corner. And, in the middle of the ceiling, among it all, glitters a single, incongruous disco ball.

The Kid loves this place. He's working the bar. He's of medium build, not tall, with big chocolate-drop eyes framed with curling lashes. He has PTSD eyes, although he does his level best to hide them with humour. I've seen them before and I'll see them again and again before this thing ends—brown, green, blue, big, small, smiling, bloodshot. PTSD eyes somehow have the look of a dog that's been left alone outside for weeks in a yard that's been concreted over. PTSD are quick to tears.

The ageing locals who have come to dance twostep out the back of the RSL club all know him by name. He knows what everyone drinks. As his hand flick-flick-flicks the beer tap, gold and beaded with condensation, filling a pot, he looks at me, part bashful, part sceptical.

He's working there for a few shifts to fill in while he's doing his university exams. He says he's got one tomorrow and I feel sick, apologising for the timing. He's nervous and we're both conscious of the weirdness of the situation. We strike up an immediate rapport, but he's deeply wary. Every time he opens up, he shrinks back again. At times he talks in riddles. I don't take notes as a gesture of goodwill. He wants to know how I found him, who is my source?

'If I told you who my sources were, you wouldn't trust me with what you tell me. I need people to know that I won't burn them and I won't give away their names to anyone else.'

'The thing is, I've got trust issues. I would trust you more if you just told the truth,' he says.

I tell him I'm sorry and that an investigative reporter wouldn't last long in this game if she started doing that.

He looks at me and says, 'I know you are an investigative journalist—I know the work you do, I watch your show every night and I think you are excellent at what you do. If I was going to talk to anyone, it would be you, but I just can't. Don't you understand? This is really serious.

'This is about me and it's about him. That's all I can say. And by "him" I don't mean Pell.'

'Are you saying that George Pell wasn't your abuser?'

'No. I'm not saying that. I'm not saying anything at all. Just that it's about me and it's about him. That it's important. You have to understand, I have a good life, I love my community, I'm the good guy, the guy that everyone can count on. But my mental health is hanging on by an absolute thread.' He pinches his finger and thumb together. 'The only thing that is keeping me together is the idea of his head on a platter. But I'm not saying any more. Now you know I'm the guy. Okay? I'm the guy. I'm the guy. I've given you that. That's more than anyone else knows. No-one else has found me. But that's it. That's all I'm saying. That's more than I'll tell anyone else, but I'm not saying any more.'

His mum and her partner turn up. My stomach hits the floor. She's going to tell me off for hassling her boy. I imagine myself as a mother in that situation. But they go into a back room and he follows them. I sit and wait, he's in there for a while. Reassuring them. I don't see them again.

'What do you know about me anyway?' he asks when he returns. I exhale deeply. I tell him that I know that there was another boy with him, but that's about it—I don't know any of his circumstances. He blanches at this. 'So you know? Fuuccck.' He presses down on the bar with his hands. He shakes his head. 'How do you know this? You need to tell me.'

'I know he's not living any more,' I gingerly admit. His eyes fix on me with a hard look for a second, then dart off to the side. 'And I'm really, really sorry,' I say softly.

He nods vigorously, the trauma now apparent, his jaw clenched, the snap of the beer tap now deliberate. He flick-flick-flicks and pours himself another schooner.

I sit there for a while and hope he'll fill the silence.

'Okay. You know that. Well, you'll know why this is so important to me. I can't fuck this up for some journalist, don't you understand that? As much as I like what you do and I respect you and I can see that I like you, I can't fuck that up for anything. It's too important.'

'I understand,' I tell him. 'I really do. Do you think that he'll ever come back? There's no extradition treaty with the Vatican. He's already said he has a heart condition. I'm just not sure it's ever going to happen.' I want to say more, but I can't snap this thread.

'That may well be true, I hope it's not,' he continues. 'But you've got to understand how important this is to me. I'm traumatised. I know I seem like I'm a happy-go-lucky guy, but it is a facade. This is the mask I wear every day and I'm really good at wearing it. But until the Taskforce comes and tells me that it's not a goer, I'm not talking to anyone. But if they tell me it's not happening, I'll come straight to your door.'

I tell him I am so sorry to put him through this. I say it's for a good cause. I tell him loosely what information I know, which to be frank, at that point, is scant. I say that I feel sad that the very thought of me may be triggering because I am now inextricably linked with the story of his childhood. I say I have been in that situation with others before and it saddens me because he's clearly such a decent guy.

He tells me that I am 'on the right track' and intimates that there is more to this.

'More than Pell? Another priest?'

My eyes widen and he looks like he's going to say more, but then he stops. He's shaking his head and looking at the ceiling. I tell him I'm sorry. He tells me to keep investigating. 'You have to keep going—there is so much more to this.' I say I won't hassle him.

We go outside for a while. He asks me more about what I know. I understand why—it would drive me nuts. I tell him I know about a witness, I know about his situation, I know that there are others. I don't know how many. I have heard there are lawyers with clients. I don't know anything about those clients, just that they exist. He keeps shaking his head, clenching his jaw, grinding his teeth.

At the end, I give him a hug and tell him to look after himself. We part on good terms. My heart's in my throat, but this is not that rush of adrenaline you get from a scoop. It's the feeling you get when you're a little kid and you lift up a rock in the yard and a whole lot of bugs scurry out and you throw it down. As I drive home through Melbourne's northern streets, streetlights flash a sickly green through my windscreen.

Across town, a little boy and girl have gazed out their bedroom window like they do every night and looked for their star. They have found it and blown it a kiss goodnight. Their star is their uncle, The Choirboy. He was there that day that changed The Kid's life. It changed his life too. Immediately and irrevocably and brutally. If, as The Kid had said in a sworn statement to Victoria Police's Taskforce SANO, The Choirboy knew George Pell's ugly secret, he carried it with him to his untimely grave. In May 2016, when I meet The Kid, he is thirty-two. His friend, The Choirboy, would have been the same age. But he's been dead two years.

2

LORD HIGH EVERYTHING ELSE

Probably the most popular actor was George Pell as Pooh-Bah, who sustained his part as Lord High Everything Else from start to finish with never a blemish and was responsible for many a laugh.

St Patrick's College annual, 1958

There he is, always in the middle of the back row. The eyes inevitably find their way to him. He is tall and he is handsome, towering above the others. He's rarely smiling, but then again, almost none of them are. His shoulders are broad, his hair shining and meticulously swept to the side. His eyes are wide set, clear chips of blue ice. Many of the others look like typical teenage boys—a little gormless, perhaps a bit pimply, with that pubescent thing where their teeth are ever so slightly too big for their heads. They're the sons of Bungaree potato farmers, country funeral merchants, the freckled youth of what was still a pretty small town. You flick through the St Patrick's College, Ballarat, annuals from the late 1950s and he's always there, always the young-man-most-likely. In among the appeals to Good Catholic Parents for funds, and the advertisements for 'Foot Rot and Foot Abscess Remedy for Sheep', he's there. Flick past the blurb for Harman Bros Catholic Emporium—'Devotional Requirements for the Church, School and Home'—and you'll find him. But George Pell doesn't look like he's from this place. Pell looks like a film star. There must have been some broken-hearted debutantes in Ballarat when Pell decided to go to the priesthood.

Here's George, thirds in the rowing; there's George, as school prefect. In his senior years at St Patrick's, he was on the committee for the literary society and the debating team. He forcefully argued as first speaker that the State Should NOT Provide Free Secondary Education for all. And yes, his team won. A talented footballer who 'used his height and weight in the ruck' and would ultimately be selected to play for Richmond in the Victorian Football League. One of his former classmates put it more bluntly: 'anyone in his way would get skittled'. See him sitting, turned out in white singlet emblazoned with a green shamrock, posing for the athletics team photo. His impressive dash in the hundred yards singled him out as one of two boys who helped St Pat's take home the Ballarat School Sports Championship *for the eighth successive year.* He won the prestigious Purton Oratory for two years running. He seemed drawn to matters of national pride. For 1958, his topic was 'Australia Fair', for 1959, 'An Australian'. He won a scholastic prize for Christian Doctrine, the Sir Hugh Devine prize for Impromptu Speaking, first prize at the Catholic Speechcraft Festival and was on the Our Lady's Sodality Executive. The devoted sons of the Blessed Virgin met every Friday. He was also in cadets. And he wasn't just *in cadets.* He was the Cadet Under Officer. While all the other boys in the 1958 photograph are standing, wearing berets, bare-handed, Pell is sitting in the middle, his fists clenched tightly on his lap in black leather gloves, wearing an officer's peaked cap. His expression suggests he is not to be messed with.

But they were salad days too. Young George starred in a school production of Gilbert and Sullivan's *The Pirates of Penzance.* 'George's superb acting and solo work singled him out as one of the best in the cast,' the 1957 annual declared. He can be seen dressed as a policeman, between two other boys, who are dressed as ladies, each motioning to kiss him on either cheek. Those were innocent years. The following year, the editor of the annual was even more gushing about George's role as a haughty and self-important nobleman, swathed in silken robes, in *The Mikado* (Gilbert and Sullivan operas were clearly all the rage in late-fifties Ballarat). 'Probably the most popular actor was George Pell as Pooh-Bah,' the annual's editor, the Reverend Brother FB Archer wrote, 'who sustained his part as Lord High Everything Else from start to finish with never a blemish and was responsible for many a laugh.' Lord High

Everything Else. Prophetic, one might think.

George Pell. Two short words, two soft syllables. George was a war baby—born on 8 June 1941. He shared his Christian name with the sitting King of the Commonwealth. He was much-wanted and much-loved—twin siblings had tragically died as babies before him. A sister, young Margaret, and a brother, David, followed him. His father, George Arthur Pell, was a goldmine manager who went on to own Ballarat's Royal Oak Hotel. The pub was built in 1866 and its architectural austerity, uncharacteristic of the Victorian goldrush town, was offset by the salmon pink and mint green of the paintwork on its facade. 'Always Buy Ballarat Bitter', a sign on the side of the building declared. 'Rich in Malt and Hops.' A working man's pub.

George Pell Senior was a heavyweight champion boxer and a non-practising Anglican, and from him it is said his son learned his pugilistic instincts and his street smarts. But George's mother Margaret Lillian (nee Burke) was of Irish Catholic stock and regarded her religion with a great piety. A portrait of the great and formidable Archbishop Daniel Mannix hung on the wall in the Pell home and Pell had an auntie who had been given Mannix as a middle name. Pell's official biographer, Tess Livingstone, wrote that every Wednesday Mrs Pell would attend the Novena to Our Lady of Perpetual Help with the local monsignor, Leo Fiscalini. Monsignor Fiscalini, as it happens, was to have a key role in Pell's life, and later not an altogether positive one, many years after the older priest's death. Like her son later would be, Margaret Pell was a student of the Catholic Democratic Labor Party (DLP) set up by politico-cultural warrior Bartholomew Augustine Santamaria, BA in his journalist by-line, Bob to his friends. Mrs Pell undoubtedly sent up many Hail Marys for young George—who had twenty-four operations to attempt to remove a growth in his throat. Livingstone says the stoic young Pell used his convalescence to become an avid reader. So even from that early stage, Margaret Pell saw greatness in her boy, and he did not disappoint.

While he was initially offered a professional football contract to play for Richmond, young Pell joined the minor seminary instead while still at St Pat's. Pell made it his mission to acquire as much knowledge as he could.

His bishop, James (or 'Jimmy' as some of his priests fondly called him) O'Collins, a former plumber who had risen through the ranks of the Church, had Pell marked out as special. Pell became head prefect at Corpus Christi seminary at Werribee on Melbourne's western fringe. One of the priests who went through the college said it was at that time a 'ghastly environment': an 'extremely regimented, authoritarian seminary and George fitted in perfectly'. And writing in the Jesuit journal *Eureka Street* in 1997, Pell's classmate Brian Scarlett remembers a strict regime—rising at 5.55a.m., being permitted nothing except water in between meals, no visitors at all allowed from the start of the seminary year until Easter, no radios and no newspapers, meals eaten in silence, lights out at 10p.m. There was a list of banned texts, including, for reasons other seminarians are at a loss to explain, Steinbeck's *The Grapes of Wrath.* Needless to say, copies were furiously smuggled in. 'Another irritant was the discovery that Fragonard's *The Swing,* a romantic piece of frippery in which a couple of gallants look at the ankles of a girl on a swing—had been excised from a book in the library,' Scarlett writes. The height of daring was to sneak out and hitchhike to Geelong for a cheeky hamburger, to short-sheet a guy's bed, or to carefully loosen the lid of a salt shaker in the hope that it might tumble out and spoil the unwitting victim's soup.

Another trainee priest at the time, Paul Costigan, who was a year above Pell, hated it. During that time, there were about two hundred and eighty students, thirty or so to a year level. The youngest of them slept in three dormitories, which were converted classrooms, eight beds to a dorm. 'It was absolutely freezing,' Costigan remembers. The salty water had rusted the pipes in the heaters, so they were permanently on the blink. 'It was the one advantage of wearing a soutane,'

Costigan says. 'You were covered from head to foot so it helped with the cold.' In order to cope, he would sneak out for cigarettes or hitchhike to Melbourne to the footy. 'There were times when I walked out to the front gate on my own and thought "what the hell am I doing here?"'

Costigan says they were treated like children and underlying much of it was a fear of sex—be it homosexual or heterosexual. One of the professors would caution his young charges to 'beware the Daughters of Eve', much to their private mirth. Costigan remembers a spiritual director whom they all called 'Duck Butt'. Duck Butt would give them a warning. 'He would tell us "be careful about going back to the parish tennis club",' Costigan, who was a tennis ace, remembers, 'and, he would say, "if you do, don't play mixed doubles" ... That was the sort of ridiculous advice we were given.'

The trainee priests were also discouraged to befriend each other with a 'No Particular Friendships' rule. 'I thought it was bullshit,' says one of Pell's contemporaries, Kevin Larkins.

'Intimacy was an issue which was not only avoided, it was spoken against.' As they got older and were allocated their own quarters, they weren't even allowed in each other's rooms. 'Looking back at it, there was a huge fear in the authorities of homosexuality,' Costigan says. Corpus Christi also had a *noli tangere* (Latin for 'no touching') rule. 'I used to joke that that's why we became such vigorous footballers,' Costigan says with a laugh. 'Because that was our chance to belt the daylights out of other students.'

Dr Michael Leahy, now a political philosopher who was two years behind Pell at Corpus Christi Werribee, says intellectually and socially the formation in the seminary fell short of need. 'It was not the kind of preparation for a life in the secular world that was obviously ideal,' Leahy says. 'The idea that you could pop out of this isolated incubator and feel at home with the realities of everyday secular life was an illusion.'

His classmate Larkins says the seminarians remained caught in a sort of 'underdeveloped adolescence'.

'There was a tension between the threat of misery and the expectation of happiness because of the fact you were committed to an austere and isolated way of life,' Leahy says. 'No relationships with women outside visiting days. There was always that element of sacrifice that was present in your life. But nobody compelled you to be there. You were there because you were committed to becoming a priest and achieving a high ideal.'

Having said that, all of the men I spoke to, even those from later years, remarked on the incredibly close bonds they formed with one another there. So much so, that they all regularly catch up through a group called the CCC (Corpus Christi College) Guys. Many of the CCC Guys never got to the stage of being ordained, or left the priesthood behind, but still feel the pull of their seminary mates.

Leahy says despite being an environment of learning, the syllabus was selective and incomplete. 'The study was slavishly dependent on the Catholic Church. It reduced philosophy and psychology to short chapters in a textbook. It reduced (intellectual) adversaries to one or two sentences of their position. It made no attempt to address the intellectual currents that were flowing through the world at the time.'

But as for Pell, well, Costigan says that he thrived at Corpus Christi. 'He revelled in it,' he says. 'The whole pomp and ceremony of it. Wearing the soutane all the time.' The seminarians said many were intimidated by Pell's hulking presence and he rather enjoyed his head monitor role. 'Look,' another tells me, 'George was known as "The Bully". He was a bully on the football field, he was a bully all round in life.'

'I never knew anyone who liked him,' Costigan says. 'But then, I probably never walked in those circles.' He confesses that he was never a fan either. 'I found him to be a very arrogant, overbearing, patronising type of person.' But Leahy says he rather liked Pell and found the strapping boy from Ballarat had a good sense of humour at that time despite their ideological and theological differences now. 'I was two years behind George at Werribee and [later] in Rome, and in many ways, we shared similar interests,' Leahy remembers. 'We were both intellectually inclined and reasonably good at sport. We were thrown together by conditions like that.'

Dr Brian Scarlett, who lectured in Philosophy at the University of Melbourne from 1975 to 2005, was in Pell's year and even shared a room with him for six months. He says Pell was always civil, they got along well and never had a cross word that he remembers. He and Leahy both think it's possibly an overstatement to call him a bully at that time.

'George was a rules man and I don't think he found it hard to be a rules man,' Scarlett remembers. 'He was a little censorious about those of us who had a more freewheeling attitude. I think he set his sights on a career in the clerical world very early on.'

Larkins, who was in Leahy's year, says Pell took his role as head prefect seriously. 'He did not take kindly to us and our attitude,' Larkins says of his year level. 'He thought we had no "year spirit"—you know, esprit de corps, like his mob supposedly did.'

Leahy says Pell then, as now, was 'up for any sort of challenge and he relished challenges, be they physical or intellectual'. 'It was a succeed-at-all-costs approach,' Leahy says. 'A great deal of his ego was built around living up to ideals and modelling himself on what he took to be heroic figures'.

'Once he set out in pursuit of a cause—whether it be possession of the ball on the football field or winning a debate, he was unstoppable.

'That was his style,' Leahy says. 'And that's how, rightly or wrongly, he earned his reputation of being a bully. He could be utterly ruthless in his pursuit of any objective he set himself or, more importantly, any objective that the institutions upon which he depended had set for him as an ideal to be pursued.'

One of the more memorable examples of George the Unstoppable was on the football field. Whatever the social niceties of Corpus Christi, they played their footy hard. Larkins, who went on to become a senior health bureaucrat and now runs executive leadership courses, says it was so bruising that he copped five dislocated shoulders and had to leave his playing days behind. He and many of the others say none played harder on the field than Pell. He and Leahy remember one day when Pell 'flattened' another bloke on the field. The other players were aghast.

Larkins was umpiring that day. 'George was like a behemoth,' he remembers, laughing, 'cutting a swathe through anyone who got in his way. And my whistle had absolutely no effect on him.' Leahy let Pell have it, and Larkins says 'Mick' pounced on Pell and, as the smaller of the two, was 'like a gnat on his back—George just shook him off'. Leahy says he then howled a series of expletives at Pell in defence of the player Pell knocked down. Leahy himself can't remember exactly what he said, only that the language was colourful. But Larkins does. He reckons Leahy called Pell a 'great cunt'. Larkins tried to stop the game, but he says Pell was having none of it.

In 2016, during an interview for Sky News with Andrew Bolt, Pell said something very telling about his football days. Bolt was quizzing him on his inability at times to show empathy and he referred to a 'dimension' of himself that might explain this. 'I wasn't a bad footballer,' Pell said.

'It sounds like you were a bit of a thug!' Bolt countered.

'Well, I was *very* fiery,' Pell replied. 'I've got a formidable temper which I almost never show. But the discipline that is needed for me not to lapse in that way, I think helps explain my wooden appearance.'

Leahy muses that young Pell was in fact a very 'vulnerable' person.

'I think it's a combination of his own psychology and that it's borne of the kind of education in which greatness was thrust upon him. Because he has always had greatness thrust upon him, he has never been given the opportunity to develop any independence of judgement and behaviour. Opportunities were fenced in by the institutions that gave opportunities to him.'

Pell's first cousin Henry ('Hank') Nolan had also gone to Corpus Christi earlier. Nolan would later retreat to the the Ballarat Diocese and would become a keeper of secrets. Nolan is now dead. Pell's close friend in the seminary was Denis Hart—now Archbishop of Melbourne and Pell's anointed successor. A tall, blond alumnus of the elite Melbourne Catholic boys' school Xavier College, his nickname was 'The Duke' and he is one of the few people the seminarians remember being really close to Pell.

There was a strange phenomenon around the time that Pell went through Corpus Christi—and the years preceding and following. The institution turned out a remarkable number of priests who turned out to be paedophiles. It is something that in equal parts devastates and stumps the men who went through with them. Not one says he was remotely aware that men who would go on to commit such evil lurked in their midst and most are at a loss to explain exactly why it happened. The best they can offer is that as a supposedly celibate lifestyle, it offered a cover for people who were already disordered and would, in their later work, provide easy access to children. They say that that collided with the monastic lifestyle, which turned out young men grossly unprepared for life in the real world and the pastoral duties of dealing with real people. The whole topic of sexuality was, some like Larkins say, dangerously off limits. 'If you look at the rest of the community, it is not comfortable with talking about death, but it talks about sex all the time. We were entirely comfortable with the notion of mortality, but we were not comfortable at all with the idea of sex.' The combination of those factors created, the former seminarians suppose, a perfect storm. But at the time of their priestly training, none got wind of anything untoward.

Ballarat's Gerald Ridsdale, probably the country's worst serial paedophile priest, was five years ahead of Pell. So too was Wilfred 'Billy' Baker—a priest in the Melbourne Archdiocese and, say his fellow seminarians, 'a nauseatingly pious creep', who was later convicted of seventeen counts of indecent assault and gross indecency over a 20-year period. Michael Glennon, who was a few years behind Pell, was convicted five times with fifteen victims. He was charged with ten further counts just nine days before he died.

Glennon's room-mate at the seminary was Terrence Pidoto—who went on to be convicted of eleven offences against four boys—although there were seven accusers. One was former altar boy Richard Jabara. Jabara told me that one night when he was a 13-year-old altar boy, Pidoto, by then a priest who had left the seminary years before, in fact took Jabara back to Corpus Christi to abuse him. He told Jabara, '"I'm going to take you where they make priests, which is a very special place, because you're a very special boy" and when I got there, there were five seminarians waiting for me in their underwear.' When young Jabara protested, Pidoto took him to the dining room. 'He said, "We're ... we're not going to leave until this is done".'

Bob Claffey was another Ballarat seminarian three years behind Pell at Corpus Christi—he's pleaded guilty to abusing fourteen children, although I personally know of more allegations against him. Like the others, he'll die in jail. Paul Goldsmith was also a few years behind Pell and the archbishop refused to ordain him. But he went on to teach at a Marist Brothers school in Tasmania and committed sex crimes against twenty boys. He ultimately fled in 2012 to Tanzania, where he died in 2016.

Then there was Anthony Salvatore Bongiorno, a relatively mature-age trainee who was in Pell's year and was something of a class clown. Tony Bongiorno was accused of abusing three boys in Melbourne. But, as was the case in many of the paedophile clergy trials, the Director of Public Prosecutions split the trials. Two juries, unaware of the other two complainants and given the historical nature of the case, acquitted Bongiorno. The third trial was thrown out, but the victims were later awarded Victims of Crime Compensation and payouts from the Church. Another intellectually disabled boy told police he was abused by Bongiorno, but his mother was murdered in a bookshop in

Thornbury before charges could proceed. In 2013, police re-opened the cold murder case and Bongiorno, who had died in 2002, was at first a suspect in that cold case. But the DNA did not match up and Victoria Police announced in 2016 that he was no longer in the frame.

Leahy, Costigan, Scarlett and Larkins all say Bongiorno (not to be confused with Paul Bongiorno, the Channel Ten political journalist who also went through Corpus Christi and later worked as a priest in the Ballarat Diocese) was very matey in the seminary with Pell. 'He was a good friend of George's and they were great repartee partners and very much enjoyed each other's company,' Leahy says. One seminarian in Pell's year seems to remember Pell and Bongiorno going on holiday together one summer. And when Pell was just entering his twenties, in the summers of 1961 and 1962, the seminarians remember that the pair volunteered at an altar boys' camp in Smiths Beach at Phillip Island. That was to become a fateful trip for Pell, but not for a good forty years, when it threatened to bring him undone. As Scarlett and many others note, paedophilia is by its very nature secret and none of them were to know. Pell also hotly denies that he too can be counted in the number of clergy abusers who went through Corpus Christi. His alumni find it hard to reconcile the idea of the Pell they knew as a child abuser. He just didn't seem the type.

Of course, at the time of writing, Pell, unlike the other seminarians, has never been charged or convicted of any crime. There is no legal judgement to prove that he isn't as horrified as the rest of his innocent alumni at the people that the likes of Bongiorno became. He has made public statements expressing his sorrow at what went on.

Reflecting on the sordid group of sinners who *have* been convicted of multiple crimes many years later, it occurred to Leahy that, oddly, the paedophile set seemed to cope much better in the seminary than the others did. Working in prisons many years later, Leahy bumped into one of them regularly who was by that time an inmate and he said the institutional nature of the criminal justice setting similarly suited this man.

Pell's classmates say that he, too, seemed very happy in the seminary although they had been equally convinced he was not, in the language they used at the time, 'a shirt lifter'. Whatever he was, he flew much higher than many of his fellow seminarians. He set a clear-eyed focus on achieving greatness in his Church. He was clearly in many ways a remarkable young man.

After Corpus Christi, Bishop O'Collins sent young George to Propaganda Fide university to study Theology. It was, as Archbishop Fisher later put it, 'Rome's finishing school for priests' and O'Collins was fond of sending his young charges there.

In the name of good fun, the seminarians had a sort of benign ritual for the guys they were sending off to the Holy City. After a footy match, they were thrown in a horse trough. Scarlett took photos of Pell and two other seminarians who were going to Propaganda being unceremoniously dunked. 'We didn't throw them into the horse trough at the same time,' Scarlett says with a chuckle. The photograph shows Pell, with a good-humoured look of dismay on his face, flat on his back in the trough, long, muscled legs akimbo, outstretched arms trying to lift himself out. But when Scarlett published it in 1997, along with pictures of two other seminarians who were given dunkings, with a droll piece about seminary days in the popular Jesuit magazine *Eureka Street,* 'George was not too happy,' he says. Pell was by then Archbishop of Melbourne. Scarlett was surprised as he meant no malice and the article was not about Pell—he had simply used the photograph as an illustration. The pair met at an academic function soon after 'and he said something about my being in rude health, with a heavy emphasis on *"rude",*' Scarlett says. 'Perhaps he thought the photograph detracted from his dignity as a bishop. If I thought about it at all, I might have considered that it could enhance his credit as a man for all seasons.'

I spoke to one of the other young priests who studied at Propaganda Fide at the same time. 'We all regarded

George as very, very ambitious,' said the former student of the university who was with Pell in the early 1960s. 'George always took himself very seriously. He was very pompous and arrogant.' Like some of the Corpus Christi seminarians, the Propaganda Fide student described Pell as a bully. 'He could be very cutting with people,' the former student said. 'He ignored day-to-day dialogue. And if you disagreed with him, he would put you down.'

Leahy followed Pell to Propaganda and they would sit in the same lecture theatres for half of their time there. There were two key theologians—one a conservative pre–Vatican II scholar, the other a young leader of the progressive movement that was sweeping the city and the world.

As Pell himself told the Royal Commission into Institutional Responses to Child Sexual Abuse fifty years later, the 1960s 'was a turbulent time' in the Church and society in general—with the introduction of the contraceptive pill provoking profound social change that filtered through to the young scholars.

The Second Vatican Council came to be known as 'Vatican II'. Called by Pope John XXIII, it was an ecumenical council of Catholic leaders—the first of its kind in a century—which sat between 1962 and 1965. It introduced sweeping changes designed to bring the Church into the modern world—such as the Latin mass being replaced for the first time with English or the local language.

Paul Costigan's brother Michael, who was also a Catholic priest but was a decade older than Paul and Pell, remembered meeting the 'very tall and handsome' Pell when he was sent as a journalist for a Catholic newspaper to cover the second Vatican Council. He remembers that it was an incredibly exciting time—it was, he says, the most exciting assignment he ever had.

Leahy was similarly thrilled by the revolutionary zeal. 'During that time, virtually all of us Australians went through a conversion from a pretty conservative political and theological viewpoint,' Leahy says. 'By the end of all of our time there we had undergone a total conversion politically and theologically. George, well he drank from the same well as the rest of us.

'He was a great ham. He would introduce us to the antics of the conservative theologian by taking him off in the most entertaining way. When George graduated from Rome, he had come closest he has ever come to achieving some liberation from the conservative views that had been thrust upon him.'

Pell himself remembered this many years later when giving evidence to the Royal Commission. 'There was a whiff of revolutionary spirit about,' the Cardinal recalled. 'A lot of good people decided to follow other paths,' he said, referring to the many trainee priests who abandoned their vocation either before or after ordination.

While Pell sniffed the wind, he did not go with the revolution. Young Pell, ordained a priest at St Peter's Basilica in December 1966 to the strains of Bach's *Fantasia in G,* would embrace rigid orthodoxy and reject the primacy of the conscience. And, like his old mentor and benefactor Bishop O'Collins, he embraced BA Santamaria.

Eric Hodgens, a retired priest of the Melbourne Diocese, says O'Collins sent Pell, whom he describes as a 'conservative warrior', to Oxford 'to get a doctorate in order to joust with the progressives on his return'. Pell's thesis was on 'The Exercise of Authority in Early Christianity from About 170 to 270'. 'Jim [O'Collins] wanted someone who could take on the likes of Max Charlesworth—a leading academic progressive voice,' says Hodgens. And how Pell thrived.

Pell was based at the Jesuit college of Campion Hall. His great friend at Oxford was an Anglican, Peter Elliott, who was, like Pell, another anti-communist Santamaria devotee. Elliott subsequently converted to Catholicism with Pell as his sponsor. Livingstone reports that in the 1960s on campus the firm friends were known by the Marxist set as 'The Big Australian Bastard' and 'The Little Australian Bastard'. The little one, Elliott, is now an auxiliary bishop of Melbourne. In 2015, Bishop Elliott told *The Age* he did 'consultancy work' in the field of exorcisms for Catholics who have been possessed by the devil.

In 1971, the publican's son returned to Ballarat with a doctorate in Philosophy from Oxford. 'I was one of the first, perhaps the first, Catholic priest to take a DPhil in the theology faculty since The Reformation,' Pell years later reminded the Royal Commission early in his evidence. The Reformation in the sixteenth century, that is.

The good burghers of Ballarat could not have been more proud of their favourite son. It's impossible to overstate how large this young man loomed in the town's consciousness upon his return.

Pell's brilliant career in the country diocese started modestly enough. It must have been a huge comedown for young Father Pell to be awarded a doctorate at Oxford and then to make his way to the tiny, isolated parish of Swan Hill at the north of Victoria's Western District, where he was appointed assistant priest. But by 1972–73, he was back in Ballarat, living at the presbytery of St Alipius, the

Ballarat East parish where his parents had been married. That was before St Alipius earned its reputation as the centre of a culture of rampant child abuse, both physical and sexual, by a ring of paedophile Christian Brothers and the predatory parish priest, Gerald Ridsdale.

Pell lived out his thirties and early forties there from 1973 to 1983. He infamously shared the presbytery with Ridsdale for a year and much has been made of the 'optics' of this, but even his harshest critics wonder what he could have known in a busy presbytery where there were constantly clerics and other visitors coming and going. Most priests think it is utterly simplistic to entertain the notion that he definitely knew what was happening there. Terry Laidler, who was also a priest in the 1970s but left the priesthood and became an ABC broadcaster, shares this view. 'It is quite plausible to me that he didn't know [what was going on in that house],' Laidler says. Laidler, too, had lived in busy presbyteries like St Alipius and says it was quite possible to hardly see the other priests at all.

Having said that, the presbytery was also next door to St Alipius Boys' School, where the paedophile brothers terrorised the children in their care. Pell later acknowledged he'd heard vague rumours about brothers being over-affectionate, such as kissing children on the lips. But he says that was it.

During those years, like the rest of his career, Pell packed an enormous amount of work and achievements into his life. Andrew Collins, a survivor of child sexual abuse in Ballarat, was a family friend of Pell's. His grandmother lived on the same street as Pell Senior's pub. 'I remember my grandmother, she used to work at the presbytery,' Collins recalls. 'She said to me, "If you ever have any trouble with the Church, George is the man to go to".'

Collins' friend, Peter Blenkiron—also a survivor of abuse in the diocese, in his case, at Pell's old school of St Patrick's—also remembers Pell well at both his primary school, Villa Maria, and his high school, St Pat's. 'Not only did he work the room,' Blenkiron says, 'he worked the diocese. He was in all the places all the time, getting well known, pushing himself.'

Pell became director of Aquinas College—the Catholic teachers' college. He was there for ten years and was considered an excellent administrator who boosted the profile of the campus enormously and enhanced its academic credentials.

'He has always been a politician—an ecclesiastical politician,' says Father Hodgens. 'His appointment [to Aquinas College] introduced him to wheeling and dealing with governments and unions.

'Ballarat's Aquinas College became a campus of the newly created Australian Catholic University with George as a key participant in the negotiations between Church and government.'

As one senior member of a religious order with similar academic qualifications to Pell noted to me, because Pell had not worked as an academic before, this would have been enormously challenging and busy work. That factor led the priest to believe Pell's much later evidence in the Royal Commission that he was too tied up with his work at

Aquinas to notice or have time to turn his mind to the sexual abuse crisis that was unfolding in the diocese under his nose.

When Bishop O'Collins was succeeded by Ronald Mulkearns, Pell was Mulkearns' Episcopal Vicar for Education—responsible for schools across the diocese. He was also on Mulkearns' board of consultors, whom the Bishop consulted on priestly appointments and movements throughout the geographically huge diocese—which sprawled right across Victoria's Western District to the South Australian border. Pell was also for five of those years editor of the diocesan magazine, *Light*.

He coached the rowing team at his alma mater, St Patrick's College. And, of course, he managed to say mass at St Alipius every Sunday and St Martin's in the Pines during the week and to be on a confessional roster. In the warmer months, he would spend the afternoons and evenings at the Eureka Pool, where he'd swim laps and then horse around with the boys in the pool. It's exhausting just thinking about it, but Father Pell was up for it all. If you speak to any Catholic who was a child at the time in Ballarat, they remember him as this seemingly omnipresent character, towering over everyone else, with this booming voice, just *everywhere.* Certainly, several pages from his diary tendered to the Royal Commission and penned in his distinctive hand are packed with events in Ballarat and in far-flung parts of the diocese, not to mention his trips back and forth to Melbourne. He was a mover and a shaker. A connected, ambitious, competent and fiercely ambitious man. The publican's son was going places.

All the while, a crisis was brewing. And Pell was living, working, praying, right in among it. He furiously maintains that he had almost no idea of what was going on. But, says the town's survivor community, he would say that.

3

THE AUXILIARY

Ride on! Rough-shod if need be, smooth-shod if that will do, but ride on! Ride on over all obstacles, and win the race!

Steerforth in *David Copperfield*

Ultimately, Ballarat was too small for George Pell and could scarcely contain his ambitions. As he launched into his forties, Pell's positions mirrored those of the fabulously charismatic, theologically conservative Pole, Karol Wojtyla, who had been elected as Pope John Paul II in 1978. And so Pell, who continued to cultivate his Roman contacts, was being noticed. 'By 1985 it was Ballarat's turn to provide a rector for the [Corpus Christi] seminary. George got the job—another good career step,' Father Eric Hodgens, who is older than Pell, remembers. So, Pell set off to Melbourne, the archdiocesan jewel in the Australian Church's crown, to make his way in the world.

'I think George has always been a political animal,' Hodgens tells me. 'His claim to fame has been his ability to be street-smart. He sniffs the wind and he knows which way to go. He's a loyalist to the institution—you just keep the rules and you don't ask why, you just keep them.'

Corpus Christi had now moved on from its bucolic Werribee mansion setting to drab suburban Clayton, but Pell rolled up his sleeves and got down to the business of getting some order back into the place—as far as he was concerned, it had abandoned the stricter protocols of his era and had adopted a more laissez-faire approach. Seminary numbers had halved since the beginning of the seventies and were in freefall. Pell's biographer Tess Livingstone reports that Pell spent his two years there reinforcing practices like 7a.m. masses and commitment to prayer. But while at times he crossed swords with many of his colleagues and students, he was right in line with Rome.

His discipline and obedience paid off. He was appointed Auxiliary Bishop in 1987. He would now be referred to as 'His Grace'. His star had risen. His time had come. Some of his priestly colleagues were aghast—particularly since the word was that Archbishop Frank Little had, they said, put up other names to Rome and Pell wasn't one of them. But it's said that Rome told Archbishop Little that Pell had to be on the list. From that time on, say the priests past and present I have spoken to, Little's relationship with Pell became decidedly frosty.

As the Cold War raged, the wind in the 1980s bellowing from the Vatican brought with it the return to a more orthodox conception of Catholicism. It fit with the times. Wojtyla had been, in Poland, an anti-communist champion. When elected Pope, John Paul II was a hero to the *Solidarno´sć* or Solidarity—the non-violent movement in Poland which was pivotal in the demise of the Eastern Bloc. Pope John Paul II had a thousand-watt smile and a message that resonated. He was much loved by the flock. Despite the affection for the Pope in Australian parishes, both laypeople and priests were still riding the wave of a different social movement—the progressive post-Vatican II spirit of optimism, hope and openness. For the traditionalists in their midst, those were marginalising times, when they watched mass numbers dwindle and felt intellectually bored by an atmosphere of 'holding hands and singing "Kumbaya"'.

Melbourne's Archbishop Little was a spiritual father more of the 'Kumbaya' set than the Wojtyla-led neo-cons. He was, however, a man of great contradictions. He was an archbishop who ultimately accepted and, it is said, was somewhat cowed by Roman authority—much to the detriment of some parts of his ministry, most spectacularly in his gross mishandling of child abuse cases. As his Vicar-General Hilton Deakin later said, 'one of the things that motivated the Archbishop to do what he did ... was his fear of the reach of Roman Canon Law; knowing that, if a priest possibly was found guilty, he would appeal to Rome, and the Roman authorities, knowing in the most limited way what they knew about this sort of thing, would find in favour of the priest and against the Bishop'.

But Little also had his own ideas about how to do things, and in many ways they clashed with Pope John Paul II's teaching. Little was loved by his priests, who now are at a loss to explain exactly why he, like some other bishops in other dioceses, chose to cover up the crisis that was quietly fermenting in his archdiocese. But on other pastoral matters, the priests say Little was all for openness and embracing the laity.

During his period as Auxiliary Bishop, Pell also ran Australian Catholic Relief—what is now Caritas Australia—the Catholic Church's overseas aid organisation. And he is widely considered to have done an excellent job expanding operations and raising money through the fundraiser Project Compassion. Pell has always been considered an excellent administrator—most likely the reason why Pope Francis chose him many years later, in 2014, to reform Vatican finances. But back in the 1980s, Pell was particularly involved in work in the ruins of post–Pol Pot Cambodia, which was recovering from a brutal genocide where up to two million people were murdered or forced to leave their homes. 'I think he made a very important contribution,' former Archbishop of Hobart Adrian Doyle told me. Doyle took over from Pell's successor at Caritas, Bishop Hilton Deakin. 'It was something [George] was very interested in,' Doyle says. 'He was very supportive and very committed to the whole humanitarian exercise. I think once he puts his mind to something, he intends to see it through.'

Michael Costigan, whose brother Paul had been at Corpus Christi with Pell and who had also been a Catholic priest, left the priesthood and became a journalist and religious commentator. He also worked for many years for the social justice arm of the Australian Catholic Bishops Conference. 'I would have to pay tribute to the job that [Pell] did,' Costigan says. 'He showed compassion for the poor of the world and showed concern for their plight.'

Being face to face with the human consequences of the Cambodian Killing Fields, where churches had been reduced to rubble, was clearly something that struck a deep chord in Pell, as Livingstone records him writing in 1989:

> Evil is nearly as deep a mystery as saintliness, as heroic goodness, and much more of a problem. But in Cambodia nature did register a protest. Under Pol Pot, the misery and hunger were so great that the people, in their battle against famine, ate all the wild birds. More than ten years later there are very few birds in Cambodia; in many places, no birds sing.

There were those who came later to Caritas leadership who were somewhat dismayed by aspects of Pell's approach—Pell wanting, for instance, to use the money to build churches. 'It was meant to be a body to help people—to feed them, to help them with hospitalisation, to help them stay alive,' one remembers. 'Never to build churches. But that's what he wanted to do.'

Although Costigan was, by his own admission, associated with the 'centre left' of the Australian Church, he says Pell was 'supportive of me in my role'.

'People say of him that he enjoys a bit of conflict—he enjoys the carry and thrust of rigorous debate,' Costigan says. 'I think I can say that in my time of working close to him, we did not have any difficult difference of opinion.

'Sometimes we would disagree but it was always in a friendly way. I heard one of the bishops use the term "bully", because it's been used fairly widely about him. But if you are asking whether I would say that, well, I am a charitable journalist. There might be an element of that in his character and style, but I didn't experience it. Except once or twice during meetings where things were not going his way, he could be forceful in putting his agenda.'

As Auxiliary Bishop, Pell wasted no time making his presence known on the Bishops Conference floor, making a splash in the media and being, well, forceful in his agenda.

Bill Morris was Bishop of the Diocese of Toowoomba and he watched the Pell ascendancy with interest. 'George was always very political,' says Morris, who joined the Bishops Conference in 1993. 'He was a mover and a shaker and would keep going until he got what he wanted in an area of policy or procedure. He did not always win though.'

Morris and many others in the Church I have spoken to say Pell always only had a small group of supporters on the floor who were like-minded and they would often sit together on their own. 'The vast majority were ambivalent to him and the rest were actively opposed or even openly hostile,' Morris says.

'George never won a popular vote in conference. He was never elected chair of the conference—he would have loved to be chair of the conference,' he says. Pat Power, who was Bishop of Canberra-Goulburn until 2012, confirmed this—saying Pell's name never got the simple majority of the secret ballot, even when in 2003 he became Cardinal. 'The Cardinal was normally elected,' he says. Pell's three predecessors: Cardinal Norman Gilroy (1946), Cardinal James

Freeman (1973) and Cardinal Edward Clancy (1988) were all, Power points out, elected president of the conference. It was, say others, a slap in the face for Pell not to get the nod.

Archbishop Emeritus Adrian Doyle was not close to Pell, but caught up with him at the Bishops meetings and had some admiration for his fortitude. 'He's a man that in the views he holds, he holds them very strongly,' Doyle says. 'He's prepared to stand up and put his position as bishop in the Church.

'He has a very powerful mind, a very strong personality. But I think there's a gentler side to him. He can be a very compassionate and understanding person. People don't see that very much.'

Doyle says while other bishops might have disagreed with Pell, the meetings were civil. 'This is a group of 40-plus people—you can't expect everyone to be the same,' Doyle reflects. 'I think the group got on remarkably well.'

Pell began, even as mere Auxiliary, to make himself known as One to Watch in the Church. His appointment to the Vatican's Congregation for the

Doctrine of the Faith was, says Hodgens, a 'golden opportunity'. 'He was immediately mixing with the bigwigs in [what is effectively the Vatican's] Department of Ideology,' Hodgens says. That included the man who would succeed Pope John Paul II, Cardinal Joseph Alois Ratzinger, who was cut from a similar theological and ideological cloth to Pell. The time of Pope John Paul and Ratzinger, who became Pope Benedict XVI, is described by Hodgens as a 'counter-reformation' and dashed the great hopes of all those in the Church who had been buoyed by Vatican II.

Of course, Pell would argue that this was returning the Church to what it should be, to an acceptable orthodoxy which would arrest the terminal decline in numbers it was already beginning to see in the late 1980s and early 1990s. In fact, Pell has said of Hodgens himself that he belonged to a 'swinging sixties' set of post–Vatican II priests whose liberalism had 'emptied churches' across the western world. Pell's publicly stated view was, essentially, that morally and particularly sexually, society was going to hell in a handbasket. The laity needed to listen less to its own misguided conscience and more to, well, people like him—people who spoke the word of Truth, the word of God. To effectively disseminate his message, the young Auxiliary, just forty-five when he was appointed, embraced the bright lights of television.

How a person goes into battle tells you a lot about them. Auxiliary Bishop Pell, then as now, clearly relished the odd skirmish.

After Penny Chapman's *Brides of Christ* miniseries appeared on the ABC in late 1991, Pell dismissed it as a 'religious soapie'. It was, however, immensely popular—discussing the Church battles it explored was the water cooler discussion of the day and so, despite deeming it beneath him, Pell deigned to go on a panel on the ABC's *Couchman* program to discuss the state of the Church in light of the issues thrown up by the miniseries.

ABC broadcaster and then-Catholic priest Paul Collins was also on the show. 'I think the thing that the conservatives were most upset about was that I called him "George",' he says. (I have noticed in my research for this book that none of the priests I have spoken to have ever referred to Pell as anything other than 'George'. Irking George's perceived delusions of grandeur seems to be a bit of a blood sport in the Australian clergy.)

Collins—who more traditional Catholic commentators have written off as a leftie, complaining that he gets too much airtime on the ABC and too many Fairfax column inches (this dismissal is a common fate for anyone who comes up against Pell)—was dismayed by Pell's demeanour on the program. He says he didn't believe the Bishop was hearing what a number of people on the panel were saying about their negative experiences with the Church—particularly its rigidity around issues such as celibacy of priests and the ban on oral contraception. He was most angered at Pell's reaction to the Australian actress Colette Mann, a former star of the television hit, *Prisoner,* who was sitting next to Pell on the program. Mann had, Collins says, given a heartfelt recount of her divorce and how desperate she had been for comfort and support from the Church.

Addressing Pell directly, Mann said, 'I made a mistake, I married this man in 1974 and it was a big mistake.' As she said it, Pell visibly leaned away and peered down at her. 'I want to be forgiven for that, and I have married another man, but I am not forgiven for that, because I am not even considered to be divorced, I am considered married to the first man!' She said both she and her ex-husband were now very happy in their new marriages. 'And I can't see why the Church can't embrace me, with that happiness, but it can't.'

Collins remembers, 'There was sheer pain in her voice and there was pain and hurt in her whole attitude and she was speaking from her heart. If George had just reached out to her and touched her on the forearm and said something like "I am so sorry", people would have said, "He's a decent human being, he has to say what he says as a bishop, but he's a nice man". But no. He hasn't an ounce of empathy. So, he just sat there as stiff as a board and said nothing.'

The comedian Geraldine Doyle joked darkly about the 'industrial-strength nuns' who had taught her when she was at school. When the camera pulled out wide, many other panellists were seen laughing heartily. But not Pell. The Bishop's hands were crossed, his face, once a film star's, now 50-something and well fed, was sullen as he stared at the floor.

Similarly, he had no time for the musings of former priest Don Burnard. Burnard said when he began to study Psychology while still in the priesthood and to question things, he was constantly being hauled over the coals by 'the hierarchy and the clergy that were ambitious'. Questioning things is something that Pell, the most ambitious of them all, constantly railed against. But Burnard continued. 'There are some wonderful men among the clergy. There are some very dead men among the clergy,' he said. From his body language, the discussion was clearly beginning to irk Pell.

'The real question today is that neo-paganism has failed,' Pell declared. 'If we followed Christian ethics, there would be *no* AIDS epidemic. If we had stuck closer to Christian ethics, there would not be as many marriage break-ups. Not as many suffering children. The argument against artificial contraception comes from the essential link between family, sexuality and love. And the fact that those three elements have been broken apart so radically in our society.'

This preoccupation, a constant fixture in Pell's dialogue at the time and for many years later, is fascinating in light of the child sex allegations he now, decades later, faces.

As Pell continued, he was reinforced by Liberal Catholic politician Peter McGauran. McGauran made the women on the set apoplectic with rage by his assertion that because Christ did not appoint women as apostles, there couldn't now be women priests. 'Men and women are equal in the Church,' McGauran said to gales of disbelieving laughter from the gathered nuns and other prominent Catholic women, current and lapsed, 'but they are equal in different ways.' It brought to mind Orwell's *Animal Farm,* in which the dominant pigs haughtily announced, 'All animals are equal, but some animals are more equal than others.' Pell had McGauran's back. 'We are not a social welfare agency, to be refashioned in each generation. We are part of an ongoing tradition and our basics have come from Christ,' he said, pointing out that Christ was, after all, the son of God. 'So Christ's teaching is not negotiable.'

Thanks to a combination of, he believed, Pell's preposterous arguments and what he perceived as the Bishop's lack of empathy for Mann and others, Collins saw red. 'And so, I thought, "the gloves are off",' he remembers. 'I decided to go in, boots and all.'

Collins, who was behind Pell, said all 'reputable scholars' agreed it wasn't historically correct to say that Christ had instituted the Catholic priesthood and that it was an office that really began in the third and fourth centuries. 'To simply say that Christ set up the hierarchical Church and the ordained priesthood is nonsense!' Collins said. Pell pursed his lips, fidgeted with the gold chain to his pectoral cross and looked to the heavens, shifting uncomfortably in his seat. Collins got even more fired up. 'You really do sound fundamentalist, and that's what worries me about people like you in powerful positions making statements that are fundamentalist.'

At this point, the smoke practically billowed out of Pell's ears. He reminded all present that he did his doctorate at Oxford in early Church history so he knew what he was talking about (ergo Collins—no slouch, who did his own post-graduate studies at Harvard—didn't). 'Because a man says what he means and means what he says, he should not be condemned as a fundamentalist, that's a classic put-down from people who want to dissolve the basis of the faith to suggest that anyone who is hanging on to what Christ taught is a fundamentalist.' Pell did, at this point, entertain the idea that somewhere in the future there might be married priests, although he wouldn't be pushing for the concept. '[But] that's quite different from the ordination of women,' he said to the largely female panel, with a dismissive flick of his hand, 'which is quite impossible.'

Collins felt a bit guilty at the end for going after Pell. 'After the show, I thought I better go and do the good Catholic priest thing and make friends,' Collins says. 'I did that, but he just said, "Oh yes" and walked off.'

The *Brides of Christ* experience did not deter this gladiator, Pell, from entering the televisual fray once more. When in August 1993 Pope John Paul II released his papal encyclical *Veritatis Splendor,* the ABC's *Four Corners* program chose him to go head-to-head with the more liberal Provincial of the Australian Jesuits, Father Bill Uren, on the impact of the controversial document—which reasserted papal authority and addressed some of Pell's favourite topics at the time like birth control and assisted fertilisation. It was a fiery exchange held in October 1993 in front of a small studio audience of carefully chosen Catholic stakeholders. Uren was a lecturer in Bioethics at the University of Melbourne and, like Pell, an old boy of Campion Hall at Oxford, although he had taken Philosophy instead of Theology.

When the late journalist Andrew Olle asked Pell whether, in light of the encyclical, there was any room for dissent in the clergy now, there were gasps in the audience as the Bishop replied. 'Well, I'm not so sure there is,' Pell began, 'because the purpose of the encyclical is to reassert the moral teaching of Jesus Christ who, the Pope says, is the word of Truth about good and evil.

'The situation has certainly deteriorated since the Second Vatican Council which never at any stage suggested that a person was free to follow his own ... his or her, own conscience. And what the Pope is doing is reasserting the basic moral teaching of the New Testament, which is common to all the mainline Christian Churches.'

Uren disagreed wholeheartedly—priests like him were not, as Olle described them, to become 'moral puppets'. While Uren agreed that the Pope's encyclical should be treated with 'great respect', there was still room for disagreement.

'Is that good enough, Bishop?' Olle asked Pell.

'No way,' the Bishop drily replied. Pell rejected Olle's assessment that the Vatican was keeping priests like Uren 'under the thumb', though.

'Not at all,' Pell said. 'What we're doing is presenting the teaching of Jesus Christ. Whether it has a tag of a particular type, I think is quite secondary. The real point is whether Christians believe that when the Pope says he is repeating and explaining the teaching, the moral teaching of Jesus Christ, whether in fact in the bases of the encyclical, whether in fact Catholics accept that he's doing that, and they will honestly say yea or nay, and then the Church knows where everyone stands.'

There were strident supporters of Pell's view in the room, principally laypeople who even thought he was not going far enough and that dissenters should be weeded out and punished. But there were also fierce critics, and his response again drew guffaws from some nuns and priests in the room, including another feisty Jesuit, Father

Michael Kelly, who had recently spoken out about the Auxiliary Bishop in the media and who on *Four Corners* that night got stuck into Pell.

'Haven't you in fact already been told, Father Kelly, that you have to toe the line now, you have to pull your head in?' Olle asked Kelly, who was sitting in the audience.

'By the same Bishop,' Kelly, who at times has something of a terrier-like disposition, snapped back. Pell was having none of it. 'That's absolutely incorrect,' he told Olle.

Kelly refused to back down. 'George, there were only two of us there. That was what you told me. You told me to watch out.'

'What I said was there might be a gear change. I mean, I was quite surprised ... I was quite surprised to see a private conversation quoted in the press, but what I said was that I thought there might be a gear change and, given that I'm a friend of Father Michael's, I said "be careful",' Pell responded.

If Kelly was ever Pell's friend, he wasn't showing it. 'George, if I may ...

I mean, with respect, for a bishop to be telling a priest that he'd better watch out, is a pretty serious matter.'

'I didn't say that,' Pell replied.

'Would you like to explain to me what you did?'

'I just have. I just said "be careful".'

The 'be careful' exchange referred to by Kelly took place after he and Pell were in a studio, this time for an ABC radio interview in October 1993, following the release of *Veritatis Splendor,* to debate just what the encyclical meant. Kelly was at that time the founding publisher of *Eureka Street.* As soon as the segment began, and before Kelly could speak, Pell launched into a monologue about 'the genuine crisis in the Catholic Church' which he thought was 'the result of a greater moral confusion in the wider society', but he also immediately got stuck into a rather taken aback Kelly. 'I think evidence of that confusion,' Pell began, 'is the fact that I am here with Father Michael Kelly, the Jesuit. Now I don't know what Father Michael is going to say, but if in fact he's going to rubbish the encyclical, then I think that would be most inappropriate, because, Father Michael, as a priest, like me, he's bound by the encyclical as much as I am. And also, of course, if he was going to attack the encyclical, it would be particularly unfortunate, because the Jesuits have a fourth vow of obedience to the Pope.'

Before Kelly, who did not even know that Pell would be in the studio, could say anything, Pell went on to argue that priests were essentially bound by a notion akin to Caucus or Cabinet confidentiality and should have their debates behind closed doors rather than in the public domain. 'It's destructive and inappropriate for you to go into the public domain with it,' he cautioned. '[The Pope] is very much opposed to orchestrated and public dissent. It has done great damage to the Church.'

When the journalist Sharon O'Neill asked Kelly if he was a dissenter, he wryly observed that 'George and I did not touch gloves as we walked into the studio, and I am certainly not here to do what George is fearing I am doing'. Kelly managed to keep his cool and to present a counterargument to Pell which did not involve the outright dissent that the Bishop had implied.

Pell launched into another spate of the old faithful: finger-wagging at the deplorable sexual mores that had seen society as he knew it fall apart.

'We have had an epidemic of abuse of the Pill. There are more abortions, also, within the Catholic community, more broken marriages, more single mothers, more homeless and unwanted children, because of the selfish and contraceptive mentality that an unthinking use of the Pill has produced. I think we need to look closely at what has happened in our own society.'

Contraceptive mentality. At this point O'Neill pointed out that Catholics were ignoring the Church on that one. They had been for generations. Despite this, here was Pell, in 1993, when we all thought we were frightfully modern, describing the defiance of those who chose to take contraception as 'unfortunate' and saying 'I think they, like all of us, need to reassess the situation'. Kelly disagreed, but declined to get into an argument with Pell and therefore confirm the Bishop's earlier attack on him. He said that the Bishop's comments were a misinterpretation of *Humanae Vitae,* the papal encyclical which had reinforced the then Pope's opposition to contraception.

But when the two priests left the studio, Kelly describes to me the full force of Hurricane George. 'He said, "People like you better watch out,"' Kelly tells me. 'And I said, "Pardon, George?" And he said, glowering at me, in *that* voice [Kelly does a pretty solid impersonation of Pell's booming, sonorous voice], "People like you are endangered species, there's been a gear change in the Church and people like you are on the way out."'

Kelly was floored and angered. It prompted him to, on the later *Four Corners* program, 'put a stake in the ground'. 'I know the vast majority of people in the Church across Australia agreed with Bill [Uren] and me and we wanted to give some recognition to that point of view,' Kelly says. And he also wanted to put on the record what Pell had done. 'So I did it to two and a half million of my closest friends,' he says, chuckling sourly. 'And it was career-altering. He was determined to do me in after that, and ultimately, he did.'

Three years later, Uren's successor as Provincial of the Australian Jesuits, Father Daven Day, called Kelly in to tell him he had been let go from his job running Jesuit Publications. He was removed, incidentally, in April 1997—two months after Brian Scarlett's photograph of Pell, legs akimbo in the horse trough, appeared in the magazine. Kelly suspected the hand of Pell. He was dismayed but not surprised. 'That's the way he's always done things,' Kelly says. 'That's his style of Catholicism.'

There appeared to be consequences, too, for Uren, for publicly crossing swords with Pell. Uren is now Rector of Newman College at the University of Melbourne, but was blocked from the job when he applied for it in the 1990s after he stepped down as the Jesuits' Provincial. Newman College is controlled by the Melbourne Archdiocese, of which Pell was archbishop when Uren applied for the job.

The stories of Kelly and Uren bring to mind a remark Bishop Bill Morris once made to me. 'George was always very pleasant as long as you stay away from religion,' Morris says. That makes me laugh, given we are discussing a Catholic priest, talking about religion was pretty unavoidable. He laughs too, but then he's also deadly serious. 'Bring religion into it and George was a bully. How George played his football is how he plays his religion. It was always "take no prisoners".'

Kelly says the take-no-prisoners approach was classically in the style of BA Santamaria, mentor to former Australian Prime Minister (and former seminarian) Tony Abbott as well as to Pell, although both men had their points of difference with Santamaria. 'Santa', as Abbott has sometimes affectionately called him, was an anti-communist, a social conservative, who set up what's known as 'The Movement', which later became the National Civic Council and would split the Australian Labor Party to form the DLP. The Melbourne Press Club, which inducted Santamaria into its Hall of Fame, described him as a 'brilliant but divisive polemicist'. Thanks, for many years, to the benevolence of

Frank Packer and his son Kerry, he was a strident and eloquent broadcaster, whose monologue *Point of View* would appear on Channel Nine on a Sunday morning. As Australians prepared their roast lunch and waited for the wrestling on *Wide World of Sports* to come on the box, they'd be treated to a soliloquy where Santamaria would deliver without autocue, barely stopping for breath, his sermon on the issue of the day as he perceived it. One memorable tirade in 1985 concerned the hotbed of 'radical feminism and homosexuality'—the ABC—whose presenters were 'with few exceptions ... protagonists of aberrant sexual practices'.

Santamaria was very close to Rome through its papal nuncio to Australia—effectively, its man on the ground—Franco Brambilla. When Santamaria was on his deathbed in 1998, he was visited by both Brambilla and Pell. When Prime Minister John Howard granted Santamaria a state funeral, it was Pell who gave the eulogy at St Patrick's Cathedral in Melbourne. 'You have to see George in the context of the culture wars,' Kelly says. 'George is a defined culture warrior and it's a position mapped out for him by Bob Santamaria. He has done what Santamaria did and it's black and white, good and evil, right and wrong—you know, "our guys are right and all the others are dissidents"—it's the politicisation of religion. Santamaria was the greatest practitioner of the demonisation of anyone who disagreed with him. Anyone who disagreed could only be evil.'

These days, people get their giggles out of watching retro Santamaria clips on YouTube as old Santa thunders on about the scourge of 'gays' and other contributors to the downfall of civilisation as we knew it. So as befits the times in which he has found himself, it is arguable that Pell's polemical approach is somewhat more nuanced than Santamaria's. Somewhat. But back in the eighties, Auxiliary Bishop Pell was far less subtle. He vigorously defended his Church against criticism and dissent, going at the doubters like a mallee bull. With a front, as they said in those days, 'the size of Myer'. But there is evidence to suggest that there was a deeply serious flaw in that overarching confidence. And that it was sometimes exercised at the expense of exposing the child abuse epidemic that was exploding around him.

4

THE FIXER

I'm a Christian, I'm a priest. Now I might have put the Church first for a while rather than the victims. But I'm certainly not here to put myself first. We're not into that.

Cardinal George Pell in Sky News interview with Andrew Bolt, March 2016

When the Most Reverend George Pell was still Auxiliary Bishop of Melbourne, he had the passing acquaintance of a priest in his region called Father Noel Brady. Brady is now parish priest at Resurrection Kings Park, a thriving western suburbs community where he ministers to a distinctly multicultural group of worshippers. He is an understated man and he blanches from any colourful descriptors of Pell or indeed of Pell's motives. Brady says he prefers to stick to the facts. And the facts he alleges fly in the face of everything Pell now says about what he knew about paedophilia and how he handled it in the Catholic Church before becoming Archbishop of Melbourne in 1996. Brady is not the only one putting his concerns on the record for the first time.

Brady was ordained a priest in 1992 and his first parish, where he worked as assistant priest, was St Mary's, Dandenong, in Melbourne's outer south-east. Dandenong was in the southern region for which Pell was responsible for ministering as Auxiliary Bishop. Brady was appointed to St Mary's on 8 July 1992, and that date is significant, he tells me, for reasons which shall become clear. About four months after Brady arrived at the parish, he says a young couple who were parishioners came to see him after mass. They were extremely concerned about the husband's brother, who lived a bit further out in Narre Warren. The young man was a victim of the serial paedophile priest, Father Kevin O'Donnell, and Brady went to see the victim. 'I will never forget walking around the property with [him] and the telling of his story reducing us both to tears,' Brady later wrote.

O'Donnell was by then a retired priest who was still living in a house on Church property at Dandenong. 'It was awkward to say the least,' says Brady of the living arrangement—particularly since O'Donnell was good friends with Brady's superior, the parish priest. In a 1989 confirmation ceremony video at Sacred Heart in Oakleigh, where O'Donnell was ministering at the time, Pell praised O'Donnell and another priest 'for all the work they are doing here': 'It is obviously a great and strong parish with a proud Catholic tradition, and I know you will work to maintain this just as your priests do, and I look forward to many, many more years of work from Father O'Donnell in the Church here.'

There is no evidence that Pell knew it as early as 1989, but O'Donnell was a dreadful man, who later pleaded guilty to abusing eight, and then a further twelve, children over decades at pretty much every parish he went to. His most well-known victims, and certainly the most tragic story associated with him, are Emma and Katie Foster. The Foster sisters' lives derailed after their abuse at Sacred Heart Primary in Oakleigh to the point where Emma died of a drug overdose and Katie, drinking to numb the pain of her abuse, walked in front of a speeding car and was left with permanent physical and intellectual disabilities. Their parents, Chrissie and Anthony Foster, have been ardent campaigners for justice; they later in a Victorian parliamentary inquiry described Pell as having a sociopathic lack of empathy in his dealings with them. But Brady, on the other hand, was very empathetic and was disturbed by what he heard about O'Donnell. 'I eventually met ten or twelve of his victims,' Brady says. 'I helped them and I told them to go to the police.'

Brady says child sexual abuse has always been something which he abhors and feels should be spoken out about. He always believed the victims who came to him and, as it turned out, he was right to. 'The common response, twenty or thirty years ago, was just "get over it, get on with your life". But there is so much pain and hurt,' he says.

Back in 1992, Brady made a bold decision for a Catholic priest at the time. He decided not to be silent. 'I spoke out about it at Dandenong in mass in November 1992 and I was given a round of applause,' Brady says. He continued to make it known to his parishioners and to survivors of O'Donnell that he could be trusted and he would advocate on their behalf.

Two years after Brady's appointment, in 1994, a parishioner made a complaint to head office about Brady for, the parishioner said, the heretic charge of questioning the virginity of Mary. Saints preserve us! 'I got a phone call from George,' Brady remembers. It was a Friday and Brady says he had a lunch and a dental appointment that day, so he made time to call Pell back later on the Friday.

The parishioner's complaint turned out to be false, and Pell, Brady says, soon discovered that. 'After he conducted his heresy trial', Brady says Pell made a startling comment.

'He said to me, "You've been speaking out about sexual abuse at Dandenong and you should not be doing that."

'He then said either "you are too close to the scene" or "you might be too close to the scene".' Brady can't remember which of the two versions it was, but he believes that is immaterial. 'That is definitely what he said,' Brady says.

'I said, "George, you cannot be more wrong, more so in Dandenong than anywhere."' Brady meant that Pell could not be more wrong in his assessment that he, Brady, should not be speaking about this scourge and it was particularly vital to speak out about it at Dandenong. Brady wanted his parishioners to know that they were believed and that if they had a complaint, he could be trusted to help them manage it. Brady believes that Pell's warning connoted, first of all, that Pell was trying to shut down discussion by him of child sexual abuse, and second, that he knew there were issues with O'Donnell, who was on the 'scene' at Dandenong.

The words, says Brady, are 'seared in my memory'. 'I don't want to comment on what it says about George, I just know what's true. I know that in July 1994, George Pell told me not to speak out about sexual abuse in Dandenong.' And unlike many witnesses and complainants in this sexual abuse saga, trying to recall incidents decades before, he can pinpoint the date exactly. 'I can pinpoint it exactly because I said in relation to the heresy allegations, "I have been at Dandenong two years to the day and you hardly knew I existed, and then one complaint and I am summoned on the same day".'

So, in 2015, when Brady realised that this information about Pell was particularly significant, he went back to his dentist—one of the appointments he had earlier on that day that required him to delay returning Pell's call—and asked if there was any way of checking his records for 8 July 1994—two years to the day of his appointment at St Mary's Dandenong. As it happens, there was. 'They said you had two procedures done and you paid the bill in cash,' Brady says.

Back in 1994, Brady ignored Pell's warning not to speak out at Dandenong about sexual abuse. He thought it crucially important that he did. And as it happens, two months after the conversation he recounts with Pell, on 7 September 1994, Victoria Police charged O'Donnell with thirty-two incidents of indecent assault at four parishes.

Brady had always shaken his head at the way that Pell had spoken to him back in July 1994, but it wasn't until June 2015 that he felt compelled to do something about it. Jesuit priest and social commentator Father Frank Brennan had written a piece for *Eureka Street,* republished in *The Australian.* It was headlined 'Call off the Cardinal Pell Witch-Hunt'. Brennan is no great fan of Pell's, but he has frequently written of his dismay at the way Pell has been treated by some commentators. 'Many Australians are baying for Pell's blood,' Brennan writes. 'It's time for a dispassionate consideration of the facts.'

As part of that dispassionate consideration of the 'facts', Brennan says this: 'Between 1987 and 1996, Pell was an auxiliary bishop to Archbishop Frank Little in Melbourne. Pell has constantly claimed he knew nothing of abuse in those days and was therefore in no position to do anything about it. No evidence has been produced proving that Pell knew anything at that time.'

Reading this made Brady sit upright in his chair. He searched his conscience and decided it was best that he put his knowledge on the record. So, Brady wrote to the Royal Commission into Institutional Responses to Child Sexual Abuse. I have that letter, and the replies to Brady from Darren Latimore, the Australian Federal Police officer who is seconded to the Commission to work with victims and other witnesses. '[Brennan's] article contained an assertion that George Pell did not know anything about clergy sexual abuse in Melbourne until he became Archbishop in 1996 [July],' Brady writes. 'I know that not to be true ... My only motive is the truth be known and the chips then can fall where they may.'

For reasons best known to the Royal Commission, Brady was never called to give evidence, either publicly or privately in camera. He was verbally told that the Commission was very busy, had an awful lot of potential witnesses and they had to make a judgement call on who they could manage to fit in or leave out. Another Royal Commission source suggested to me that it could have been an oversight by the legal team and there were 'any combination of reasons, not always good ones, why some things have been overlooked because they deal with a vast amount of information from many, many sources'. Brady's ears pricked up again when he watched Pell give evidence to the Royal Commission from Rome in February 2016. So much so that he wrote to Latimore again: 'Having listened to the evidence given by George Pell to the Royal Commission, I think the point raised in my email still has some relevance.' However, again, the Royal Commission did not call him as a witness.

Father Noel Brady did not approach me; I found him. He thought very carefully about contributing his conversation with Pell to this book. But he says in the end, he is just committed to the truth.

'People can handle the truth,' Brady says. 'It's the cover-ups that really hurt.'

There are other evidentiary alarm bells which suggest Pell knew about O'Donnell long before Pell became archbishop in 1996. These are found first in the minutes of the Melbourne Curia—the diocesan governing body—from the early 1990s. In among the discussions about whether kissing the crucifix during what's known as the Veneration of the Cross could spread HIV and talks about a public relations (PR) strategy for 'special issues' (that's the euphemism they used for sexual abuse of kids) and undertakings to keep written discussions of special issues to a minimum (lest they be discovered in legal proceedings) are a number of references to Pell's work. They show Auxiliary Bishop Pell was a committed and detailfocused local bishop who was regularly involved in priest and parish matters in his region. In the minutes from April 1991, there are two relatively oblique references to O'Donnell. The first is headed 'Oakleigh Parish': 'Bishop Pell said that Father Kevin O'Donnell is happy to stay alone in the parish, provided adequate supplies can be arranged.' During the next April meeting, that sentence is amended. '[The reference] should read: 'Bishop Pell said that Father Kevin O'Donnell is *prepared* to stay alone in the parish, provided adequate supplies can be arranged.'

So, what was that all about? Well, two documents give a clue. And they suggest that Pell was a kind of fixer in the whole O'Donnell saga. The first is a meeting many years later between Pell's later lawyer, Richard Leder, and a Father John Salvano. Salvano was assistant priest to O'Donnell. Salvano couldn't bear O'Donnell. It says in the typed notes of this conversation that Salvano had four or five meetings with Pell's colleague, the Archdiocesan Vicar-General Hilton Deakin, as Leder wrote, 're unhappiness'. Salvano was unhappy with the 'way he treated children, women', said O'Donnell was 'an abusive personality' and 'I found his behaviour around children quite inappropriate'. Salvano said while he never saw anything happen, O'Donnell would 'focus on a couple of kids at a time', brought one boy on a holiday to Queensland, gave kids money and Salvano 'had a gut feeling all was not right'. While initially nothing happened after Salvano's discussions with Deakin, he notes that eventually 'something did'. 'Because they sent Pell to see Kevin [O'Donnell] and confront him. Then [O'Donnell] retired. My understanding is that it was a forced retirement. I know he was not happy about retiring.'

Deakin in 2015 gave evidence that he was the one who actually went down and told O'Donnell that he was being stood down—'it was a command, an order', Deakin said. But, by Salvano's account to Pell's lawyer, Pell was part of the reason that O'Donnell was no longer at Sacred Heart Oakleigh and in fact was at a house in Brady's parish in Dandenong. Deakin too appeared to support this notion in his evidence. At the time that Deakin was remembering the events at Oakleigh he was eighty-three, and he confessed that his memory was hazy. 'George was going, was doing his own thing as he believed he should do, and spending a lot of time and I understand ... that he went out to Oakleigh a few times and on occasions he was bruised publicly.'

In 1999, Salvano gave more detail of what he had told the hierarchy about O'Donnell in a statement to a solicitor who was representing Chrissie and Anthony Foster, parents of Emma and Katie—the little girls abused by O'Donnell. Salvano, who is now dean of St Patrick's Cathedral in Melbourne, looked over the statement for Chrissie Foster some years later and agreed to her making it public. Salvano had an awful time working with O'Donnell. In his approaches to Deakin about O'Donnell, he cites cases of serious violence—O'Donnell punching Salvano and having him in a headlock, guns and ammunition being kept all over the presbytery, large amounts of parish money being given to boys, boys constantly being present—day and night—and O'Donnell 'mauling' boys in his presence: 'physical contact with the boys in an inappropriate way by hugging them, holding them around the shoulders or waist'. Salvano thought it 'incongruous for a man [O'Donnell] who was otherwise so cold and aggressive and not demonstrative'.

He described the behaviour to Deakin as 'highly abnormal' and believed that boys had keys to the presbytery and were letting themselves in at all hours. Deakin informed Little. Salvano also told Deakin he believed that O'Donnell was 'emotionally dependent' on the boys. At one point during the year, O'Donnell announced that a boy who was a frequent visitor to the presbytery was moving into the priests' house for the rest of the year. Salvano went straight to Deakin about that, too, and when he got home that evening, the boy had moved out. Chrissie Foster's solicitor notes at the end of the record of interview that Salvano became quite tearful having relived the O'Donnell years. He made clear that if anyone had ever come to him about O'Donnell sexually abusing children, he would have gone straight to the police.

The Salvano statement also says that despite the eventual decision to retire O'Donnell, the first response of the hierarchy via Deakin was to offer to find alternative accommodation for Salvano. Salvano refused—primarily because he was concerned about the situation between the children and O'Donnell. This was galling for the Fosters, whose daughter Katie was abused during the 7-month period between when Salvano first began to raise the alarm and when Pell came and got O'Donnell out. Chrissie Foster believes that Little, Deakin and Pell were 'responsible for the abuse which took place in those seven months by Father Kevin O'Donnell, who had an insatiable sexual appetite for primary school aged children which spanned the fifty years of his priesthood'. And after they participated in the process of getting O'Donnell out? There is no evidence to suggest that any of them ever went to Victoria Police about O'Donnell.

Pell has never admitted any personal liability in this, nor any other child abuse cover-up. In some cases, he has alleged a conspiracy of others. Deakin, who is not, incidentally, a friend of Pell's and disagrees with many of Pell's positions, has been more forthcoming. In late 2015, Deakin agreed that as a member of the Curia of the Melbourne Archdiocese, he belonged to a culture 'motivated by a desire to protect the Church's reputation', that 'collectively forgot about the primary need to protect children'. He admitted that the Archbishop had 'secret files' and said that he was instructed to only tell Little verbally, when they were alone, about these cases. But he also said they had 'covered up especially the evil deeds of certain men against children ... There were meetings, for instance, where everybody voted on things; like, for instance when a priest was moved or retired, it was because of ill-health or something, when in fact it was because of child abuse.'

There is another person who says she and her family bore the brunt of Pell's efforts to sweep the abuse problem under the carpet during his reign as Auxiliary Bishop and, again, lecturing a priest about not getting involved. Her story about Pell has also never been told. Her name is Eileen Piper. Her history is strange and tragic.

When I first meet her in the autumn of 2016, Eileen Piper is ninety-one—a sprightly woman who seems about ten years younger and is as sharp as you like. She has dancing eyes, often claps her hands in exclamation, calls you 'darling' and insists on feeding you slice and tea cake she's baked that morning. Eileen has been holding on to her story about Pell for more than twenty years.

Eileen Piper has faced the sort of tragedy that would make many others collapse into bitterness. She and her husband struggled to have children and eventually adopted two. One was her daughter Stephanie. Eileen and her husband were very committed Catholics—Eileen was the proud sister of a monsignor, Kevin Toomey. Stephanie too was very active in the life of the parish of St Christopher's Syndal in Melbourne's eastern suburbs. 'She had very strict morals and she wasn't a worldly type of girl,' Eileen remembers.

But sadly for Stephanie, when she was a teenager in the 1970s, she came into the orbit of one Gerard Mulvale. Mulvale was a Pallottine brother who became a priest. He was based at the Syndal parish and would run the youth groups. While Eileen had had some concerns about Mulvale at the time, it wasn't until 1993, when Stephanie was thirty-two, that Eileen says she realised that the concerns were well founded.

Stephanie attempted suicide. And after she did so, she told her mother what she had been hiding for many years, that she had been a repeated victim of Mulvale's—culminating in a final incident in which Stephanie alleged she had been locked in the boot of his car and later savagely raped. 'It was torture, what he put Stephanie through. And the fear, the fear ... He strangled her with fear,' Eileen says, looking off to the side sadly, 'and she didn't want to tell us what was happening.'

Mulvale eventually pleaded guilty to the abuse of one boy in Stephanie's youth group and was convicted of abusing another. A fourth complainant—a girl in the youth group—pulled out of the police prosecution. Stephanie also made complaints to both police and the Catholic Church's Special Issues

Committee about Mulvale, but her mother says she was belittled and not believed by the man who took her statement for the Church, the now-deceased Vicar-General of the Melbourne Archdiocese Gerry Cudmore.

After leaving the interview with Cudmore in 1993, Stephanie broke down crying and said, 'What's the use? Nobody will believe me.' In August 1993, the committee found Stephanie's allegations could not be substantiated. In November of that year, Stephanie made a complaint to the Victoria Police Rape Squad. Mulvale has always strenuously denied the rape, and even made complaints, from prison, to the Victorian Ombudsman when Eileen later went to the media.

When Stephanie went to police, Mulvale was charged with her rape and he was later charged with offences against the others. One of the others, Neil Bourke, who was terminally ill during the trial, made a statement saying Stephanie had made the whole thing up and while he was a victim of Mulvale's, she was not. Eileen says that this was done under duress from the

Catholic Church. Bourke later retracted that statement during his court case and said Stephanie had told the truth. Bourke told the court that a Pallottine priest at Syndal, Father John Flynn, instructed him to sign a statement for the Church 'that we had to put Stephanie Piper down and make her seem thoroughly horrible ... The object of this letter was to make Stephanie the villain,' Bourke told the court. Father Flynn 'told me what to say and how I was to say it'.

In 1993, the court heard, Bourke received a letter from Cudmore, thanking him for signing the statement. 'I was doing what Father Flynn told me was correct and I believed him as a priest.'

But by then it was too late for Stephanie. In January 1994, before the case even got to trial and she could give evidence, she took her own life. 'She gassed herself at two o'clock in the morning,' Eileen sighs. 'She was a terrible mess, poor darling. She never really had any chance of living a normal life.'

Bourke was devastated. 'I felt that [my Church] statement drove Stephanie to suicide,' Bourke later told the court, admitting that the guilt of this had driven him, too, to attempt suicide soon after.

Eileen's husband was also sick at the time and he died that year too. After their deaths, but before Mulvale was brought to court, Eileen went to look after her brother, Monsignor Kevin Toomey, who was in poor health. She was at Toomey's house in Mount Eliza in outer Melbourne one day when, she says, the telephone rang. Eileen says on the other end was Pell. 'Kev said that "the big boy" was coming down,' Eileen remembers. At that time, Pell was based in Mentone, about half an hour from her brother's home, but she says he seemed to arrive very quickly at Toomey's door.

'And I saw George Pell beckon with his hand, to tell me to go out, to get out of the room.' Eileen did what she was told. 'I sort of skittled into the bathroom, which was the adjoining room.'

Eileen says she was shocked by what happened next. 'I heard George Pell say to my brother, "Don't you dare have anything to do with your sister's case, now that's an order".' Eileen says that Pell left shortly after. 'He just came to say that, and he was in a dominant mood and I heard him say that,' she says.

'I came out of the bathroom crying, breaking my heart. Because I thought he was threatening Kev not to do anything about Stephanie, I was getting no help.'

But fortunately for Eileen, she says her brother chose to ignore the orders of his regional bishop and to stand by his sister. 'Kevin was beautiful, and he told me not to be upset, he would support me in any and every way I needed him and he would be there ... we appeared in the court, we went together.' Toomey also wrote to Cudmore on Eileen's behalf.

Eileen says she's furious that Pell tried to bully Toomey over his niece's case. 'The Church let Kevin down,' Eileen says of her brother, whom she now regrets gave his life to the institution. 'He worked so hard for the Church and to be told to do that, to save them, at my expense, it makes me feel that the Catholic Church,' she shrugs darkly, 'has got a lot to answer for.'

'It destroys your faith in the Catholic Church. They're there as a beacon of right from wrong, but to me, it's manufactured. There's nothing really deeply genuine about it at all. It's just surface. It's all on the surface.'

Eileen went through the Church's Melbourne Response, which was set up when Pell became archbishop, to try to get justice for Stephanie and to have her name cleared. Pell's Special Commissioner Peter O'Callaghan, QC, found there was an absence of corroboration, variations in Stephanie's story and also, in his words, an 'inherent improbability of a brutal rape as alleged, occurring without complaint being made, or any injury or distress observed'.

O'Callaghan was also concerned about the changes to Bourke's story—and to be fair to O'Callaghan, Bourke's initial written claim that

Stephanie's complaint was false was emphatic and unequivocal. Bourke said that as 'a homosexual', he could 'recognise similar traits and other men of my own inclinations' and would find it 'very difficult to believe that Father Mulvale would have sexual relations with a member of the opposite sex, especially forcing on them'. However, it should be pointed out that the other female complainant had come forward, but withdrew her charges after, Eileen says, seeing what was done to Stephanie. O'Callaghan decided that he would not uphold the complaint. As of early 2017, the Melbourne Archdiocese stood by that position, despite the Pallottine order paying Eileen $20 000 in an ex gratia compensation payment in 2002. A Change.org petition initiated after I featured Eileen's story on the ABC TV's *7.30* program (minus the Pell part of it) hit more than fifty thousand signatures in favour of Eileen's fight for justice. She delivered it to Archbishop Denis Hart when he appeared before the Royal Commission in 2017. Hart said while he would 'pray' for Eileen Piper, he would not change his mind.

As Eileen's lawyer Judy Courtin says, 'How my client feels is, "They're just waiting for me to die and go away." But [Eileen] says, "I'm not going to go away. I'll fight as long as I need to fight."'

As for Pell, Mulvale wrote a letter to him while Pell was Archbishop of Melbourne and before O'Callaghan made his determination. It was sent from Ararat prison, where Mulvale was then detained. Curiously for the time, when archbishops were typically referred to as 'Your Grace' or 'Archbishop' in correspondence—particularly from a much more junior priest who was a convicted criminal—Mulvale was much more familiar. He addressed his letter 'Dear George'. Eileen had been in the media talking about Stephanie's case and Mulvale was most upset about it, saying she 'appears to be taking her place in the line-up for a compensation pay-out'. He referred to Cudmore's earlier investigation which had found Stephanie's claims to be 'without substance' and he—Mulvale—was, astonishingly, looking at 'litigation' against Eileen. There is zero remorse in the letter for any crime he committed—two of which he had been found guilty of—but he is full of righteous anger at the grieving mother of a young woman who had killed herself after alleging that he raped her. One might think that an archbishop who was doing his job as a Christian and an effective leader might have reminded Mulvale, a convicted sex offender, to come off his high horse and get his priorities right. Eileen obtained a copy of Mulvale's letter, but she has no idea whether 'George' ever replied, and if he did, what he said to Mulvale.

Eileen has never forgotten Pell's conversation with her brother that day, but fearing it might hamper her attempts to get justice for Stephanie because Pell was so powerful, she has never spoken out about it before now. It is contained in a statement she has written which has been used in correspondence with the Catholic Church as she fights for an apology for Stephanie.

'He has hurt me. It has hurt me. It's a wound that won't heal, until I can get justice for Stephanie,' Eileen says.

Then the dark cloud lifts from her face and she breaks into an almost beatific smile. 'I hope I can live long enough to do that.'

Eileen Piper's and Noel Brady's assertions are just the latest examples of these sorts of allegations about Pell to go public. In 2002, a former teacher called Genevieve Grant from the St James Primary School in the sand-belt suburb of Gardenvale, also in Pell's jurisdiction, came forward to *The Sunday Age.* Grant told the newspaper she tried to raise concerns with the Auxiliary Bishop in 1989 in the school staffroom during his visit to the school, but he 'brushed me aside' and 'didn't want to know'. Pell countered in a statement to the paper that 'no teacher spoke to me alleging sexual improprieties by Father Pickering on students'. Father Ronald Pickering, a serial paedophile, fled the jurisdiction in the middle of the night in 1993 with litigious victims on his tail. A memorandum by then-Vicar General Gerry Cudmore, tendered many years later to the child abuse Royal Commission, said: 'I got word from

Bishop Pell and he said "I think you better go down to Gardenvale, I have heard that Pickering's gone..." So, I went down and I think [Pickering's housekeeper] was a bit stunned, she didn't quite understand what happened. He rang during the night and I came the next day and she is still trying to put it all together, but she implied that the police were on his tail.' Pell said in 2016 that he did 'not recall' hearing that the police were on [Pickering's] tail. 'I just might have, but I've got no such recollection.'

Pickering fled to the United Kingdom and moved in with another paedophile priest—from the Ballarat Diocese—Paul David Ryan. The Melbourne Response compensated Pickering's victims. But Pickering himself also continued to be compensated, while in England, living out his days. He was paid a monthly stipend by Pell, by then Archbishop of Melbourne. Pell argued that he had an 'obligation to pay out all priests who are not laicised, even if they are convicted'. Pell's successor Denis Hart did not feel that same obligation. When he took over from Pell he cut off the money supply until Pickering shifted off this mortal coil in 2009.

If these accounts of people being warned off speaking the truth by an archdiocesan fixer are true, they suggest Pell was a man used to getting his own way, to throwing his weight around with the priests below him and who, even as Auxiliary Bishop, not yet in the top job, felt comfortable in exercising raw power, and was dismissive of those beneath him. But not just that, it goes against the image he has carefully tried to construct in the years since he did become archbishop—an image of a white knight who was determined to clean up the sexual abuse crisis in his archdiocese. A man of principle and honour who might at times lack social skills, but made up for it with fortitude and courage. As one of the most senior priests on the Curia of the Melbourne Archdiocese at the time remarked to me, 'Look, to be frank, I don't think very many people had that view of George Pell. I don't think George Pell had it either.' When I push the senior priest to tell me what Pell was then, if not a pioneer on child abuse, he is blunt: 'To be honest, I don't think anything of him. He was an ambitious man and a bully and all the things I don't think bishops should be.'

5

A TWEETER BEFORE TWITTER

And the angel said to them, 'Be not afraid'.

Luke 2:10

The announcement in July 1996 that Pell had become Archbishop of Melbourne was a huge surprise to the priests of the city. It was no secret that many of them did not care for his style. It was equally apparent that Pell himself was unburdened by this and felt that he should get on with reforming an archdiocese which he considered to be foundering under Frank Little.

Terry Laidler, who had by then long left the priesthood, was doing the evening shift on Melbourne's ABC local radio talkback station, then known as 3LO. After the fax carrying the announcement of Pell's appointment had rolled off the machine, he remembers staring at the press release, wondering if he was reading it right. No-one saw it coming. He called his friend, the parish priest at Belgrave, Phil O'Donnell. O'Donnell remembers, 'Terry says, "Frank's resigned, George is Archbishop of Melbourne!" And I said, "Piss off Laidler, I've got a meeting to go to." And he said, "No, Phil, I'm serious" and he and I could not believe it.'

Laidler faxed the press release through to O'Donnell and, O'Donnell says, 'I just sat there, stunned and then I went out and said to the finance guys, "We've got a new Archbishop".'

For the next days, the phones rang hot on the priestly grapevine. 'People were just shocked,' O'Donnell says. The thing that really shocked them was that Little was just seventy—five years younger than the usual age in which an archbishop submits his retirement. Like most septuagenarians, he had a few health complaints, but nothing so serious as to be a significant impediment to his ministry. There had been no warning signs that it was coming. And his successor stood proudly for a form of clerical Catholicism which

Little did not at all support. 'Others do the choosing,' Little famously said.

'To use a contemporary parallel, for us, it was kind of like Trump following Obama,' O'Donnell muses. One of the curiosities of those years for outsiders looking in is that Little was considered a gentle, decent and inclusive operator by the priests and parishioners of his archdiocese at the time, however unkind history has rightly been to his appalling handling of the sexual abuse crisis. 'And then you get the Big Man come in,' O'Donnell remembers. 'And I thought, "Wow, it's not going to be dull".'

Dull it most certainly was not. O'Donnell says most of the priests he knew in the archdiocese were not happy about Pell's appointment, although at the time O'Donnell said he had a very cordial relationship with the Archbishop and they always got on 'very, very well' in person. He remembers Pell coming to stay at his parish for three days in the early years of Pell's tenure in the top job. 'I was a bit apprehensive because we were at different ends of the spectrum of the Church, so having George as a house guest—I didn't know how it would be,' O'Donnell says. 'But I do have to say it was an absolute pleasure having him and he was very good company—very convivial and very respectful. I think he and I have had plenty of points of debate and discussion around various issues, but it was a very positive experience. I have got some very serious criticisms of George, but not on a personal level. On a personal level, I found him to be very good.'

So, what happened? How did Pell become archbishop out of the blue? The word among Melbourne priests of the time was that Little had in the January of that year visited Rome, asking the Vatican to appoint a coadjutor, or, essentially, anointed successor, so that when the time was right for him, he could move on with a smooth succession plan in place. That is what had always happened. But when Little went to Rome, he was told that that was not to happen. He came back, tail between his legs and six months later, the Pope appointed Pell, a man with whom he had little common ground and with whom his relationship was civil at best; as Pell himself said much later, 'we were not close friends in any sense'.

'Frank never had any time for Pell but got saddled with him [as Auxiliary],' says Eric Hodgens, who was a senior priest in the archdiocese at the time. Hodgens points out that it's significant that Pell was at that time a member of the Congregation for the Doctrine of the Faith—allowing him to become a player in the Vatican. 'This job involved regular participation in Roman meetings and wheeling and dealing in Vatican politics,' Hodgens writes for the Catholic website *Catholica.* 'George became a recognised figure in Vatican corridors.'

When, years later, Pell was asked about Little's retirement in the Royal Commission into Institutional Responses to Child Sexual Abuse, he was highly critical of Little and indicated that his covering up of child abuse, including keeping secret files on paedophile priest allegations, had something to do with Little's early retirement—four years early.

He said that 'it would not surprise me if Archbishop Little was requested to put in his resignation'. Pell declined to say who might have made this request, but agreed that the Apostolic Nuncio Brambilla would have had the power to do this and it 'would have been done in consultation with [Little]'.

'It wasn't worked out in consultation with *you?*' the Counsel Assisting the Royal Commission, Gail Furness, asked him tartly.

'No, it wasn't,' Pell replied.

The priests he was to lead at the time were sceptical of whether the child abuse mismanagement by Little was the real reason, believing instead that Pell was simply the Pope's Man in Melbourne. One way or the other, it was recognised that the child abuse issue desperately needed to be addressed.

Little had secret files and allowed accused priests to stay in their posts, like the infamous and dangerous Peter Searson at Doveton. Pell's publicly stated spin on this is that liberal, lax morality allowed this to happen and the only cure for it was a return to rigidity. In his words, 'a colossal failure of leadership'.

Whether you believe that interpretation, the clergy, even those who had no knowledge of what was going on, had been in complete denial about child abuse as an issue. Even some urbane, intelligent priests I have spoken to say that until the late 1980s, they are mortified to admit they had absolutely no understanding of child abuse—they thought it was simply a 'moral failing' of which a person could be 'cured'—not an incurable criminal addiction and something that would cause lifelong trauma in its victims. Some revealed that at that time they conflated abusing pubescent boys with homosexuality. They also say that this was a wider societal phenomenon and, certainly, it was common for familial abuse at the time not to be reported to police. My constant refrain to this is that these were crimes on the statute books. They say they know that, but are ashamed to admit they didn't have a real understanding of it then. Some were quite desperately naïve about matters sexual. And homosexuality was a crime on the statute books too.

These are decent men and they are speaking from the heart. But it can't help but stick in one's craw that at the time they were living under this gross misapprehension, their own Church, and the celibate men schooled in remote seminaries like the Corpus Christi of the fifties and sixties, was so incredibly prescriptive about how adults should live their lives—no contraception, no abortion, no sex outside marriage, no homosexual relationships. Also, not all of them were labouring under this dangerous falsehood. Father Noel Brady was advocating for survivors and knew what was happening was wrong. Phil O'Donnell was travelling the length and breadth of the state to hear from victims and to help them negotiate their complaints to the Church or the criminal justice system. Why did it occur to them and not others? When I ask these questions, the priests are embarrassed, but often a bit stumped, as to the answer. Some of the older ones go silent or change the subject or fluff the answer or plead their age. Right and wrong, as I have found out, are often sticky notions.

I remember an incident from my own childhood when I was about six years old that causes me to reflect on this collective ignorance. I was living in Scotland and attending a Catholic primary school in a small and unsophisticated regional town. It was at some point during, I think, 1979 or 1980. I was at the bottom of the playground with two friends and a man approached us from the other side of the fence and wanted to lift us over. He told us he had a little boy at home who was having a great time and had lots of sweets. We could get sweets too if we came with him. We told him we would not go and we did not like him, but we were kind of hypnotised with repulsion–attraction. We couldn't take our eyes away. We didn't notice the bell ring, the other children file inside. Eventually, the teachers realised we were missing and set out to find us. The man ran off and we were whisked away. The police were called and we were all given a lengthy lecture on stranger danger. The only telling, classically 1970s, aspect of this is that they neglected to tell my parents.

The point is, if a Catholic school in a forgettable little town in Scotland knew that potential child abuse was enough of a problem to call the police, surely the clerics of a large metropolitan archdiocese in Australia did too? It's hard to escape the feeling that the difference here is that the offenders were their own, that it was hard for them to think that a man of God, the fellow charged with, like them, telling the rest of us what to do, could suffer from the same human frailty as a creepy stranger.

Not long after Pell settled into the top job, he set about radically changing the way the archdiocese worked. He employed a slick corporate public relations firm, Royce Communications. Royce, under the careful stewardship of Peter Mahon, has been there with Pell ever since. Whether it or Pell comes up with the headlines is hard to say, but the Archbishop went with punchy, newsworthy messaging, big time.

'Think the religious equivalent of "jobs and growth" or "stop the boats"—Pell was gifted at simple messaging,' Hodgens says. Policy and theology translated into simple and digestible grabs. David Marr lists some of them in his Quarterly Essay, *The Prince,* written about Pell in 2013: 'Mail Order Divorce' and 'the spread of gay propaganda', and others include: 'our contraception culture' and 'the bland leading the bland'.

'Oh, George was a tweeter before Twitter,' Hodgens says. 'And he was doing that when the whole of the established authority of the Church in Rome was on his side—that explains his whole rise.'

The clever messaging extended to every part of the operation. For example, as Livingstone reports in the Pell biography, for his archbishop's coat of arms, 'Pell dispensed with the traditional Latin, choosing instead *Be Not Afraid,* echoing Christ's words to his followers in the Gospel'. But it was also in keeping with Pell's pugilistic style of Catholicism—the son of a boxer who owned a pub who had that very take-no-prisoners approach to theology and to ministry. It was perfect. Pell seemed like a guy who wasn't afraid of anything.

And he wasn't all talk—one of his first moves as archbishop that year was to clear out the entire staff at Corpus Christi seminary. Pell wanted to revamp the place, with a greater focus on prayerfulness, a return to a more monastic daily order, and a tightening of what he saw as liberal attitudes. The official version of events was that they resigned, but the bottom line is, every single member of staff resigned in a day—they believe they had no choice and so really, they were sacked. The decision rocked the archdiocese. It made international news.

The rector of the seminary was Father Paul Connell. Connell is an exceptionally bright, Oxford-educated theologian who still teaches at the Catholic Theological College in Melbourne. I met him at his presbytery at St Oliver Plunkett's in Pascoe Vale in Melbourne's northern suburbs, where Connell is parish priest. Connell has wrestled with his conscience and decided to set the record straight about what Pell did to him and his colleagues. 'It's been just over twenty years,' Connell told me. 'I think it's time.' In 1996, he sat down and made forensic contemporaneous notes about what took place with Pell. He put them away for safekeeping and only showed them to his closest confidants. In February 2017, he decided that the time was right to put them in the public domain and handed them to me across the little coffee table in his parlour.

Connell's account says he first learned of his and his colleagues' fate on Saturday 9 November 1996, when he met Pell at Mentone, where Pell had been living as Auxiliary Bishop, to discuss another matter. They had a brief discussion, and then Pell handed Connell a document. 'Now to more contentious matters,' the Archbishop declared. The document proposed that the seminary be moved from the Clayton site and proposed a radical overhaul. While the Archbishop indicated that there had been some discussion about whether the changes be delayed, he had 'decided a few weeks ago to cross the Rubicon and do it now'. 'I suppose it would be difficult for you [the present seminary staff] to implement this,' Connell says the Archbishop told him.

Connell could only agree that the Archbishop was right.

Connell was snookered and he knew it. Under Connell, the seminary had a central focus on the key goal of human formation, in line with Pope John Paul II's 1992 exhortation *Pastores Dabo Vobis*—what Connell describes as a 'magnificent document'—'effectively the Magna Carta for seminary formation'. The document argues, Connell says, that despite the decline in priestly vocations that was happening at the time, it was still primarily important that seminaries were forming priests as mature human beings.

These principles had guided the original design of Clayton, and Connell felt that they would be put at risk under this new system. Pell had already put some thought into where each of them might go—one priest could have a 'good parish', another could continue his academic work at a university, and Connell would be treated with 'dignity' and allowed to continue lecturing Theology.

Connell went back to see his staff. 'Well, we've been sacked!' he told them.

The following Tuesday, the trustees of the seminary met—that is, all of the bishops of Victoria and Tasmania. When Connell arrived at 4p.m., he sensed the bishops had had a 'testing' day. The other bishops wanted to protect the reputation of the seminary staff and so a compromise deal was sought with Pell whereby the present staff could stay on for a year, but only if they did so under the new Pell model. 'Apparently, George had begun by holding a gun at their collective heads. If they rejected his proposals, they were welcome to continue to conduct Corpus Christi, but he would withdraw and start his own seminary for Melbourne. Since he controlled about two thirds of the proprietorship and financial resources of the seminary, and each other [bishop] just a fraction, this amounted to fairly crude blackmail,' Connell wrote. The other bishops were, Connell said, being challenged to put at risk the unity of the region. He said they were in an 'intolerably difficult position'.

'Such pushing through of his own agenda with unseemly haste is again a typical tactic of George,' Connell wrote.

'Little time is allowed for any effective opposition to develop, and his thick-skinned blustering style invariably wins the day.'

Connell went back to his staff with a heavy heart. They did not want to work under 'an excessively forceful and interfering chairman' like Pell. They did not want to be used for a year, then simply cast aside. And resignation was a 'particularly galling prospect', because they felt they were doing good work.

So, the staff resolved to refuse to resign and to force Pell to sack them—then 'George would have to bear the public consequences of carrying out his own original decisions in this whole affair'. But when Connell told Pell of this decision the following day, Pell replied that that was most certainly not to happen. 'You have to resign,' Connell says the Archbishop blustered. 'The motion's designed for that.' Snookered again, Connell acquiesced. Connell announced at a meeting of staff and students that the entire staff had decided 'that we have no option but to resign'. At dinner that night, Connell says Pell described the meeting as 'one of the more difficult things I've had to do'.

Of course, it was far more difficult for the staff. But Connell was determined not to let that show or to stoop to a tabloid-style public spat with the Archbishop. The Archbishop was convinced that this was going to drive enrolment numbers up. While seminary numbers had, admittedly, dropped enormously since the 1970s, Connell was committed to the screening processes he and his staff had implemented to make sure that the right people were entering, people who were temperamentally suited to becoming priests. 'George's views were more akin to the older practices of accepting almost anyone and "letting the seminary sort them out".' The dreadful legacy of the seminary of the fifties and sixties—that is, the scourge of paedophilia—shows just how important screening was. And it shows that the seminary most certainly did not sort them out. Pretty much every priest I have spoken to for this book—whatever their theological or philosophical persuasion—believes that it's more likely that this vocation was seen as a 'safe haven' for someone with paedophiliac tendencies, rather than the seminary being a place that created paedophiles. If that's true, then good testing and vetting procedures for the seminary are and were vital.

Dr Michael Leahy, who is friends with some of those who lost their jobs, says there is no other way of putting it than they were 'summarily dismissed'. Despite his warm relationship with Pell in their seminary and Propaganda Fide days, Leahy thinks this type of exercise of power by Pell and other 'ruthlessly destructive' examples he has been told of over the years by priest friends, 'can be characterised in no other terms than those of a bully'.

'You might be tempted to think that the exercise of authority in this way is not altogether surprising in a notoriously authoritarian institution,' Leahy says. 'In fact, it is even more scandalous than it would be in a secular institution. The Church is in its very essence supposed to be a community of love. The tyrannical exercise of authority thus always violates this essence and thus harms the faith of those who see it and suffer it.'

Be that as it may, the seminary numbers began to climb again in the years following and, as of 2015, *The Age* reported, the intake was back to fifty-nine seminarians—the largest number since the 1970s. Some Catholic commentators believe the positive influence of Pell has been lasting. But the *Age* article makes the point that one of the real 'pull' factors now is the charismatic Pope Francis and his infectious message of love and kindness. As Connell pointed out, since Pell's changes, the rigorous screening processes that he and his colleagues had employed were gone.

Father Peter Matheson, who is now parish priest at Cheltenham in Melbourne's sand belt, believes Pope Francis, not Pell, is definitely the dominant factor in those that are coming forward with vocations now. But he says the idea that the seminaries are filling again to any significant degree is overstated. He says there is a 'desperate' shortage of priests and those who are left work extremely hard.

He says that the Pell–Hart legacy has left a different complexion in the clergy in Melbourne too. 'A lot of the young priests that are coming through are very, very conservative,' Matheson says. 'We are basically Vatican II priests and I think they are waiting for us to die off. The young guys are what we call "sacristy priests"—they are more interested in things like canon law than they are in the people or putting people first before the law. They like wearing their soutanes and their collars—it's a very clerical model, different to our model, which was about working with people.' He says that the model reflected in the younger priests was popularised and encouraged in the era of Pell in the 1990s and 2000s.

Matheson was in 1996 chairman of the Diocesan Liturgical Commission, which worked with the parishes on issues like how the mass would be told—for example, how much parishioners were involved, which music would be chosen—and it also ran a diocesan magazine. He says he was immediately removed when Pell came in, to be replaced by Pell's friend and later successor, Denis Hart. 'The basic reason was that we were discussing what we were going to do when there were not enough priests to celebrate masses—how the liturgy would be celebrated and how we might assist the laypeople of a parish to conduct a lay-led mass,' Matheson remembers. This was not so much a desire of the commission, but rather a recognition, he says, that it was a realistic possibility given the rapid decline of vocations. 'We thought that would have to happen in the future,' Matheson says. 'But George said that [a lay-led mass] was not happening in any archdiocese of his. Our vision of the future was not his.' Matheson was philosophical about his demise in the role—but said it was yet another of the decisions that symbolised the shift under Pell and created a Church in Melbourne that was radically different to what had come before.

6

TOWARDS HEALING?

Broadly speaking, my aim in introducing the Melbourne Response was to make it easier for victims to achieve justice, and to seek financial compensation and counselling, without needing to establish legal liability. I believe that it was the first scheme of its kind implemented anywhere in the world to respond to victims of child sexual abuse. I was, and remain, proud of its establishment and the assistance it has provided to victims since 1996.

Statement of Cardinal George Pell, August 2014

The percolating child abuse crisis was to be much harder to fix than dumping the staff of a seminary or cleaning out one's ideological or theological adversaries from Church bodies. The media was going after the issue in a big way. The victims were becoming emboldened. It was becoming a dominant narrative: terrible PR for a Church whose mass attendance numbers were already in freefall. It was potentially costly in terms of compensation payouts. And in 1996, it was unclear just how many priests Pell as archbishop might lose to criminal prosecutions, but suffice to say they were falling over like dominoes. Little before him had quietly folded the issue into a neat little box and stuffed it at the very bottom of a decidedly deep, too-hard basket.

Jeff Kennett, the then-Victorian premier, was on the warpath. Kennett had in some ways a similarly can-do, crash-or-crash-through, Steerforthian personal style to Pell. There are also parallels between how their legacy is viewed. Kennett may have closed a lot of schools and been antagonistic to opponents, but by god, they say, he got things done: Kennett got an ossified and financially crippled state moving again. Similarly, with Pell, he may divide opinion, many say, but at least he's got muscular, traditional ideals, at least he's a man of action, at least he's out there fighting for the one true apostolic Church, none of this wishy-washy bunkum. Kennett told Pell at a meeting that something must be done about the abuse issue. The former premier was asked about it in *The Australian* in 2015. The newspaper said Kennett 'liked Pell' and quoted him as saying, 'I don't think that George has ever run away from it'.

'I was not one of the [Catholic] flock and I said to him, if he doesn't fix it, I will. I said that not as a threat [but] as an encouragement.'

But when I called Kennett in late 2016 to take me through what happened, Kennett, who has in the past been happy to cooperate with me on other controversial stories and to say things that upset powerful people, blanched. I told him I was just interested in getting the history right, did he mind if I asked why he was refusing to comment? 'Oh quite frankly, Louise, because I can't be bothered,' Kennett said. 'Anyway, good luck with your project, I'm quite busy, have a good day, bye!' This was after I had published a series of allegations on the *7.30* program about Pell.

Whatever Kennett's motives were, the 'I can't be bothered' refrain is a common one from people who have refused to speak to me, or, at least, have refused to speak to me *on the record,* for this book. Many say it's too hard to step into the fray with either Pell or his bullish band of defenders; it is an exhausting business, sometimes accompanied by legal letters, inevitably followed by outraged columns or poisonous tweets from his supporters. 'You never hear the end of it,' one priest complained. 'I've been down that path before,' another former seminarian demurred. 'To tell you the truth, I'm completely Georged out,' said a third.

Of course, Kennett wasn't the only person in Australia who had worked out that there was a veritable tsunami of child abuse claims coming at the nation's Catholic Church. The Church hierarchy, too, had realised it had to act. The Victorian Governor at the time, former judge Richard McGarvie, also had a word to Pell. He told him in 1996, 'You are going to have to deal with this problem resolutely. If you don't, it will bleed you dry for years—emotionally, and more importantly than that, it will bleed away the good standing of the Church.' McGarvie suggested something akin to a 'Catholic Royal Commission'. In fact, more than two decades later, a worldfirst report by an actual Royal Commission—into Institutional Responses to Child Sexual Abuse—found that 7 per cent of Australian priests working between 1950 and 2010 had sexual abuse complaints made against them to the Church. That's far higher than the international figure of 2 per cent as the quantum of paedophile priests offered by Pope Francis to Italy's *La Repubblica* newspaper in 2014. For Christian Brothers, the figure was a whopping 20 per cent. St John of God, 40 per cent. Of the complaints at that time, ground zero was the Archdiocese of Melbourne which Pell oversaw. Between 1950 and 2010, 8.1 per cent of 859 priests were accused of sexual abuse. While there were other dioceses where the percentage was higher, they were in places where the numbers of priests were far lower. Melbourne had more paedophile priests than any other place in the country. And most of them operated during Pell's time in Victoria as priest or bishop.

Pell is proud of his record in being the first Australian bishop to respond to the child abuse crisis. He consistently cites it when he is being scrutinised in the media and points out that he was probably the first in the world, let alone here in Australia, to boldly go where no other bishop had dared to tread. In 2016, he said: 'When I became Archbishop, I turned the situation right around so that the Melbourne Response procedures were light years ahead of all this obfuscation and prevarication and deception.'

You have to wonder, then, what this religious leader who was so zealously committed to rooting out child abuse was doing in March 1996—just four months before his appointment as archbishop—at the funeral of one Nazareno Fasciale. Fasciale was parish priest at Yarraville in Melbourne's inner west. In the preceding December, Fasciale had been charged by Newport detectives with multiple counts of indecent assault and gross indecency against four victims who had been assisted by the newly formed victims' advocacy group Broken Rites. The priest had been remanded to appear in court the following February. As the new year arrived, the Newport detectives discovered that there was another file on Fasciale with three further victims in the nearby town of Geelong, and police had planned to apply to the Office of Public Prosecutions to combine the cases. When the matter came to court in February, a Church solicitor applied for an extension of time, alleging poor health on the part of Fasciale. The date was set for six weeks later. Fasciale was dead within a month.

Fasciale's skirmishes in the criminal justice system right before his death did not deter his priestly colleagues from giving him a glorious requiem mass send-off at St Mary's in West Melbourne. The archdiocese published a death notice, ending with the words 'caring for those who cared'. Four bishops, along with an extraordinary sixty priests, attended the funeral. The Auxiliary Bishop of Melbourne Peter Connors led the ceremony, referring only obliquely to Fasciale's crimes. 'The life of our brother Nazareno Fasciale was not without its own fair measure of pain and suffering,' Connors conceded. 'He would be the first to confess that he too was a sinner. So often a priest has to struggle alone.' The mass booklet was adorned with a photograph of Fasciale, head thrown back in an infectious smile. It was written in Italian as well as English: *'Nelle tue mani, Padre clementissimo, consegnamo l'anima del nostro fratello, Nazareno...':* 'Into your hands, Father of mercies, we commend our brother Nazareno ... in the sure and certain hope that, together with all who have died in Christ, he will rise with him on the last day ... Open the gates of paradise to your servant and help us who remain to comfort one another with assurances of faith, until we all meet in Christ and are with you and with our brother forever.' As the Almighty opened the gates of paradise for Brother Nazareno, one of the four bishops at the funeral was Pell. The Master of Ceremonies was Pell's best mate in the Church, Denis Hart.

As one of the senior priests of the day told me: 'I don't think any priest would apologise if he was to pray for the repose of the soul of a sinner—whether that sinner was a priest or otherwise.' I countered to this priest that the same consideration was not given by many of those priests present to the little kids who were abused. Then or even now. Maybe Pell just didn't know that Fasciale had been charged with indictable offences against little kids. Priests, he would often later chide, don't gossip. This was not, I might say, my experience, in writing this book. They love a yarn and are wonderful storytellers. They'll sit on the phone to you for ages. They'll give you the blow-by-blow lowdown on who's who. Information is currency in the priestly world.

Two years before the funeral, in 1993, when Fasciale resigned for euphemistically titled 'ill health and stress' after, handwritten archdiocesan notes attested, being 'shocked and repentant' about what he had done to children, Pell was on the Personal Advisory Board which accepted the resignation letter. Pell agreed that of the five members of the board that day, three—Archbishop Little, Monsignor Gerry Cudmore and Monsignor Hilton Deakin—were aware of child abuse complaints against Fasciale. So, was Pell? Did they tell him? 'I can't remember whether they did or they didn't. It is possible that they did,' Pell much later said.

The funeral of Fasciale occurred about three years after the fateful day when Pell accompanied serial paedophile Gerald Ridsdale to court in Warrnambool. The photograph will haunt Pell to his grave—it is used by the media every time there is a discussion of him and child abuse. On a kind interpretation, Pell was just doing what real Catholics do, walking with a sinner at his darkest hour. Having grown up Catholic, I can absolutely see that could have been the case. But from the Ridsdale victims' point of view, this 'priestly act of solidarity', as Pell much later called it, is nothing more than a slap in the face to them and their enormous suffering. Moreover, they say, the magnanimity that Pell extended to

Ridsdale has not been extended to victims. The Fasciale business suggests that perhaps Warrnambool didn't represent a one-off, well-meaning, priestly brain snap, that it represented an attitude.

Whatever he thought in March 1996, by Pell's account in July, his resolve had hardened against this dreadful paedophile scourge. He launched the Melbourne Response at a press conference attended by his Special Commissioner Peter O'Callaghan, QC, his spin doctors at Royce, and his lawyers, Corrs Chambers Westgarth, who drew up the scheme. For the first time, he apologised unreservedly to victims. It seemed like this was a turning point. The scheme included, apart from the Special Commissioner, a compensation panel led by Alex Chernov, QC—later a Supreme Court judge—which could award the victims up to $50 000, and an independent counselling service known as Carelink. At the end of the process with the complainant, Pell would sign a letter of apology.

Victoria Police released a statement welcoming the Melbourne Response, saying it was 'a positive step in tackling this very sensitive community issue'. In his much later statement to the Victorian parliamentary Inquiry into the Handling of Child Abuse by Religious and Other Institutions in 2014, Pell wrote that as archbishop, he knew he had to act immediately. 'This was an issue that needed urgent attention and ... we needed to do much better in our response,' the Pell statement says. 'At that stage no decision had then been taken by the Australian bishops to set up the Towards Healing procedures. This was decided at the November 1996 meeting of the Australian Bishops' conference. The Towards Healing Protocol was published in December 1997.'

While this is all strictly true, it's a pretty selective analysis of the facts. In 1996, the Australian Catholic Bishops Conference was working on a scheme called Towards Healing and had been developing it and consulting with stakeholders for three years. The man charged with running it was the

Auxiliary Bishop of Sydney, Geoffrey Robinson. Robinson, importantly, came from the other end of the priestly ideological spectrum to Pell. He was from the Vatican II primacy-of-conscience set.

The history of how this took place is significant, because Pell's immediate refrain whenever he is questioned about his handling of child abuse matters, is that he was, through his Melbourne Response, the first Catholic bishop in Australia, and anywhere in the world, to come up with a comprehensive program to tackle the child abuse question.

Pell was most certainly not the first person in the Catholic Church to decide to address the issues, he just got in at the last minute, before the national response was about to be released.

In the 1980s, the Church's euphemistically titled 'Special Issues Committee' was headed by, of all people, Bishop Ronald Mulkearns from Ballarat, who had covered up the offending of priests in his diocese for decades. However, the committee began to mature as the realisation dawned on the Church internationally that something must be done. Robinson said that at first psychiatrists told them they could cure paedophile priests, but that changed as the profession came to terms with the incurable nature of paedophilia. Robinson was appointed to develop a new protocol, which was to become Towards Healing. One of the questions often asked of the Church is why develop a protocol at all? This was, after all, a criminal justice issue—why not direct the complainants to the police? But Robinson says the majority of complainants he met at that time were not interested in going to the police.

So, Robinson set his mind to developing an alternative forum for victims to get some sort of restorative justice, not to mention making sure that none of the accused priests remained in service with access to children. But turning around the attitudes of his colleagues was a massive effort. 'There was always this loyalty to the priest question that was there,' Robinson later said. '[And] for a lot of the bishops the fault was a moral one and sin was a sexual sin. That was the big mortal sin. The harm that might have been caused to the minor was not treated as seriously.' He bore the brunt of some of the bishops' ire. 'One bishop called me a fanatic, another an avenging angel, and yet another accused me of "acting like Adolf Hitler in the way you harangued and bullied the bishops".' Having said that, of the forty-one bishops present at a vote in April 1996, only five voted against the protocol.

As one of the senior people involved with the developmental stages of Towards Healing remembers, getting the protocol drawn up was a tricky business: 'It had been going on for three years. Every time we drew up a protocol, Geoff Robinson would rightly insist on taking it to the victims' groups and understandably, it was never good enough [for them] and we had draft after draft after draft.' Robinson also had to get diverse dioceses and religious orders, each with their own leaders who had differing views, to come together as one. It was a massive task.

'So instead of having this thing in 1994 as we expected, it had dragged on to November 1996. George came in as archbishop and because he thought we were taking too long, he decided he would introduce his own protocol,' the person told me.

Auxiliary Bishop of Canberra Pat Power was involved at the time as a bishop on the conference floor who observed proceedings. Power, who is now retired, says that matters had come to a head in April 1996. There had been a conference at the University of Sydney called the International Conference on Sexual Abuse. Robinson and the senior Brigidine nun who was working with him, Sister Angela Ryan, gave an 'excellent' workshop at it, even though 'the Catholic Church had come in for a lot of flack at that workshop'. 'Someone asked Geoff Robinson, "What has the Vatican done in response to all of this?"' And Geoff paused for a while and eventually said that there was very little. That was the grab that got in the news.' Power says that Robinson thus came in for criticism in some quarters of the Church.

Robinson, incidentally a victim of child sexual abuse himself who was forced to confront his own painful history by speaking to so many victims, wrote about this in his 2008 book, *Confronting Power and Sex in the Catholic Church.* He said the failure to act went to the highest levels of the Church—to the papacy. 'I was one of many people crying out for strong and compassionate leadership on this matter and trying to do my best without the support of that leadership,' Robinson wrote. 'I felt that here was the perfect opportunity for the papacy to fulfil its most basic role of being the rock that holds the church together, but this did not happen and the church fractured.' Robinson said the public comment he made at the workshop about the Church's response attracted a letter from the Congregation for Bishops in Rome citing 'ongoing concern' that he had 'expressed views that are seriously critical of the magisterial teaching and discipline of the Church'.

'I was told that "in a recent audience, the Holy Father has been fully apprised of your public position on these issues and He has shown 'serious preoccupation in your regard".' Two months later, [16 October 1996—the month before the Australian Church was to meet on Towards Healing and very soon before Pell made his announcement about the Melbourne Response] I received a further letter informing that "the relevant documentation will be forwarded, for its information and review, to the Congregation for the Doctrine of the Faith", implying that I was suspected of some sort of heresy.' Pell was, of course, a member of the Congregation for the Doctrine of the Faith.

But Robinson carried on, determined to get the Towards Healing protocol out to in some way address the pain of the many victims whose tragic stories he had borne witness to during those years. 'Geoff sent out about ten things trying to achieve consensus before we were all due to meet in the November,' Power recalls. 'Then out of the blue, George Pell comes up with his own thing. When he claims that he was the one that gave the lead, he really just broke ranks with everyone. Certainly, the thing of him coming out early was something everyone felt very critical about.'

'The Melbourne bombshell,' Robinson later called it, confirming that Pell had been there for all of the discussions on Towards Healing, all of the motions, but hadn't said a word against it. Robinson knew nothing of the Melbourne Response until Pell made it public without telling any of the other bishops. 'He later would claim that he was the first person in Australia to have such a protocol, he was ahead of everybody, in other words. I mean, that's only a very partial truth ... Melbourne was the biggest [diocese in Australia, because Sydney is divided into parts] which meant that we no longer had that unanimity that we were all working together.'

Bishop Bill Morris, who had joined the Bishops Conference in 1993 as Bishop of Toowoomba, says the other bishops were very disappointed. 'Well, this is George, George will go his own way because George wants to reform the Church according to George Pell,' Morris says. 'This is the way he will operate and he is not going to be told. He believes his approach is the best approach. No-one will tell him what to do. That's George. It's unfortunate.

'It would have been much better for the Church in Australia to act as one to bring in a national approach and I am sure those who were close to George would have said that to him.'

The November 1996 meeting, which included bishops from every diocese in the country, as well as the leaders of all the religious orders such as the Jesuits and the Christian Brothers, was the day that the bishops approved the Towards Healing protocol—a united Church front to make an attempt to address this scourge. Some who were present were particularly furious at Pell's lack of consultation with others—especially his failure, as they put it, to hear the opinions of the religious leaders who would be operating in the Melbourne Archdiocese.

One of those was Bill Uren, Provincial of the Jesuit order. When, in the weeks before the conference, Uren heard that Pell was bringing in his own scheme, he rang Pell's archdiocesan business manager, Ted Exell. Uren and Exell went way back—they were altar boys together in the 1940s. Uren told Exell that it would be good if Pell consulted with the religious superiors of Victoria before making a final decision. Exell told his old friend he would mention it to the Archbishop. Uren also made a phone call to a mutual legal contact whose firm worked closely with Pell, a man Uren had known since boyhood too. The lawyer reportedly said he'd see what he could do too. Uren never heard back but has no doubt that the messages would have been passed on to Pell.

The big meeting was at Kensington in Sydney on 22 November 1996. On the conference floor, Uren's blood began to boil because when Robinson would mention 'the protocol' (Towards Healing), Pell would interrupt and say, 'there are two protocols'. After it happened several times, Uren saw red. He jumped to his feet and confronted Pell across the conference floor for not consulting the religious leaders of Victoria before going ahead with the Melbourne Response. Pell replied that he did consult them, but Uren said to Pell he believed the only one Pell had spoken to was Brother Paul Noonan—who was then the head of the Christian Brothers. Uren had received the information in one of those typical Catholic coincidences—his personal assistant was the wife of the Christian Brothers' lawyer. Uren told the conference about consulting Exell, and went on to correct Pell about the 'consultation', saying it was simply a statement informing Noonan that it would be happening. It was said that you could have heard a pin drop. Uren really got going then, saying that the rest of them had been working on Towards Healing for three years and had been gazumped by Pell without any consultation with the religious leaders.

After the meeting, sources told me the two went toe-to-toe in the doorway, where Pell is said to have told Uren he objected to being called a liar in front of his fellow bishops. Uren was undeterred. He asked why Pell hadn't consulted the provincials and Pell is reported to have said 'because of the sort of provincial you are'. Bill Morris remembers the confrontation on the conference floor and the scene in the doorway. 'You see, Bill Uren, like George, is a big man. The two of them reminded me of two big bull seals, you know? Fronting up to each other in Antarctica.'

Uren finished up as Provincial of the Jesuits the following month, in December 1996. Ironically, and much to Uren's dismay, his successor, Daven Day, was the only religious leader (or bishop) in Australia to opt to go with Pell's Melbourne Response, rather than Towards Healing.

Morris and many others I have spoken to in the Church believe that Towards Healing, while certainly not perfect and in many ways wanting, had a more pastoral outlook than the Melbourne Response, which was set up under the auspices of a Queen's Counsel and had a more legalistic framework. Nonetheless, many have a great respect for O'Callaghan and said they believed he was motivated by decency.

'What [Pell] came up with had a lot to recommend it,' Robinson says, 'but I had big problems with it too. The major one was that the very first point of contact for a victim was a QC in a city office, that's who he had to go and see, and I felt that that was just too much for victims altogether. Towards Healing, on the other hand, had a person go and see the victims in their own homes.'

Pell's argument is that the situation was so dramatic that he had to act swiftly. He later told the Victorian parliamentary inquiry, 'in light of the urgent need for an effective system to respond to victims of abuse and the uncertainty at that stage about initiatives for a national response, I moved quickly'. To be fair to Pell, things in the Catholic Church move in a byzantine and sluggish way. He knew the job needed to be done. But many of his colleagues believe that in going about it the way he did, he undermined the national process with an inferior scheme, and that unity was vital when addressing such a vexed issue. Moreover, as the Royal Commission was later to find in its report into the Melbourne Response, because Towards Healing did not cap the financial payment to victims as the Melbourne Response had—at $50 000—'it may have and has resulted in more generous payments to survivors than the Melbourne Response'.

Pell later said that when he was Archbishop of Melbourne 'the Catholic authorities worked from the principle that the needs of victims must be our first consideration'. With respect to Pell, that is not in my experience how the victims felt they were being treated. Pell said that he had only a handful of 'relatively minor complaints' about the scheme and 'on the contrary, over time I received many positive comments about the system'. In covering the later Royal Commission and speaking to survivors, solicitors and advocacy groups, I found that the response to the Response, from the people it was meant to help, was overwhelmingly underwhelmed. This was a position later reflected in the Victorian parliament's Betrayal of Trust Report by the Parliamentary Inquiry in the Handling of Child Abuse by Religious and Other Institutions of November 2013.

One of the issues some survivors had, including Chrissie and Anthony Foster, was that the counselling service Carelink was run by a psychiatrist, Professor Richard Ball, who had provided treatment not just to victims, but to priests of the archdiocese, including their daughters' abuser O'Donnell, and had also provided expert witness statements on the priests' behalf. The Fosters believed this was 'not fair' and the Royal Commission later agreed that while it did not question Ball's integrity, 'where there is a power imbalance, perceptions matter a great deal'.

Then there is the fact that Leder from Corrs Chambers Westgarth, who is Pell's solicitor and acts for both Pell and the archdiocese to the time of writing, was given medical and psychological reports and assessments of the victims (albeit 'on a confidential and without prejudice basis'), and was involved with each component of the process, at the same time as he was acting on behalf of the archdiocese in the civil matter the Fosters took. The Royal Commission later found the fact that Corrs was performing these dual roles raised 'clear potential for conflict. It also raises difficulties with confidentiality.' The Commission questioned the independence of the Melbourne Response—something Pell was always so publicly defensive about—'when the lawyer for the Archdiocese was a common and key element and was involved in all major steps of the process'.

A common refrain from survivors was that while they found O'Callaghan himself superficially pleasant enough, they found the framework set up by the archdiocese patronising, incomplete and insufficient; people said to me that they felt like it was set up 'to shut me up'. They often felt intimidated by the fact that interviews were conducted in O'Callaghan's barrister's chambers, which presented another power imbalance when, as a victim of child sexual abuse, power imbalance is something to which you are acutely sensitive. O'Callaghan himself rejects this as an issue. In the Melbourne Response's official documents, it cautions complainants that while they 'remain free to use the normal court processes' for civil compensation, such proceedings would be 'strenuously defended'.

Leder told Chrissie and Anthony Foster's daughter, Emma in his $50 000 compensation letter that it was provided as 'a realistic alternative to litigation which will otherwise be strenuously defended'. He later agreed that this would 'frighten the average person' and 'the language was inappropriate'. When the Fosters did eventually sue, it *was* strenuously defended in the sense that the Church, much to the Fosters' confusion and dismay, at first would not even admit the abuse in their defence to the Fosters' statement of claim. Leder was asked about this many years later, in 2014, by the Royal Commission's Counsel Assisting Angus Stewart, SC. 'Did you not see at the time that, whatever the technicalities about the legal structure of the Church and the breach of duty of care, the one thing that would hurt the most would be for the Church to deny that there had been abuse?' Leder's answer was dazzlingly legal. 'We didn't deny that there was abuse, sir.' What they did, Leder said, was *not admit* the abuse. He said he believed that it was up to the lawyers for the Fosters to explain the difference between 'do not admit' and 'deny'. The Church ultimately settled with the Fosters.

When many people think of the Fosters and Pell, the immediate thing that comes to mind is the well-told story about the couple going to see Pell, and being confronted with what Anthony Foster described (under parliamentary privilege in the Victorian Inquiry in 2013) as his 'sociopathic lack of empathy'. The headline-hitting moment was the Fosters showing Pell a photograph of Emma, after she had slashed her wrists, with Pell saying, 'Hmmm, she's changed, hasn't she?'

But what is less well known is the wrangling that went on for years, before a settlement was reached. The lengths the Church went to, through its Melbourne Response and the legal wrangling, demonstrated to the Fosters, Chrissie tells me, that 'I was a good Catholic and yet it meant nothing. I meant nothing, my girls meant nothing.' She says that she has not come across 'one single survivor who has had a positive experience of the Melbourne Response' and is scathing about the fact that, unlike Robinson with Towards Healing, victims were not consulted by Pell to set up the Melbourne Response. Foster believes it was a top-down, paternalistic approach, and 'a pathetic scheme'. She is also concerned that the scheme operated with impunity—with no regulation from government. 'The government allowed this to happen, there were no checks and balances, they were not accountable,' Foster says. 'It was a monopoly and it was basically "take that",' she says, referring to the ex gratia payments, 'or "get lost".'

Indeed, when I ask about the Melbourne Response, survivors invariably roll their eyes, or say, 'don't get me started on that'. One example is Julie Stewart. In a statement, Stewart said she had not expected the 'hostile cross-examination' to which she was subjected and was very troubled by being made to sit facing her abuser at the parish of Doveton, Father Peter Searson. She was required to sign a deed of release to waive her right to future compensation in order to be paid the $25 000 she was awarded and she also had to sign a document which she believed to be a confidentiality agreement. She left the hearing in tears. 'I felt that the whole process re-traumatised me,' Stewart wrote in her statement. The documents which were interpreted by survivors to be non-disclosure agreements were later abolished, but not before many felt that they had been used to silence them.

Another example is Paul Hersbach, who, along with his father, uncle and brother, was abused by the priest Victor Rubeo. I met the Hersbachs in 2014 and they are a lovely family but are deeply scarred, particularly Paul's dad, Tony—who feels so guilty that Rubeo's grooming of him continued to the point where the priest also preyed on his sons. O'Callaghan told Paul Hersbach that 'due to the "unsurprising haziness" of [Paul's] memory, there would not appear to be much point in taking his matter to the police'. Paul was awarded a $17 500 ex gratia payment by the Melbourne Response. As Paul Hersbach much later said, 'signing it helped me emotionally at the time, but now causes me angst. The Catholic Church has taken so much from me over the years. I feel like the Church has exerted complete and utter control over my life. I find it ironic that at the point where I finally wrested control back, I signed a document giving up my rights and putting myself again under its control...

'I want the Church to acknowledge that the deeds of release signed by victims through the Melbourne Response may add to a victim's burden and exacerbate the very problem they were designed to alleviate.'

Hersbach is one of the lucky survivors for whom the child sexual abuse he suffered has not been something which has dominated and destroyed his life. He thinks about it every day, but he has a lovely family and he's a senior executive at Australia Post. He says that Pell has become a lightning rod to which people attach their anger—sometimes without real justification. 'It's like a pantomime where they want to boo and hiss when he comes on stage,' Hersbach muses. But that said, he believes a dispassionate analysis of the Melbourne

Response is not at all favourable to Pell or those who designed it.

For instance, that compensation cap—$50 000—was a fraction of what the complainants might have expected to receive in a civil court had they been successful. Indeed, it was far less than what they would have received under Towards Healing, had Pell and his band of legal advisors (who were raking in a small fortune through their involvement in the scheme) not jumped in ahead of Robinson and the other bishops.

Between the start of the scheme, in October 1996, and March 2014, the Melbourne Archdiocese spent just over $34 million on the Melbourne Response. But the breakdown of figures is instructive. It paid $9.7 million in ex gratia compensation payments to survivors. The average amount received by a survivor was $32 000. Its Carelink scheme—to direct survivors into external counselling—cost $11.1 million (largely staff and administrative costs). But the biggest cost of all was the legal bills. The combined cost of paying for O'Callaghan (and his successor Jeff Gleeson, QC) and Corrs Chambers

Westgarth was $12.5 million. And that didn't count the other legal bills to Corrs and other silks to defend the Church in any compensation cases that were brought civilly or, for instance, to write solicitor's letters to people the Archbishop deemed defamatory. '[The legal bills for the Melbourne Response] were worth it,' Chrissie Foster says. 'He saved the Church hundreds of millions of dollars in what he would have had to pay in the courts.'

To be fair, a civil process would have taken years for a survivor to complete. Especially since civil claims were strenuously defended by Church lawyers—the same lawyers that were helping to run the Melbourne Response. The scenario is darkly comical. A Church happy to admit abuse if you take $20 000, but will not admit it if you claim $750 000.

Rightly or wrongly, survivors told the Royal Commission that they also felt deeply suspicious of O'Callaghan's motives when he cautioned them about difficulties he warned they might encounter if they went to the police (which, he did say, they were free to do). The Royal Commission found that O'Callaghan had discouraged some victims from going to the police and 'this advice was not appropriate'. O'Callaghan told complainants that if the police process commenced, the Melbourne Response process would terminate. The complainants were also not appointed lawyers—if they wanted one, it was their own responsibility. And while the Church would pay for a complainant's lawyer if the complainant asked, O'Callaghan would not offer it, and certainly nothing was offered in writing. The Church provided legal representation for the accused priests, no questions asked.

The more or less universal opinion of those I have spoken to—people whose childhoods were robbed of them—not to mention their legal representatives and other advocates, is that the Melbourne Response as it operated under Pell was nowhere near good enough. And if you are not pleasing, or even re-traumatising, the very people you supposedly set out to help in the first place, whether or not it was well intentioned becomes somewhat beside the point.

Francis Sullivan, from the Church's Truth, Justice and Healing Council, is the lay Catholic tasked with cleaning up after this almighty mess. As Sullivan conceded to me in an interview for the ABC *7.30* program, 'the Church, I don't believe, is up to looking after these matters internally'.

'Individuals who are either left confused or without information, who are left on the long handle and not responded to, who feel frustrated by the Church's processes, who sometimes are thwarted because they can't get information they need, all of that is the result of the Church investigating itself,' Sullivan says, his eyes shining.

So, when Pell says he was a trailblazer in handling the sexual abuse crisis in Australia, you have to take it with a grain of salt. As Paul Hersbach says to me of the fact that Pell jumped in ahead of the other bishops, with a scheme that limited how much victims would be paid and required deeds of release to be signed, 'history is littered with cases of he who wins the battle controls the story'. Hersbach, for one, is not buying that story. Pell may have won that battle, but he has not won the war. And as for the idea that Pell has been a white knight who came to the rescue of victims? Hersbach is scathing. 'I find that kind of offensive.'

7

BIG GEORGE

Your appointment was the biggest thing that has happened to Sydney since Plugger Lockett came to town.

Michael Costigan to George Pell

If Pell's handling of the Melbourne Response upset his fellow bishops, it had absolutely zero impact on his standing in Rome. The Archbishop of Melbourne continued, with the Pope's blessing, his ideological crusade. A key example of that mission was his handling of the 'Rainbow Sash' movement—a group of gay Catholics who wanted more acceptance from their Church. That acceptance was not forthcoming from Pell and matters came to a head on Pentecost Sunday, 31 May 1998. A group of Rainbow Sash protesters turned up to St Patrick's Cathedral, where a confirmation mass was taking place. They said their sexuality should not preclude them from participating actively in the mass. Pell refused them holy communion and upbraided them for disturbing the service. The congregation treated the Archbishop to a hearty round of applause. The protesters were crestfallen, and, as Bishop Pat Power remembers, felt 'further alienated'.

Rainbow Sash turned up to Power's own church in Canberra the Sunday after they had been to St Patrick's and Power regretfully informed them during his homily that Church teaching forbade him, too, from granting them the blessed sacrament of communion, which he said was one of the hardest things he had ever done in his thirty-three years as a priest. 'We need to find new and better ways for the Church to enunciate its teaching on sexual morality,' Power told the gathered congregation. 'I recognise the pain of you homosexual people here today, as I recognise the pain of too many other groups of Catholics: of Catholics in irregular marriages, of some of my dear friends who have left the active ministry.'

But the powers that were in the Vatican lay with Pell, not Power. Nothing encapsulates this more than an episode in the late nineties known ominously as The Statement of Conclusions, released at the Oceanic Synod (a meeting of bishops from the Oceania region) in 1998 and signed by the presidents of eight of the Roman congregations. The statement was a document which essentially outlined the Vatican's thoughts on the parlous state of the Australian Church. 'It was dreadful,' Power says. The criticisms contained in it echoed the sentiments often expressed by Pell, although the other bishops have never been able to prove that Pell had a hand in it.

Pell, like the other archbishops of the day and secretaries and chairs of bishops committees, was involved in dialogue before the Oceanic Synod and Power says they told him it was a good meeting and they felt positive about the future. Then, at the Oceanic Synod, Power, like all the other Australian bishops, had the opportunity to make a statement in front of the Pope and their ecclesiastical contemporaries and,

Power says, 'we all felt very liberated'. Some of the issues the Australian bishops brought up related to married priests, homosexuality and an expanded role for women in the Church. As Sister of Mercy and social justice advocate Sister Margaret Hinchey told *Four Corners* the following year, 'I was thrilled with that—thought, "This is wonderful, that the bishops are saying a lot of the things a lot of us are saying, they obviously are concerned".'

Power also felt hopeful. 'I remember someone making the comment one time that George has not had much to say, and someone else said, "George knows the real action is elsewhere",' Power tells me. 'Now, I don't really know what that meant and I have no evidence that George was responsible for this, but George would have been very well-connected among those people in the Vatican.'

The bishops' hopes were dashed. The Statement of Conclusions from Pope John Paul II basically rejected everything they were saying and criticised the egalitarian nature of the Australian Church which, the Pope supposed, could undermine the authority of the clergy. The bishops felt that the egalitarian nature of the Australian Church was its very strong point. Archbishop John Bathersby of Brisbane admitted to 'terrible disappointment' when he saw it and felt 'sad' and 'somewhat depressed'. 'But ultimately ... I prayed. I prayed about the document and because I did carry hurt and pain, and then said, "No, well this is coming from the leader of the Church. I have to take it seriously."' When, on the ABC's *Four Corners,* journalist Andrew Fowler asked Pell after The Statement of Conclusions was released what Pell thought was the biggest threat to the Catholic Church at that time, Pell replied, 'Oh, that we'll just merge into the background'. Merging into the background was, of course, the last thing Pell wanted for himself or his Church. '[I fear] that we'll just take on the colours of our society,' and added his memorable slogan, 'that we'll become the bland leading the bland.'

It was around about that time that a lay group based in Sydney and led by the conservative lawyer Paul Brazier started sending out spies to parishes around the country to see if priests were conducting group confessions through the Third Rite of Reconciliation. The Third Rite allowed Catholic mass-goers to have their sins absolved en masse rather than be required to visit the confessional alone with a priest. In what will be a mystery to non-Catholic readers, it was a great source of debate for Catholics in the 1980s and 1990s. It had been favoured by Pell's predecessor, Frank Little, but was not supported by Pope John Paul II. The conservative spies duly reported back the results of their spying on the Third Rite to Rome. Archbishop Len Faulkner of Adelaide, who is now ninety and retired, confirmed to me that this was happening in his archdiocese, where he had opposed the spying, and also raised concerns about the theologically conservative Catholic groups Opus Dei and the Neo-Catechumenates taking a foothold in South Australia. Faulkner is tired and not wanting to buy into the old debates any more, but he confirmed that such spying was against the spirit of the archdiocese he was trying to lead: one of openness and dialogue.

The Statement of Conclusions and its aftermath essentially confirmed that as far as Rome was concerned, the theological position championed by Pell, which railed against the primacy of conscience, had won. Pell was winning at home too. On 26 March 2001, he was appointed to the most important archdiocese in the country. Pell was made the eighth Metropolitan Archbishop of Sydney.

'I remember he would much later repeat back to me what I had said [at the time],' Michael Costigan remembers. 'Which was that "your appointment was the biggest thing that has happened to Sydney since Plugger Lockett came to town".'

'Plugger' was, of course, Tony Lockett, the dazzlingly talented AFL player who had played full-forward for St Kilda but had defected to Sydney in the nineties. '[Pell] thought that was pretty funny that I said that—he enjoyed it,' Costigan says.

'But the Plugger thing was kind of symbolic as well. Plugger was big, he was tough, the opposition would be making a mistake if they got in his way. He was a big player and he was a very good one. No-one in the game has kicked as many goals as he did. He was a very strong player and he did not take prisoners. You made a mistake if you stood in his way when he was charging through. And of course, that was like George.'

By the following year, 2002, Pell had become a true Catholic celebrity. He had friends and allies in high political office like Tony Abbott and Prime Minister John Howard. And despite the stern authoritarian pronouncements on how his flock should live their lives, he was nonetheless something of a social butterfly. He dined with an elite circle of Sydney Catholics and wowed his dinner companions with his charming banter.

One of those people was a good friend of mine from *The Australian,* where I then worked: Jane Fraser. She had a weekly column, 'Plainly Jane', a wicked sense of humour and a fabulous harbourside mansion where she would serve champagne to guests on the terrace. Jane, a member of the *Catholic Weekly* Board and a regular at St Mary's Cathedral, loved Pell. When Jane died, Pell said she was 'a dear friend, great company and good to be with'. She would often speak of him—she'd sometimes discuss dinners where matters of the day would be mulled over with Pell and other prominent Catholics. Jane said Pell was jolly good fun, incredibly bright and maintained 'the knockers' just didn't get him.

But in the middle of that year, the Carnival of George came to a sudden and grinding halt. In June, the Nine Network's *60 Minutes* program featured a story about abuse victim David Ridsdale, who claimed that Pell had tried to stop him from going public about his long-running abuse by his uncle, serial paedophile Gerald Ridsdale. The Ridsdale allegation turned into something of a saga, which went on for more than a decade.

On 7 August, an article appeared in a much less august publication that would nonetheless cause far more of a headache for the Archbishop than the slickly produced *60 Minutes* effort. The story landed in a little-known leftist website called *Indymedia*. The author professed to be one 'Xavier O'Byrne' of 'Parramatta'. He said Pell was being accused of child sexual abuse. At first blush, it had all the hallmarks of a conspiracy theory, a hateful slur. And had it not been for the white noise created by the *60 Minutes* piece, it may not have attracted the attention it ultimately did. Pell only heard of it when informed by his solicitor the following day. Leder promptly fired off legal letters to the website's editors.

But the mainstream media got on board. Newspapers including *The Age* were chasing the story and demanded an official response. The narrative got away from the Church. On 20 August, two weeks after the obscure website first broke the story, media outlets across Sydney were informed that at 5.30p.m., just before the commercial television deadline, the Archbishop would make an announcement. That announcement was to be that Pell would step aside as archbishop while the Australian Catholic Bishops Conference held an arm's length inquiry into the allegation. This wasn't merely a scurrilous, made-up story by a marginal online publication. It was a genuine complaint. As to whether the *substance* of the complaint was also genuine, the retired Supreme Court justice who was appointed to oversee the inquiry would determine that. His name was Alec J Southwell, QC.

The Archbishop felt wrong-footed and wounded by the whole fiasco and made it known. He believed that others in the Church had deliberately kept him in the dark, because they had known about the complaint for a good two months and hadn't told him. The complainant had, at the advice of his parish priest, gone to Towards Healing, and met, through that process, with Sister Angela Ryan of the Church's National Committee for Professional Standards (NCPS) on 11 June. Pell's Auxiliary Bishop in Sydney, Geoffrey Robinson, who was also on the committee, had also been aware as he had had several telephone calls with the complainant, but to the Archbishop's chagrin, neither the Bishop nor Ryan had kept Pell in the loop.

Pell came out swinging in a *Sydney Morning Herald* interview, titled 'Pell the Victim of Cruel Treatment', by columnist Miranda Devine. Devine is a conservative Catholic, one of Jane Fraser's gregarious dining set, and has always been a loyal defender of Pell. Pell complained to Devine that he had suffered an 'appalling lack of due process'. 'If there are procedures in the Towards Healing process, we should follow them,' Pell told the columnist. 'The [accused] person should be informed as soon as possible.' He also later told a press conference he thought the timing was 'remarkable'. And when a reporter asked the Archbishop whether not being informed earlier 'damaged' his case in any way, the Archbishop declared 'it certainly didn't help it'.

However, the NCPS had found itself in a terrible bind. The advice to Towards Healing from the state police forces with which it liaised was absolutely unambiguous: it should not, under any circumstances, inform the alleged offender of the fact that a complaint had been made about him or her. That, the Church officials were told, was a job for police. But in this case, the victim did not want to press charges—despite several phone calls with Robinson in which the Bishop begged the complainant to go to the police, the complainant declined. Robinson's view was that it was absolute folly for the Church to investigate a complaint of this nature—it was much too high profile and fraught. The Church could only find itself accused of a whitewash or a cover-up. A police investigation was the proper approach.

The problem with a police investigation was that the complainant, it transpired, had good reason to feel that he might not get a fair hearing. The complainant was not for turning. As these negotiations were taking place, the *Indymedia* piece appeared online. The wagons began to circle. The NCPS assumed at the time that the complainant had leaked it—but he says he did not. One way or the other, the NCPS had to act. And the Archbishop found out in the worst possible way: public humiliation.

The complainant was to discover that Pell does not respond well to public humiliation. As one of Pell's former priestly colleagues in the Church told me, 'George is like a bulldozer. His way of defending is to attack'. And attack he did.

Pell's complainant, Phil Scott, met the young man he says abused him in 1961 when Scott was a 12-year-old altar boy from the working-class parish of Christ the King in Braybrook in Melbourne's west. Pell was a 20-year-old Corpus Christi trainee priest. Scott's devoutly Catholic mother struggled to make ends meet and was delighted when her young charge was invited to an altar boys' camp on Phillip Island, supervised by a priest and a handful of seminarians. Several of the seminarians told me that Pell was accompanied on the camp by his good friend Tony Bongiorno, who was later outed as a paedophile priest. One former seminarian even later pondered if perhaps the complainant had mistaken George for Tony. But George and Tony looked nothing alike.

The camp was at Smiths Beach, a pretty rocky inlet looking out onto Bass Strait. While the little kids slept in a dormitory with one or two seminarians, the bigger ones like Scott and the remainder of the trainee priests slept in military-style tents. It promised to be a boy's own adventure.

It was in one of the tents that Scott alleges the seminarian, whom the boys referred to as 'Big George', first got at him. He says that during activities like pillow-fighting or wrestling, Big George, while facing him, put his hands down the inside of young Phil's pants and got a 'good handful' of his penis and testicles. It happened, he says, on several occasions. Scott was shocked at this behaviour: first, because before that he had regarded the trainee priest as 'a fun person, a gentle person, a kind person, he was a terrific bloke', and second, because while Big George was doing this to him, he says other boys were also in the tent, horsing around and seemingly oblivious. Scott maintains he believed Pell positioned himself in such a way that the others would not have seen. The 12-year-old boy did not know what to do, the 53-year-old Scott later explained, remembering back, except pull the man's hand away each time.

But Scott says it didn't stop at that. On a further two occasions, he alleged, the seminarian took Scott's hand and guided it down his own pants. Scott says he whipped his hand out before it could touch Pell's genitals. There was another time, when the boys were all on an evening stroll, walking 'Indian file', and Scott remembers Pell grabbing him from behind and putting his big hands down Scott's pants. And then there was the time when they were swimming. As Scott jumped through the waves fizzing onto the beach, he says Pell put his hand down inside Scott's bathers and touched him again. For reasons that will become clear later, as I re-read this particular detail fourteen years after Scott went public, the hairs on the back of my neck stood up on end.

Catholic Church officials who were used to dealing with the classically predatory grooming behaviour of other paedophile priests—a tired and sorry script repeated over and over—later saw the detail of the complaint and found it distinctly odd. Scott did not describe a lead-up. The priest hadn't cosied up to him, hadn't heaped him with flattery, hadn't showered him with presents, talked about 'our little secret', made him feel like he was the 'only one'. In short, there was no real grooming. Scott's allegation was, one Church official mused, 'just straight-out grabbing'. 'It was pretty unique,' says the official, who concedes they genuinely don't know what happened on that camp, but felt at the time that Scott was believable. 'But if there was ever anyone who would offend in this way, I can imagine that George might.'

'Why's that?' I ask the official, bemused.

'Because that's the kind of person he is. He's not a very subtle person,' the official replies. To be clear, this person is not saying Pell *is* an offender, but rather, if it was proven that Pell *was,* it wouldn't be a shock to learn that this was the way Pell chose to offend.

Scott says the only person he told at the time about Big George was his friend, who was known simply in the Southwell Inquiry as 'A', whose real name was Michael Foley. Scott claims to have also seen Big George molest Foley in the same way. He said Foley turned away from Big George and told him to 'fuck off'. Scott says the boys discussed the abuse on the camp and one day, it all just got too much for his friend. Foley ran away and when Scott says he found him, Foley had a box of matches and was threatening that he was 'going to burn the place down'. He says they then lit a fire. It became a grass fire, he remembers, and was brought under control by the Country Fire Authority. Sure enough, it was later proven in the Southwell Inquiry that the CFA had indeed extinguished a grass fire near Smiths Beach on 13 January 1961.

The first time Scott told anyone outside his family about Big George was when he called the Broken Rites victims' support group. He spoke to former historian Bernard Barrett. That was in May 2000, say Scott and Barrett, who gave evidence in the inquiry. Barrett says Scott told him that, watching television, he had recently recognised the Archbishop of Melbourne to be the seminarian who had molested him almost forty years before. The Archbishop of Melbourne, said Scott, was 'Big George'.

8

SOUTHWELL

It was a stark reminder of how differently our press treats vulnerable accusers and powerful men who stand accused.

Ronan Farrow, discussing allegations levelled by his sister against their father, Woody Allen

I went to see Father Bob Maguire many years later to discuss what happened to Phil Scott when he came up against George Pell. By that time, Maguire had long been 'managed out' of the Catholic Church by Pell's successor and old ally Denis Hart. I went to Maguire's office in South Melbourne. Maguire doesn't have a parish any more—they took that away from him. Instead he inhabits this ramshackle shopfront, where he runs his charity. I sat and waited for him on a nineties plaid armchair covered in dog hair from Maguire's poodle. Eventually, the priest called me in. 'Oh no,' he said in his slightly comical drawl, rolling his eyes, when I told him who I was. 'I've told you, I can't bloody help you.'

When I insisted I'd like to have a chat anyway, he ushered me into his office. For someone who didn't want to help me, Maguire could chat the hind legs off a donkey. His conversation goes in complicated loops. And every now and then, say, three-quarters through the loop, he says something absolutely compelling and quoteworthy, but you can't prick up your ears, can't change the expression on your face, because then he's onto you. He's onto the fact that maybe that is something you might want to use and he'll recalcitrantly change the subject.

Maguire won't soon forget Phil Scott coming to him with his problem in 2002. The priest listened to his parishioner, whom he'd known for a number of years through Scott's work with street kids, in silence. 'He didn't want to go to police,' Maguire said. 'He was a former Painter and Docker,' he said, speaking of the union to which Scott belonged, which in the 1980s was caught up in enormous controversy in the Costigan Royal Commission. 'Phil didn't want compensation. All he wanted was for George Pell to be in the room with him, man to man, and look him in the eye and apologise for what he did. And of course, that's not what happened. But it's not for me to discuss this with you. Read my book. Read my book.'

His book is a biography by journalist Sue Williams. In it, she says Maguire admired Scott for 'having risen above a past riven by alcoholism and crime'. In 2002, it says, the 53-year-old Scott was 'a respected figure whom [Bob] bumped into regularly at Collingwood football games and seemed genuine in his belief about what had happened. He said he wasn't after publicity or money—he'd been tortured by the memory of what he recalled having happened and wanted the Church quietly to acknowledge that, and perhaps have a meeting with George Pell, to lay his demons to rest'.

Scott's situation left Maguire, his biography says, with a 'terrible dilemma'. 'On the one hand, he found this accusation very hard to believe,' it says, referring to Maguire's prima facie assumption that his fellow priests, especially one that had risen to such dizzy heights as Pell, were of sound and good character. 'On the other, he'd worked with abused kids long enough to know that those in authority often didn't take their claims seriously and, in the case where they were telling the truth, scepticism and a refusal to investigate could cause them sometimes even more damage.'

But despite the nervousness of getting involved with a complainant who was taking on someone like Pell, Maguire had another motivation to help Scott, the book explains: 'He wanted his beloved Church to be free of the taint of ever trying to cover up any kind of allegations involving the evil of child abuse.' Maguire had good reason for this—he had been working in the very same parish with an abuser, Vincent Kiss, and had been stung by the revelation that the priest had deceived him. Kiss was jailed in 1993 for defrauding four charities. When he left prison he was promptly re-arrested for child sex charges and pleaded guilty to abusing four boys. Scott too knew of the publicity around the Kiss case. 'The Father Vincent Kiss case had been a sickening jolt for [Father Bob] and he was determined that the Church always be prepared to be accountable for any past and present sins, however unlikely.'

'What was I to do?' Maguire told his biographer of the Scott dilemma. 'I couldn't turn my back on the bloke who came to me. I was in a position of trust, and he'd come to me for help. I couldn't tell him to go away and just shut up about it. But I knew that if I supported him, I could be making a powerful enemy too. That could be the end of me, and my work.'

Maguire changes his mind depending on when you talk to him about whether the Scott business was the straw that broke the camel's back in ending his career as parish priest at South Melbourne. Whether the powerful enemy he made in Pell was, as he said it might be, the end of him and his work. Certainly, when the priest turned seventy-five in 2009, Pell's anointed successor and great friend, Denis Hart, personally arrived at Maguire's parish presbytery and told him to hand in his resignation. This was a departure from the usual protocols, which require that the priest hand in his resignation, but then very commonly the Archbishop will refuse to take it (that's what happened with Pell himself as Cardinal in the Vatican in 2016—the Pope refused his resignation). Maguire was given a stay of execution until 2012 and Hart released a statement saying the decision to ask him to go was because of financial mismanagement. Maguire thought it was largely because his more liberal Vatican II- style ministry clashed with the rigidity of the likes of Hart and Pell.

One way or the other, Maguire's decision to back a complainant against Pell can't have helped when he was pleading his case against Hart. But as we spoke in his South Melbourne office that day, he said something interesting about the psychology of a priest that has stayed with me and informed my responses to revelations about abuse by paedophile clergy. 'We priests,' he explains, 'we're psychosocially damaged.

We're crystallised in adolescence. Of course we are. How could we be any other? We haven't had mature adult relationships. We're stuck, in many ways, at the age when we entered the seminary. So we have problems. Don't let anyone tell you we don't. Not having meaningful relationships does something to you. It stunts your psychological growth, being celibate, being alone. I'll admit it.'

It's a brave admission, and no doubt one that some priests would passionately dispute, but, truth be told, you can see it in him. He flits from subject to subject. He is a compassionate, thoughtful and intelligent man, but engaging on a deeper level one on one sometimes just seems to get the better of him. His eye contact is patchy at best. He changes the subject, makes jokes, obfuscates, plays a part and does his razzle-dazzle, funny, witty, slightly mad priest routine.

But despite his eccentric demeanour, the business about being psychosocially damaged rings true. Several other priests—some still serving, some laicised, to whom I have spoken for this book, have also mentioned this limitation. Those who have left say it has taken years to readjust as they emerged, 30- or even 40-year-old virgins. And in the Royal Commission into Institutional Responses to Child Sexual Abuse, Father Eric Bryant, who was in Ballarat a colleague of Pell's on Mulkearns' consultors committee, put it this way:

> The Church, like a lot of other male institutions, are places for people to hide ... For the priesthood, a lot of young people went into the priesthood 15, 16 years of age and were not mature enough, they didn't know their own sexuality or anything else like that. They say a male doesn't develop that knowledge until he's 25 or 26 nowadays. And we had young people going in who were just out of school, they were taken away from their families, and I think things happened there.

Michael Leahy, who went through Corpus Christi just behind Pell, told the Royal Commission in a submission that by compulsorily depriving men 'of healthy, holy sexual relationships' over a period of centuries, it establishes the clergy as a 'caste within the Church'. And 'it is very difficult to see how the members of that caste can avoid distorted views of such relationships and of sexuality generally,' Leahy says. The priests are, he says, denied 'opportunities to confront and express rationally one's own sexuality', but more disturbingly, a 'hiding place' is provided 'for those wishing to avoid confrontation such as rationalisations in religious terms of deviant inclinations'.

Pell was, of course, one of these people whisked away (by his own ardent volition) from his family before he reached significant maturity. Pell is not the sort of person I can imagine ever admitting to a weakness like being psychosocially damaged. But I think that day, when Maguire rambled in his office, that this is what he was getting at—that this applied to Pell too. And this is one of the reasons why, apart from the respect he had already developed for Phil Scott in his community, and his priestly duty to support people in their hardest hour, that it was Maguire who made the first phone call to the Church's National Council for Professional Standards on Scott's behalf.

The timing of the phone call was provoked by Scott seeing something in the papers which piqued his interest. On 8 June 2002, the Melbourne and Sydney archdioceses had put full-page ads in the metro newspapers, apologising to all Church abuse victims and giving a Church telephone number for survivors to call. The staff at Broken Rites noted sardonically that the ad provided no corresponding phone number for police sexual offences units, where victims could report allegations.

The ad got Scott's blood boiling again. That day, he telephoned Broken Rites again. It had been two years and one month since his previous call. Scott said he still intended to make a report to Church authorities about what had happened on Phillip Island in 1961. The Broken Rites advocate told Scott about Towards Healing, and how he might proceed. Scott got back on the phone to Maguire. And Maguire got on the phone on his behalf.

After several phone calls with Bishop Geoffrey Robinson, Scott was offered a sit-down meeting on 11 June with Sister Angela Ryan. While the transcription of that meeting was being checked and corrected by Ryan and Scott over the course of following days, both Maguire and Scott spoke to Robinson again, who was still very keen to get the police involved. It is not an exaggeration to say that there was much angst at NCPS headquarters. All concerned realised that there were no winners in the present scenario—including themselves. No matter how delicately they trod, they were likely to put a rather sharp stiletto onto a toenail. They had a jittery complainant who didn't like cops, a respondent in Pell who was, frankly, terrifying. And a media that was likely to go completely feral.

On 19 June, after Scott received the finalised transcription of his interview, he waited to see what the NCPS was going to do. And waited. Five weeks passed in which he heard nothing. On 13 July, Scott picked up the phone again to see what was going on. Robinson told him that the case could not go through Towards Healing because the rules forbade a complaint against an archbishop. On 17 July, Scott wrote to Robinson, expressing his disappointment at the NCPS' failure to act. Robinson wrote back with a compromise solution, a compromise which Robinson felt was inadequate. 'All I could offer you was to set up a process that would imitate the process of Towards Healing, that is, it would appoint assessors who would question the two parties and witnesses and give them a finding ... [However] if he [Pell] denied everything, this process would not have teeth and would not be able to enforce its finding,' Robinson wrote.

By August, the rumour mill had started. Journalists were starting to make calls to Church officials to ask if there was to be an inquiry into Pell. On 1 August, Robinson contacted Scott through Maguire and said that he was setting up an 'imitative' inquiry, that is, like Towards Healing. Scott was told that there would be two 'assessors' appointed. Both of the assessors, it transpired, were former police officers. One of them was a former member of the Gaming Squad, who, Scott said, had charged him in the early 1980s. Scott was most displeased. Scott smelled a rat, but it could well have just been a coincidence. Broken Rites staff pointed out that as Towards Healing promises that assessors be independent of the Church authority, the complainant and the accused, this would have constituted a breach of protocols.

On 7 August, the *Indymedia* piece appeared. The campaign by newspapers to find out more stepped up. And then, on 19 August, *The Age* faxed a bunch of questions to the Sydney Archdiocese. The archdiocese did not send answers, instead saying there would be a big announcement the following day. When the stories appeared in the newspapers as they dropped in the wee hours of 21 August, the counterattack on Scott had already begun. Who dug up the dirt has not been revealed. But the Church was already using 'assessors', who were essentially private investigators employed in these sorts of investigations. One way or the other, the first newspaper reports which broke news of the announcement referred to Scott's criminal past.

'Church sources said last night that the man making the accusations against Dr Pell had a long criminal history,' *The Age* reported on 21 August. 'He had been convicted of various offences including drug trafficking.' As the slaying of Scott's reputation began, Pell accrued some very powerful public cheerleaders. The Prime Minister, no less. 'I believe completely George Pell's denial,' John Howard told reporters. 'I rang him this evening and spoke to him. They are, of course, very serious allegations and he's done the right thing in standing aside and the Church has done the right thing to have the allegations fully investigated.' Pell's friend and fellow Santamaria-devotee Tony Abbott, then Workplace Relations Minister, also weighed in. He told reporters Pell was 'the most combative, forthright and most effective ecclesiastical leader Australia has seen since Danny Mannix'.

'That means George Pell is a target for all sorts of people, some well-meaning, some malevolent,' Abbott said.

'It should not surprise any Christian that there would be people who want to make unfair, wrong, mischievous, malevolent accusations against the strongest and most public Christian of the time. I'm more than ready to accept Pell's testimony.'

Of course, just like all the other people who jump to the prima facie defence of alleged child abusers before they know *any* of the details of the case, Howard and Abbott couldn't possibly know what really went on because they weren't there and didn't know the detail. They were just springing to support the person who was accused as the abuser. It's a fascinating and pervasive social phenomenon and not one you can really demonise Howard and Abbott for because it is so incredibly widespread. People don't want to believe that someone they know—especially an eminent and high profile person they have respected—has damaged little kids. But here's the thing: it's a decidedly handy social phenomenon if you happen to be white, male, powerful and an abuser of children. Because generally, people seem to somehow find it difficult to believe an accuser's word against these sorts of men.

Scott told Maguire he just wanted to be believed. And he wanted Pell to own up. Pell, on the other hand, was furious at what he was describing as a mendacious slur. At best, a delusion. At worst, a sinful lie. But Scott's lawyer Peter Ward reflected that the gross imbalance of power between a former wharfie and one of the Catholic Church's most senior figures was profound. Dr Pell, as he was still then known before he made Cardinal, had obtained the finest legal counsel money could buy. Jeff Sher, QC, had been at the bar four decades, three as silk, and was known for his tenacity and toughness. He was described by his colleague at the bar, now a Supreme Court Judge, Kate McMillan, SC, as having a 'reputation as a clinical, merciless courtroom interrogator and infighter'. He had a list of wealthy and powerful clients and in his civil work had won the largest damages payouts ever recorded at the time. Colleagues joked that Sher despised mediation—this was a Queen's

Counsel who was built to fight and win. Pell and his solicitors don't muck about when they appoint counsel.

The Southwell Inquiry commenced on 30 September 2002 and ran for five days at a Melbourne hotel. The retired Supreme Court justice Alec Southwell was chosen carefully. It was important that he was not a Catholic so it was not considered a stitch-up in favour of Pell. While on the bench, he was considered a 'straight shooter' and his judgements in sexual assault matters had not been entirely predictable. For instance, he disagreed with his colleagues on the Full Court of the Victorian Supreme Court when they freed paedophile priest Father Michael Glennon because they determined that a 'name and shame' campaign by then-broadcaster, now-Senator, Derryn Hinch prevented the priest getting a fair trial. In his dissenting judgement, Southwell said the court was creating 'legal history by finding that in a large city, adverse media publicity must be held to have had the result that a person charged with a serious offence will never be called upon to face trial'.

However, Southwell was also one of the Full Court Judges who decided that raping a prostitute was a lesser crime than raping a 'chaste' woman.

During the hearing, Southwell heard from a string of witnesses. No-one—not the other seminarians, nor the students who could be contacted—could remember any abuse, as described by Scott, taking place. Scott's mate Michael Foley, whom he said had also been abused, had died seventeen years before in a bar fight. Foley's family was contacted by private investigators hired by the Pell camp and some members of the family told *The Age* they were most displeased at this intrusion. But they said that Foley had not disclosed anything about the Smiths Beach allegations to them.

There was, though, one witness, known to the inquiry as 'H', who did have some recollections, which suggested very strongly that all was not well at the camp. H remembered both Scott and Pell being at the camp. He remembered 'various frolicking activities' and also a night walk where the boys were walking in a spread-out fashion

('Indian file', Scott called it). He remembered the 1961 camp as being his last, although Southwell pointed out in his report that parish records show him on a camp in 1962—demonstrating 'the great difficulty of fact finding in relation to incidents occurring 40 years ago'.

H said he remembered Foley well. He said that while Foley was several months younger than he, Foley 'always tended to look after me a bit'. And there was something else. 'He came up to me and he said to me one day, "Just watch out for Big George".' After that incident, H told the inquiry, he gave Big George a wide berth. 'I didn't get too close to him.' He didn't inquire further about what Foley meant when he cautioned him about the seminarian, because, he said, 'it was the way he said it. I assumed.'

Other former altar boys gave evidence that Pell was popular, and Scott said he was kind and gentle, and was not a disciplinarian, not given to violence. Thus, Southwell later reasoned in his report, Foley 'had no reason to think that H was at risk of a belting or some other unpleasant punishment'—that is, the 'watch out' was not ambiguous. The 'watch out' had a sexual connotation. And that is what H said in his signed statement—he 'presumed there was a sexual context of the warning'.

The evidence of H is the sort of thing that causes journalists and other students of true crime to prick up their ears. It seems to corroborate. It's a pretty astonishing recollection, all those years later. *What? Another kid was warned about Pell? That kid was told Pell was dodgy?* But alas (for Scott, at least) in a criminal trial, Sher pointed out, that evidence would not have been admissible. And even though this wasn't a criminal trial per se, the judge agreed. 'Evidence of what an eleven-year-old boy "assumed" about a possibly misunderstood "warning" is no sound basis for adverse findings in an inquiry of this nature,' Southwell later wrote. However, the judge admitted that he wrestled with whether the warning itself should be included. He decided, 'not without hesitation', that 'given the very serious nature of this proceeding, and the possible ambiguity of the warning, I should put it aside'.

Southwell also put aside another thing which to a lay observer seems pretty compelling: that H heard that Foley had lit a fire at Smiths Beach. 'This inquiry is not, of course, investigating the question whether [Foley] was molested, and the only evidence of that came from the complainant,' Southwell wrote in his report. 'There is, in my opinion, too tenuous a connection for that evidence to go into the scales against [Pell].'

A crucial witness who gave evidence to the inquiry was Phil Scott's first wife, known to the inquiry as 'Mrs C'. She and Scott had children together, but had separated in the early 1990s—a decade before the inquiry. She was important because she could give what is known in these cases as 'evidence of first complaint'. Mrs C told the inquiry that she had a 'clear recollection' of Scott first having a conversation with her in 1975 or 1976—so it was about fourteen years after the Phillip Island camp took place. Mrs C remembered that Scott said that when he was an altar boy at a camp at Phillip Island, he had been interfered with by 'a big bastard called George'. Mrs C also told the inquiry that Scott had informed her that Michael Foley had been 'involved in it'. Mrs C was 'shocked' by what her then-husband had disclosed, but as soon as it had been raised, the topic of conversation was abandoned again and it was, she said, 'swept under the carpet'. Mrs C heard little else of Big George until she received a telephone call, she said, from her former husband, in about July 2000. Scott expressed astonishment to her on the phone that he had just recognised that the man he knew as Big George, his molester, was George Pell. Mrs C hadn't the faintest idea who Pell was. 'He's an archbishop,' her husband replied, she told the inquiry.

Sher tried to discredit Mrs C's account. 'How could she remember a common name like "George" after all those years?' Sher mused in his closing address. But Southwell dismissed that thought. 'I regarded her as an impressive witness,' the judge found, 'who had a clear recollection of a startling statement.'

Southwell said that the recollections of Mrs C, which he believed, certainly could rebut the suggestions by the Pell camp that Scott was motivated by a desire for compensation. 'In 1975 there was no compensation scheme such as is now in place ... There really could be no valid suggestion of any evidence pointing to a desire,' the judge mused. He also noted that the first time that compensation ever came up was when Scott talked to Bernard Barrett of Broken Rites—who informed Scott of his rights under the Melbourne Response. Despite the fact that Mrs C's evidence might not have been admitted more generally in court, the judge decided that it should stay 'in', as it were. It could, Southwell found, be used in a criminal trial to rebut evidence that the 'Big George' allegations were a recent invention.

There were issues with some aspects of Scott's recollection—for instance, Scott remembers that when he saw Pell on television and recognised him to be 'Big George', he believed the Archbishop was wearing purple robes. But the priest who was responsible for dressing Pell gave evidence that while at some formal functions he did wear a purple robe, it was covered by a white surplice. Sher also tendered videotapes of television programs in which Pell had been seen that year and guess what? No purple robes. It was, Sher told the inquiry, highly unlikely that Pell had ever been seen in any purple robe on television at any time.

Memory does strange things when it comes to visual descriptions of people.

Southwell had clearly given these issues some thought too, because he did not hang his hat on the verity of the purple robe memory. 'I do not accept it as disproving that at some time around the middle of 2000, the complainant observed the respondent on television,' he said.

There were also issues with Scott's interview with Sister Angela Ryan—he at first told her that he had seen Pell on television in 2000 because he was being appointed Archbishop of Sydney; however, Pell had not been appointed to Sydney until March 2001. Scott later said he thought Ryan was 'leading' him. But he had signed off on the changes made to the transcript of his interview and, indeed, made some corrections. This was the only part of Scott's evidence where the judge thought that perhaps Scott was not being entirely truthful. The judge believed Scott had been caught out and was trying to backtrack. But again, the judge did not think it meant that Scott was not telling the truth in other capacities. 'The fact that I think his evidence concerning the [Ryan] interview was unsatisfactory does not lead to a finding that the whole of his evidence must be rejected,' Southwell said. 'But it does mean that where credit assumes the very great importance that it does in this case, I must view all his evidence with caution.'

As for Scott's motive for complaint, despite the best efforts of the Pell legal team and, undoubtedly, the private investigators employed by it, Southwell noted that they had not unearthed any evidence which suggested some other 'spite or malice' on the part of Scott towards Pell or even the Church in general. The judge pointed out that, on the other hand, Pell had a 'strong motive to push memory of these fleeting incidents by a 19-year-old to the recesses of the mind, from which there could be no recall'. If this was a judge 'completely exonerating' someone, as Pell would claim, then it didn't read like that.

The journalists who first wrote about the Southwell Inquiry when it was initially announced were leaked fairly scant information by 'Church sources' about Scott's past. Then, on 6 October, the *Sunday Herald Sun* exposed the lot. 'Altar Boy's Life of Crime', the headline blared. There in a 2-page spread was the full, inglorious criminal history of Scott. Scott was infuriated to see they had also photographed him from behind outside his home.

There is no escaping the fact that Scott had not been an angel. Far from it. The Southwell Inquiry heard that he had had thirty-nine convictions from twenty court appearances. The vast bulk of these were drink-driving and assault convictions in the 1970s when he was an alcoholic. Scott's problem with alcohol ended more or less at the end of the seventies and from the 1980s, he began to attend Alcoholics Anonymous. But there were other offences in the 1980s—relating to SP bookmaking. He was also hauled before the infamous Costigan Royal Commission in relation to his time as a member of the Painters and Dockers union (Scott was on the union's executive for six years) and was fined for contempt for failing to answer questions. He avoided tax and he had several bank accounts to aid in pursuing his bookie business.

But perhaps the most serious issue for Scott was his 1995 conviction for dealing speed, for which he served two years in prison. At that time, the sentencing judge acknowledged, Scott was sober, a good dad and generous with his time to those less fortunate than him. So dealing amphetamines was a major slip-up, to put it mildly. If it hadn't been for the drug dealing, Scott could have said his criminal past was ancient history. But the drug dealing was just seven years before. He'd done time. It was really, really embarrassing.

For his part, Southwell thought Scott's criminal record was more notable for 'alcohol and violence than dishonesty'. 'However,' continued the judge, 'there is sufficient evidence of dishonesty to demonstrate that the complainant's evidence must be scrutinised with special care.' And it would be difficult, he believed, to support Scott's version above Pell's without the supporting evidence of other witnesses, or circumstantial evidence.

In the end, Southwell was not convinced that Scott was a liar. The character assassination did not succeed on that front. 'I did not form a positively adverse view of him as a witness,' Southwell said. The judge accepted the evidence of Michael Tovey, QC, the smooth and skilled advocate who was appointed Counsel Assisting the inquiry, who said that Scott, when talking about the events at Phillip Island, 'gave the impression that he was speaking honestly from an actual recollection'. But the judge still couldn't find that the complaint was upheld. He had the same view of Pell. '[Pell] also gave me the impression that he was speaking the truth,' Southwell remarked.

That being the case, the judge had to return to several issues surrounding the credibility of the parties: the very long delay, 'some valid criticism of the complainant's credibility', the lack of corroborative evidence. Southwell had to find that he was 'not satisfied that the complaint has been established'. So in the end, the character assassination of Scott was successful—it achieved its intended aim—to keep Pell as Archbishop of Sydney.

Pell has always described this result as his exoneration. 'I am grateful to God that this ordeal is over and that the inquiry has exonerated me of all allegations,' he said at the time. 'There's no mud to stick, I've been exonerated.' Even though many lawyers who have studied the finding will tell you it was most certainly not an exoneration. It was nil-all. Or one-all.

Which is why, despite the humiliation of having his life analysed, his criminal record exposed, being photographed unknowingly outside his home, and forever being tagged as the altar boy who turned to a life of crime, Scott was happy with the Southwell finding. He felt, Scott's solicitor Peter Ward tells me, that Southwell had been fair. He hadn't expected a fair fight and he hadn't expected a fair finding. But he got the fair finding, he thought. Southwell believed him. That is, he thought he was telling the truth. For Phil Scott, that was enough.

Ward believes Pell's lawyers made a huge tactical error in closing submissions. Southwell gave the parties a choice before he retired to consider his finding. He could, he said, give them simply the finding—that is, whether or not the matter was substantiated. Or he could give reasons for that finding too. Ward thinks that Pell's lawyers expected a roasting of Scott and that it would play very well for their client for the reasons to be published. So they opted for the reasons. It did not play very well for their client. Had the simple fact of the finding been published, Pell would have been right in saying he was completely exonerated, but the reasons showed the judge's decision was qualified. There were passages in it that were not helpful for Pell. The judge believed the kid from Braybrook, who turned into a guy with a criminal record. But there just wasn't enough contemporaneous corroborative evidence to legally find that it definitively happened.

This detail was reported at the time, but for a huge story like that, its impact was blunted. Because in October 2002, a massive news event eclipsed everything in its path. A great tragedy for hundreds of people became a blessing, of sorts, for Pell. On the Saturday night of 12 October, Jemaah Islamiah terrorists set off bombs in the Sari nightclub in Kuta, the tourist district of Denpasar in Bali, killing 202 people including 88 Australians. It was the biggest Australian news story in years.

The Southwell Inquiry had concluded its deliberations on 4 October. It's unclear who dictated the terms of release, including the date, but it was an inquiry run by the Catholic Church. The Church released the report to the media on Monday 14 October. The Bali bombings were on the Saturday night and the report landed 36 hours after the attacks—on the Monday. It's not to say that the Southwell report wasn't covered—it was. But a story that would otherwise be huge was buried. The victims' rights groups believed that it was an example of 'taking out the trash'—like when a government releases a negative departmental report just as the horses are entering the barriers for the Melbourne Cup. It rolls off the newsroom fax machines and pops into the email inboxes just as the nation's heads are collectively turned.

Whether or not it was a deliberate trash-taking exercise, in many ways it worked. The simple message conveyed was that Pell would still be Archbishop of Sydney. He was 'cleared'. It is certainly how I, who was at the time a young reporter very wrapped up in the aftermath of the bombings, saw it.

Archbishop Pell's first job after being reinstated at St Mary's Cathedral was a mass for the victims of the bombings. Afterwards he told columnist Miranda Devine:

'One of the unusual Christian teachings is that you can draw good out of evil ... For someone with no religion, suffering is a brute fact you have to try to ensure with dignity. For a Christian, you can hope this suffering can be transmuted into something of benefit—if not for you, but for others.'

Devine surmised that Pell's darkest hour had only strengthened him. It most certainly did not impede his path to ecclesiastical glory. Almost a year to the day that the Southwell Inquiry had commenced, Pope John Paul II appointed George Pell a Cardinal.

9

EMINENCE

Laws are like cobwebs, which may catch small flies, but let wasps and hornets break through.

Jonathan Swift

For many years, the memory of the Southwell Inquiry fell away. In the mid-2000s, His Eminence Cardinal George Pell resumed his position as what the priests somewhat disparagingly referred to as Captain Catholic.

One of Pell's first tasks in coming back on the job in Sydney was behind the scenes, a rather troublesome matter of a John Andrew Ellis. Ellis had made a complaint to the archdiocese of abuse by a Father Aidan Duggan, who had been a priest at Christ the King parish at Sydney's Bass Hill, among other locations.

Duggan had for a time worked in Scotland at an exclusive Highlands boarding school, Fort Augustus Abbey, on the banks of Loch Ness, where it was later alleged a cluster of Benedictine paedophiles including Duggan abused boys. A BBC investigation in 2013, which spoke to fifty former students, said one of them had made accusations against Duggan. One of the other accused priests was another Australian, Father Denis Alexander, whose extradition proceedings to Scotland to face charges have only just commenced at the time of writing in 2017. But Duggan returned to Australia in 1974. There is no evidence on the public record to prove that the Sydney Archdiocese knew about his history. The year following his return, Duggan met a quiet and intelligent young altar boy, John Ellis, who was fourteen. The grooming began almost immediately. The abuse would go on for twelve years.

By the time he first made his complaint through the Towards Healing process in 2002, Ellis was in his forties and had made it to salaried partner with the large city law firm Baker McKenzie. He was the sort of lawyer who might have had a brilliant career had he not had, essentially, a breakdown, where his teen years came crashing down on top of him. When Ellis first complained to the Archdiocesan Professional Standards Office, the office wrote to Pell to express that on the balance of probabilities the evidence did not corroborate the facts as Ellis alleged them. It was supposed that a criminal proceeding would go nowhere because Duggan was by then in hospital with dementia and in 'no position to plead', and Ellis' prospects of a successful civil case were dim given the fact that the abuse alleged carried on into adulthood. From the very start, the protocols that had been carefully worked out through Towards Healing were not properly followed—for instance, Ellis was told there was a $50 000 cap on compensation (like the Melbourne Response) when Towards Healing had no cap. But that was just the tip of the iceberg in a hugely telling and regrettable course of conduct which was to involve Pell's inner circle and his lawyers.

In December 2002, just a couple of months after he had returned to work after his own accusations were settled by Southwell, Pell wrote a signed letter to Ellis. Ellis received it on Christmas Eve. It told Ellis that 'the facts of your matter cannot be established'. Pell brought up the priest's ailing health and also stated, very clearly, that 'we have no other record of complaints of this kind against him'.

Except, well, that wasn't true. In 1983, another former altar boy, only known as 'S', had made a complaint of the abuse that he had suffered at the hands of Duggan at the same time as Ellis. He had complained to the dean of St Mary's Cathedral.

S only found out about the Ellis case three years after Pell wrote that letter. He contacted Ellis and then swore an affidavit in the NSW Supreme Court that he was abused between 1980 and 1982 and that the following year he made a statutory declaration to Father Michael McGloin, who was the St Mary's dean. Duggan was brought in to discuss the case and at that point, McGloin left the meeting and left S alone with Duggan, much to S's humiliation. S was 'devastated' at the handling of the matter and the fact the complaint went no further. He was also aware of Ellis' relationship with the priest and had suspected that Ellis, too, had been abused.

When Ellis' lawyers sent this affidavit to the Church's lawyers and they checked it out, it turned out McGloin had no recollection of the meeting (poor memory is a common affliction among Catholic priests of a certain era and predilection) and had been on the wrong side of the Towards Healing process himself. In the words of John Dalzell, a Corrs lawyer working for the Church, McGloin had 'a complaint file as big as the New Testament ... including some under age sex'.

Corrs then wrote to the Catholic Church's insurer to say 'unfortunately ... this fresh allegation would suggest that the Archdiocese (or its agent) was on notice of Duggan's predilection for young men and did nothing to stop it'. To be clear, nothing has been found which suggests that Pell's office knew this when Pell sent the letter in 2002. Nonetheless, when Corrs next wrote to Ellis' lawyer, it made no mention of

McGloin's own troubles and only said that the statutory declaration that S had signed had not been located. Problem was, Ellis' wife Nicola worked at the Catholic Schools office in the nearby diocese of Broken Bay. And she knew all about the complaints against McGloin.

'Good heavens! How did that happen,' barrister Stephen Rushton, SC, who worked for the Church, wrote to the archdiocese when he got the news that Nicola Ellis knew about McGloin. 'I think our clients need to be very very careful how this is handled. Whatever her role in father McGloin we are snookered.'

This all happened in the context of a lengthy and vexed litigation process. By August 2004, Ellis had elected to sue Pell as representative of the Catholic Church in the Sydney Archdiocese, having found the Towards Healing process entirely unsatisfactory—it was exceedingly lengthy, poorly executed and he had only been offered $30 000 in compensation because, he was told by a Church official, 'they don't consider your abuse to be that serious', and with it he was required to sign a deed of release. Ellis felt compelled to commence litigation because under the statute of limitations, his time was about to run out.

The litigation was similarly poorly handled by the archdiocese—something many involved have now admitted. But even back in December 2005, unbeknown to Ellis, the matter was starting to seriously irk other factions of the Catholic Church. The Church's insurer, Catholic Church Insurance (CCI), was not so much upset about what Pell's people were doing to Ellis, but about the hundreds of thousands of dollars they were shovelling off a cliff. Standing at the bottom of that cliff, catching the cash as it fell, were Corrs Chambers Westgarth and the pricey barristers they had taken on to fight the case. CCI had had enough. It wrote to Pell's business manager, Danny Casey, to say that the bill at that stage for the case was $367 215. By comparison, in another 'vigorously contested' case against the Church and, ironically, McGloin, the bill to get all the way to the conclusion of an appeal was $120 000. CCI was cranky at what it saw as double handling and overspending. 'Clearly CCI can't allow the present position to continue ... CCI will not meet the current Corrs fees in full.'

It was decided that the archdiocese would run a defence saying that, effectively, Ellis could not sue Pell because he was not archbishop at the time that Duggan was in the employ of the archdiocese and was not, therefore, the proper defendant. The Archdiocese argued he could not sue the Trustees of the Archdiocese because they had, effectively, no legal personality. As Pell's private secretary Michael Casey conceded in an internal email, 'Just saying that the Archdiocese cannot be sued because it doesn't exist does present a serious pr [sic] challenge...' But the good men of the archdiocese, spurred on by their lawyers, pressed on. PR be damned.

The archdiocese was undeterred. Ellis was vigorously cross-examined about the abuse, despite the archdiocese's earlier offer of compensation to him.

When the first judgement a couple of months later was unfavourable to the Church, Casey encouraged the lawyers to 'Go full steam ahead' to appeal. Pell won the appeal the following year. The court accepted the Church's argument. The case is therefore thought to have enshrined a principle now known as 'The Ellis Defence', a precedent which has made it exceedingly hard for victims of child sexual abuse to sue the Catholic Church if the bishop or archbishop who made decisions around the employment of a paedophile priest is no longer living. The Ellis Defence also means that the Trustees of the Catholic Church are only considered to hold its considerable assets in regard to property matters, and can't be sued in respect of abuse that occurs on that property. It also held that the Church is not considered to be responsible for its priests, because technically, it does not employ them. As Andrew Morrison from the Australian Lawyers Alliance told the ABC *7.30* program when discussing this case, that is not the situation anywhere else in the common law world.

A jubilant Casey wrote to his boss. 'Eminence,' he began, and then outlined a quick note on the outcome of the case. 'Danny [Casey, the business manager] and Ted Exell delighted with the treatment of the proper defendant issues by the court.' Ellis decided to appeal to the High Court. 'Many hundreds or thousands of people may [have been] disadvantaged if the Court of Appeal decision were allowed to go unchallenged,' Ellis later said. 'I made a conscious decision to risk everything I owned to do what was right.' The High Court refused Ellis special leave to appeal and Ellis fell apart.

Astonishingly, the Church, a billion-dollar organisation, and its wily lawyers turned their attention to recovering costs against this broke, heavily mortgaged and under-employed plaintiff. In December 2007, the archdiocese commenced steps to recover costs in the court proceedings. A letter to Ellis requested payment within one month. The costs amounted to more than $700 000 and the lawyers for the Cardinal told Ellis they had instructions to take formal enforcement action if the costs were not paid.

Dalzell, the Church's lawyer at Corrs, wrote an email about it to CCI, which was later tendered to the Royal Commission. 'I should say from the outset that [Corrs Partner] Paul McCann has a number of significant concerns about pursuing the plaintiff for costs,' Dalzell wrote. 'He has considerable experience of bearing the brunt of negative publicity caused by clients attempting to recover costs at the end of hostile litigation. The test Paul applies is whether you would be prepared to accept the risk of this story appearing on the front page of the Telegraph newspaper.' He noted, however, that Pell's private secretary Michael Casey was concerned 'we are potentially giving away a considerable amount of money'. The archdiocesan finance guy Danny Casey said he'd entertain forgoing costs if Ellis promised not to go to the media again. The insurers supposed that would look like 'hush money'. As for Dalzell, he was prepared to wear the 'Telegraph Test' negative publicity because 'it would also have the effect of sending a clear message to potential litigants that the Church takes these matters seriously and that they will not be given a free kick'.

The insurance company got back to the lawyers and while it had earlier complained that their fees were too steep, it didn't resile from forcing Ellis to pay them. However, as a compromise, to water down the bad press, it suggested going to him and offering, effectively, a discount. To do that, Ellis would be required to set out his annual income, his assets and liabilities and any directorships of companies he may have.

Ellis' lawyer wrote back, essentially begging for mercy for his client, whom he said was 'traumatised' by the judgement, in poor health, at risk of self-harm and 'physically and emotionally' devastated by the tragic death of his 18-year-old son that year. His lawyer had 'genuine and grave concern' for Ellis' welfare if the costs letter was sent to him. He asked Corrs to please ask their client—i.e. the Cardinal—to take all of this into account. When Michael Casey showed 'HE' (what the in-crowd called His Eminence) the letter, HE thought it best to leave it a few months before going back to Ellis to demand costs, but instructed the lawyers to obtain 'more details' about their client's health.

Ellis' solicitor duly sent back a letter from a psychiatrist who had grave concerns for his client, particularly the stress of the court case and the resultant financial problems he would have from a costs order. The Cardinal expressed his concerns about the negative publicity of bankrupting Ellis and also the prospect he might self-harm. But his advisors countered that they didn't want to look like they would just roll over any time someone said they couldn't pay costs. So, they kept going. They asked Ellis' solicitor for proof of just how broke his client was. The solicitor, David Begg, replied 'as you are aware, the prospect of your client enforcing the costs judgement and forcing our client and his family from their home is cause for considerable stress and is adversely affecting his wellbeing'. But he set out his client's modest financial position—including a heavily mortgaged home which was badly storm-damaged and falling into serious disrepair.

At the end of May 2008, Corrs wrote to Ellis' solicitor and said the archdiocese had decided to 'defer' the question of costs, knowing, as an email actually said, that it would 'infuriate' the Ellis camp because it gave no finality. As Ellis' solicitor pointed out, the psychiatrist had said one of the greatest stressors for Ellis was having the financial threat 'hanging over him'. And this was precisely what the archdiocese was continuing to do.

In utter desperation, Ellis wrote a heartfelt letter to his Holiness Pope Benedict XVI in June 2008, who was due to visit Sydney for Catholic World Youth Day the following month. He told the Pontiff that he was on a substantially reduced income, suffering from severe mental health issues and had therapy twice a week. He would lose his home if forced to pay the Church's costs some time in the future. He asked, among other things, that the Cardinal formally forgive his costs permanently and that Pell come to meet with him in an attempt to restore the faith in the Church he had lost. Pope Benedict never replied.

Eventually, the Church began to pay some of Ellis' psychiatric bills and told him the costs would not be pursued, although this would never be put in writing. In 2009, Pell agreed to meet John Ellis. At that meeting, Ellis told Pell that his original request for an ex gratia payment had been just $100 000. The Church eventually paid seven to eight times that amount to Corrs Chambers Westgarth and the silks and juniors they engaged. Pell told Ellis he had no idea that that was all Ellis had originally sought—he believed it to be millions and what he had been through was 'legal abuse'.

'I will make sure this does not happen again to anyone,' Ellis says Pell told him. The Sydney Archdiocese began to make payments on Ellis' house repairs and eventually spent hundreds of thousands. It also contributed to his medical bills. But the money dried up when Ellis spoke out on ABC TV about the abuse, the litigation and the response of the archdiocese.

Ellis later said that his meeting with Pell led him to believe that the Cardinal was not aware of what had gone on. But the references to 'HE', 'Eminence' and 'Cardinal Pell' dotted throughout the hundreds of pages of correspondence I have read between the various parties—to which Ellis did not have full access when he made that statement—suggest that 'HE' was being briefed. He was involved in twenty significant steps of the Towards Healing process. The Royal Commission much later found, essentially, that he was not telling the truth when he said that he didn't know that Ellis' original request was only for $100 000. His Monsignor, Brian Rayner, gave sworn evidence that he *did* tell the Cardinal about it. And as the Commissioners found, 'it seems unlikely' that he would not have been told.

As for the legal hammering Ellis received from the archdiocese, again, it's inconceivable that Pell didn't have a significant hand in it. His private secretary, his business manager, his solicitor, his insurers, as well as a number of priests who worked closely with him, were all in the loop. It is implausible, especially given the money expended and the vexed nature of the litigation, that Pell was not a party to discussions. And part of his reason to instruct Corrs to vigorously defend was, he later admitted, to dissuade other abuse complainants from litigation.

As Begg tells me, reflecting back on those dark days, 'it was like BHP was suing Rio Tinto and this was about the law and nothing else,' he says. 'There was no appreciation that we were dealing with a human being ... a plaintiff who had a significant illness. I think, unfortunately, they dealt with him as a gifted lawyer and that was the blinkers through which they viewed the claim.'

This sorry saga went on for seven years. In the process, it nearly broke a man who was already a victim of the Church. That Church obsessively pursued a technical legal defence of a person it had already accepted was abused. It accepted, in the midst of that process, that another man, S, coming forward, significantly strengthened Ellis' case, and yet never reconsidered disputing it.

Pell, a leader of a faith-based organisation, acquiesced in a process where his rolled-gold lawyers, whom he instructed to go hard, spent an inordinate amount of money defending Church coffers against a man who had been abused by a dodgy priest with other victims—not just here, but, it transpires, in Scotland. Even the Church's own insurers blanched at the legal bills. The lawyers and the people closest to Pell kept haranguing a man to the point where his lawyer had to warn them he was at significant risk of self-harm. In the end, it seems the PR risk got to them—they say that in the documents. They couldn't have a bankrupt victim of child abuse top himself. Best pull back.

While Pell's archdiocese was supposedly saving money by spending it hand over fist on legal bills, it and the state government of New South Wales were also splashing the faithful's cash on a much more positive and life-affirming event. Pell had scored the coup of bringing Catholic World Youth Day to Sydney—an all-singing, all-praying international Catholic conference for young people, starring the person Ellis had hoped to intervene in his matter, and Pell's old ally, Pope Benedict.

Despite concerns about over-spending ($86 million) by a state government that was on the nose and hadn't spent enough on infrastructure, the twenty-third Catholic World Youth Day itself, the first in Oceania, was a success. A million people came to the weekend mass to see Pope Benedict, with young pilgrims attending from 200 countries. Pilgrims belted out 'Alleluia, Alleluia! Receive the Power to be a light unto the world!' with former *Australian Idol* winner Guy Sebastian who sang the official song. Press releases said 200 000 meat pies were distributed to the faithful. A busy trade was done in baseball caps and rosary beads. 'There's nothing immoral with a little commercialism,' Pell told reporters. '[P]eople have got a right to make a living out of doing a good thing, which is spreading Christ's message in a modern way.' All in all, it was largely agreed that the whole thing was a credit to the Cardinal—another example of his excellent organising skills.

But there was a flip side to an emboldened Cardinal. The exercise of power became a constant feature of those years. And those who disagreed with Pell on matters theological or spiritual felt thoroughly marginalised. As the 2000s wore on, it was not just a case of Pell necessarily exercising the power himself, but that he had remade the Australian Church in his image. Dissent was actively discouraged, discussion about subjects he had declared off limits was avoided.

Bishop Robinson, who had retired in 2004 as Pell's Auxiliary, later said of Pell's relationship with his priests in the archdiocese at the time, 'the most common word you might have heard was "disengagement". Priests simply forgot the diocese, put their heads down and looked after their parishes, because [Pell] had lost the support of his priests ... [Pell had] lost the majority of his priests and that alone made him an ineffective bishop ... The majority of the priests wished he would get transferred somewhere else ... So the diocese became separate parishes rather than any unified body. [The effect of that was] a lack of effectiveness, a lack of diocesan unity, a lack of working together, a lack of real loyalty to the bishop. It was a difficult time.'

Much of it was bound up in Pell's overarching position that truth, not conscience, should be the primary driver of human endeavour. Truth set down, as it happens, by Rome and, the Cardinal would argue, by extension, Jesus Christ. Tolerance, Pell believes, is a vastly overrated concept. Particularly tolerance of those who happen not to fall into his world view. As he wrote in an essay in May 2005, 'The Inconvenient Conscience':

> 'Tolerance' is often something of a weasel word. Of course, all human beings should tolerate the foibles and weaknesses of their fellows. But by 'tolerance' many now mean 'never judging.' And this is a much more debatable proposition. In fact, believers in tolerance themselves usually acknowledge unspoken limits. Tolerance rarely means refraining

from judging racists, or sexists, or pedophiles, or political cheats—naturally enough: these are morally wrong and should be judged so. But the contemporary love of tolerance is severely limited. In effect, the only things we must be tolerant of are people's sexual choices, or perhaps their choices about such life issues as abortion or euthanasia.

Why do people strain to accommodate absolute sexual freedom as a matter of conscience? Why does no one plead for the right to racism or sexism as a matter of conscience? Could it be because the liberal concept of conscience has been specially formulated in order to facilitate the sexual indiscipline that our culture upholds?

It still all comes back to sex in the end. As for Pell, he believes that anyone who criticises this should just take a look at themselves:

> When a lapsed Catholic says 'I have a problem with the Church' his real problem is a contradiction

within himself. In truth, most real-life dilemmas are not between the inner person and external authority but between competing desires and reasons that the person has trouble reconciling. As a way of sidestepping the terrible tension a moral dilemma can create, people may identify one side of the dilemma with their own conscience and the other with an external power such as the Church.

See what he's doing there? He's saying it's your problem if you don't like what the Church says. It's not ours. We represent inviolable truth. You just haven't found it yet. I remember as a cadet at *The Australian* interviewing his friend Denis Hart when he replaced Pell as archbishop in 2001; I asked what he thought about the fact that I didn't know anyone with whom I went through Catholic school who still went to mass. What sort of indictment was that? 'You're all just lost,' the Archbishop replied, beaming magnanimously. 'You'll come back.'

The Church of Hart (at least at that time) and Pell (then and now) is a monolith whose structures must be fortified. Doubt or dissent or even basic questioning cannot be allowed to permeate any part of it. Those who question it are to be pitied, shunned or, in some cases, actively punished. It was exemplified in Pell's speech in Cork, Ireland, where he asked the assembled audience 'Where Have All the Fighters Gone?' and urged Ireland, like he had Australia, to reject 'cafeteria Catholicism' and promote 'authentic renewal'.

Father Eric Hodgens had a public tit for tat with Pell in 2011, writing in the Catholic journal *The Swag* on the current trend for orthodoxy in the Church—including World Youth Days—that reasserted 'an old model' which wasn't working and was causing a drought of priests and the loss of the younger generation.

Pell responded, 'The now aged liberal wing of the Church, which dominated discussion after [Vatican II] and often the bishops and the emerging Church bureaucracies, has no following among young practising Catholics or religious.' In a western world dominated by secularist media, he said, 'liberalism has no Catholic progeny'. But Pell pointed out that it is the 'mainstream orthodox' trends attracting the younger generations who were flocking to the new orthodox religious orders and seminaries, and that the well-worn 'liberal' agenda had lost its cachet. According to Pell, all the cool kids in the Catholic Church these days are committed conservatives. Questioning is, like, so 1967.

Robinson, who of course had been running the Towards Healing program and was at odds with Pell's conception of Catholicism, resigned, seeing that his position could only be untenable given their inability to agree on key matters. But when his friend the Sydney Marist priest Michael Whelan sought to promote discussions by Robinson for Whelan's progressive Catholic organisation, Catalyst for Renewal, he hit roadblocks.

Catalyst for Renewal had already given up on trying to house its events on Church property—it had been made clear to the organisation by Pell's archdiocese that that would not be tolerated. But even the Sydney diocesan magazine, *The Catholic Weekly,* which

Whelan assures me is strongly controlled by the Archbishop, took measures against them. When Robinson was lined up to give a speech for Catalyst for Renewal at one of its events, Whelan says he approached *The Catholic Weekly* to buy advertisements for the talks. '[I] got a deal for two Sundays in a row for ads. To tell you the truth, I was gobsmacked when they printed the first one,' Whelan says. 'Then they called me and I got an embarrassed apology. They told me "we shouldn't have done that, we can't publish the second one".'

As late as 2014, while Pell was still, just, archbishop responsible for Sydney, when Catalyst for Renewal brought out former Irish president Mary McAleese, who was studying canon law and had progressive views, for instance on women in the Church, *The Catholic Weekly* also informed Whelan that it could not be advertising such a person in its pages. A former Irish President. Whelan wrote a letter to the editor, and, to be fair, *The Catholic Weekly* printed it.

> As Editor, you spoke with me on the phone and explained to me

that you would not run those advertisements because Ms McAleese, in previous talks, had expressed views not in line with current Church teaching. You have the right to make that decision and I accept that. However, I would like to tell your readers that in more than 42 years as a priest, I have never known anyone with the willingness and ability to 'speak the truth in love' (Ephesians 4:15) as Ms McAleese does.

The sexual abuse tragedy has confronted us with at least two terrible truths and at least one urgent question. The first truth is that some of our number abused people. We had to be cajoled, embarrassed and threatened into accepting this. The second truth is that our handling of the complaints ranged from the naïve to the criminally negligent. Alarmingly we sought first and foremost to protect the Church. We paid scant attention to the victims until we were forced to. Many of those victims have had their lives wrecked.

Why did these things happen? This urgent and troubling question requires us to critically and radically examine the Catholic culture—its theology of ministry and the training of priests, its self-understanding as part of society, history and culture, its ideal of holiness, its attitudes to sexuality, its structural and personal ways of exercising authority, and so on...

Prophetic people like Mary McAleese must be welcomed into a dialogue that allows the truth to emerge.

Of course, Pell and his supporters are entitled to their opinion of Mary McAleese and to shout it loudly from whatever rooftop they desire, but when the official diocesan magazine of a city of 4.8 million people, more than 28 per cent of whom identify as Catholic (higher than the national average) does something like this, it raises troubling questions. Saying it cannot advertise a speech talking about Catholic issues, by the former president, a Catholic, of a heavily Catholic nation, whose ties are stronger to Australia's local Catholic community than perhaps any other, suggests something is going terribly wrong.

Whelan had had his run-ins with this sort of mindset before. Whelan is a Marist father and the order has since 1868 had the care of the historic St Patrick's parish in The Rocks on Sydney's waterfront. St Patrick's is always a busy church and has long been considered a jewel in the crown of the Church in Sydney. Whelan's name was submitted by the Provincial of the order in the mid-2000s to Pell, who was expected, as usual, to appoint the name submitted. But the Archbishop of Sydney has always had a technical right of veto. Pell, says Whelan, chose on this occasion to exercise that right.

'The reasons [Pell] gave to [the Provincial] were fabricated and spurious,' Whelan remembers. 'He said that Father Michael has "many talents" but does not always use them in the service of orthodoxy.

'He said that to appoint Father Michael as parish priest would be to make a statement. And he might upset the faith of the simple folk.'

The sort of orthodoxy that saw an Irish president denied advertising in a major Catholic publication also saw a bishop in a large Queensland diocese dumped by Rome for speaking out about matters it didn't want discussed.

Bishop Bill Morris of Toowoomba was asked to resign by a papal representative, Archbishop Charles Chaput, in 2011 after he started speaking out about issues like contemplating the possibility of accepting gay parishioners and women's ordination. On the other hand, Morris was later praised by the Royal Commission and others for his diocese's exemplary handling, with its strong pastoral focus, of child sexual abuse complaints.

'He was the consummate team player who planned his pastoral strategies in close consultation with his presbyterate and the various consultative organs he set up in the diocese,' Jesuit Frank Brennan later wrote in *Eureka Street*. 'As the people of Toowoomba continue to live faithful lives as Catholics, they still hold Bill in high esteem; meanwhile all the people in Rome are now gone ... It was "a poor decision based on poor advice".'

Pell spoke out when Morris got the sack. 'He's a very good man. He had a lot of pastoral strengths. He's got a lot of good points. He's done a lot of good work. He's got quite a strong following in the diocese,' Pell conceded. 'But the diocese was divided quite badly and the bishop hasn't demonstrated that he's a team player.'

'That's quite a claim coming from an archbishop whose own auxiliary Geoffrey Robinson had cause to say, "He's not a team player, he never has been",' Brennan pointed out.

'I think part of the problem has been that in our Church people have had in mind two separate teams. There is the Roman curia team, and there is the local Church team. There are those like Cardinal Pell who have played with the Roman curia team providing exclusive avenues for reporting on the local team, and then there are those like Bishop Morris who have played with the local Church team knowing little about the workings of the Roman team. One message of [Pope] Francis is that it's time to bring both teams together, and the Roman team is not always right.'

Pell preferred to hold the rigidly orthodox line—the line that says you're either with us or agin us: 'Catholics stand with the Pope as the successor of Peter and his role is to strengthen his brothers and to defend the apostolic tradition, and it's now Catholic teaching that women cannot be ordained as priests. That's not an optional belief; it's now part of the Catholic package,' Pell said.

'I think [Morris' demise] will be a useful clarification for people that Catholic doctrine is there to be followed and bishops take promises to defend the integrity of Catholic teaching.'

Despite many murmurs around the Australian clergy that Pell was conniving with his Rome contacts in the removal of Morris, Morris himself won't buy into that, but he acknowledges that Pell used his removal to reinforce his message. Morris is adamant that the sort of Church that Pell represents must change if the Church in Australia is to survive.

'There needs to be a new paradigm for the priesthood,' Morris tells me. 'We need to understand what the priesthood is all about. There *has* to be married clergy and there has to be women clergy and until we have these conventions we are going to run into little dictators who come out of the seminary ... Until we change it we are going to keep running into trouble.'

10

TWO COUNTRY COPS

I believe we must do everything we can to make sure that what has happened in the past is never allowed to happen again.

Julia Gillard, 2012, announcing the creation of the Royal Commission into Institutional Responses to Child Sexual Abuse

In 2012, two things happened in the Australian media that lobbed grenades into the Church's power structures and, in the process, straight at the nation's most senior Catholic, George Pell. They both concerned country cops who could no longer bear the burden of picking up the pieces of child sexual abuse in their districts.

The first cop put together for the first time a series of suicides, principally in Pell's home town of Ballarat. The second was a police officer from New South Wales who came forward with what he knew. He had nothing really to do with Pell, but would change the life and Church of the Cardinal.

On 13 April 2012, *The Age's* investigative team splashed on page one a story which shocked anyone unfolding the broadsheet with their morning coffee. 'Confidential police reports have detailed the suicides of at least 40 people sexually abused by Catholic clergy in Victoria, and have urged a new inquiry into these and many other deaths suspected to be linked to abuse in the church,' the story began. The leaked police report the newspaper had obtained was written by Ballarat detective Kevin Carson, who had been for decades investigating the likes of Father Gerald Francis Ridsdale and the paedophile Christian Brothers of Ballarat's St Alipius.

Carson, who was not quoted in the story, was weary of, with his colleagues, finding bodies with slashed wrists in baths, prising men out of cars crashed in single vehicle accidents, cutting down blokes on ropes, attending at the homes of mothers and wives and brothers and sisters who would wail at the loss of their loved one. He and some of his Ballarat colleagues were sickened by the silence of the Catholic Church. The victims who had survived this torrent of abuse in that town and in Melbourne were calling for an urgent inquiry into the Church. The story featured a series of photographs of those who had died and quoted Dr Vivian Waller, the dogged lawyer who represents probably more victims of abuse than any other solicitor in Victoria, saying any inquiry would discover an 'epidemic of abuse'.

This story would go on, some years later, to spark an ugly series of events, but when it landed, it forced then-Victorian Premier Ted Baillieu to act. Four days after the story was published, Baillieu announced a parliamentary Inquiry into the Handling of Child Abuse by Religious and Other Organisations in Victoria. Survivors at the time were happy that finally someone, somewhere, was going to investigate the obfuscation, the corruption that they had borne the brunt of. The inquiry was chaired by a no-nonsense Liberal non-Catholic, Georgie Crozier. Her deputy was

Christian Brothers–educated Frank McGuire, the member for the working-class electorate of Broadmeadows. The inquiry was not limited to the Catholic Church, but its report, Betrayal of Trust, said the majority of the evidence heard related to the Church's parishes, schools and homes.

Later that year, on 8 November 2012, the comments of another country cop impelled another politician to finally call the Royal Commission that survivors had been demanding. The second country cop came from another ferociously Catholic diocese, Newcastle. His name was Chief Inspector Peter Fox. The politician was the first female prime minister of Australia: Julia Gillard.

Peter Fox was a 30-year veteran with the force and he went rogue, writing a letter to NSW Premier Barry O'Farrell, and appearing on an interview with the ABC's Tony Jones on *Lateline.* He spoke of the rampant culture of sexual abuse by clergy and the cover-ups by the Church's Newcastle Diocese.

It was a stark interview. Fox, in a dark suit and burgundy tie, sat and gave Jones a horrific catalogue of things that he knew.

'I think most people would be absolutely crumpled up in tears to hear it,' Fox began. 'Whether you're the Premier of New South Wales or you're just somebody sitting back watching this on TV tonight, it's got to move you. It can't but move you. It's terrible.'

Fox, who had been collaborating with *Newcastle Herald* journalist Joanne McCarthy—who later won the Graham Perkin Australian Journalist of the Year Award for her work in this area—wrote to O'Farrell that day: 'I can testify from my own experience the Church covers up, silences victims, hinders police investigations, alerts offenders, destroys evidence and moves priests to protect the good name of the Church.'

It was the sort of thing that at that time, you would almost never hear a police officer go on television to say without the approval of his bosses. Fox had no such approval. He made some alarming allegations about police colluding with the Church—ultimately the NSW Special Commission of Inquiry set up immediately after the interview aired found that those could not be substantiated. Margaret Cunneen, the silk appointed to oversee the inquiry, ultimately found that Fox was not a credible witness because essentially, like many whistleblowers, he'd become clouded with emotion and lost objectivity. It was a bruising experience for Fox.

However, many of the Fox allegations about the Church would be stacked up by Cunneen. Not just that, it was glaringly apparent that what was going on in the Newcastle Diocese was but a microcosm of what had taken place in dioceses across the country—and none more than the diocese that made Pell—Ballarat—and the archdiocese that Pell remade in his name—Melbourne.

Within three days of Peter Fox's first appearance on *Lateline,* basically as soon as she got back from an overseas engagement in Bali, Prime Minister Gillard announced a Royal Commission into Institutional Responses to Child Sexual Abuse.

'Australians know ... that too many children have suffered child abuse, but have also seen other adults let them down—they've not only had their trust betrayed by the abuser but other adults who could have acted to assist them have failed to do so,' Gillard told reporters. 'There have been too many revelations of adults who have averted their eyes from this evil. I believe we must do everything we can to make sure that what has happened in the past is never allowed to happen again.'

It was perhaps to be Gillard's most lasting legacy—one that could not be substantively peeled back by successive governments from the other side. 'At a time when we were being hammered in the press for no matter what we did,' her Deputy Prime Minister and Treasurer, Wayne Swan, tells me, 'Julia was determined to do the right thing. She did not flinch or agonise, she just did it.'

But Swan was right about the hammering. Even at the time, some portrayed it as a distraction from the real issues, as policy on the run.

'The dismal, populist and doomed quality of Australian governance has been on display this week with Julia Gillard announcing an in-principle royal commission into child sexual abuse, a panicked Tony Abbott falling into line and an ignorant media offering cheer upon cheer,' *The Australian's* Paul Kelly proclaimed in a column after the announcement. 'This decision has plunged Australia into a multi-jurisdictional, multi-institutional, state-church, high-cost shambles where nobody knows how the massive expectations of victims can be satisfied.'

Kelly was also critical of Pell, whose press conference in reaction to the Royal Commission announcement he described as a 'catastrophe'. 'Pell is unable to project a convincing sense of compassion, reform and healing,' Kelly wrote. 'Pell looms as a huge liability in the institutional crisis now facing the Catholic Church in Australia.'

Pell had privately and publicly thanked Gillard for not confining the whole thing to the Catholic Church and said he welcomed the Royal Commission. But the press conference

Kelly referred to was widely received as a car crash.

'We think it's an opportunity to help the victims; it's an opportunity to clear the air, to separate fact from fiction,' the Cardinal began. 'We are not interested in denying the extent of misdoing in the Catholic Church.'

But. But. But. 'We object to it being exaggerated, we object to being described as the "only cab on the rank".'

Peter Blenkiron, an alma mater of Pell's old school, St Patrick's, who was abused by Brother Edward Dowlan, a serial predator who got pretty much every kid in Blenkiron's class, was watching. '"The only cab on the rank"—he used a trucking analogy,' Blenkiron says, his pale blue eyes widening at the thought of it. 'He seems to have a mentality where he is completely dissociated from the impacts and his ability to look at the reality.'

Blenkiron's friend Andrew Collins, a survivor of a shocking four abusers, says the cab on the rank analogy also misses the point. 'Well yeah, they weren't the only cab on the rank but they essentially legitimised all the other abuse, because if the clergy are abusing kids, it can't be that bad.

'If the police are aware that Father So and So is abusing kids, it can't be such a bad thing, can it, if the highest moral authority on the planet's doing it?'

Later in the press conference came Pell's old trope: the siege mentality.

> There is a persistent press campaign against the Catholic Church's adequacies and inadequacies in this area that does not necessarily represent the percentage of the problem that we offer.
>
> In other words because there's a press campaign focussed largely on us it does not mean that we are largely the principal culprit.
>
> I certainly very much regret the general smearing [that] "the church is covering up, the church has done nothing". Because that's not the case, it's demonstrably not the case.

Had the Church done 'nothing'? No, the Cardinal was absolutely right. Had the Church covered up? Yes. Again and again and again. In almost every diocese where paedophile priests roamed. What Pell would characterise as a 'smearing' would turn out to be an unabashed statement of fact. As the Royal Commission would later find, between 1950 and 2010, a staggering 4444 people alleged incidents of child sexual abuse to ninety-three Catholic Church authorities concerning 1880 perpetrators. The average age of victims at the time of the abuse was 10.5 for girls and 11.6 for boys. The average time it took for them to come forward was thirty-three years. And when they did come forward? Obfuscation. Cover-up. Excuses. Lack of empathy. 'The statistics kept hitting me one after another, to be perfectly frank,' the Truth, Justice and Healing Council's Francis Sullivan told me in February 2017. 'These are extraordinary numbers, they absolutely undermine our whole sense of what people are doing in religious life. They undermine our confidence in the whole vocation of the priesthood.

'And for decades, inside the Church, individuals and leaders have known these sorts of numbers. And they haven't, frankly, done enough, to demonstrate that they want the Church cleaned up.'

Sullivan told me that he was looking forward to the Commission being over. That day, he had fought back tears as he gave a statement. 'You know, I'm a Catholic, I actually believe in the show,' he told me.

'Still?' I said, looking at the crumpled man in front of me.

'Still. And that's pretty profound when you have to stand there and face what is such a hypocritical history.'

If Pell hoped that sorting the fact from the fiction would paint things in a more positive light for his Church, that would prove not to be. But back in 2012, he shot the messengers. The messengers seated in front of him in that press conference.

'One question I think that might be asked is just to what extent the victims are helped by the continuing furore in the press over these allegations,' he began. 'The pursuit of justice is an absolute entitlement for everyone. That being said, to what extent are wounds simply opened by the re-running of events which have been reported not only once but many times previously?'

The Royal Commission was to discover many stories that had never been heard before. And of those that had, it was in the mountain of documents that the real truth began to emerge. The previously legally privileged material which showed the lengths that the Church and its lawyers went to, for instance, to stop Ellis from being compensated. Sometimes the tell is not so much in a single bombshell, but in the drip, drip, drip of bitchy asides, spectacularly insensitive legal letters, the revelations of just how much money went to lawyers in defending this whole damned mess and obstructing anyone who tried to get justice.

As Chrissie Foster, who will forever grieve the death of her daughter Emma and be responsible for the care of her other daughter Katie, says to me, all of the galling information that has since been discovered about the gross cover-up of the destruction of countless lives of little children would never have come out were it not for the fortitude of the victims, the fearlessness of the whistleblowers and the media who told their stories. Only that forced the politicians to finally act. Only that meant that there ever was a Royal Commission. When people from the Catholic Church complain, for example, that airing allegations against Pell constitutes a 'trial by media', they might remember that.

11

ON DEFENCE OF THE INDEFENSIBLE

A lot of people here really miss you, Georgie, they really think you ought to just get on a plane. We all just want you to come home, Cardinal Pell, I know you're not feeling well, and being crook ain't much fun, even so, we think you should come home.

Lyrics by Tim Minchin, 'Come Home (Cardinal Pell)'

On the final night of February in the leap year of 2016, a sleek car delivered a septuagenarian to Il Quirinale, the highest of Rome's seven hills. Il Quirinale is home to the Italian presidential palazzo. The septuagenarian who walked through the softly falling rain into the 4-star Hotel Quirinale was not a president, nor a pope, although at times he did have a rather majestic way about him. He was Cardinal George

Pell, Prefect for the Secretariat for the Economy in the Holy See. And to put it extremely mildly, his presence was highly anticipated.

Pell was to give evidence about two Royal Commission 'case studies', which involved his time in Ballarat in his earlier years, and also his time in Melbourne as an auxiliary bishop. Pell hadn't meant to be in Rome. He was supposed to be giving evidence in Melbourne and it had been set down for December the year before. It had carried over from when the Commission sat in Ballarat in May, when attempts to hear his evidence by videolink had been highly unsatisfactory, with the feed constantly disrupted.

There had been much disquiet in Ballarat when it was discovered that just before that videolink hearing, Pell had 'secretly' returned to his home town—and therefore could have provided the evidence in person. During that visit, he toured St Patrick's College with principal John Crowley, and appeared in its glossy magazine, *The Shamrock.* Crowley was at the time very new to the job and came to regret the inadvertent message it sent—given his school was already smarting from the revelations in the Royal Commission that it had in the 1970s been an epicentre of abuse by a ring of Christian Brothers. Crowley has since quietly reached out to many survivors—even offering personal financial support to the sick and cash-strapped. His school has been a model of how to address child protection, and as one survivor said to me 'it's probably the safest place in the country a child can go to school now'. Crowley believes the Cardinal is of course entitled to visit his alma mater, but knows that that photograph caused great pain to the men who had been abused there as boys. The fact that he turned up, unannounced, just before he gave videolink evidence, angered his home-town community.

As to the Cardinal's December cancellation, it came from nowhere. On 11 December, the Auxiliary Bishop of Brisbane, Brian Finnigan, was being cross-examined when, after the luncheon adjournment, Pell's legal team indicated they had an application to make. Ears pricked up around the courtroom. Allan Myers, QC, addressed the bench, saying that he was applying for his client to give his evidence by videolink—that is, he would not return to Australia. 'The grounds of the application are based upon the health of Cardinal Pell.' The room went into uproar. 'Get him a fucking air ambulance!' yelled one woman. The Chair, Peter McClellan, was forced to try to calm the room, to make sure that 'Mr Myers has a proper opportunity to put his application'. A medical letter was provided to the Commission, written by one Professor Patrizio Polisca, director of complex emergency care medicine at the Tor Vergata University Teaching Hospital in Rome. Somehow, between April and December, Pell had developed a heart condition so troubling that he could not fly back to Australia. Polisca cited 'hypertension, ischemic heart disease, complicated by previous myocardial infarction and cardiac dysfunction'. He said a long flight risked heart failure in his patient. Pell later said that he had collapsed twice after getting off long-haul flights from Australia.

Google the name Patrizio Polisca and what comes up first is not medical journal articles, but religious ones. For Polisca, a cardiologist, had been head of Vatican Health Services. In 2014, Polisca was on hand to help the Congregation for the Causes of Saints to unanimously declare a miracle by the late Pope Paul VI, who had interceded in an 'inexplicable' healing of a patient, according to Professor Polisca. Paul VI was beatified in October of that year—the first stage in becoming a saint. The first Google image search result of Polisca brings a picture of him shaking the former Pope Benedict's hand. Pope Benedict being the former Cardinal Joseph Ratzinger, Pell's great promoter in the Vatican. Polisca was on staff until 2015 as the Pope's personal physician. Polisca was removed by Pope Francis eighteen months before Pell asked not to fly, but remained as Ratzinger's official doctor. He also remained on the Congregation for the Causes of Saints job, lest a medical opinion might be sought when another miracle ought to be declared.

The Royal Commission's Chair was, like so many people who find themselves up against Pell, snookered. While Justice McClellan noted that people with Pell's condition did fly, the Commission couldn't exactly force the Cardinal to come back and risk him dying on the plane. However, many argued that there were other options available—such as having a medical specialist accompany the Cardinal home, first class, in short stages, with breaks in between. Seems, prima facie, like a lot of money to spend. But Pell always flies first class anyway. He, via the Church, can afford to splash around $20 000 a day on his Queen's Counsel, Allan Myers, not to mention the rest of his legal team.

Not only that, Pell was offered the services of local medical specialists. Dr Richard Sallie, a gastroenterologist from Nedlands in Perth, dashed off a pitch-perfect missive to the Cardinal via the letters section of *The Sydney Morning Herald:*

> I hope you get well soon. However, on a practical note, I am a doctor with experience in

transporting critically ill patients on long-haul commercial flights. To ensure that your critical testimony to the Royal Commission isn't misconstrued and the Catholic Church unfairly vilified as a result of any inaccuracies that might result from the video testimony, I would happily travel to Rome to escort you safely back to Australia. I am certain a team of other doctors could be quickly organised to ensure your travel safety. Furthermore, as I understand you only travel first class, I'll happily pay for your tickets. Please let me know.

'Well played, Dr Richard Sallie,' they said on social media. 'Well played.'

The online tabloid *Daily Mail Australia* had a field day, sending a paparazzo to the Piazza Navona to catch the Cardinal munching on a fried steak and chips, washing it down with a pint of lager and accompanying it with a generous bread basket. 'Heart condition improving then, George?' said the headline.

As it happened, the eventual cost to the Royal Commission (and therefore, the Australian taxpayer) of the eleventh-hour determination that the Cardinal was simply too ill to fly is estimated to be in the region of $250 000.

Survivor Peter Blenkiron was sitting in court that day, and he says his first response was black humour. 'I knew if I didn't laugh, I would have cried,' Blenkiron says. But as he left the court, Blenkiron, a very mild-mannered and pleasant fellow, felt the rage start to rise in him. 'What sort of condition was it where he was still able to work?' Blenkiron wondered. 'I just thought, "This does not make sense. This does not have a ring of truth."'

It was not publicly known at this point, but eight days before Pell's solicitors sent the medical letter to the Royal Commission, a raid had taken place. A raid by detectives of Victoria Police's Taskforce SANO, which investigated institutional abuse cases. The detectives went to St Patrick's Cathedral, St Kevin's College in Toorak and 'other properties believed to be linked to the Church'. Victoria Police later confirmed to *The Age* that the offences related to 14-year-old boys in the cathedral. The detectives told the newspaper that they wanted to speak to 'victims or anybody with any information relating to any alleged sexual assaults at the cathedral between 1996 and 2001'. Those years just happened to correspond with the years of Pell's tenure as Archbishop of Melbourne. The article also made a point of saying that the Church's buildings in East Melbourne also housed Caritas Australia and the Cardinal Knox Centre (the archdiocese's administrative offices). Caritas, of course, being Pell's workplace for some years in the 1980s.

Pell was not named in the article. But given that it was the seat of power of perhaps his closest friend in the Church, Denis Hart, and that, more generally, it would have caused quite a stir among staff that the detectives had turned the place upside down, it is within the realms of possibility that news may have travelled back by some method or another to Pell by 10 December that something was afoot. There are those in the criminal justice fraternity who are absolutely convinced that it did. The detectives, of course, were looking for information about Pell himself. They were looking for something, anything, that might shed light on a complaint about Pell during those years. They were searching for clues about Pell and The Kid and The Choirboy. When Pell made his announcement that he wasn't to fly, it took twelve days for the carefully worded article in *The Age* to surface. It had an official comment from a Police Media operative. It was clear that the cops wanted Pell to know they were circling. And as I have interviewed a number of complainants who allege child abuse by Pell, everyone involved with that investigation was absolutely gutted when he didn't come back.

The tide of public opinion crashed against the Cardinal like a monster wave. Like Blenkiron, the other survivors and families of Ballarat and Melbourne who had been waiting to eyeball the Cardinal during his evidence were incandescent. They determined that somehow or other, they would get to Rome.

Comedian and composer Tim Minchin released an absurdly catchy charity song, 'Come Home (Cardinal Pell)'. I remember the first time I heard it and gasping as the audacity increased with each verse. The initial lines are innocuous enough—'Come home, Cardinal Pell, come down from your citadel, it's just the right thing to do, we have a right to know what you knew'. But then it builds in intensity—hurling insult after insult at Pell: 'You spent year after year, working hard to protect the Church's assets, I mean, with all due respect, dude, I think you're scum!' It gets worse—Pell is called a 'pompous buffoon', tarred with 'ethical hypocrisy' and 'intellectual vacuity'. 'And your arrogance don't bother me as much as the fact you turned out to be such a goddamn coward. You're a coward Georgie. You're a coward Georgie.'

Perhaps the most brazen bit—the bit where he plays Pell at what so many say is his own bullying game—is at the end, where Minchin gives a metaphorical two-fingered salute, taunting the

Cardinal to come home and sue him if he doesn't like it.

'Oh, Cardinal Pell, my lawyer just rang me to tell me this song could get me in legal trouble. Oh well, Cardinal Pell. If you don't feel compelled to come home by a sense of moral duty, perhaps you will come home and fricking sue me.' The song was played on the Network Ten program *The Project,* and a website set up by Ballarat local and *The Project* presenter Gorgi Coghlan and comedian Meshel Laurie. It raised just shy of $200 000 in four days. The proceeds left over from funding the survivors' trip to Rome were given to Ballarat's Centre Against Sexual Assault—which has always done a brisk trade in the abuse-scarred town. *The Project's* co-host Steve Price thought the song was disgraceful. 'I think it is really disgusting the way he has resorted to personal abuse of George Pell,' Price said. 'This guy is a Cardinal, regardless of what you make of it ... To use your talent to simply abuse someone from a distance, I think it's pathetic.' *Herald Sun* columnist Andrew Bolt, who would go on to be granted an exclusive interview with Pell, said Minchin was 'desperately unfair and cruel' and 'bases his case for the damnation of Pell on one untruth after another'. He was, said Bolt, 'a man of no real intellectual integrity or moral courage'. While the song was a huge hit, in some ways it could be said that its coarse qualities played into Pell's hands—that it gave him the moral high ground, made him look like a victim.

Two dozen survivors ultimately flew to Rome to hear the Cardinal's evidence. It became a massive international media event. The survivors were interviewed by news organisations across the world. As Blenkiron, who was one of them, says, ironically, the Cardinal's decision not to fly was 'in hindsight, the best choice he could have made'. It turned enormous international attention to their cause, helped by the fact that the film *Spotlight*, about *The Boston Globe's* investigation of the cover-up of clergy child abuse in its own city, had just been released. 'And if that's what it takes to keep children protected and no communities like ours destroyed in the future,' Blenkiron says, 'then it was worth it.'

Blenkiron noticed, however, something surprising about the man declared to be in such perilous health, when he met the Cardinal at the close of his evidence: his handshake. 'I was shocked by how strong he was for a man of his age,' Blenkiron says. 'I'm 90 kilograms and he almost took me off my feet.'

The Cardinal was to give his evidence in the Quirinale's Giuseppe Verdi room, a vast parqueted space, named after the Italian composer of operatic classics such as the 'Triumphal March' from *Aida.* As it transpired, the Cardinal's evidence was to be far from a triumph.

When Pell walked with his familiar stooped gait into the Giuseppe Verdi room, filled with Blenkiron and his fellow travellers, another survivor, Paul Levey, says the star witness did not make eye contact with them once. Instead, Pell sat with a gaze glued on the monitor of the videolink screen for a good ten minutes while Royal Commission staff organised the feed.

Having sworn on the Bible to tell the truth, the whole truth and nothing but the truth, 'so help me God', he rebuffed any suggestion that he was the number three man in the Vatican, a common and clearly tiresome misconception. 'People like to make hypothetical lists,' Pell shrugged. 'Some people would see the financial affairs of the Vatican as very low on the list.'

Not he, though. Goodness, no. It is highly unlikely that Pell himself ever saw himself or his title as low on anyone's list, anywhere. He was 'something equivalent to the Treasurer'. He had walked into that building surrounded by an entourage and bodyguards. The bodyguards sat in the room where he was to give his evidence, flanking the survivors, wearing suits and earpieces like they were guarding an American president.

'I think it's very important that Church money is used efficiently, that the donations are used for the running of the Church, and for the helping of the poor, that they're not wasted,' the Cardinal declared.

Counsel Assisting the Royal Commission that day, beamed from Governor Macquarie Tower in Sydney back to the Hotel Quirinale, was Gail Furness, SC. A flinty, blonde barrister, Furness possesses a dry, whip-smart intelligence that creeps up on the witness slowly and seemingly innocuously, then wallops him over the head without warning. Then it bashes and bashes and bashes. Beating the unsuspecting witness to a bloodied pulp. 'She's not exactly what you'd call a people person,' someone who works around the Royal Commission told me. 'But she's bloody good at her job.'

This first day started maddeningly slowly. But Furness was building her case.

Furness asked Pell if he or those he reported to in the Vatican had thought to set aside funds for victims of abuse when dioceses had run out of money. In a word: no.

'As a preliminary clarification, my authority touches only the Vatican. Unlike most other Vatican councils or congregations, that is, departments, they have some sort of authority around the world.' That is, whatever money flowed into the Vatican, whatever money it had collected over centuries through prudent financial and real estate decisions, would not flow out.

When Furness asked what might happen in the event of there being insufficient funds, where the people who were seeking to be compensated would go, the Cardinal replied that he wasn't sure 'we've ever been in that situation'.

'And the Vatican,' offered Furness, 'as you see it, doesn't have a role?'

'No.'

Gail Furness brought up the inquiries around the world, which had focused on clergy abuse and exposed the inaction of the senior clergy.

The Cardinal paused slightly and leaned in towards the microphone. 'Let me just say this as an initial clarification, and that is, I'm not here to defend the indefensible. The Church has made enormous mistakes and is working to remedy those, but the Church in many places, certainly in Australia, has mucked things up, has made ... let people down.'

Mucked things up. The survivors gasped for the first time. *Mucked things up?*

'Unfortunately, original sin is alive and well; the tendency to evil in the Catholic Church too, and sometimes it's better, sometimes it's worse, for good or for ill the Church follows the patterns of the societies in which it lives.'

'So you wouldn't suggest that it's just a case of a few bad apples, as it were, within the Church?' Furness asked.

'I've never suggested that,' the Cardinal replied.

'And you wouldn't think that it's the case of a few weak or inactive leaders in the Church?'

'No, unfortunately, they weren't necessarily few.'

This was clearly a more conciliatory tone than Pell had previously adopted. The survivors felt quite heartened. Perhaps there would be more admissions. However, the Cardinal refused to admit that the problems were structural. 'I think the faults overwhelmingly have been more personal faults, personal failures, rather than structures.' With 1880 accused perpetrators over sixty years, and most of them never brought to justice by the Church, that's one truckload of personal failures.

Continuing in his conciliatory tone, he also admitted that the Melbourne Response and Towards Healing 'have been shown to be imperfect' and added that he would like to see a national redress scheme—something that victims are desperate for.

Furness brought the Cardinal to his return to Australia after his education at Oxford—when he went back to Ballarat.

'It seems that education and the education of children became an area of particular interest to you?' Furness asked.

'The Bishop asked me to take a role in that area and I did so happily,' the Cardinal replied. The role was Episcopal Vicar for Education.

Here, Furness began subtly to sharpen her knives. She cited a letter in 1984 from Pell to Bishop Ronald Mulkearns, in which Pell wrote that he was part of 'the essential link between the Bishop, priests, parents, teachers and students'.

Furness asked, 'Now, that is how you saw the role, isn't it?'

To which Pell responded, 'I would be very interested to see where I said that; I think it somewhat overstates my role, it was not the director of education.'

Furness showed him the document, dated 20 September 1984, where he addressed 'My Lord'—Mulkearns—on 'some thoughts on the role of the Episcopal Vicar for Education' 'the bishop's representative in all areas of education'. 'Through this clerical/religious presence education is seen as one vital part of the church's apostolate; the essential link between Bishop, parents, teachers and students is also emphasised.'

Despite being one part of this 'essential link', Pell said he only 'very rarely' visited diocesan schools.

'Perhaps more the opening, the blessing of a wing or an extension,' Pell explained. 'I had no regular such role because I was a full-time academic in the Institute of Catholic Education.' This is certainly not the recollection of students at St Alipius, from Villa Maria, from St Patrick's College, where almost every one I have spoken to knew who Pell was when they were a child at school and said Pell was a fairly regular visitor.

Furness asked if, as part of his role, any teacher, parent, principal or child approached him about problems at their school. The Cardinal replied that they did. She asked if the problems were in relation to teachers being 'overly affectionate or in some way touching' students.

'Well, it's a long time ago, but I can't remember such complaints, and normally they would have been addressed to the Education Office, not to the Vicar ... I can't remember any such, ah, examples, but my memory might be playing me false, I–,' he stopped short and looked at the screen.

Furness went in: 'Why might your memory be playing you false?'

The Cardinal clasped his hands: 'Because I don't have perfect recall.'

The steel-trap mind was at play here: 'Cardinal, I was just repeating what you said in different language; what you said was "I can't remember any such examples but my memory may be playing me false". That's the answer you give?'

'That is the answer. No more and no less,' Pell responded.

Reflecting on this during an interview I had with him later on that night, a tired Andrew Collins, who had been watching this exchange in the Quirinale, was sceptical.

'I mean, he's a very, very intelligent man. Very smart man. He doesn't strike as the sort of person who would have his head in the sand over these things.

'So I do find it unbelievable that he didn't know. I would probably find it more believable that he may not have wanted to know,' Collins said. 'But he would have had to have known, I'm sure of it.'

Furness took the Cardinal to some of his previous publicly reported statements on his time in the Diocese of Ballarat. For instance, that the general attitude of the Church to disclosures of sexual abuse was 'generally not to believe the child'—did he accept that?

He did not accept that. He qualified it. 'I think that, no, I that, I would now say that that is an overstatement, but it certainly was much, much more difficult for the child to be believed then.' Furness asked if the predisposition was to be 'dismissive of those complaints'.

'If they were not presented clearly,' Pell replied. 'Too many of them certainly were dismissed and sometimes they were dismissed in absolutely scandalous circumstances ... Very, very plausible allegations made by responsible people ... were not followed up sufficiently.'

Furness wondered whether this was about asset protection, but Pell countered that it was about shame. 'The instinct was more to protect the institution, the community of the Church, from shame.' But he admitted that asset protection 'did' become an issue later on.

The Cardinal did agree that the culture was to not report to police. And to think that offenders could be treated, to 'overestimate what could be done through psychological and psychiatric treatment'.

Here, without warning, Furness went in for the kill. 'It's the case, isn't it, that you were aware during the 1970s and early 1980s, that the Bishop was sending [Ridsdale] off for treatment for sexual offending against children?' Gerald Ridsdale is, of course, the former Catholic priest of the Ballarat Diocese who is thought to be Australia's worst serial paedophile. The Royal Commission had seventy-eight formal claims against him for child abuse when it did a data analysis in 2015. In April 2017, he pleaded guilty to a further 20 charges against eleven children. But the numbers of victims are thought to in reality go into the hundreds. Pell wasn't biting at the suggestion that he knew that his former Bishop, Ronald Mulkearns, was sending Ridsdale to counsellors, then on to the next parish, instead of sending him to police.

'No, that's certainly not correct ... I wasn't aware of Mulkearns sending anyone off for sexual offending,' Pell said.

When Furness asked if he knew of anyone sent off for 'sexual offending of any type', Pell became archly definitional.

'Well, an offence is, I presume, something against the law. If a priest is engaging in sexual behaviour, either heterosexually or homosexually, that's incompatible with his continuing as a priest, and it's possible that people were sent off—but once again, I'd have to hear who or what, say, to reply specifically.'

At this point, the Chair of the Commission for the first time showed a hint of frustration, which would become, in time, exasperation: 'Cardinal, all that counsel is asking you for are the names of any priest you can remember who were sent off for treatment by Mulkearns, that's all...'

'It was long after I'd gone from the diocese, but Ridsdale was sent off for such treatment to the United States.'

Mulkearns had, of course, destroyed documents in relation to paedophile priests. Pell said that he only found out during Victoria's parliamentary inquiry in 2014 that this had happened. 'The way he was dealt with [it] was a catastrophe, a catastrophe for the victims and a catastrophe for the Church,' the Cardinal said.

'If effective action had been taken earlier, an enormous amount of suffering would have been avoided ... He shifted—gave him chance after chance after chance, shifted him around, and initially at least trusted excessively in the possible benefits of psychological help.'

But the Cardinal was adamant that he was unaware at the time that this was taking place: 'I did not know it at the time ... I didn't know that Mulkearns knew, let alone anybody else.'

When Pell commenced his priestly duties as an assistant priest at Swan Hill, he served under parish priest Bill Melican, who was to become very significant to the Royal Commission.

About 230 kilometres from Swan Hill, but with no significant towns in between, was the similarly isolated neighbouring parish of Mildura. It's there that an incorrigible sex offender, Monsignor John Day, was abusing children with the protection, it's now clear, of the local police. Pell remembered during his evidence that he knew of rumours and 'gossip' in regard to this. But Day had made denials of such behaviour. Day was later moved on by the Bishop when parishioners and some police confronted him. 'I must say, in those days, if a priest denied such an activity, I was very strongly inclined to accept the denial,' the Cardinal admitted to the Royal Commission.

Day was granted twelve months leave of absence on the guaranteed minimum salary. Then, in 1973, Mulkearns appointed him to the tiny Western District dairy town of Timboon. 'Yes, I am critical of it,' Pell told the Royal Commission. Day died in 1978, leaving a swathe of victims in his wake. Mulkearns gave him a glowing homily, admitting only to his 'flamboyant' ways.

In 1973, Pell of course moved on to St Alipius, another parish notorious for its child abuse. Ridsdale was at one time parish priest at St Alipius, where he famously lived for a period in the presbytery with Pell, as well as a string of other young priests, including Father Paul Bongiorno, who would later become a political editor for Channel Ten news.

The ring of paedophile Christian brothers at St Alipius beat, stalked and abused the children. They favoured nude bike riding, skinny-dipping at Lake Bungaree, kisses for the boys on the lips. They'd sit the children on their knees and stroke their hair at one moment, belt the living daylights out of them the next. And that was just the supposedly innocuous stuff. A whole generation of Ballarat kids was affected by what went on at St Alipius. So Furness was curious to know what Pell knew, and how much involvement he had with the school, in his Episcopal Vicar role.

'Almost nothing,' Pell replied. The St Alipius school is right next to the St Alipius parish where Pell was required to say mass. The presbytery where Pell lived is on one side of the church, the school, a stone's throw away, on the other. The buildings are in very close proximity. And Pell admitted he did know all the brothers who worked there.

Did anyone complain about any of these brothers? 'There was talk about the eccentricity of Brother, is it Fitzgerald? ... But there were no specific accusations ... I think he used to—it's alleged he'd—when some of the boys were leaving he'd give them a kiss. He was very strange, old-fashioned, but a good teacher; there were things like that.'

'At the time, did you see him kissing the children as sexualised behaviour?' Furness asked him.

'No, it was common knowledge, and the general conviction was, it was harmless enough ... People were aware of it and they weren't insisting that anything be done.'

Pell estimated the first time he heard there were problems with Brother Ted Dowlan was the early 1970s—the problems were at St Patrick's College, up the road on Sturt Street.

'What sort of problems?' Furness asked.

'Unspecified,' Pell replied, 'but harsh discipline and possibly other infractions too.' When pushed, he admitted that 'other infractions' were problems of a sexual nature.

Father Lawrence O'Toole, a friend of Pell's who was also an assistant priest of St Alipius in the seventies, says he knew of 'sexualised conduct' by the Christian Brothers at the school.

'He didn't mention that to me,' Pell assured the Royal Commission.

O'Toole also gave evidence that a monsignor who had been on the Bishop's consultors' committee, which Pell later joined, and whom Pell knew, had had parents speak to him about another Christian Brother at the school 'exposing himself to a child'. 'Did that come to your attention?'

'No.'

He'd heard about the nude bike riding, the skinny-dipping and 'one or two fleeting references' to 'misbehaviour which I concluded might have been paedophiliac' by Dowlan.

Survivor Tim Green, who gave evidence to the Royal Commission that he told Pell of Dowlan's behaviour when Green saw Pell in the change rooms at the Eureka Pool in 1974, said he found it 'inconceivable that none of the

Brothers, lay teachers, the nurse, or even some of the parents knew about the abuse by Dowlan. It was just so blatantly obvious and every boy in the class knew that their turn was going to come up at some stage.' That sentiment has been echoed by every St Patrick's alumnus from that period whom I have spoken to—including several whose names I plucked from yearbooks and who are professionals who have never 'come out' as survivors of Dowlan.

Pell says his information came to him from 'a St Pat's boy ... A fellow at the school. Yes, one that I remember,' he said, adding that he still knew the boy's name.

'He recollected it years later, but I remembered him as a good and honest lad and I didn't think he'd be telling—I couldn't remember the actual incident, but I didn't think he'd be telling lies.' Pell later said, in his second, headline-making PR failure, that the boy 'wasn't asking me to do anything about it'.

Pell agreed with Furness that the evidence showed that there were students, more than one teacher, the principal of St Paul's Technical School, parents and probably Mulkearns who knew of the goings-on at St Patrick's College.

'You'd agree, would you, that the knowledge of the sexual offending by Christian Brothers at St Alipius School and St Pat's School was known by a significant number in the community; would you agree with that?' Furness asked Pell.

'I would agree that it was known to all the people whom you've mentioned and they do constitute a significant number.' But as to the Episcopal Vicar for Education? Well, he heard nary a whisper.

He heard nothing when Brother Paul Nangle, the headmaster of St Patrick's, went to see Mulkearns because he saw a brother in bed with two boarders. Nangle also went to see the Christian Brothers' Provincial, Brother Patrick Naughtin, and the Provincial took the offending brother out of the college and informed Mulkearns.

He heard zilch about Ridsdale from Swan Hill, Pell's first parish, even though there had been just one assistant priest between Ridsdale's and Pell's placements there. As the next few days were to show, there was so much that Pell didn't know. Despite being in so many places where he might find out.

12

A SAD STORY THAT WASN'T OF MUCH INTEREST

I didn't know whether it was common knowledge or whether it wasn't. It's a sad story and it wasn't much interest to me.

Cardinal George Pell on the rumours about serial paedophile priest Father Gerard Ridsdale's prolific offending at the tiny town of Inglewood

From the moment George Pell's midnight-blue Volkswagen slid down Via Nazionale and pulled up at the Hotel Quirinale slightly before 10p.m. on the first day of the Italian spring, the Roman night was abuzz with expectation. The Cardinal had met that day with Pope Francis. And as he strode into the hotel, it was clear that the meeting had gone rather well. 'Cardinal

Pell! Did you meet with the Pope today? What did the Pope say?' a reporter called out to him from the media pack as he entered. The Cardinal did not turn around, but he waved his hand back at the reporters as if to bat them away like pesky blowflies at a barbecue. 'I've got the full backing of the Pope,' he declared. From the very start of his evidence that day, it appeared that full backing had left him emboldened. He seemed less concerned with appearing humble and conciliatory, as he had the day before, and absolutely determined to defend himself at all costs.

The following four hours contained a comprehensive series of alibis, excuses, defences, qualifications, exceptions. A dazzling display of a steel-trap mind that is resolutely made up. These were principally framed around why Pell, as a member of the priestly college of consultors of the Ballarat Diocese in the late 1970s and early 1980s, determined with Bishop Ronald Mulkearns and the other consultors to move the priest whom we now know was a serial child predator, Gerald Ridsdale, from parish to parish where he would abuse ever more children. And why Pell, in a community where the list of people who knew and were awfully concerned about Ridsdale was ever growing, had apparently no idea what was going on.

Pell was, for instance, 'deceived' by Mulkearns and other consultors. And of course, consultors were merely 'advisors' to the Bishop, not decision-makers. More generally, priests just weren't gossips—they had more noble and godly preoccupations. He led an awfully 'busy life'. And even though he was the Episcopal Vicar for Education in the Diocese, he was terribly distracted by his full-time job as an education academic. Yes, parishioners and parents and nuns and teachers were writing to, meeting with and calling the Bishop about Ridsdale's offending. But there were no mobile phones in the diocese, no social media, so word travelled surprisingly slowly. This was the 1970s and early 1980s, you see. And there were 'enormous social inhibitions' on discussing matters like paedophilia.

The people surrounding Pell who knew about Ridsdale during this time included his Bishop and some of the priestly consultors—one of whom was well acquainted with Pell's mother. There was another lifelong priestly friend, two nuns he knew professionally and personally, and even the retired and elderly bishop he lived with. Not to mention that he had lived with Ridsdale himself for a period at the presbytery at St Alipius. But Pell knew nothing. None of those people thought to breathe the merest hint to him. Even when he was meeting with them and they were discussing Ridsdale himself. But more of that later.

It is hardly an exaggeration to say that this line of defence left Ridsdale victims grossly disappointed and, indeed, furious. One of Ridsdale's victims was from the town of Warrnambool, which lies on Victoria's Great Ocean Road. It's surrounded by emerald-green cliff-top pastures with dry-stone walls. Bluestone cottages are battered by winds from the southern ocean. It's perhaps Australia's closest thing to the west coast of Ireland. Warrnambool's people are Murphys and Barrys and Delaneys and it is resolutely Catholic. The sort of place where priests were revered and, so, well suited to Ridsdale. A witness known to the Royal Commission as 'BWA' was, over a period of two years at the ages of fourteen and fifteen, digitally raped and forced into oral sex in the garage of his family home at Warrnambool.

The teenager, who felt he could not tell his parents, ran away to Adelaide, and when he returned, he told a priest called Tom Brophy, known to him as 'Broph', what had happened.

> I told Broph everything in pretty graphic detail and he basically sat slumped on the chair. He looked at me and said, 'it can't be true'. I said, 'I can give you a dozen names of other kids involved' ... Broph assured me that he would put a stop to it. He was someone I believed in implicitly. He told me that he and Monsignor Fiscalini would go to Bishop Mulkearns in Ballarat.

That was 1972. Broph died suddenly in 1974 and never spoke to BWA again about the matter, but years later, he says another priest, incidentally a friend of Pell's—Father Brian Finnigan—confirmed that Brophy had passed on the information as promised. When Finnigan was quizzed on this in a public hearing, he said that BWA was an honest truth-teller, but he, Finnigan, could not recall telling BWA this. That was one of many things Finnigan could not recall.

Furness quizzed Pell on that. 'So it seems, doesn't it, from this document, that Bishop Mulkearns and Monsignor Fiscalini moved Ridsdale to Apollo Bay with knowledge of that earlier complaint against Ridsdale [by BWA in Warrnambool]?'

'That is correct,' replied Pell drily, who agreed the conduct of the Bishop and the Monsignor was 'unacceptable'.

Chillingly, when BWA discussed the matter with Finnigan in 1989, Finnigan recommended a clinical psychologist to BWA. That psychologist was a Father Dan Torpy. Torpy had been a consultor to Mulkearns along with Pell in the Diocese of Ballarat during the crucial period when Ridsdale was being shunted about. If the most unforgiving interpretation of the consultors is found by the Royal Commission—that is, that they colluded with Mulkearns to move Ridsdale from parish to parish with knowledge of the reasons why—then Torpy had a pretty good motivation for encouraging victims of Ridsdale not to come forward to police. And that, according to BWA, is precisely what this clinical psychologist did when BWA sought his advice about getting back into the Catholic Church community:

> He said that the first thing I had to do was learn to forgive as that was what the Church was built on. He also said there was no need to report Ridsdale's offences to the police. There was no way I was going to forgive Ridsdale ... After this conversation I basically got up and walked out. Father Torpy's words made me feel like it was still my fault.

The day before Torpy, who told the Commission he counselled clergy for the Church as well as victims, was due to give public evidence, he slammed his car into a truck. In April 2017, he pleaded guilty to reckless conduct endangering serious injury. Torpy, now a lay psychologist, helps his wife run a child abuse charity. He never did give that evidence.

After BWA's complaint, Ridsdale was moved to nearby Apollo Bay. But he didn't last there either. The priest himself told police he left Apollo Bay after a drunk man came to see him at the local pub.

'I got rid of him as quickly as I could and in the course of the conversation he said, "they are saying things down at the pub about you and kids",' Ridsdale said.

And so Ridsdale put in for a transfer. The Bishop and his consultors committee, which did not yet include Pell, duly obliged. They obliged with Fiscalini and Mulkearns knowing of the serious sexual assaults on BWA. Ridsdale was packed off to the tiny inland town of Inglewood outside Bendigo.

In his evidence, Pell was critical of this decision by the Bishop, saying even by the standards of the time, it was poor. He said that at the time, the practice, at first instance, was to send priests away for counselling 'and for help with the possibility of return'. And even that hadn't happened. Furness jumped on this admission. Did he then know that paedophile priests were being sent off for counselling? No, Pell assured her, he didn't know about this contemporaneously: it was 'something I discovered subsequently'. How subsequently, exactly, he 'couldn't say precisely at all'.

Not surprisingly, things went pear-shaped for Ridsdale at Inglewood too. A Victoria Police detective, Col Mooney, was approached by an Inglewood local making a complaint about Ridsdale and kids. The talk about the town had got so fierce, according to local police and indeed to Ridsdale himself, that the priest packed his things and left town at midnight, never to return. This was 1976. Pell chose his words carefully when asked about his knowledge of something that was clearly widely known in the town and beyond—he couldn't say that everyone knew. He knew some people knew.

At some point, between the events in 1976 and Ridsdale being charged in 1993, Pell discovered that some people knew what Ridsdale was up to at Inglewood. And it was while he was trying to explain this, that he made his worst public relations gaffe of the evidence.

'I–I couldn't say that I ever knew that everyone knew,' the Cardinal began. 'I knew a number of people did. I was—I didn't know whether it was common knowledge or whether it wasn't. It's a sad story and it wasn't of much interest to me.'

The Cardinal looked skyward as angry gasps and guffaws echoed through the Quirinale and the Sydney courtroom, which he could clearly hear. 'Oh, what?!' said one survivor. 'You've got to be joking!' spat out another. Melbourne survivor Julie Stewart turned to me and widened her eyes. She folded her arms tightly across her chest. In Rome, a collective gasp echoed around the room. Vanessa Beetham, who was there as a support person for the survivors, said they sat back in their seats in dismay. She said conservative commentator Andrew Bolt, who was there to report for the pay TV news channel Sky, sat with his head in his hands, rubbing his eyes. 'He might have been tired,' she says wryly. 'I don't think so.'

'What wasn't of much interest to you, Cardinal,' Furness asked, archly.

Pell became flustered, he started blinking and looking at the floor. He knew immediately that he had misspoken. It was to be his gravest mind snap of the evidence. 'Umm ... The suffering of course was real and I very much, ah, regret that,' he began. 'But I had no reason to turn my mind to the extent of the evils that, ah, Ridsdale had perpetrated.'

Furness went in for the kill.

'In order, Cardinal, to not have the offences and misconduct of the past repeated, doesn't one need to understand the circumstances in which those offences were committed and the structure and personnel that permitted that to occur?'

Pell returned to combative form: 'Yes, and obviously you approach such a task differently according to the level of responsibility that you have.'

But Furness wasn't giving up.

'Isn't the case, Cardinal, that every adult in the Church is responsible for ensuring the safety of children going forward? It's not a question of structural responsibility; it's a question of being an adult and being responsible, isn't it, Cardinal?'

Pell wasn't biting. 'Well, an individual can only do what is possible to do and everybody has a responsibility to try to preserve the moral health of the community in ways that are real and practical.'

'But it's the case, isn't it, within the Church that every priest or ordained person is responsible for ensuring the safety of children who are taken in by the Church to be looked after?'

Well, according to Pell, not exactly. 'No, that's much too general a statement.'

The 'sad story' line made international headlines. Pell was pilloried because of it. He later said he was 'muddled' during that part of the evidence. 'I'd just say in a little bit of self-defence,' he told Bolt, 'nineteen and a half hours of evidence is ... it ain't nothing!' The pair chuckled.

Pell described the situation at the time as a chain of command—parish priest responsible for his parishioners, bishop for his diocese. But what if the priest was a paedophile and the bishop was turning his back on the children against whom the crimes were committed, simply moving the priest from parish to parish? Who was the responsible adult then?

'It's very difficult to answer these questions where we swing from one extreme to the other. Everybody has some sort of general responsibility. Individuals, and especially office holders, have particular responsibility for their area of concern.'

So a neighbouring parish priest who had heard of this had no responsibility?

'Well, very obviously I said nothing of the sort ... I'm not suggesting for a minute, especially in a neighbouring parish, that a neighbouring parish priest would have no responsibility at all. I never suggested that.'

But clearly, his belief was that it was a diminished responsibility. And it certainly seemed to contain the wriggle room that allowed for the odd blind eye to be turned.

'I think office bearers have greater responsibilities and of course people can do something, and that depends on the role and position and location they have.'

Watching on at the Hotel Quirinale, Ballarat survivor Peter Blenkiron said he felt that Pell was not only being evasive and defensive, he believed the Cardinal was being deliberatively provocative.

'At times it was sort of like an onslaught of statements where we felt it was trying to inflame us to lose our shit,' Blenkiron says. He adds that it was particularly difficult for the men who were directly affected as children by the denials being covered by this evidence.

'For them to keep their shit together and to not call out [was incredibly hard]. As a group, given everything we've been through, I think we did an amazing job of keeping it together. It was lucky we had the counsellors there and the support people. Because every resource was drawn on. I think we were all a bit fearful that some of the guys who hadn't had much counselling and stuff were going to lose it. And it would have taken just one of us to lose it...'

Pell took on the role of consultor to Mulkearns in 1977 and, as foreshadowed, it was to become pivotal to what he knew or, in his view, what was kept from him, about the activities of Ridsdale. It became a sustained line of attack during the second day of the hearing. The consultors met, as was their practice three or four times a year, in July 1977. Minutes of the meeting were taken, but as one of the consultors later told the Royal Commission, the raw notes of these meetings were 'destroyed' and Mulkearns urged confidentiality about the discussions.

Present at that meeting with Pell and Mulkearns were Monsignor Fiscalini, who already knew about Ridsdale's proclivities, and Father Torpy, who would later advise the victim BWA that there was no need to go to the police. Also there was Father Frank Madden, who later served with Ridsdale at the parish of Horsham and wrote a glowing character reference for Ridsdale when he was later facing multiple child sex charges in 1993:

> Fr. Ridsdale has been quite an outstanding priest in almost every facet of his work. He has been blessed with real talent which he has used with exceptional energy and zeal.

In fact, Madden had not a single bad word to say about Ridsdale in 1993 and did not once mention the allegations that were the reason he was required to write this character reference. Two other priests—Fathers McKenzie and Arundell—made up the numbers. In the Royal Commission, Furness was keen to find out what Fiscalini, who of course knew about BWA, had told Pell during the 1977 meeting. 'If Monsignor Fiscalini was doing his job properly, he would have told you all of what he knew from 1972, wouldn't he?'

'He should have,' the Cardinal replied.

'And Bishop Mulkearns would have told you what he knew from 1972 and 1976?'

'Yes, well, he certainly didn't.'

'He didn't?'

'He did not ... I can't remember what reasons were given [for Ridsdale being moved], but there are many possibilities other than paedophilia for the removal or the translation of a priest.'

'Well there may be, but in this case it was paedophilia, wasn't it?'

'In this case, we now know it was paedophilia.' The survivors in the courtroom shook their heads.

Furness reminded him that each of the other consultors had knowledge of sexual assault allegations against at least one priest.

'That is correct. Yes,' he drawled. 'That is correct.'

'And yet you say that none of those people shared with you any knowledge they had about Ridsdale?'

'That is correct.' Pell reminded Furness that it was simply 'not discussed' at the consultors' meetings and 'that is the—close to the—unanimous evidence of the consultors'.

But the Cardinal chose his words carefully. 'Close to'. Not unanimous. The reason for that phrasing was the evidence of one Father Bill Melican. Melican, an octogenarian priest, had given evidence to the Royal Commission just shy of three months before, in December 2015. Melican broke ranks. Melican's memory of the meetings themselves was hazy and he said he could not remember the content of discussions. But unlike Pell, he was willing to accept Justice McClellan's suggestion that the consultors had discussed the real reasons for Ridsdale's unusually high pattern of priestly appointments to different parishes, including unexplained temporary postings, agreeing with McClellan that it was 'a problem peculiar to Ridsdale' and it was 'well-known to the consultors'.

When McClellan asked Melican whether the consultors would have known about the moves and 'presumably, known the circumstances of the move', Melican replied 'yes'. Melican said he couldn't remember exactly what he was told, but agreed that 'in the normal course of things that's what would have happened'.

But unlike Melican, Pell stuck ferociously to his guns. Mulkearns and Fiscalini had, 'unfortunately', deceived him.

'It's hard to imagine a greater deception, isn't it?' a sceptical Furness asked.

'Well it probably would be possible to imagine a greater deception, but it is a gross deception.'

At this point, the Chair made the first of what would be a series of interjections, which became increasingly exasperated as the hearings progressed, asking the Cardinal whether he thought Ridsdale's pattern of movements was 'strange'.

'Why, when you were sitting at that meeting, did you think that Ridsdale had been moved in this irregular way?' McClellan asked.

It was then that the Cardinal made his first admission.

'Because, obviously, there was a series of difficulties, but it certainly was not stated that those difficulties touched on paedophilia and crimes.'

'Did you ask what the difficulties were?'

'I can't remember specifically asking, but there would have been some generalised explanation.'

'Generalised explanation? Could you help me to understand what that might be?'

Pell answered that it could have been difficulties with the school principal, of personalities, of an inappropriate adult relationship, or it could have simply been restlessness.

Pell repeated this to Andrew Bolt, when he granted Bolt an exclusive interview in Rome. 'It was obvious that he was restless, or had some sort of personality problem,' he told Bolt. But when Bolt pressed him on what sort of personality problem it might be, and what people had called it in discussions, the Cardinal quickly said, 'I can't recall any specific discussion, ah, like that. Umm, and I can't remember any specific discussion of a personality problem of Ridsdale.'

'They certainly did not tell me,' he told the Royal Commission, 'that the reason he was being shifted was because of paedophilia ... I can't remember exactly what was said, but it would have been quite clear that there were difficulties of some sort.'

Justice McClellan peppered Pell with questions. 'It must have been somewhat notorious now, in the mind of at least Fiscalini, that there had now been two complaints in relation to Ridsdale and they had both been of a serious nature.'

'Correct.'

'And given that notoriety, it would be surprising, given that priests do talk among themselves and gossip, that there was not the subject of discussion with others including yourself?'

'Well, I think you are making a number of jumps there,' Pell replied. 'There is a saying in the Church and elsewhere that those who know don't say and those who say don't know. Priests, because they hear confessions, can be and must be about certain matters the most secretive of people. I do not remember much discussion about the secret failings of priests, and certainly at that stage there was never any discussion in my presence about the dreadful story of Ridsdale.'

In his evidence, Melican contradicted this 'priests don't gossip' trope of Pell's.

When Counsel Assisting, Angus Stewart, SC, said a number of priests had told the Commission that they did in fact gossip, Melican somewhat sheepishly admitted, 'It's pretty hard not to agree, isn't it?' During private evidence in July 2015—which he did not think would become public—Pell's friend Bishop Finnigan said he was not sure he'd 'call it gossip, always, but [priests] talk about these things'.

The Chair returned to the 'common knowledge' of Ridsdale's activities at Apollo Bay and Inglewood. 'Now to suggest, Cardinal, as you have repeatedly, that knowledge about Ridsdale was secret is just not true.'

Pell replied that it wasn't known to him and he believed 'it wasn't known to quite a number of others'.

The Chair asked if he could think of 'any reason why Bishop Mulkearns would choose to deceive you about Ridsdale's behaviour?'

The Cardinal did speculate as to some possibilities. '[Bishop Mulkearns] would realise that I didn't know and he did not want me to share in his culpability. And also, I think he would not have wanted to mention it to me and some—at least some of the other consultors because, at the very minimum, we would have asked questions about the propriety of such a practice.' In other words, Mulkearns was at once protecting Pell and the others from his terrible knowledge and worried about what they, who were clearly far more morally upright than him, would do.

That theory might wash if the record didn't show that the Bishop had nothing to worry about in relation to the other consultors, at least when it came to Mildura offender Monsignor John Day. A female survivor, known to the Royal Commission as 'BPI', was nine when she was molested by Day. In 1993, in light of the publicity about Ridsdale and Day and the revelations about Mulkearns' appalling inaction, she wrote a blistering letter to Mulkearns, in which she said that the abuse of her and others in the northern Victorian town of Mildura had cost her faith in the Catholic Church and in any religion at all.

> I reckon the Church owes me for all this stuff. I'm not sure it owes me money but maybe in today's currency, that is how debts are measured and paid. If that is so, then perhaps that'll have to do. I'd prefer answers. I'd prefer honesty. I'd prefer an admission of guilt, a confession.

Two months later, Mulkearns wrote a rambling and defensive reply to her, trying to justify his actions in reappointing Day to another parish after he removed him from Mildura. He said that Day had vigorously denied the accusations and Mulkearns said something *very* telling about the consultors:

> The Diocesan Consultors of the time who were advising me felt that there was no alternative but to give him the appointment which he sought. Accordingly, I appointed him to Timboon in January 1973.

This letter was led during the Melican evidence. It shows a very different type of bishop–consultor relationship than was described by Pell. While the role is still advisory, it shows that the Bishop, Mulkearns, was more than ready to accept their advice and, in fact, he felt bound by it. It shows that consultors, some of whom were still in place when Pell came on board, were happy to proffer their opinions about matters—in this example, that there was 'no alternative' but to give him a job he was seeking. None of this was lost on Justice McClellan.

The Chair fixed a laser gaze on the monitor where the Cardinal could be seen. 'You see, you speak of the Bishop's culpability. If we were to come to the view that you did know, you would be culpable too, wouldn't you?'

'That's correct.' But the Cardinal then passed the buck again. 'It is very clear, of course, that the decision is one of the Bishop's, that the consultors only have an advisory capacity and, of course, all of us have to respect the evidence.'

People in the courtroom again raised their eyebrows at this last statement—Pell appeared to be lecturing the Chair of the Royal Commission on how he should treat evidence. If this angered McClellan, he did not allow his features to betray him.

Furness returned to the microphone to ask if Pell knew, in his Episcopal Vicar of Education role, of the claims of a Sister Kathleen McGrath. Sister McGrath had given evidence that a parent at Edenhope told her that she had been warned to 'just mind your children' in relation to Ridsdale.

Pell, of course, was terribly busy. 'I would like just to repeat, as I have said previously, that I had a full-time job as an academic and, therefore, the amount of time I devoted to my duties as Episcopal Vicar was limited,' he said.

Furness' reply was wry, clipped, playing to Pell's hubris: 'You are not suggesting you didn't carry out your job as Episcopal Vicar to the best of your ability, are you?'

'I am suggesting that I was able to devote very little time to it, and this was understood by the Bishop and all concerned.' Pell did not, as suggested by Furness, offer to give up the episcopal vicar job because he was too busy. He said he was 'quite happy with the limited amount of time [he] was devoting to' the job.

This was the point in the Cardinal's evidence where it became apparent that this was not a man who is used to taking instruction, to being questioned, to being doubted. Doubt is a foreign concept to Pell. It grates on him.

'I would—could I suggest—could I suggest that for both of us the obligation is to study the words in the document and to conclude from that?'

Furness had his measure. 'Thank you, Cardinal. I suspect some lawyers have an understanding of that concept.'

The consultors met again in 1979. At this meeting, the minutes show a discussion of Ridsdale asking for study leave at the National Pastoral Institute in 1980. The handwritten consultors' meeting minutes say 'Father Gerry will be attending NPI in 1980'. He wished to resign as parish priest at Edenhope and, on his return, desired a central parish. He had only been at Edenhope for two years. Furness pressed that a consultor who was 'effectively and efficiently doing his job' would be asking why this man was continually changing parishes. But Pell said the Bishop would have given 'some reason', like he wanted to take leave 'for a bit of prayer and reflection. That was not in itself cause for alarm.'

Furness asked, 'You knew, didn't you, that the reason he had applied for study leave was to remove himself from parish work? You knew that?'

'That view is much influenced by hindsight. I think it's a jaundiced view.'

But interestingly Melican didn't appear to think that interpretation represented a jaundiced view when he gave evidence on 8 December 2015. His answers were simple and direct.

'It stands to reason, doesn't it, from what we do know that [the reason he went to the National Pastoral Institute] was to get him out of parish work?' Counsel Assisting, Angus Stewart, SC, said.

'Yes,' said the priest.

'Essentially to keep him away from children?'

'Yes.'

'And that was known to the consultors at the time?'

'Yes.'

13

EDENHOPE

Happy is the one who seizes your infants, and dashes them against the rocks.

Psalm 137:9

Pursing her lips and shaking her head as she watched Pell's evidence live from her home near Bendigo in Australia was a woman named Donna Cushing. She had grown up Donna Harrison, the eldest of seven siblings. Her brother Mark Harrison was also watching Pell's evidence. He'd travelled to Rome with the survivors. It was a big step for Mark, who has never spoken publicly about what happened to him and has struggled with it all his adult life. Mark decided it was time to finally break his silence and spoke with me about what happened.

The deliberations of the consultors in 1977 and 1979 discussed by Pell were crucial to the Harrison family.

Essentially, if Ridsdale had been sent to the police or removed from the priesthood at that point, Donna and her siblings would never have been victims. It is an extraordinarily difficult pill for the Harrisons to swallow. 'I can't believe that George Pell did not know about Gerald Ridsdale: why he was being moved,' Cushing said, after watching the evidence.

'Everybody else knew: like, the police knew, parents knew, schools knew. The Catholic communities knew. I cannot understand how,' she said, swallowing, 'he couldn't have picked up on that, put two and two together. He is a smart man.'

The Harrison kids met Ridsdale in 1979, the year of that second consultors' meeting that allowed the priest to be shuffled on from Edenhope to the National Pastoral Institute in Melbourne, or, as Broken Rites has termed it, 'the sin bin'. The Harrisons had just moved to Bendigo, another goldrush town north of Ballarat.

I first met Donna Cushing at her home outside of Bendigo in May 2015. Cushing is, as her lawyer Viv Waller describes her, a sweetheart. She has large, doll-like blue eyes, curling blonde hair that frames her open face and a girlish voice that belies the fact that she is now in her mid-forties.

'We were a very vulnerable family. We didn't have an active father figure around at the time,' Cushing told me as she sat on a plaid sofa in her lounge room, her hands clasped tightly in front of her. She was nervous and apologetic. It is not a story she had ever told to a journalist and the family had not discussed it widely with friends. It was too painful. The pain was thrust upon this family after the Ballarat Bishop, in the presence of his consultors twice made the pivotal decision not to tell the police about Ridsdale, and instead moved him on to the next parish, to the next set of kids whom he would mark out as his victims. Cushing and her siblings would become four of those victims.

In a depressingly familiar scenario, Ridsdale seemed like a wonderful man when the family first met him.

'One night this man came to our door and he introduced himself as

Father Gerry. He came with a great big hamper of food—and that was amazing for us, because generally we would have food when it was payday. He was such a big, booming, gregarious man,' Donna remembers. Family snaps from the time show a smiling, bearded priest, in relaxed open-necked shirt and sunglasses, in some pictures helping the children pan for gold, in others, giving one of them a hug.

'You instantly took a liking to him because he was smiley and happy—very affectionate. Took great interest in all of us children. He would give us cuddles and kisses and whiz the boys, the little boys, up into the air. Do all of the playful things that a father would do, which we didn't have at that time,' Cushing says. Of course this was the classic Ridsdale grooming modus operandi. Like many paedophile clergy of the time, he would target vulnerable families—widows, single mothers with lots of kids, children who were recently bereaved.

He soon became a constant fixture in the children's lives and indispensible to their mother, a staunch Catholic who, by Cushing's estimation, didn't really know what paedophilia was. So her mother thought nothing when, in the summer of 1980, the priest offered to take the four oldest children off her hands for the week. Donna was twelve, her younger brother Sean eleven, and the twin boys Mark and Simon were nine.

'He was going to give us a really lovely holiday,' Cushing remembered. 'So we were all excited and Mum told me recently that she went to so much trouble. She made sure that we all had really nice clothes and she packed us all up so beautifully.'

The memory of packing the children off in their Sunday best has haunted Cushing's mother for decades. Not to mention the four children. As Cushing describes it, the buoyant mood evaporated as soon as Ridsdale bundled the children into the car. 'The atmosphere changed—it became very tense,' she says.

His chosen destination was the parish of Edenhope.

'When we got to Edenhope, it was really difficult. The time there, I felt like

I was walking on eggshells,' Cushing says. 'He seemed angry with us all the time. And we hadn't done anything wrong and I remember feeling that I just didn't understand why he was angry with us. He was pouncing around the house and he was a big, booming man. And he would take up a lot of space and he was ... very intimidating.'

The story she tells is a grim insight into the way that Ridsdale overpowered his victims.

Early on in the piece, he began to make advances on the 12-year-old Donna. Pictures of her from the time, enclosed in those walnut oval frames everyone used to have, show a girl who looks younger than she is. 'He would come into a room and ask me to give him a kiss and then he would give me one and it was not at all what I had experienced in my life,' she says.

'I could describe it as wet, sloppy and disgusting. I felt like I was kissing a wet eel. I remember thinking, when he pulled away, "What was that?"'

Cushing, who was very innocent about the ways of the world, was terrified.

'I feared that any time he would come into the room I was going to have to do that. And there was a time when he wouldn't ask me for one, he just came charging at me. So he was a big man and there was no way that I could fight that off. I just stood still and let it happen.' She purses her lips and nods. Her blue eyes have filled with tears.

She had noticed when they arrived on the first night that the sleeping arrangements were odd. 'He showed us our room and there were three mattresses on the floor.

'And he said, "One of you will have to sleep in my room tonight".' Donna was annoyed. 'Because I thought, "How could he have overlooked that? He knows that there are four of us and yet he only made up the three beds,"' she said.

'It didn't feel right that one of us would have to sleep in his room. It wasn't like the twins were babies. They were nine.'

And yet one of the twins did sleep in Ridsdale's room that night.

'I remember one of the boys bringing out five dollars the next day. Because he'd spent the night in Father Gerry's room. That was a lot of money to all of us—we never really had money.'

For each of three nights, a different boy had to bunk in with the priest.

'And then one morning at breakfast he said it was my turn to sleep in his room,' Cushing said.

'And I was like … I froze, I guess. I didn't want to do that. There's no way I felt I needed to do that. I was a big kid. I didn't need settling and I certainly didn't feel comfortable sleeping in a room with a grown man.

'I didn't know how I was going to get out of it. I was distressed the whole day, I was visibly crying and beside myself—I didn't have a voice to know that I could stop it or say no. And so I just cried and cried all day, very visibly. And he did see me crying and then he said I didn't have to sleep in his room.'

It was a decision that would both save young Donna Harrison and haunt her for the rest of her life. She was acutely aware that her brothers hated being chosen to sleep in Ridsdale's room, despite the 5-dollar reward in the morning.

'They grizzled when it was their turn, I remember them grizzling. I can still hear them grizzling today. And see their faces. About not wanting to. And I feel terribly guilty, because obviously I had got out of it.

'And I hadn't cried enough for the boys to have gotten out of it.

'I felt responsible. Because I was their big sister and I didn't look after them on the holiday. And I should've.' Cushing is openly crying now and I'm struggling not to, at the thought of those little kids with vile Ridsdale and the terrible burden on a 12-year-old girl.

'He took me to a farm and he asked the couple while we were there visiting if I could stay the night,' she says. 'So he basically got rid of me.'

When she returned, Cushing remembers being taken on an outing to a lake. She was wearing a purple bikini and her budding breasts were starting to develop. 'I just remember his eyes fixated on me. I felt really uncomfortable. That wasn't normal.'

When they returned, she went to have a shower.

'I'd got out of the shower and I was starting to dry myself, so I was bent over and I was drying my legs and the door opened and Father Gerry walked in,' Cushing remembers.

'And I remember quickly saying, "I'm in here!" thinking he hadn't realised I was in there, but he made no motion to move. He just stood there and looked at me. And I didn't know what was going on. I just stood there.'

The priest had enforced a cruel roster of sexual assault on the boys each night that they stayed in Edenhope that week. But none of them spoke of it. Even to this day, Cushing cannot bring herself to say the words. But County Court Chief Judge Michael Rozenes did, in his sentencing remarks when Ridsdale was prosecuted for the offences against the Harrison children and ten other victims.

> Your method of offending as against the two brothers was the same: you invited each boy to your

bed to cuddle where you committed sexual acts upon them. These acts included fondling, fellatio, masturbation and digital anal penetration. You provided cash to the boys to buy their silence and called each of the boys your 'special friend'.

When Donna was twenty-one, she was nursing in Melbourne and she discovered that one of the twins, Simon, who was in his final year at school, had disclosed to his teacher what had happened in Edenhope. Mark Harrison remembers that they were on a school camp.

'We had a retreat and we split off into little groups. The teacher said if you wanted to talk about something to get it off your chest, you could. That's when Simon told her about Ridsdale and Edenhope,' Mark says. The teacher told the twins' mother immediately.

Donna's mother called her back home.

'And Mum flew straight at me and said, "Donna! What happened? In Edenhope? The twins have told me this. And what happened to you?"', Donna remembers. 'And I was just like bombarded.'

Mrs Harrison brought the boys to police at Bendigo. Simon made a statement, Mark spoke verbally. Nothing happened. Years later, they tried to get a copy of the statement or minutes of the interview with Mark and Victoria Police told them they had no record of them. 'I think they just threw them in the bin,' says Mark.

Cushing hands me a black and white photograph of her brother Sean taken ten years after the abuse. In all the childhood photos that predate Edenhope, he's a tanned and freckled seventies Aussie kid with a sunny smile. In this one, the young man wearing work overalls has wide, almost startled, eyes that look off into the middle distance, his skin is alabaster and his smile is forced. He looks deeply troubled. He was. Sean took his own life about two years after the boys went to the police. He was twenty-one. The family later found out that he'd told his grandmother he couldn't cope with what Ridsdale had done. The memory of it is almost too much for Cushing to bear. She wept as she told me.

'I felt responsible,' she said. 'And because Sean was on that holiday and 'cause he took his life when he was twenty-one, I never got to talk to him about that.

'And I felt bad because, because when he did take his life, if he blamed me because I didn't stick up for him when I—I just cried for myself, to get out of being in Gerald Ridsdale's room and I didn't do that for my little brothers. I feel bad that I can't say sorry for that.'

'You were only a little kid, Donna,' I offer as she weeps. She nods.

'But we will never get Sean back. And even though we are survivors of what's happened, surviving's not living.'

Mark Harrison's life has been plagued with depression and he's had two failed marriages. 'I had an eating disorder for five years—bulimia that became anorexia,' Mark says. 'I had really low self-esteem. There was cutting and self-harm.

'Because it was a guy, Ridsdale, that did this to me, I didn't have friends that were male—I just didn't trust them. I would never go to the urinals—I would always go to the cubicles. I had nothing to do with men, really, and it really affected my social life.'

Mark also made several suicide attempts. The first, in 1990, shortly after Sean died. Then, again, in 2000. His third attempt was in 2012.

'I took 101 Panadol and went to sleep and my ex-wife called an ambulance. I stayed in hospital for a while after that.'

When Mark came out of hospital, the family resolved to go to the police. Their complaints formed part of a larger brief against the priest. Ridsdale was charged and convicted of thirty-four offences against children between 1961 and 1980. This was the fourth time he'd been convicted over multiple child sex offences.

'I think it's quite possible that Gerald Ridsdale is Victoria's sort of worst career paedophile. He was a person who was repeatedly placed in positions of power and authority and respect as he was a parish priest of the Diocese of Ballarat,' Cushing's solicitor tells me. Waller, a no-nonsense Melburnian based in a converted warehouse in inner-city Collingwood, has when I meet her, thirty clients with claims involving abuse by Ridsdale. She has about five hundred clients who are survivors of Catholic clergy abuse more generally, gathered over the past twenty years. It's her life's work.

'It's quite devastating when you stop and think about how many people have been harmed by Catholic clergy,' she says.

'Many of my clients report quite profound, long-term psychological impacts from the abuse,' Waller says. 'Sometimes the full impact is not realised until later in life. It can have the effect of derailing someone's education, it can unravel their faith, it can undo the fabric of their family if the parents trusted the offender.'

Despite her sunny disposition, the abuse has had an enormous impact on Cushing and her family too. 'It's always there in the forefront of your mind,' she says. 'Of everything you do. And everything you believe and everything that happens in our life. Because we are Catholics.

'I get so troubled and stressed out when I see the priests because they have this gown on and I remember Gerard Ridsdale when he would take us to mass on that holiday and he would have his big gown on and I thought, "He's representing to the people goodness and behind closed doors, he was none of that". And I was troubled by that and I've always been troubled by that.'

Mark Harrison went through the Towards Healing scheme. He met with the Bishop of the Ballarat Diocese Peter Connors.

'I think I got $20 000 in compensation,' Mark says sourly. 'Bishop Connors told me that the most ... I could have got was more than that, but he told me what happened to us was far less significant than what happened to a lot of other people. Can you believe that? Not only that, Bishop Connors told me I was not to contact a solicitor—yes—that's what he said. Everyone was hushed up to resolve it as quickly and cheaply as possible. It was pretty low.'

When the Ballarat survivors announced their intention to go to Rome to witness Pell's evidence, Mark Harrison decided this was his time to come to terms with what had happened to him as a child. But it was also personal with Pell.

'The big thing for me was that picture of him walking Gerald Ridsdale into court—that man destroyed our lives and here he was supporting him. So many people have been abused and have committed suicide. The ripple effect on family, friends, society in general, is huge. It's terrible.'

He doesn't buy the line that Pell supporting Ridsdale at court was consistent with Jesus' message of loving even the sinners, saying the Catholic Church 'just makes their own rules to suit themselves as they go along'.

'I felt quite disgusted that Pell made so many excuses not to attend the Royal Commission here in Australia or in Ballarat. It was just excuse after excuse. I thought it was important that the survivors see him in the witness box.'

As he watched, Mark Harrison says he felt that Pell was not giving honest testimony. 'He was just trying to protect the Church and his own reputation. There was so much evidence against him and he was just deflecting it away from himself.'

The Chair of the Royal Commission, Justice Peter McClellan, also seemed troubled, or at the very least irritated, that March afternoon in Sydney, thirty-six or so years after the Harrison children were taken to Edenhope. Counsel Assisting was grilling the Cardinal about his knowledge as a consultor of Ridsdale's movements. The Chair interjected as the Cardinal explained that the consultors had met three or four times a year outside the meetings in 1977 and 1979 whose minutes outline the movements of Ridsdale.

'I assume that you, on many occasions, had met with the Bishop between those two dates, either on a personal occasion or on an official occasion?'

The Cardinal again minimised his role. 'Perhaps not as much, not as frequently as you imagine. We both led busy lives and most of my life was spent outside parish life.' Always so busy.

But the Chair was undeterred. 'As you have said, you were party to gossip within the diocese from time to time; correct?'

Goodness, no. 'I would like to think that I was very rarely part of gossip. I did hear things, but I have explained that myself, like many priests, did not indulge ourselves in that type of conversation.'

'As far as Ridsdale is concerned,' the Chair continued, pressing him, 'at least in two parishes in the diocese, the secret was out ... And you are saying to this Commission that between 1977, when you say you were deceived, and 1979, you never heard anything in relation to the misbehaviour of Ridsdale?'

'I am saying that,' Pell replied, much to the disdain of Mark Harrison and Donna Cushing. 'I would like to remind Your Honour of course we are talking about a different age. There was no social media; I don't think there were mobile telephones; we are talking about a country diocese. There was certainly not the flow of information in society that there is now, and certainly on a topic like this, there were enormous social inhibitions on discussing such matters.'

McClellan wasn't buying it.

'But there were telephones in the diocese, weren't there?'

'Of course.'

'And priests spoke to each other by telephone?'

'Of course.'

The Pell eveidence was turning out to be what the journalists call 'a cracking yarn'. But for Donna Cushing, it was crushing.

'Absolutely ridiculous,' she said of the evidence. 'He is completely distancing himself. It's crazy. I don't believe that at all,' she said. She felt the Cardinal was 'twisting things', not getting to the point, and 'wasting the Commission's time'.

'They are making it really difficult for us to just try and find out what they knew at the time. It would be so much more helpful if they came out and told the truth from the word go.

'I am furious. The fact that they could have stopped the children being hurt so much earlier and they chose to do nothing just to keep Ridsdale invisible, to protect their name ... it broke our family apart.

'I really liked watching him squirm in his seat and be under pressure because when I was in Edenhope, Gerald Ridsdale put me under a lot of pressure and I didn't know how I was going to get myself out of that situation,' Cushing said.

'It feels good to watch George Pell in the same situation because that is how I was and I was only a little kid, and, um,' she said, her voice faltering, 'he is a fully grown man.'

14

MORTLAKE

Cardinal George Pell: Because something is wrong, you can't wave a magic wand and correct the situation easily in every situation. Counsel Assisting the Royal Commission, Gail Furness, SC: You don't need a magic wand; you just need a group of adults who are responsible, don't you?

Royal Commission, March 2016

Incongruously, the approach to the town of Mortlake along the Hamilton Highway, in the middle of far-western Victoria, begins with an Avenue of Honour. The Monterey cypresses were planted for the fallen soldiers after the Great War, and now provide a thick canopy with patches of sunlight glinting through. 'Mortlake: Australia's Olivine Capital,' a peeling sign declares, bearing a picture of a peridot, the gemstone that olivine becomes. Every country town has to be capital of something.

For Mortlake, it's a rock-forming mineral and, though not advertised on the roadside, for a short but bleak period at the start of the 1980s, clergy abuse. The town is flat and empty. On the Friday when I drive through on the way to the coast, not a single soul is to be seen and scarcely a car is on the road. Crows swoop over unlovely buildings. Mortlake is where Father Gerald Ridsdale did some of his worst work. If what went on with Donna Cushing and her siblings at Edenhope was a tragedy, what went on at Mortlake was an annihilation. And by this stage, it was becoming increasingly implausible that the consultors of Ballarat's Bishop, including Pell, didn't know what was going on.

Anyone with knowledge of what went on in the Ballarat Diocese shudders at the thought of Mortlake, where the Royal Commission has heard Ridsdale abused every boy he could lay his hands on at the local school, St Colman's. It happened at sleepovers. In his pool room. In his bedroom at the presbytery. At the school. Dr Wayne Chamley, from the advocacy group

Broken Rites, tells me it devastated the community. 'Mortlake imploded over the Ridsdale saga,' Chamley says. 'Sons fought fathers because the fathers didn't believe the sons had been abused. The whole family networks just started tearing themselves apart because of what had happened: the shocking tragedy in that town.' Royal Commission statistics released in 2015 showed seven men from Mortlake had made official claims of child sexual abuse. That's more than 20 per cent of the boys at the tiny school who made a claim against Ridsdale.

But they were just the ones who claimed. Evidence to the Royal Commission from survivors, parents, teachers, clerics and the nun who was school principal suggest far more than seven were abused. Internal Church documents suggest every boy in one class was affected. Another parishioner said none of the altar boys went unscathed. 'A stream of parents [came] and [said] this had happened,' the principal, Sister Kate McGrath, told a Catholic Church Insurance loss assessor.

'How many boys would you have had in [Grade] 5 and 6, roughly?' asked the loss assessor in 1993 in the lead-up to Ridsdale's first criminal trial.

'I suppose twelve or fourteen,' McGrath replied.

'Do you think they could have all been molested to some extent?'

'The possibility is certainly there, yes.'

'How many would be in Grade 7 and 8, boys?'

'Fewer there, perhaps between the two classes, there would have been eight or ten...'

'A lot of children to have been affected by one man, isn't it?'

'Well the school was only something like sixty-eight children. If you took half of those boys that's thirty. I think I added it up at one stage and it was a possibility of twenty of them having been molested.'

In another CCI interview in 1993, Ridsdale himself admitted that he 'went haywire there. Altar boys, mainly. They came over to the presbytery.'

'It was no secret around Mortlake eventually about me and my behaviour;

there was talk all around the place,' he said.

Mortlake is an instructive case study in just how badly things went in the Ballarat Diocese during those grim years that Ronald Mulkearns was Bishop and Pell was, among others, one of his priestly consultors. Ann Ryan was a teacher at St Colman's who became painfully aware of the extent of the problem, and the scale of the ensuing cover-up. I met her in July 2015 at St Patrick's Cathedral in Melbourne. We chatted as we both walked through its grey grounds on a freezing day. I'd looked up every Ann Ryan in western Victoria (not surprisingly, in those Irish Catholic towns, there are many) and when I stumbled upon her in the phone book, she said, 'I'm so glad you've found me'. Ryan is profoundly disturbed by what happened to the children in that little town and how terribly it was handled. And she had a bad feeling about Ridsdale from the start.

'He had a very strutting style when he came amongst us,' she told me. 'And I just, well, no, I just didn't like him. Couldn't put my finger on it, but didn't like him.' Teaching the boys at the school, she began to notice a change in their behaviour—petulance and an over-curiosity about matters sexual. A part-time librarian as well as teacher, she noticed much giggling behind hands, lads looking up sexual terms in the Funk and Wagnalls. All of a sudden Ridsdale was removed. Ladies were asked to bring a plate for his hastily organised leaving do. Ryan did not know the reason why, until several weeks later when a parishioner told her after mass that he had been 'interfering with boys'. Ryan was gobsmacked. A few weeks later, the impressively brazen Ridsdale returned for the school fete and Ryan noticed many parishioners who had been his friends were now shunning him.

Part of the reason Ridsdale had been found out was because McGrath was told by parents that Ridsdale was abusing their children. That same day, she arranged for another nun, Sister Patricia Vagg, to inform Mulkearns. Ridsdale was removed almost immediately. But Mulkearns didn't tell police. He also failed to provide any assistance for the child victims. Documents tendered to the Royal Commission show that McGrath tried to arrange counselling for the families:

> Some of the parents wished to hold a meeting. The bishop said 'no', there was to be no meeting. I asked that something be done for those children and to the best of my memory the response was that we could do nothing for the children.

Ryan says in recent years she's had conversations with McGrath about that, and McGrath said that Mulkearns told her 'that would be admitting guilt, to do anything for the children or to do anything at all'. When I asked Ryan what she thought of that, she paused and drew breath: '*Horror* ... Yeah. It's just a totally inhumane response.'

Seven years after Ridsdale left, another parishioner dissolved in tears and told Ryan that her son had been badly sexually abused by Ridsdale. Ryan decided to write to Mulkearns. She brought those letters to St Patrick's to show me. She rolled her eyes reading them in 2015—at the copperplate waffling, the simpering tone towards the Bishop: 'I must say how terrific it is to see you at our Diocesan Pastoral Planning meetings', 'Yours sincerely in the work of Jesus', etc. But when she gets to the point, Ryan makes it abundantly clear that the children's safety had been severely compromised.

> Some years back (1980–81) some very unfortunate happenings took place between the parish priest of the time and some young schoolboys ... Both horrified and sickened, I was stunned into a state of shock as were many others, including parents of those concerned. For years now, the fact that this happened in our parish and was virtually swept under the carpet has concerned me ... Some might say 'let sleeping dogs lie', but would Jesus? And are the 'sleeping dogs' at peace?

The Bishop's response, tapped out on the diocesan typewriter, left her stunned:

> I am sure that you will appreciate that it is simply not possible to enter into

correspondence in any detail concerning the matters to which you allude. I assure you of my own concern for all members of the diocesan community. However, it is difficult to reach out to specific people when one hears only vague rumours of a very general kind.

Ryan could not believe the dismissive tone of the letter. She simply shook her head when I told her that at that very time, 1989, as he wrote that he could not do anything about these 'vague rumours', Mulkearns was sending Ridsdale to New Mexico for 'treatment' for his paedophilia.

'I had no idea. Absolutely no idea,' she said. She sent four letters in all, to no avail.

Finally, Mulkearns turned up a few months later to Mortlake to officiate a sacrament. Ryan and one of the victim's mothers marched up to the presbytery after the service to see the Bishop. The parish priest who came to the door said the Bishop declined their request. Ryan kept up her letter-writing campaign to Mulkearns and to other priests in the diocese for many years. Her job was threatened by a later principal at St Colman's and the parish priest. The message was, essentially, to shut up about the abuse. She lost her faith entirely due to the cover-up and she says she'll never go back to the Church.

Paul Levey lived at Mortlake, although not really of his own choosing. Ridsdale actually met him through Levey's Irish-Catholic mother, when the priest was at one of his many postings—the National Pastoral Institute in Melbourne, before Ridsdale's Mortlake stint. Levey is absolutely disparaging about Pell. And he doesn't believe for a single second that Pell didn't know around that time about him or what happened in that town. Ridsdale first abused Levey in the isolated far-western New South Wales mining town of White Cliffs, in 1980 when Levey was twelve, the same year his parents split up. Ridsdale discovered on a visit to Melbourne that Levey had been truanting. In fact, Levey now believes that his disengagement with school was because of the abuse he had already suffered.

But Ridsdale's discovery of the truancy led to a decision, in 1982, by Levey's father and Ridsdale. They cooked up a plan to send the boy to live with Ridsdale to bring him into line. In Easter that year, Levey went to live at the Mortlake parish presbytery with Ridsdale. Ridsdale essentially kept him prisoner. A little camp mattress was set up for the boy in the priest's room.

'He was sexually abused all the time, just about every day,' Gail Furness told the Royal Commission as Pell's second day of evidence wore on.

'Yes, a terrible and sad story,' Pell responded.

Levey describes that he always slept in Ridsdale's room and that there was a housekeeper and always people coming and going, including people having parish meetings at the presbytery. He says it was common knowledge in Mortlake 'that I lived at the presbytery'. '[I was introduced] to everybody that was there [at the presbytery]. We'd go out to different families around the place and I'd be introduced there and I'd be introduced at the school and the presbytery,' Levey says, agreeing that those visitors to the presbytery included other Church officials who had meetings there.

He tells me he'd try to get away—making excuses to stay at other kids' homes for sleepovers at any opportunity. He now feels guilty about the children he brought to the presbytery, in the hope that he would be spared a night of sexual abuse—knowing now that they, too, were abused by Ridsdale during those sleepovers. Ridsdale, meanwhile, would threaten him.

'He'd say, "you'll get thrown out of school, and your mum and dad don't want you" or, "we need to keep this secret because no-one will like you",' Levey says. 'He made out that I was consenting to it and later in life it's something that I found very stressful and confusing—you know, you ask yourself, "Was I consenting to it?"'

No-one came to collect Levey. He remained with his priestly predator from Easter to Halloween. Ridsdale even requested that his mother send the family allowance she received from the government to him. She refused.

Unbeknown to Levey at the time, his mother, Beverley, had tried to get him out several times, by calling Mulkearns.

'I did not like the situation at all,' Beverley Levey told the Royal Commission. 'I was devastated because they had taken my son away.' Beverley Levey called Mulkearns' office repeatedly, and finally said she would not stop calling unless Mulkearns spoke to her.

'When I finally spoke to Bishop Mulkearns, I said, "How can you let a child live in a presbytery with a priest? That's not appropriate. I want Paul taken out of there." Bishop Mulkearns said there was nothing he could do as Ridsdale had Paul's father's approval. He hung up on me.'

The last time she spoke to Mulkearns, she threatened to get the police involved if he didn't do something about Paul and Ridsdale. Mulkearns hung up on her again. But Paul was moved out to a nearby Mortlake family. George Pell's cousin, Monsignor Henry Nolan, had an active role in getting Levey out,

'Bishop Mulkearns' response here was nothing short of scandalous, wasn't it?' Furness asked Pell.

'That is correct,' replied the Cardinal.

Levey never told a soul about the abuse until the 1990s, when broadcaster Derryn Hinch 'named and shamed' Ridsdale as 'the worst paedophile in Australia'. That's when Levey told his dad, who accompanied him to the police station. At first, Beverley Levey wanted nothing to do with it—then a staunch Catholic, she thought he was bringing down the Church. But since she gave evidence in December 2015, and in Paul Levey's words 'watched all those priests get up there and lie', she hasn't been back to mass. After seventy-six years in the Church, the lies and obfuscations finally became too much for Beverley Levey.

The Church vigorously defended a civil action Levey took in the 1990s. A Church document written by Monsignor Glynn Murphy, who is at the time of writing a defence force chaplain but was then working for the Ballarat Diocese, gleefully discussed handing the writ over to the Melbourne Diocese 'who will probably send it back to [solicitors] Blackburn, making them chase around a bit more!!' The glib tone recalled some of the correspondence during the John Ellis case in Sydney, or the Fosters in Melbourne. The Church made Levey wait two years before it ultimately settled his case. During that process, he never received an apology, never had a meeting with Church officials, was never offered counselling.

Levey, who was in Rome with the other survivors as Pell gave evidence, was scandalised by what Pell had to say as he watched on. At times his head was buried in his hands, at others, on his wife's shoulder. He managed to keep his cool, but only just.

'I had to get up and walk out at one point when they were discussing me,' Levey says. 'I had to take a few deep breaths until I calmed down.' When he returned to the room, he noticed that one of the Cardinal's security guards had sat in the seat beside him.

'I don't know whether they thought I was going to punch him in the head, or what, but I wasn't,' Levey says. A worker from the Ballarat Centre Against Sexual Assault came and sat between Levey and the security man. 'And I managed to control my temper.'

'Paul has a lot of anger, a lot of justifiable anger, and he was very angry at the time,' says his fellow survivor Andrew Collins.

'Especially when he heard that stuff about him, he found it hard to remain composed. But he didn't go off. He had the support of all of us around him. He didn't jump up and make a scene.'

Supporter Vanessa Beetham, who runs a survivors-of-suicide group for the Ballarat community, was watching Levey and the other men struggle to maintain their composure and marvelled at their self-control.

'I wish that every Australian could have seen those men in that room,' Beetham says. 'These men in that situation, the way they were so dignified, and so composed, are like, for me, the new folk heroes. So brave, so courageous.

'The things that were being said by Pell, that they had to sit through, there were moments when I felt like I was going to jump across the room. And it's unrelated to me. But for them to sit there with that dignity and composure. Amongst his bodyguards. Amazing.'

While Levey was still living with Ridsdale, Pell was director of Aquinas College and principal of the entire Institute of Catholic Education. He was living with the ailing retired Bishop of Ballarat James O'Collins, who also had knowledge of Ridsdale's offending, but was sliding into advanced dementia. Pell agreed with Furness' comment during his evidence that he would have thought a boy living in a presbytery 'most unusual'.

'It was imprudent,' the Cardinal told the Royal Commission, 'and even in the most innocent of relationships, it could have given rise to gossip.' The Cardinal agreed that he had never heard of such a living arrangement and did not approve of it either.

So Furness asked him the obvious question: 'If you had discovered that a 14-year-old child was living in a presbytery, you would have done what you could to take the child out, wouldn't you?'

Pell's answer was not precisely an affirmation. 'Well before that I would certainly have wanted to know why the child was there and what precautions were in place and whether this was something that was temporary or permanent.' The Cardinal agreed that if there had been complaints about Ridsdale of 'a sexual nature before the child was placed in the presbytery', he would never have put the child there.

Furness insisted that once he discovered that there was a child in the presbytery, 'it would be wrong to do anything other than take the child out; isn't that right?'

Pell agreed, but qualified: 'If it was in my power to do so ... I would do whatever was in my power in such a hypothetical situation.'

Furness at this point began to adopt a slightly disdainful tone. 'It is not a question of power or authority or structural responsibility when it comes to children, Cardinal, is it?'

But for Pell, perhaps, yes it was—he said he believed we are 'all surrounded by real constraints' and even if a recommendation was made, sometimes it would be rejected. 'Because something is wrong, you can't wave a magic wand and correct the situation easily in every situation,' he told Furness.

A hint of vexation again returned to the Counsel Assisting's voice.

'We are talking about the safety of children, Cardinal. Does that answer apply to the safety of children in the Church?'

The Cardinal paused for a few seconds. Then he leaned forward to the microphone. 'Ah, ah of course it does. Everything practical must and should be done to provide for the moral and physical safety of children.'

'You don't need a magic wand; you just need a group of adults who are responsible, don't you?' Furness said.

But Pell would not bite. 'I have explained that different people are able to do different things in different situations and what I am attempting to say is that nobody can do the impossible. Everybody has an obligation to do what they can to provide appropriate safety precautions.'

Furness was not minded to give up—she asked him whether in the 1970s and 1980s, the Ballarat Diocese, the Church 'collectively failed to protect children'. But Pell sheeted it home, effectively, to Mulkearns, who was at the time of Pell's evidence close to death: 'Well, in the Diocese of Ballarat there—certainly was a gigantic failure of leadership.'

Furness said it was surely more than just leadership. 'It was all parish priests, assistant priests, advisors, consultors who all collectively failed to protect children who were living and under the care of the Church in that diocese in the 1970s and 1980s?'

By this time Pell's pugilistic instincts had well and truly kicked in—the ghost of heavyweight boxer George Pell Senior floated around the room: 'I think that is a vast and misleading overstatement. It goes far beyond any evidence. Where there is evidence that people knew of misbehaviour, where they knew of a practical danger, they should have acted. We are not permitted to go beyond the evidence.'

Levey didn't buy this for a second. 'He had to have known—he was at those meetings,' an emotional Levey said that night. 'It was common knowledge the whole time I was at Mortlake that other clergy knew I was there. This has been the hardest part of it all so far.'

Pell's thesis on all of this in his final submissions to the Royal Commission, and indeed any knowledge that he may have had in relation to Ridsdale's movements and why they took place, is that there is not a scintilla of evidence, neither documentary nor spoken, to actively show that he had been told. It was rather convenient that those people proven to have known were either dead when the Royal Commission was sitting—his cousin and priest Henry Nolan and Monsignor Leo Fiscalini—or on their deathbed and completely discredited—Mulkearns (who ultimately did die in April 2016).

During the hearing, Furness pointed out to the Cardinal the 'collective failure in the diocese', which included parish priests, advisors and consultors who knew about Mortlake and Ridsdale, beyond just those three.

'There was clear evidence that there was knowledge amongst all the people that you have mentioned,' the Cardinal replied drily. 'I am not aware of evidence that other people, other clergy, knew these things.' He drew Furness' attention to the difference between a universal failure and a collective failure. 'For those who were ignorant, I think it is improper to impute responsibility to them.'

At this point, the relationship between Furness and Pell became positively arctic. It did not recover. 'So any consultor who you say knew nothing has no responsibility, including moral responsibility, for what happened in the diocese in relation to Ridsdale; is that your view?'

Pell dropped all pretence of professional conviviality with his interlocutor. 'That is stated very badly,' he said, disdainfully, 'but when there is ignorance, when the ignorance is not wilful, when the ignorance does not represent somebody not doing their authority, I can't see that responsibility be imputed to them.'

Furness took her moment. 'Is it the case, Cardinal, that all your answers over the last little while have been designed to exclude yourself, in your mind, from any responsibility in relation to Ridsdale and the Diocese of Ballarat?' Everyone in the courtroom leaned forward.

'My answers were designed to answer your questions accurately and completely.'

The survivors gathered in Rome and in Sydney had been waiting for some sense of ownership of the consultors' failings, some admission that Pell accepted some responsibility, any responsibility, for Ridsdale being moved from parish to parish. But when Furness asked the Cardinal if he accepted any responsibility as a consultor, his reply was succinct: 'No, I don't.'

Getting back to Levey, Pell said he didn't know that Levey, or any boy, was living at the presbytery at Mortlake. But other priests in the diocese did. Father Lawrence O'Toole gave evidence to the Royal Commission in December 2015 that he knew that Levey was living with Ridsdale at the time, when O'Toole was based half an hour away at Warrnambool. He said he didn't think it was 'discreet', in fact he thought it was 'dangerous ... because it could lead to aberrations, sexual aberrations'.

O'Toole later went to zone meetings attended by some of Pell's fellow consultors. But he claims he told neither them nor the Bishop. O'Toole knew Pell—he'd lived with him at the presbytery at Ballarat East in the 1970s. When Furness asked the Cardinal if they'd kept in touch after that when O'Toole moved to Warrnambool, the Cardinal replied 'once or twice a year'.

While Pell said he had no recollection of O'Toole telling him there was a boy living in the presbytery, he did say he heard about it 'plus or minus 1990'. When pressed on this point, Pell replied that he couldn't recall precisely when he had heard about 'the cohabitation'.

Several days later, at the close of Pell's evidence, Levey was the only survivor in Rome who didn't go to meet with the Cardinal. He was just too furious. This was despite the fact that he had been the first survivor who arranged to go to Rome after receiving a private donation from a benefactor and arranging beforehand with the Cardinal's office to have a private meeting.

But the evidence he heard made Levey feel that any meeting with Pell was utterly futile. 'It was just a media stunt,' he said. An Australian Catholic official who was at the Quirinale at the time asked Levey why he wouldn't be going to the meeting with the other survivors. 'Why not? Because he is a fucking liar,' Levey shot back.

15

ALL THE BISHOP OF BALLARAT'S MEN

Faith, here's an equivocator, that could swear in both the scales against either scale; who committed treason enough for God's sake, yet could not equivocate to heaven.

The Porter in *Macbeth,* Act 2, Scene 3

To examine what George Pell really knew during his time as a consultor of the Ballarat Diocese, you have to take a forensic look at the state of knowledge of those around him. One of the most instructive figures to examine is Brian Finnigan. At the time he gave his public evidence to the Royal Commission in December 2015, Finnigan was Auxiliary Bishop of Brisbane. But for many years, Finnigan had been a priest in the Ballarat Diocese, and a friend of Pell's, and although they haven't seen each other for a few years, the Cardinal says they remain friends to this day. Finnigan was Bishop Ronald Mulkearns' secretary. During those consultors' meetings, Finnigan took the notes. Besides his public evidence in December 2015, Finnigan also gave evidence to the Royal Commission in a private hearing in July 2015. In that evidence, he made some shocking admissions—including that back in the 1970s, he and other priests didn't consider things like touching boys' penises, masturbating and even anally raping them as crimes.

> Certainly a moral fault, I don't know whether I'd consider them crimes, because one of the things that puzzles me about all of this matter that we are dealing with, is poor old Bishop Mulkearns gets, as it were, blamed for everything, it's good to dump everything on him, but many policemen knew about this activity and they didn't press charges or anything.

'Poor old Bishop Mulkearns', without whose dreadful inaction dozens of children in the Ballarat Diocese would not be victims of Ridsdale. Paul Levey and the Harrison kids to name but five.

Finnigan knew that young Levey lived with Ridsdale at the presbytery at Mortlake. When asked if he thought it untoward that a priest had a child bunking in his living quarters, Finnigan replied that it was 'a bit unusual, but not unusual', adding that a priest had recently had approval for a relation to stay in his presbytery.

'This isn't a relation, this is a young boy staying at the presbytery,' Furness snapped back, '...The rational explanation is that you were blind and naïve and stupid in those days, is that it?'

'If you want to put it that way, yes.'

When Furness asked Pell if Finnigan 'at any time' told him that he knew there was a boy at the presbytery, Pell replied, 'I don't recall him doing so'. And when asked if it was brought to his attention by Mulkearns or O'Toole, Pell replied, 'I don't think so'.

Some of those watching believed answers like this—which dominated Pell's evidence as well as Finnigan's and many of the other priests—to be a form of 'mental reservation', or *mentalis restrictio* in the Latin. It's a theological strategy dating back centuries, which involves the idea of truths 'expressed partly in speech and partly in the mind'. As the theory goes, lying is considered a sin. But a Christian's ethical duty is to tell truth to God—reserving or restricting part of that truth from human ears is ethically sound if it serves the greater good.

An oft-cited hypothetical example of mental reservation is the priest who hides Jews from the Nazis and when the Gestapo comes to the door and asks if there are Jews in the house, the priest replies, 'they are not here' and in his mind silently says 'for you Nazis'. Therefore, he has not lied to God and has done a noble thing.

Strict mental reservation permits what is essentially a spoken untruth if the liar is telling their truth to God; the untruth to man is told for the greater good. But Catholic theology has shunned that for centuries. The jury is out, however, on so-called 'wide' mental reservation, that permits an ambiguity, as opposed to an outright lie, if the ambiguity is resolved to God in the speaker's mind and if it is done for the greater good. It is only supposed to be permitted in life or death scenarios. However, internationally, there have been situations where it appears to have been used by priests and bishops who have covered up child abuse—that is, for the greater good of the Church. The landmark Murphy Report in 2009 into sexual abuse in Ireland's Dublin Diocese called out the practice. The report quotes Dublin Archbishop Desmond Connell as saying:

> Well, the general teaching about mental reservation is that you are not permitted to tell a lie. On the other hand, you may be put in a position where you have to answer, and there may be circumstances in which you can use an ambiguous expression realising that the person who you are talking to will accept an untrue version of whatever it may be—permitting that to happen, not willing that it happened, that would be lying. It really is a matter of trying to deal with extraordinarily difficult matters that may arise in

social relations where people may ask questions that you simply cannot answer. Everybody knows that this kind of thing is liable to happen. So, mental reservation is, in a sense, a way of answering without lying.

In one example heard in the Murphy Report, the Irish Church issued a press release saying it had cooperated with the police in dealing with a paedophile priest, but when the victim's advocate inquired more fully, the archdiocese's explanation was 'we never said we cooperated *fully*' with an emphasis placed on the word 'fully'.

When viewed through this prism, many who observed the answers given by Ballarat priests including Pell to the Australian Royal Commission wondered if they did not include some form of mental reservation: 'I don't think so', 'I don't recall', 'no-one mentioned paedophilia'—answers sufficiently ambiguous to satisfy the wide mental reservation definition if the person uttering them was telling their truth to their God. Certainly, Ballarat survivors Andrew Collins and Peter Blenkiron believe that Pell was employing the strategy.

American canon lawyer Tom Doyle told the Royal Commission in February 2017 that canon law had been used 'by ecclesiastical authorities for not proceeding in taking direct action against reports of sexual abuse'. 'It has been used as an excuse for not reporting to civil authorities, and it has been used as an excuse for allowing accused clerics to continue in ministry,' Doyle said.

Kieran Tapsell, a former NSW District Court judge, seminarian and writer on canon law, says that in the Church when there is a conflict between canon law and civil law, canon law prevails. He says that until 2001, canon law had a 5-year limitation period on sexual abuse claims by children, meaning they disappeared after five years. This is problematic, given the Commission has heard that the average time to report a crime is thirty-three years.

In a report to the Commission, Tapsell also elaborates at length about something called the Pontifical Secret or *Secreta Continere.* Its origins were in 1922, when Pope Pius XI issued his decree *Crimen Sollicitationis,* which created a 'privilege of clergy'—meaning that any information obtained through canonical investigations of issues like child abuse by priests be protected by 'the secret of the Holy Office'. Tapsell writes that the Pontifical Secret was crystallised in 1974 on 'extrajudicial denunciations' and the 'process and decision' involving child sexual abuse. The secrecy was extended to the allegation itself. It requires that all who participate in cases to which it applies 'should observe the strictest secrecy, the secrecy of the Holy Office'. 'The observance of the pontifical secret,' Tapsell writes, 'made the requirements of mandatory reporting [of sexual abuse of minors] and the need for the healing of the victim more difficult. Indeed, the observance of the pontifical secret can be seen from the worldwide pattern of cover up and its consequences.' The existence of the Pontifical Secret is why the architects of Towards Healing, including Bishop Geoffrey Robinson, encouraged complainants to report the abuse to civil authorities—including police. Because once the Bishop got involved, the cover-up began.

The Pontifical Secret might go some way to explain the actions of Mulkearns. Mulkearns has been crucified in the media (for good reason) for his cover-ups and has been appointed, along with Archbishop Frank Little, Scapegoat-in-Chief. There is no question he did this. There is no question that his actions and inactions were unspeakably bad. So it surprised me to learn from many of his fellow priests who happen to be good people that there was another side to him—a gentler, decent side. Even after Pell had dumped on him royally in the Royal Commission, Pell later admitted to Andrew Bolt, 'I think he just got caught deeper and deeper and deeper and I suspect, eventually, was like an animal caught in the headlights of a car, he was trapped ... I can't give any coherent reason for it'.

Former Corpus Christi seminarian Michael Costigan remained friends with Mulkearns until the former Bishop of Ballarat's death in April 2016, and feels that in some sectors, Mulkearns was improperly vilified—with Pell the supposed hero in his handling of child sexual abuse claims and Mulkearns the villain. Costigan said there was no defending what Mulkearns did, but questioned whether there was so much distance between him and others in the Church at the time.

I question Costigan on this vigorously—I know too many people who would not have had their childhoods blighted were it not for Mulkearns' cover-up. Costigan offers the explanation that Mulkearns had a 'blind devotion to the papacy and to Rome'. Mulkearns, like Costigan, was a canon lawyer. 'If Rome told him to act in a certain way, he believed there was no alternative—it was almost a juvenile reaction,' Costigan says. Costigan spoke with Mulkearns regularly right up until the former Bishop's death and makes an admission, never before made publicly: that Mulkearns confessed to him that he 'honestly did not know what to do' about Ridsdale. 'He did not know how to handle it,' Costigan says.

It culminated, Costigan says, with what's known as an *ad limina* visit, where bishops visit the Vatican for an audience with the Pope. Mulkearns appealed to Pope John Paul II about what to do about child sexual abuse—he wanted, says Costigan, 'some direction or counselling'. 'He said the Pope would not talk to him about it,' Costigan says. 'He said the Pope turned his back and walked out of the room.'

Costigan says Mulkearns felt completely at sea and the exchange radically altered his opinion of the Pope. 'It wasn't long after he came back that he stood down as Bishop,' Costigan says.

There was, of course, no need for pontifical secrets or *mentalis restrictio* when, back in April 1993, Finnigan, who was then Vicar-General of the Ballarat Diocese, was interviewed by a loss adjustor for Catholic Church Insurance, in the lead-up to Ridsdale's first trial. This was a secret conversation which Finnigan thought would never again see the light of day.

But tellingly, CCI later refused to insure the Church for any abuse committed by Ridsdale after 1975, because of the knowledge the diocese had from Ridsdale's time at Inglewood. In the interview with Finnigan, the insurer was 'very concerned' about what had occurred in Mortlake. Finnigan indicated his knowledge of events there.

'All this is very confidential,' Finnigan began, 'but one of the subsequent [parish priests] at Mortlake would say that Mortlake is one of the real trouble spots and whether he is given to a bit of dramatisation ... All kids in a couple of classes...'

Finnigan went on to point out that a colleague or relative of his was a parishioner there and 'his son was certainly molested'. Finnigan told the loss adjustor that at the time he was the Bishop's secretary, while Ridsdale was at Mortlake in 1981 and 1982, 'three or four people' had come to him to complain about Ridsdale—who was inviting 'lads around to his place' and was 'overly friendly'.

'I confronted Gerald Ridsdale and I must say it was a very hard thing to do in the sense that he was most crestfallen. He said, "I thought I was going along very well".'

Finnigan then wrote to Ridsdale to tell him that the loss adjustor needed to see him about writs, where complainants were claiming damages against the Church for the abuse. 'Some of these fellows now see the opportunity to obtain some easy cash,' Finnigan wrote. When asked in the Royal Commission whether he 'seriously' thought 'it's an easy way to get money to go through the ordeal that people have to endure to win a trial for damages', Finnigan gingerly replied, 'No, not easy at all; drastically difficult'.

After his public evidence on Friday 11 December 2015, Finnigan found himself confronted outside court by a furious Levey.

'I told him he was going straight to fucking hell for lying,' Levey says. 'And I said, "I will be fucking here in the morning waiting for you".' Levey says Finnigan, who looked shocked, did not say a word.

Finnigan called in sick the next day and that was the end of his evidence to the Royal Commission. Levey started a petition on Change.org to have the bishop removed. When the signatures got to 5200 on 30 December, Finnigan announced his retirement as Auxiliary Bishop of Brisbane.

'From those whom I may have disappointed, I seek forgiveness,' Finnigan wrote to his flock.

Why do we need to know about Finnigan? Because of his proximity to Pell. The point about all this Finnigan business is that in the period that Ridsdale was at Mortlake, while Finnigan was on the consultors committee with Pell and was, indeed, Pell's friend, Finnigan knew there were complaints about Ridsdale with Mortlake boys and an extremely inappropriate living arrangement between Ridsdale and young Levey.

Not just that. Finnigan was also aware that another consultor, Leo Fiscalini, knew more too. 'I think there may have been something more serious than what I have mentioned, because … people from Mortlake approached the then Vicar-General, Monsignor Fiscalini,' Finnigan told the CCI loss adjustor.

So this shows not just that Finnigan, Pell's friend and fellow consultor, knew about problems at Mortlake when they were happening, but that Fiscalini had somehow made it known to Finnigan about the fact that he knew. Pell insists they uttered not a word to him.

Fiscalini had heard about the trouble with Ridsdale at Mortlake from a local farmer's wife whose children went to St Colman's. Her two youngest sons served as altar boy. 'I remember he swept the whole area when he arrived with his outgoing personality and enveloping emotions,' the farmer's wife said.

So when one of her sons came home and begged her for a weekend sleepover at Father Gerry's house, like the other boys at school were having, she allowed him and his brother to go. She knew that there was a problem as soon as she saw her pale and sullen son two days later. As she drove him home, he was slumped and silent in the back of the car. She went immediately to see Fiscalini.

> We met Monsignor Fiscalini at the front door of the presbytery. I don't think we went inside. I said to him, 'We've got a problem in Mortlake.' That was as far as we got. We didn't even get a chance

to say that it was Father Gerry who was involved. He told us that Bishop Mulkearns was not in the diocese at the time. He said, 'I will deal with it' and dismissed us. He did not ask us any questions.

The late Fiscalini, who was so greatly admired by Pell's mother and had known the Cardinal since he was very young, clearly knew what he was dealing with. He knew it was Ridsdale and he knew it was kids. He knew that, because he'd heard it all before. He knew that, because he'd colluded with Mulkearns and moved Ridsdale from parish to parish. Not long after the farmer's wife's visit to Fiscalini, her sons came home with a letter apologising to the family, although Ridsdale made no admissions to abuse as such. 'He wrote things like, "Poor me, I had a hard life. I had a hard upbringing,"' said the farmer's wife, who has since destroyed the letter.

When another mother disclosed to the farmer's wife that Ridsdale had also abused her boys, the two families arranged to go to Ballarat to see

Mulkearns—when they arrived they said they had 'problems at Mortlake'.

'Before we said anything more, Bishop Mulkearns replied "How am I to take the word of a child over one of my priests?"' The mother said, 'I think we were in his office for less than five minutes ... After this, the four of us left the premises, went to the car and drove home in basic silence.'

Pell was not surprised by Mulkearns' response. 'If there was no contrary evidence or the evidence was pretty equivocal, people would be inclined to support the priest,' he explained. 'But for this to be said after so much evidence being presented on previous occasions is astounding.'

Another Mortlake mother known to the commission as 'BAI' says not long after Ridsdale arrived in Mortlake, her son came home, looking wan, and she asked him what was wrong. He blurted out: 'I think our friend Father Gerry is gay,' adding that Ridsdale had grabbed him and said he 'wanted to feel his vibes'. She called the Bishop's palace and spoke to Finnigan. BAI gave evidence to the Royal Commission that

Finnigan told her 'Bishop Mulkearns was not available but assured us there was no problem'. Finnigan now says he has no recollection of this, but agrees that if he did say it, it was 'dishonest'. He was, he said, 'just a small-time secretary'.

BAI went on to discover that Ridsdale had abused other children in the community eighteen months after she made that telephone call to Finnigan. She also spoke to the family doctor in the town about Ridsdale.

Furness pressed Pell on this: 'We have now at this stage, in Mortlake, the family doctor being aware there was a problem with Ridsdale,' Furness began, 'a number of people knowing that there was a boy living in the presbytery with Ridsdale, and Father Finnigan being aware that one set of parents was concerned about the welfare of their child around Ridsdale ... It's getting close to common knowledge, isn't it?'

His Eminence leaned forward to the microphone: 'Certainly those people knew.'

'At this stage, can I suggest, Cardinal,' Furness put to Pell, 'someone in the diocese within the Church should have accepted responsibility to do something about Ridsdale. Do you accept that?'

'I would say that anyone, especially in a leadership position who knew what the situation was, had such an obligation.'

'And that includes Father Finnigan, Father Fiscalini and also Father O'Toole, doesn't it?'

'Yes ... They should have done what could be done to remove these dangers, prevent this awful situation.'

BAI also rang Sister Kate McGrath and told the nun, 'I believe we've got a practising paedophile priest'. McGrath did act, but Mulkearns swore her to secrecy when Ridsdale was eventually moved. McGrath told the Royal Commission she was gutted by the episode:

> I have always been angry that Bishop Mulkearns required me to keep quiet about Ridsdale's activities. This was incredibly isolating for me personally, but far more importantly, it impeded my ability to assist the victims and the

local community to deal with the impact of Ridsdale's actions. I was unhappy that nothing was done for the children affected by Ridsdale's abuse, when I thought the Church had a responsibility to support them and to help them deal with the terrible experiences they endured.

A delegation of parents also went to Mulkearns. 'He just sat there and stared at us,' BAI told the Royal Commission. Pell said this was 'extraordinary and reprehensible'. 'His repeated refusal to act is, I think, absolutely inexplicable,' Pell said.

But the circle of people in Pell's acquaintance in the Ballarat Diocese continued to widen. McGrath went to see Sister Patricia Vagg who knew Pell—her brother had gone to school with him. McGrath asked Vagg to ring Mulkearns. She did, and Mulkearns sent a delegate to deal with the situation. That delegate was one Monsignor Henry 'Hank' Nolan, Pell's cousin. Nolan was concerned about the boy living at the presbytery—he'd seen Levey sleeping on a stretcher in Ridsdale's bedroom and he said he demanded of Ridsdale that the boy be removed.

But according to Pell, 'That—that is correct, but we couldn't easily draw conclusions about how widely this was known ... Because people were very reticent to talk about these things. But, obviously, with parents whose children had been abused, they would certainly have spoken about it.'

Furness took issue with this: 'Cardinal, it cannot be fairly said that people were very reticent to talk about these things having regard to Sister McGrath's statement.'

Pell demurred, saying he was 'talking generally about society at that time'.

Furness reminded him that society at the time did not appear to have that same reticence—in Mortlake, Apollo Bay or Inglewood, doctors knew, people were talking about it at the pub; at Inglewood, the talk had got so bad that Ridsdale was more or less chased out of town.

'These matters, of course, were scandalous, weren't they?' The Chair, Justice Peter McClellan, asked Pell.

'Of course.'

McClellan reminded Pell of his earlier evidence that he had heard gossip about Monsignor Day in Mildura, another paedophile priest.

'Are you now saying that notwithstanding this spreading knowledge through the parishes in relation to Ridsdale, and the scandalous nature of his behaviour, that there weren't any rumours that came to your ears about him?'

'I certainly am.' Again, incredulous guffaws echoed around the room.

Pell later told Andrew Bolt in their interview after his evidence that his cousin Nolan was 'notoriously monosyllabic'. He said the fact that none of these people including Nolan told him was not the major implausibility.

'What is so overwhelmingly implausible is that we've got probably the worst paedophile in Australia active and we've got a bishop who didn't just give him a second chance, but repeatedly refused to act ... The Bishop and one or two of his helpers sat on this very tightly,' Pell told Bolt. 'And I think the reason for that is that if they had mentioned to the consultors why it was happening, it would have provoked an enormous discussion, and people would have said, "Well, what's going on? Can we do this? Is this appropriate?"'

The Cardinal asserted that nobody who now knew him believed that he knew and did nothing. 'I might occasionally be outspoken, I might occasionally put my foot in it, but anybody who knows me knows that I wasn't going to be sitting there saying nothing if I was aware of that.' Perhaps he might not have said nothing. He is right that it is certainly not in his style to say nothing. But that does not mean that he did not know.

Survivor Andrew Collins, watching on in Rome, did not buy Pell's argument: 'When you look at a group of people who grew up together, who were educated together, who were priests together, who were around the Diocese together, Ballarat is that central hub, the same people all meeting making these consultors' decisions, it is just unbelievable to think that Pell didn't know ... of course [he] would have known.

'Especially when you have a look and see that Pell was such an ambitious person. Ambitious people don't bury their head in the sand and not look around them. They make sure they know. Because you know everybody's strengths and weaknesses, because you want to move ahead of them.'

There was another consultors' meeting in 1982. That's when they decided to get Ridsdale out of Mortlake. So, bear in mind that by this meeting, Nolan knew, Fiscalini knew, as of course did Mulkearns. Three other priests from the diocese, along with Pell, made up the seven present. Mulkearns now had multiple complaints about Ridsdale, going back at least a decade to 1972. With that knowledge, the Bishop had moved his errant priest from Inglewood to Kangaroo Flat. From Kangaroo Flat to Bungaree. From Bungaree to Edenhope. From Edenhope to Melbourne, Melbourne to Mortlake. Underlined in the minutes of the 1982 meeting was the following:

> The Bishop advised that it had become necessary for Fr Gerald Ridsdale to move from the Parish of Mortlake. Negotiations are under way to have him work with the Catholic Enquiry Centre in Sydney.

Pell told the Royal Commission he did not remember this, nor any of the consultors' meetings. But he said that while the minutes were 'consistent' with Ridsdale being moved because of his sexual offending against children, the minutes were written to 'distract from that possibility'. And this appointment to the National Pastoral Institute would have been seen as a promotion.

Furness questioned him about the meeting: 'I suggest, Cardinal, that it is implausible, given the knowledge of three of those consultors and given the conduct of Ridsdale and the wording of those minutes, that the consultors, including you, did not know why it had become necessary for him to be moved?'

The survivors in Sydney and Rome sat up and craned their necks, waiting to see what he had to say.

'That is a complete non sequitur. We can conclude about those who had that knowledge; we cannot conclude about the minds of those who were not privy to that knowledge.'

The survivors slumped back in their seats.

Furness wondered if he asked why it had become 'necessary' for Ridsdale to move.

'I can't remember explicitly asking,' Pell said. 'One of the priests present said that the reason given was homosexuality. I don't have a recollection of that, but that would be entirely possible.'

Eyes in the courtroom narrowed.

Pell knew of the homosexuality explanation because he clearly had studied the evidence of one Father Eric Bryant, another consultor, as it seems he had with all other relevant witnesses. Not only that, his barrister had cross-examined Bryant. Bryant testified that he remembered that the reason it was necessary for Ridsdale to be moved was 'a problem with homosexuality'. He did, however, admit there were other priests he knew at that time to be homosexual, but the Bishop never thought to move them.

Bryant had earlier noticed some very unhappy young boys staying with Ridsdale at his White Cliffs property in remote western New South Wales, and now says it had brought him to tears thinking of how he might have helped them had he known. Some time after the comments about the homosexuality in the consultors' meeting, he says he started thinking of White Cliffs and wondering, 'My God, what is the story there?' But when asked by Counsel Assisting what he did about it, he conceded 'probably very little, if nothing'.

Pell said he didn't remember homosexuality being mentioned at that meeting. 'I have—don't have a clear recollection of the meeting at all, except to the effect that paedophilia was never mentioned.'

Furness wasn't buying it. 'Well if you can't recall, how can you recall that he didn't mention paedophilia?'

'Because it was the sort of,' Pell began, 'the sort of category of event which was very clearly quite wrong and a reason for removing a priest at least for treatment.'

Pell agreed that by this time, he knew that there had been an 'unusual' number of priestly appointments for Ridsdale. Furness wondered if he asked the Bishop why. Pell replied that 'would have been discussed ... The Bishop would have given some reason.' And so what, exactly, was that reason?

This is where some survivors started suspecting mental reservation. 'I can recall very clearly that paedophilia was never mentioned and the recollection of another priest there is homosexuality was mentioned. I can't recall that explicitly.'

He couldn't recall a thing. He couldn't remember a conversation. But, on the other hand, he could recall and remember that there was no discussion of paedophilia.

Furness suggested Pell and the other consultors should have asked far more questions and that by not doing so they failed in their responsibilities.

Pell adopted a tone, which again appeared to those gathered, quite frankly like mental reservation. 'I have never suggested that I knew nothing. I've never suggested that I knew nothing about Ridsdale. I've never suggested that I didn't inquire generally...

'I knew nothing about his paedophilia. I knew that he was a somewhat difficult person and obviously that he had been shifted around quite a bit...'

The evidence of Pell's old friend Finnigan about precisely what the consultors knew differs significantly from the Cardinal's.

'Bishop Mulkearns told the consultors why it was necessary to move Ridsdale, didn't he?' asked Furness of Finnigan.

'Yes. He—yes.'

Like Pell, Finnigan went on to say that he had 'no recollection that the Bishop spelt out why'. But he acknowledged that the consultors would have asked questions—they would have asked why.

Finnigan later conceded that he was 'not in a position to deny' Mulkearns told the consultors the reason for the move. And he agreed that if it was discussed, he most certainly would not have put it in the minutes—and that's why it's not there. He also agreed that it 'follows' that it was the bishop's *and* consultors' decision to send Ridsdale away from a parish, to somewhere he would have less access to children. With that admission, he went far further than Pell.

Finnigan even accepted some personal responsibility: 'I'm happy to accept blame myself for a lot of the deficiencies in our approach.'

Another consultor, Frank Madden, who had written the glowing character reference for Ridsdale before Ridsdale's first trial, was also contrite. 'I can't escape some responsibility for my role in not questioning some of the moves,' Madden said. 'I can understand that in retrospect. As being part of the college of consultors and as Vicar-General, I have to take some responsibility and I regret that ... The responsibility for not having asked more questions or being more investigative of what was going on, going along with what was proposed. I can understand that now, and you wish—one might wish that I'd done something else.'

A third consultor, Father Eric Bryant, went even further, saying he too had to 'accept responsibility on behalf of the diocese for what happened' and 'I have to own' being part of what he later described as a 'cover-up'. 'I don't think anybody knew how to handle the situation and I think the Diocese virtually took a great dive around that stage and sort of ended in the Dark Ages ... I still feel a great guilt for what's happened to people personally, because perhaps I didn't know how to handle it, I didn't ask the right questions, I didn't do the right things as far as Ridsdale was concerned, and I was presuming that all the time, I suppose, that the Bishop and others were doing what was seen to be right ... I think it was, you know, one of those dark, really dark passages of the last 20, 30 years of our history.'

The words of the other consultors in this regard draw into sharp relief the attitude of Pell towards his own role as a consultor. Very few people in the Royal Commission public gallery knew the detail of Bryant's, Madden's or Finnigan's admissions as they watched

Pell's evidence. But nonetheless, the exasperation felt after his complete failure to take any responsibility on that first Tuesday in March hung over the room like a fog.

The Cardinal's repeated insistence that he didn't know about 'paedophilia' was interrupted with a question from the Chair. 'We have heard from others that paedophilia has been understood by some in the Church as sexual activity with prepubescent children but not adolescent children,' McClellan said.

Pell quickly replied that it 'wasn't a factor' in his thinking, but conceded that he was aware of the distinction.

'It is not unknown, of course, for priests to have engaged in sexual activity with adolescent boys, is it?' McClellan asked.

'That's correct,' the Cardinal replied.

'And when, you say, the other consultor refers to the Bishop referring to homosexual activity, many in the Church would see homosexual activity as including sexual activity with adolescents who have not come of age, wouldn't they?'

Pell: 'I—I don't think people would—that's a theoretical possible classification. But in these sorts of discussions, I don't think that decision—that distinction—would have been made.'

The Chair pressed on. 'When you say you don't think the distinction would have been made, there would be, would there not, in the Church to your knowledge, a somewhat different view taken of a homosexual relationship with a post-adolescent but nevertheless minor as opposed to abuse of a prepubescent child?'

Pell responded, 'Yes, there is—I think the literature clearly distinguishes that.'

'What literature?' people in the courtroom mouthed in horror.

'And there is a recognition in the Church amongst some writers and speakers of that distinction,' Pell continued.

So the Church that lectured to people that sexual intercourse was not permitted outside the bounds of marriage, that had railed against the contraceptive pill and condoms, this same Church had made granular distinctions between how it viewed sexual relations, of whatever complexion, between adult priests and boys, depending on their age? Well, yes, it seems that it did.

In 2009, the Vatican's representative in Geneva, Switzerland, Archbishop Silvano Tomasi, was quoted as saying that the sexual abuse crisis in the United States and internationally was about homosexual priests preying on adolescent boys, rather than paedophilia per se. It was 'more correct', Tomasi said, to speak of ephebophilia, an attraction to adolescent males, than paedophilia.

According to LifeSiteNews, a Canadian pro-life news site which focuses on religious, particularly Catholic, issues, Tomasi's views were 'backed up by a report commissioned by the US bishops that found that in the overwhelming majority of cases the clergy involved were homosexuals, with 81 percent of victims being adolescent males'. The implication of this report appeared to be that the problem was homosexuality, not clergy abuse.

What point this is really supposed to make is questionable. One possibility is that they believe that if you weed the homosexuals out of the clergy, then you'll be able to fix the problem. The first issue with this is that it blames the clergy abuse problem on homosexuals, rather than the Church taking any responsibility. The second issue, of course, is that it ignores the point that by law and by all social norms, 11- to 17-year-olds are still children. It ignores the overwhelming evidence to the Royal Commission from survivors that 11- to 17-year-olds are just as profoundly affected when they are raped by an adult who is supposed to represent all that is good and holy in the world as are their younger brothers and sisters.

Back at the Royal Commission in Australia, Bryant had, in his evidence, noted that a preoccupation with sex with postpubescent boys was considered, in the 1970s and 1980s, 'curable', whereas sex with prepubescent children was considered paedophilia and therefore incurable.

Pell repeatedly referred to that word 'paedophilia' as something that he said was never discussed in the consultors' meetings. Whether the use of this term (excluding ephebophilia) was a case of *mentalis restrictio* is something only the Cardinal and his God can really know.

To be fair to Pell, the meetings took place thirty-four years before the Royal Commission hearing. Remembering the details would be extremely difficult. And it's also reasonable to think that despite the hazy recollection, if offending against children was discussed, it was such a jarring topic that it is bound to have stuck out. In those ways, his reasoning makes sense in theory.

But what makes this theory questionable is that he also claims that none of the others with knowledge, whom he knew very well, discussed it with him—George Pell, the one marked out, more than anyone else present, for greatness. Someone who was looked up to in the community. The sort of person with whom you might like to curry favour by providing him with information. Again, just a theory. But the theory is bolstered by the fact that others who were not present but were nonetheless well known to Pell also knew about Ridsdale's activities. That is what stretched incredulity like a rubber band so tightly that day in court. So tightly that inevitably, it snapped back in the witness's face and stung like a wasp.

Furness calmly proceeded. 'You do not have any recollection of what was said at the [1982 consultors'] meeting, although you have a recollection of what was not said; is that right?'

'The clear expectation was if there was criminal activity, that would be mentioned,' Pell said.

Furness asked the obvious question: 'You said in your answer that the clear expectation was if there was criminal activity, that would be mentioned. Now, what was the basis of that clear expectation? Where did you get that clear expectation from, Cardinal?' He replied that it came from his experience, his 'general way of thinking'.

The Chair of the Commission wondered whether, in minutes of this nature, given the 'sensitivity of the subject matter', 'gentle and euphemistic language' might have been used. Pell agreed it was—and that was what kept him in the dark.

Pell continued with an odd monologue in defence of the Church's conduct, describing it in a way that was the exact opposite of how witness after witness had portrayed its operation over many decades, across many dioceses. 'We do not propose to shift priests, promote them, when it's been shown they have engaged in criminal activity. That's not the basis on which the Church has ever acted,' the Cardinal declared. The incredulity wasp snapped back and stung Pell on the face, with McClellan calling it out: 'Well, it's clearly the basis on which Mulkearns acted for Ridsdale, isn't it?'

Pell conceded, 'It is, and that is totally inexplicable.'

Not so inexplicable when put in the context of what was happening not just around Australia, but also across the world, for decades. Documents like the Murphy Report in Ireland show it was the default plan.

Pell insisted that even the consultors who had known about the abuse had less of a moral responsibility for the shifting of Ridsdale than the Bishop because they had no authority, and were merely in an advisory role.

The Chair seemed to see where he was going with this. 'Cardinal, you keep referring back to authority and structural responsibility, but it is the case, isn't it, that within the Church you would expect and indeed might I suggest the community would expect—that each priest would act responsibly, regardless of their position?'

He was met again with some vintage obfuscation, capped off with a familiar Pell trope: you people just don't understand my Church. 'To understand the Catholic Church's structure and who has authority, you go to Church law, and according to the canon law of the Church, you can there identify the different levels of responsibility—it might be a jurisdictional responsibility; it might be a moral responsibility at different levels. But it's from the canon law that you decide what the situation is within the Church.'

And here the Chair got to the nub of Pell's true thinking on this, the bubble he finds himself in, where the ordinary rules of morality, decency and even criminal responsibility are leavened to varying degrees by byzantine Church structures.

This is a perspective which brings Dr Wayne Chamley of advocacy group Broken Rites to a rather stark conclusion: without knowledge of the lengths the Church went to to cover up these crimes, it might otherwise seem a gross exaggeration, even a conspiracy theory.

'I see the Catholic Church as an example of the state of anarchy,' Chamley told me. 'Not marching-in-the-streets anarchy, but in terms of members abiding by their own laws—the canon laws—and those responsible for running the show deciding not to abide by society's laws. That's the classic definition of anarchy.

'Nobody accepts responsibility for anything. And so it is allowed to go on.

'They chose to surround themselves with their canon law edicts and not do anything else and believe in that because they were held in such high esteem, by very faithful people who saw that priests could do no wrong.

'And they just let hundreds of people have their lives so impacted that it ruined them. And some of them decided to take their lives.'

Despite the initial euphoria of Rome—the recognition that the survivors received from the international media attention—Paul Levey tried to kill himself several months after returning from Rome. Fortunately, he survived the attempt and he's trying to keep positive. But like Chamley, the Church's rigid adherence to canon law baffles him.

'Everyone else has to abide by the law of the land; why does canon law put them above the law of the land?'

16

DOUBT

*Doubt can be a bond as powerful and sustaining as certainty.
When you are lost, you are not alone.*

Father Flynn, *Doubt*

Fast-forward several decades on from Pell's years in 1970s Ballarat and what he might or might not have known as a priestly consultor, and you land with a jolt in a modest motel room in the central western New South Wales town of Wagga Wagga. On 26 August 2009, a 47-year-old man punched two holes on either side of the bearings in his motel room and hanged himself with his belt. The suicide was a jolting shock to everyone that Wayne Brennan knew. Wayne was a successful businessman whose company had been subcontracted to do a big building project in Wagga, but he was born and bred in Ballarat. There was no real sign that this was about to happen. No-one will ever really know what went through Wayne Brennan's mind as he sat in that motel room and made the horrible decision to end it all. But there was a clue. It was discovered that playing that night in the motel when Wayne died was a film called *Doubt,* starring Philip Seymour Hoffman. *Doubt* is about a Catholic priest accused of sexual abuse of a teenage boy. The boy's father is abusive and his mother wants to sweep the allegations under the carpet. It was a plotline that would have rung chillingly true for Wayne. He had a tragic connection to Catholic priests, and, it's alleged, to Father George Pell, that has never been made public.

Wayne Brennan was a man's man. Generous, hard working and, by many accounts, 'the best chippie in Ballarat'. But if some people wear their hearts on their sleeves, Wayne had his in the pocket of an old jacket that he hardly ever wore, shoved to the back of his cupboard, gathering mothballs. He would be mortified to think that anyone, anywhere, ever felt sorry for him. He had a thriving building company and a wife and three adult children. His eldest son worked for him and he was the person who found his dad strung up in that motel room. It seems like a cliché, but on the surface, Wayne had everything to live for. Underneath, things were far more complicated.

Like Pell, Wayne was a St Pat's boy. He was part of a terrible cluster in the early seventies blighted by Christian Brother-perpetrated abuse and premature deaths. Wayne had for decades buried a terrible secret—and only very, very occasionally would it get the better of him and bubble to the surface. There is much more to Wayne's history than the achingly familiar story of the abuse he suffered. If true, his story suggests that Pell knew something about it, indeed, that he knew about child sexual abuse allegations in 1974. It directly contradicts the key theme of Pell's evidence to the Royal Commission: that with the exception of one 'good and honest lad' he did not know about abuse in Ballarat, that he was 'too busy' to hear or engage in gossip. If the statement that has been made to the Royal Commission about Wayne's situation is true, it suggests that Pell was directly involved in the cover-up.

Wayne's widow, Sue, runs a hairdressing business in Alfredton on Ballarat's western fringe. I first spoke to her in October 2016. She's in two minds about disclosing what happened to her husband—as are all of the people I spoke to who knew him—because he was such a private person and would hate the idea of people talking about his personal hell. Even the best man at his three weddings never got wind of it.

'If you had've rung me six years ago, I would have said I don't want to get involved. But now I think it's important that this is known,' Sue Brennan says. It's what Ballarat survivor Peter Blenkiron, who went to school with Wayne and was also 'gotten at' by the cruel Christian Brother Ted Dowlan, describes as 'popping the pimple'. The dirt of the abuse gathers beneath the surface, and then it all rises to the top with the anger of the untold story, the anger at the perpetrators, the fury at the institutional cover-up and the lack of belief and support. And then,

Blenkiron says, '"Pop." Then you can't stop the talking.' The Brennan family pimple was finally popped in late October 2016, after decades of silence, bitterness and dysfunction.

Wayne started at St Pat's in 1973, a good two decades after Pell. But Pell was living back in the diocese. It was a particularly unfortunate year, as it turns out, to find oneself under the tutelage of the Christian Brothers of Sturt Street, Ballarat. Also in Wayne's class was Phillip McAteer, who as a young man doused himself in petrol and blew himself up in his car outside of Ballarat. Tim Green, another Dowlan survivor who famously said he told Pell about the abuse of his peers at the Eureka Pool only to be brushed off with 'don't be so ridiculous', was also in Wayne's class. Green was an excellent witness and Pell was compelled to say in his final submissions that while he didn't believe Green was lying, he, Pell, had never said this. Council Assisting the Commission submitted that the Tim Green story was true.

Wayne wasn't there the day they came to take his Form 1 photo—not a surprise as his sister Joy, who is one year older, said he was constantly wagging. But he turned up for the Form 2 shot. He's standing right in the middle of the front row. Like the smallest kids in the class always were. His hair is in a neatly brushed cowlick to one side, there is a fixed grin on his elfin face.

Not long after he started at St Pat's, Wayne began to 'beg and beg' his father, Barry, to take him out of the school. Barry was a Catholic who with his wife Heather, a convert, who is now in a nursing home with dementia, fathered a brood of twelve. But Barry Brennan was also a violent alcoholic. Any time he heard Wayne complain about St Pat's, he would, Wayne's sisters recall, 'beat the living daylights out of him'.

Even before she really knew about Wayne's abuse, one of his sisters (who asked not to be named) sensed it in her bones. 'Wayne used to cry and cry and cry and say, "I don't want to go to school",' she remembers. 'Back in those days they did not listen to their children. I can just remember and it haunts me to this day.'

She says their mother spent many years fleeing to safe houses and having shots fired into the windows by Barry Brennan. As a little girl, she used to regularly crawl out the window to the phone box on the street, to call the police on her raging father after he stumbled home from his local.

The terror in the family caused fractures and silences. As the children grew up, they split into factions and carried on feuds. To this day, many of them don't speak. Sue Brennan says this and what happened to Wayne at school had an enormous and life-long impact on her husband, who refused help.

Sue says Wayne told her on several occasions about St Pat's. He told her that like Blenkiron, whom Sue has spoken to, Wayne was abused by Dowlan at the school. This would make sense, as in 1973 he was in Form 1A—the class in which for two years running, Dowlan terrorised the 12-year-olds whose destiny he was to shape. Even those who have never come out publicly as 'victims' say they did not escape his wrath. John

Stekelenburg, who is a highly successful doctor and, like Pell, is what's known as a Legends of St Pat's alumnus, says he believes there was not a single boy in his class, the year below Wayne's, who was not abused in some way. He hates to identify as a 'survivor', but remembers Dowlan brushing up against him with an erection in the corridor and delivering shocking beatings.

Dowlan's photographs show a handsome, sandy-haired Christian Brother with an open smile. But he was in reality a sadistic and emotionally manipulative creep. I spoke to several old boys from 1973–74 who told similar stories of varying degrees—from waking up with Dowlan's hands down their pants while they were in beds in the boarders' dormitory, to anal rape. These stories have also been documented at length to the Royal Commission and to Victoria Police. Dowlan, who changed his name to 'Ted Bales', is, at the time of writing, in prison serving his second sentence of eight years and five months. He'll be eligible for parole in March 2020. Stekelenburg, for one, says if and when Dowlan gets out, he'd be happy to put his hand up to 'put him back in'.

Joy Brennan and another of her sisters were unaware of what had happened to Wayne at St Pat's back when they were children. It's not surprising given the chaos at home. Wayne confided in Joy, the eldest of the Brennan clan and one year older than Wayne, just four years before his death.

'He said, "I was one of those kids at St Pat's",' Joy remembers. 'Wayne said he was raped. He was small, Louise, so small ... It was awful.' Joy volunteers this before I tell her anything that I know—my knowledge of the abuse has been passed on by Wayne's wife, Sue, and, independently, by his work colleague Pat Moran. Joy has spoken to neither of them at this point. All she knows is that I am researching matters to do with the Royal Commission and I wanted to look into some of the suicides and why they died. I tell her this initially so as not to pollute her story. When she has told me what she knows, I elaborate further.

As for another of Wayne's sisters, she says Wayne never told her 'in so many words'. But she has suspected it in her heart and had been vowing to go to Ballarat and find out more when the Royal Commission exposed the extent of the problem there. She says he did hug her tightly once, during a night of drinking and reminiscing, and say, 'I know that you know, I know that you know'. She feels sad now that she didn't ask more.

Amid the chaos at home, she, Joy and Sue say that suddenly, for some reason, Barry seemed to change his mind about forcing Wayne to continue at St Pat's and let him leave. After less than two years there, his parents abruptly moved him to St Paul's Technical College. The Brennan siblings knew little about the reason, beyond the fact that Wayne had clearly been unhappy at St Pat's. But Sue, who he was with for thirteen years before he died, says he told her the reason. The reason is shocking and it involves, Sue says, George Pell.

When the Royal Commission into Institutional Responses to Child Sexual

Abuse was sitting in Ballarat, Sue finally bit the bullet and made a verbal statement. She did so on the encouragement of her friend Dominic 'Nick' Ridsdale—nephew and victim of Father Gerry Ridsdale—Nick was one of the survivors who travelled to Rome in 2016 to hear Pell's evidence.

When I phone Nick Ridsdale to ask him about it, he discloses the shocking news with the nonchalance that only someone who has survived the madness of the Ballarat Diocese can muster. Nick announces that Wayne had told Sue that when he was making allegations of abuse at St Patrick's, Pell had gone to the Brennan house for a meeting and 'offered to pay for Wayne's education if he moved schools'.

Nick Ridsdale accompanied Sue to the Royal Commission that May. He saw her go in to make her statement. 'Sue is a very straight up and private person,' Nick Ridsdale says. 'There's no way she'd make that up.' Joy and the other sister I spoke with say that while neither of them are close to Sue, they find it hard to believe that she would invent such a story. And anyway, they say, it all made perfect sense.

Sue sighs as she tells me about Wayne. She says while her husband barely spoke of the abuse, every now and then he would become overwhelmed, usually when he had been drinking, and would spill his guts. She said she begged him over and over to get counselling, but he refused. Sue says that by the time Wayne got to Form 2 at St Pat's, he 'would not keep quiet' about the abuse. And that's how Pell got involved.

She says he 'spoke up about' the abuse at school and Pell and at least one other priest had a meeting with Wayne's parents. She believes there was possibly also someone from St Patrick's there. 'I remember Ridsdale on the telly one day and something came up about Ridsdale and George Pell [probably that famous photo of the two entering court in Warrnambool]—Wayne picked up his stubby, held it at the telly and smashed the telly,' Sue says. 'Then he said, "I remember when him and his cronies come to our place and had a chat with Mum about all of the shit that was going on",' she says.

Pell was, during the time that Wayne was at St Pat's, Episcopal Vicar for Education of the Ballarat Diocese, and was living in Ballarat as well. Many other St Pat's students I have spoken to say he was a fairly frequent visitor to the school—he coached, for instance, the rowing team.

When I ask Sue about Pell's position, she doesn't know much about him. She's unaware of the Episcopal Vicar role and she doesn't know details, she just says 'the reason [Wayne] told Pell was that he believed that Pell was in charge—if there were any problems with the priests or the brothers at the school, you would go to Pell'. This, incidentally, has been the evidence of several survivors to the Royal Commission and whether or not they were technically mistaken, it was certainly a perception that was somehow allowed to flourish. As Andrew Collins' grandmother insisted, Pell was the man to go to if you ever had any trouble in the Church. And there was, of course, the letter from Pell to Bishop Mulkearns describing the role as part of the 'essential link' between priests, parents and teachers. The Cardinal, of course, downplayed his Episcopal Vicar role during his evidence from Rome, saying he was too busy with his role as an academic at Aquinas College to get too involved in the business of the Catholic schools of Ballarat.

But Sue Brennan says the disclosure prompted Pell and two other priests or brothers to visit the Brennan home for 'a cup of tea'. She says that Wayne told her of this on several occasions, usually, like the time with Ridsdale, because he saw Pell or Ridsdale on the television. In the case of Pell, she says she remembers Wayne seeing Pell on the television and telling her, 'I remember the day that bastard was sitting at my kitchen table, bagging the shit out of me and saying that I was a troublemaker'.

'He said, "There were three of those bastards there that night". That he was in the house and overheard from another room,' Sue recalls.

'[They] said, "we will move him to St Paul's". At no cost to the parents,'

Sue says. '[Wayne said] "They classed me as a troublemaker and said I needed to be moved. [They said] I was accusing priests of unheard-of acts, accusing priests of made-up stories. No-one believed me."' She says Wayne told her that his parents believed Pell—and Pell told them they were false accusations.

'[Wayne] would say, "I don't know why they did not believe these kids. The parents idolised the priests."' She says that Wayne told her he told 'them' at St Pat's, and 'they did not believe me, and then I went home and told Mum and Dad and they did not believe me'. She says Wayne told her that his fees for St Paul's were paid until he left the school two years later.

Joy Brennan does not remember the priestly meeting, but she says that's not surprising as she spent a lot of time during those years at her grandparents' home—she had by then developed a toxic relationship with her abusive father. But she is not surprised it took place and says that at times her fees were also waived by Loreto Convent because her mother would go up to the school and beg not to pay. She says with twelve children, her parents would have been pleased to have been relieved of the burden of paying for Wayne's fees.

But her sister remembers the meeting well. And she volunteers, immediately and confidently, without me bringing up his name, that one of the priests who came to the home that night was Father George Pell.

'They come around and when they came to our house, it was like, "Oh my god, the priests are coming", it's like God was walking in, because that's how they were perceived back then,' she says. 'You know, if the priest came to your house, you were sort of higher standard than anyone else because they're coming to visit you.

'Anyway, they come to the house, and all us kids, "seen and not heard"—we had to all go to bed, the priest was here. And I remember the yelling after they'd left. And Wayne got belted ... He got the belting of his life.'

Sue confirms Wayne told her he was belted, too. 'I copped the biggest hiding of my life from the old man,' Sue says Wayne told her.

'So, why Pell, do you remember why it was him?' I ask the sister.

'Do you know, I don't know what it was,' she says. 'His voice? And just his face. His face. It just haunts me. He's got a distinctive ... He's got a distinctive face,' she says, repeating a line which people often say about Pell. And it's true, he does.

'And there was somebody else, but I just don't know who it was, I'm sorry, I just don't know.' She says that Pell had never been in the home before, but she can't forget his face. I ask her what it was about that night, that meeting, that made it stick out in her mind.

'That "Wayne's going to get into trouble because the priests are coming". Well, we didn't know initially that the priests were coming. But Wayne got into trouble because the priests were coming, he was wagging school, smoking, and not doing his homework. And that was the thing. He was causing trouble, that's what they said. That he was causing trouble and making up stories.'

I ask her if she can think of when this happened—if there are any time markers, any significant dates, which might make her remember the year. She says that the family was still at their Macarthur Street house. And the year after they moved from Macarthur Street, she changed schools—she started at that school, St Columba's, in 1975. So, doing the maths, that would make it 1974. Which the St Patrick's yearbooks show was the last year that Wayne spent at that school before, if what he told Sue was right, the priests removed him for 'making up' stories of abuse and generously paid a scholarship to cart him off to the next school.

She remembers he was far happier after moving schools, saying 'he changed, he was completely different'. She noticed some other changes too in Wayne. For example, while pretty much everyone growing up at that time in Ballarat was fairly homophobic, Wayne would fly into rages about anything to do with 'poofters'.

'Like, unusually angry ... Raging anger. Raging. It was extreme ... I [now] think it was because he was being abused,' she says.

For young boys who have been abused, 'acting out' and becoming aggressive is one of the classic trajectories. And thus the tiny little altar boy with the cowlick became known on the footy field as 'Basher Brennan'. The first person that suggested I check out Wayne's story, another St Pat's alumnus, told me of the Basher tag.

Both of Wayne's sisters whom I talked with remember another development from about the time he left St Pat's: Wayne loathed his mother from that time forward. Sue says he told her it was because Mrs Brennan didn't believe him.

His parents' lack of support caused a toxic rift between the Brennans and their son that never healed, a rift exacerbated, Sue says, by Barry Brennan's belting of his son when the priests left that night. The intensity with which Wayne Brennan withdrew from his mother especially is why Joy Brennan rang me back the day after our first conversation and said she felt that the story of him not being believed must be true—it explained Wayne's inexplicable hatred of his mother, when in fact it was his father who had beaten him and his mother.

'It just makes sense if she was told and she didn't believe him,' Joy says.

These sisters remember that Wayne left home at age fifteen and never really had much of a relationship with his parents again. His brother Paul, whom I spoke to before I met the sisters or even knew their names, told me that there was no way Wayne was sexually abused. He also said that while his dad was an aggressive drunk, it did Wayne no harm. He was immediately suspicious of me and wanted to know why I had his number (it was on the internet). He claimed that I had clearly been put on to him by his sister Joy, who had cooked up the 'lie' of Wayne's abuse because she was obviously after compensation. When I finally did find Joy, after speaking to Paul, she confirmed that she had never applied for compensation and, indeed, had never made a formal complaint about

Wayne being abused. It had haunted her all of her life, but she had taken it no further as the family was already in such pain following Wayne's death. Paul was also extremely disparaging about Wayne's wife Sue, insisting that she had driven him to suicide. Wayne's death is clearly still raw for his brother. The idea that his brother's suicide could have been caused by the women in his life is a far easier thing to contemplate than Wayne, like so many other boys in his class, having been abused by a vile paedophile Christian Brother. Life is always complicated and even more so when you have a family horribly fractured by paternal dysfunction.

Joy and her sister, who have not, when I find them, spoken in years, are both convinced the rest of their younger siblings had no idea about what had happened to Wayne because they were so much younger and he didn't talk about it to them. The memory of it all brings one sister to sudden, hot tears.

'Wayne would always stand alone. It would almost be like, he would be standing back, looking at the family, but he never felt a part of it,' she says.

'That was the family and he was here [she gestures across the table] all by himself. Where, I get that now that I know. I always thought that he was just a little bit different.'

As Professor Caroyln Quadrio, Australia's foremost psychiatric expert on the impact of child abuse on survivors, says, 'if you pile enough trauma onto any individual, there comes a point at which they can't take any more'. That point for Wayne seems to have come that August night in Wagga.

The fate of Wayne Brennan is something that now haunts Wayne's friend Pat Moran. Pat was working for Wayne on that Wagga job when his boss died. And shortly before, Wayne had confessed to him out of the blue what had happened to him growing up in Ballarat.

Were it not for Moran, Paul Brennan's thesis that the abuse was cooked up by his sister wanting money, or his widow, might hold even a teaspoon of water. But Moran is instructive. He is sober, removed, disconnected from the family dysfunction and with no axe to grind or drum to beat. A non-smoking, non-drinking ex–St Pat's boy.

I found out about Moran through a mutual Ballarat community contact who has never met the Brennans. That contact knew I was interested in investigating cases of suicide of people who had attended St Patrick's. My contact did not know at that point that one of those people I was investigating was Wayne. The fact she wrote Moran's name on a Post-it note and attached it to some documents she'd found for me on another matter was a complete and startling coincidence.

When I first ring Moran, he has not spoken to Sue since Wayne's death. He asks me how she is. He knows none of the siblings, nor anything of their factionalised family. He remembers that Paul Brennan was very tearful at Wayne's funeral, but can't remember his name. When I speak to Moran, I have not yet spoken to any of the Brennan siblings. Moran has prepared an affidavit about what he knows for the Royal Commission.

A few weeks before Wayne died, he invited Moran and another employee out after work. 'He took us out to tea,' Moran says. 'We were sitting down and the other bloke was up drinking and gambling. Wayne asked me where I went to school. I said St Pat's and I said I hated every minute of it,' he explains.

Moran hated every minute of St Pat's because of the mental and physical abuse he received. 'I was strapped over and over again,' Moran says. 'And I am absolutely convinced to this day they got some sort of sexual gratification out of giving a kid six of the best.

'There was a brother there who was absolutely cruel—Brother Ring. He gave me one of the worst beltings I have ever had. Because I had had my tonsils out and had not done my homework ... He was being investigated when he died.'

He says Wayne was not the sort to talk about matters of the heart—and especially with a group of construction hard men, but he thinks he 'had some respect for me because I was not a drinker'. When Wayne discovered that Moran, too, was a St Pat's boy in recovery of sorts, he blurted it out.

'He said it was Dowlan ... He was emotional when he told me about this—he hung his head.' He says that Wayne told him he had been sexually abused and if they'd been charged for what they did, 'they'd still be in jail'. 'And what could I do?' Moran muses. 'I just listened and let him talk.'

While Wayne did not tell Moran about the visit by the priests, he did say, 'I told my dad and he didn't believe me. I copped a belting from him for saying it.'

Moran says there is no way Wayne would make something like this up. 'How should I put this? He was not the sort of person who would make up something that would make him look weak. You know? He was a man's man. But he knew that I was someone he could trust.'

Moran also said it made complete sense that Wayne had been targeted—being from a large and dysfunctional family with an alcoholic father. 'The ones who weren't touched at St Pat's were the wealthy farmers and footballers' sons, sons of lawyers and doctors and stuff. People that had a strong family background, they would not dare touch.'

It was some weeks after the conversation between Wayne and Moran that Wayne committed suicide.

'He seemed so stable, he had a good business ... Nothing about it made sense. The union assured us there was nothing they could find—his financials and his records were impeccable.'

Moran has always felt he would like the truth about his friend to be investigated. 'It would be nice for Wayne's story not to go unnoticed,' Moran says.

Moran was so moved after Wayne's death, that he decided to go to local police, in case it would help put together a broader case. He went to Detective Sergeant Kevin Carson, another St Pat's boy who happened to have been four years below Moran at the school. The pair did not know each other, but Carson was well known around Ballarat as a cop who had investigated multiple complaints against Ridsdale and Brother Robert Best—he had been working on the matters since 1994 and secured the first prosecutions of Ridsdale. Moran had heard him speaking about it in the media. Moran thought Carson might want to know about Wayne.

As it happened, Carson was compiling his list of suicides and premature deaths of people who had been in contact with sexoffending clergy in Ballarat and other parts of Victoria. Carson added Wayne's name to that list of what became forty-three. 'I felt the need to highlight these deaths and perhaps get something done about them,' Carson later told the Royal Commission in a confidential statement. 'I thought that the Coroner might be interested in knowing about the number of deaths that appeared to be associated with clergy child sexual abuse,' his statement says.

Carson wrote a report of what he knew (which in some cases, at that stage, was fairly scant detail) and submitted it to his Superintendent at Ballarat, Andy Allen. Allen requested more detail and Carson provided what he could. *The Age* obtained a copy of the report, which Carson says he did not provide to the journalists. The newspaper splashed with the suicides on its front page. One way or the other, the story sparked the creation of the parliamentary inquiry in Victoria.

Unbeknown to Carson at that time, Victoria Police was undertaking another, top secret, investigation: Operation Plangere. Plangere was an internal 'police-in-confidence' intelligence report, which went through Carson's own investigation and, essentially, tore it to shreds. It was carried out under the auspices of the Sexual Crimes Squad and Taskforce SANO. It concluded 'only one death could be attributed to child sexual assault'.

Carson only ever saw the Plangere brief when, in 2015, the Royal Commission released it as an exhibit. The full, unredacted report, which contained the names of the people who died, was never made public. I was handed a copy of it and other files relating to the suicides by a source—not from Victoria Police and certainly not Carson.

The report says its investigations included looking at (among other things) old school records, police databases, parish centres, the Coroners Court and critically 'family, friends and associates of nominated persons'.

Reading the section that applies to Wayne is very instructive. In Carson's original report, Carson identified Moran as someone Wayne had confided in about his childhood abuse by Dowlan. Carson even provided Moran's phone number in the report to enable follow-up. No-one from Operation Plangere ever followed up with Moran, who would gladly help anyone who was getting to the bottom of his friend's death. However, in the case of Moran, the report says the following:

> Approximately three weeks prior to committing suicide, Wayne Francis BRENNAN informed an employee who had also attended St Patrick's College in Ballarat with him, that he had been sexually abused whilst at the school. According to the source spoken to by investigators this conversation was reported to Detective Sergeant CARSON a number of years ago.

I have read those sentences aloud over and over and I can only come to one conclusion: 'the source' (note, not 'a source') has to be the 'employee'. And we know the employee who went to Carson was Moran, because it's in Carson's report and Moran confirms it. But Moran has never spoken to another person from Victoria Police about Wayne, ever. 'The first person who ever made contact with me about Wayne Brennan after Kevin Carson was when you rang me,' Moran tells me. He has made a sworn affidavit to the Royal Commission to that effect. So how, I ask him, can they say that detectives had spoken to him, 'the source'? 'It's a blatant lie,' Moran says. 'The whole thing is just hideous.'

I spoke to a detective who worked on Operation Plangere and he was just as stumped why that sentence was written the way it was. He agreed with my interpretation of it, that 'the source' meant Moran. But he confirmed that while he could not remember Wayne's case specifically, he didn't ring any friends or relatives in relation to any of the suicides.

No-one from Operation Plangere ever called Wayne's next of kin, his wife,

Sue Brennan. My third conversation with her was the first time she had ever heard of Operation Plangere, or the officers involved. 'If they had've rung me, I would have told them,' Sue tells me. 'I can't see why they didn't investigate further.'

No-one ever called Wayne's sister Joy, nor the other sister I spoke to either. All of these people had information that would have helped the investigating officers discover what was known about Wayne and childhood sexual abuse by clergy. Not just that, they would have been able to piece together Pell's involvement. They were the obvious people I, a single journalist with just a laptop and a mobile phone and without their vast investigative resources, thought to call. No-one at Operation Plangere picked up the phone or left a message. The conclusion in the section of the Plangere report about Brennan is that his suicide had nothing to do with childhood sexual abuse and, moreover, it concludes: 'Childhood sexual assault not indicated'. The word 'indicated' doesn't mean it was a foregone conclusion—the dictionary definition of 'to indicate' is to have a sign or a symptom of. Those signs were there. Operation Plangere didn't look for them.

Sue says, resignedly, that none of this would have brought Wayne back. But she's perplexed. Moran is angry. And Joy suspects some sort of conspiracy.

The other sister cries when she thinks of her older brother and what he went through and the fact that he couldn't get the help he clearly needed. 'I have an 11-year-old,' she says. 'And I just look at him and think, "Oh my god" and it plays with my head.'

She tells me, eyes glistening, that she had extensive counselling after her brother died. 'I would just cry and cry because I was just broken-hearted because of what he'd been through. The hatred he had for Mum—how hard that must have been not to have a mother and son relationship.' And all that was before she really knew the truth of what happened to her brother at St Patrick's, and what he said was done to buy his parents' silence.

'And for Wayne, to have no counselling and to deal with what he did...' She trails off and sniffs back tears. 'We were robbed of our childhood.'

Sue remembers terrible arguments with her husband when she decided to send her son Ricky to St Patrick's at the insistence of her ex-husband, Ricky's father. Ricky and Wayne were very close, but one day Ricky asked Wayne to drive his trailer to St Patrick's to pick up a coffee table the boy had made in woodwork. Wayne initially refused to help. Eventually, he relented and drove back to the place that he had avoided for so many years. He came home pale and subdued. 'Geez, that brought back some haunting memories,' Wayne told her.

As for Pell, while Sue made a statement to the Royal Commission about what Wayne told her the Cardinal did, it did not choose to call her as a witness. Perhaps because she was too late to fit into the case study in the Royal Commission which looked at clergy abuse in the Ballarat Diocese. But Wayne's case is just another of those that suggest Pell decided to take it into his own hands when it came to mopping up child sexual abuse allegations in his diocese. Think Father Noel Brady. Think Eileen Piper's brother Kevin Toomey. Think Tim Green. Think Genevieve Grant. Think Hilton Deakin's evidence about Pell going in to sort out the situation with Father Kevin O'Donnell. There is a pattern here. It's the pattern of a fixer.

17

OPERATION PLANGERE

I am ashamed and embarrassed and deeply hurt by what I have been investigating these last few years.

Kevin Carson, Ballarat detective

If, as they say, an ordinary city has six degrees of separation, Ballarat has one or two. And hence, Wayne Brennan, a chippie by trade, was known around the traps by Rob Walsh, also a carpenter. And of course, both of them as children knew George Pell. Walsh was also involved in Operation Plangere—the report that has been used to discredit those that seek to highlight the extent of the child abuse problem in the Victorian Catholic Church and thus a weapon used by those who feel that Pell has been unfairly vilified. In the history wars battled in the Catholic Church over the child abuse question,

Operation Plangere has allowed some commentators to say that the entire basis for the Victorian Inquiry into Child Abuse was flawed. And that at least part of the basis for the Royal Commission was flawed. But Operation Plangere's report is seriously and curiously deficient. Not just that; Wayne Brennan's suicide is not the only case in it with a link to Pell.

Walsh attended St Alipius at Ballarat East in the seventies with his brothers, Noel and Damien, and his cousin Martin. Rob Walsh is the only one left alive. Damien Walsh hanged himself in March 2010 just as his abuser, Brother Robert Best, was committed to trial. Noel Walsh died after wrapping his car around a lamppost in 1984 in what is, accurately and yet euphemistically referred to as a 'single vehicle collision'. 'Do you want to know how Martin died?' Walsh asks me. I reply yes, on the proviso that it is not going to upset him to tell me. It does upset him, it sends him into wracking sobs, but he really wants to tell the story. 'He put a shotgun in his mouth in the bath,' Walsh says, his voice choking. 'The policeman lifted him out of the bath, his b-brain fell out. That policeman resigned from the job that day.' Martin was twenty-two.

Rob Walsh was a victim of Ridsdale and Best and he testified at two of their criminal trials. He reckons he could go back to give evidence against Edward Dowlan too, if it wasn't so bloody painful. It took ten years and he's had enough. He'll let that particular sleeping dog lie.

Walsh graduated from primary school at St Alipius and never managed to get to secondary. Being under-educated, a child victim of two predator clergymen and the only St Alipius boy of four in his family who made it past his mid-40s has left Walsh at sea. 'I'm desolate,' he tells me. 'I'm behind in my rent, divorced, you name it, I've had the lot of it ... I'll never be able to run my own building company now—I know that. I'll never reach my full potential ... Some days I just shake my head and go, "Why me? Why did I go to that school?"' But mostly, Walsh just keeps his head down and tries to keep going. He fires off emails to anyone who'll read them, phones anyone who'll listen, about the injustice of the treatment of victims of religious paedophiles—the fact 'those bastards' have spent far more defending legal claims than on helping survivors. 'You keep standing,' he says. 'In my heart I know I'm doing the right thing.' Walsh was one of the people who really pushed Detective Sergeant Kevin Carson to look into the suicides of St Alipius. Apart from his brother and cousin, he also had information on some of the others. But just like the Brennan family, Walsh heard not a peep from the detectives on Operation Plangere. 'They have never spoken to me,' Walsh says. 'And I find it bewildering. I find it just gut-wrenching.' What was going on, I wondered, with Operation Plangere? Why didn't the detectives pick up the phone?

Walsh also knows a bit about a bloke called Peter Curran. Curran was his mate and another St Alipius boy, who went on to secondary at St Patrick's in the era of Dowlan. Curran's is another name on the Operation Plangere list that has its links to Pell—not that that link seems to have been explored, if it was known, by the Plangere detectives. It's another Pell story that has so far slipped under the carpet of public scrutiny. Walsh says that some time after he first made his police statement to Carson about his own abuse, he went over to his old school mate Curran's place. He was shocked at what his friend told him.

I have Curran's handwritten statement, written for Broken Rites, about the, as he called it, 'Pedophyle Ring' at St Alipius and the abuse that he suffered at the hands of Ridsdale, Dowlan and Brother Gerald Leo Fitzgerald, who died in 1987. 'Hope they buried the Bastard face down so he can't dig his way out,' Curran writes of Fitzgerald. 'If you didn't kiss him [on the lips] you were guaranteed anything from six to a dozen cracks across the arse next day right on nine o'clock, with a splintered feather duster.'

That's in the very mild section of the statement. It goes into scarifying detail about what happened to Curran when, from the age of eight onwards, he and his mate 'Macka' moved from the junior school run by the Sisters of

Mercy to the St Alipius boys' school up the road. 'Macka', he later writes, is Philip McAteer, a St Alipius boy who, like Curran, had the misfortune of moving on to St Pat's, where he would share a class with Wayne Brennan. And for poor old Macka, life just became too much. As Curran writes, McAteer 'put 5 gallons of petrol, made himself a giant Mollotoff Cocktail, blew his car and himself away at the White Swan Reservoir here at Invermay Ballarat. This kid was [Ted Dowlan's] number one boy. Fatherless as Phil was, he was a sitting duck.'

McAteer, who was by the time of his death a diagnosed schizophrenic, is also in the Operation Plangere report, colour-coded yellow for suicide. But in the 'Confirmed Childhood Sexual Assault?' column, it says 'No. Nil Link identified [to death].' I don't think I've met a single survivor from Ballarat who doesn't bring up Phil McAteer. His story is legend. For all the saddest reasons. In Operation Plangere, he's one of those guys that fell through the cracks of, what was it? Incompetence? On a more cynical reading, it looks like a whitewash.

The treatment of Curran in the report is just as jaw-dropping. I have spoken to his wife, Colleen, and his eldest son, Blake—an upstanding young man who is a teacher and father of two—and neither of them has been contacted by a single detective from Operation Plangere or anyone else from Victoria Police, bar Carson.

Running through this entire family history was the undercurrent of Pell. Blake became so angered during Pell's evidence in Rome, he decided to put in a Freedom of Information application to Victoria Police to find out more about his dad's story. He asked for all documents pertaining to the abuse by Ridsdale, Best and Dowlan. The only one he got back was a heavily redacted document on Dowlan and some details about his father's death. Why he never received documents relating to Ridsdale or Best is unclear—Best's latest criminal trial was still being completed, but how that affected a young guy wanting to know about his dad's death is a mystery. What he did receive was page after page of whited-out documents. What, if anything, did it say about Pell? The documents refer to a 'third party' but the FOI officer writes to Blake that that information is not relevant to the scope of his question.

The chaotic life and strange death of Peter Francis Curran neatly exemplifies how the Operation Plangere report's statistical analysis of cause and effect in relation to the suicides got it spectacularly wrong. Or at least, that it was spectacularly misleading. It shows how the headline that only one suicide of the forty-three that Carson had heard about had been caused by sexual abuse was an insult to everyone involved. Significantly, Curran also had, in his latter years, a lot to say about Pell. His story about Pell is well-told in survivor circles. Like Wayne Brennan, what Curran told his friends directly contradicts the Cardinal's sworn evidence in the Royal Commission about his knowledge of abuse. But Curran died before any of it was made public. And what he had to say became another one of Ballarat's dirty little secrets.

Photographs from when his four children were growing up show Curran was a thin and wiry man with large and distracted brown eyes, skin suntanned by hours of outdoor labour, dark hair worn in a short mullet. Curran had been, by all accounts, a sweet guy, the type who would 'do anything for anyone' and who worked at the local McCain factory as a forklift driver. 'He could have been so much more than he was,' his wife, Colleen, said. 'He was a very smart bloke.' But by the time of his death on 6 September 2004, Curran had become an alcoholic mess of a man wracked with childhood pain. He died seven weeks after he suffered multiple stab wounds to his torso. But that nicely colour-coded chart that Operation Plangere kindly provides describes his death as 'natural causes'. The chart confirms 'yes' to possible childhood sexual assault, but says there is merely a 'possible link indicated' between his childhood and his death. It seems astonishing to describe Curran's situation in such a way.

What happened to Curran is spelled out in a police report obtained by Blake in 2016. It says that about 3.30a.m. on a Friday in July 2004, Curran was in bed. After persistent knocking at his door he opened the door and was met by a man who stabbed him in the chest, then said, 'Sorry mate, wrong house', pulled out the knife and left. Curran says he stayed at home for the next four days waiting for the wounds to heal, before going to hospital the following Tuesday.

The 3-page police report records that the case was reported up the line to Superintendent Paul Murnane—who ran Ballarat Local Area Command and was, incidentally, to retire to go to work for the Catholic Church's Towards Healing program. Murnane had, much to the suspicion of Ballarat's survivor community, also been, as a serving police member, on the Church's euphemistically titled Special Issues Committee. Mortlake teacher Ann Ryan describes him, in police uniform, meeting her in a church carpark with a priest when she called on the committee to come to Mortlake to investigate. Her request was refused and she wrote to

Murnane expressing her 'grave concerns'.

Curran remained in hospital and his health deteriorated. A week after the stabbing, detectives reported that his story about the incident changed somewhat. This time, there were two men at the door, one with a baseball bat. By the following Wednesday, the detectives say Curran now said that the pair were wearing balaclavas. Curran was at this point gravely ill and internally bleeding. He was, in other words, delirious.

Almost two weeks after the stabbing, police began to suspect that Curran had in fact stabbed himself. They discovered that Curran had been 'totally drunk' the night the stabbing occurred—not a surprise as he was a raging alcoholic. Shortly before Curran died, the matter was handed to the homicide squad, but the investigators had concluded by this point that because of the change in Curran's story, the stab wounds were self-inflicted 'in a drunken state in his home' and effectively, this was a suicide. Foul play had been written off.

Curran was just forty-three and left behind four children aged from seven to twenty-one. In light of this bizarre series of events, it is frankly astonishing that Operation Plangere colour-coded his death as 'natural causes'. His death certificate, given to me by Colleen, certainly does not. Under 'Cause of Death', it says 'Cerebral and respiratory failure unascertained in a person with cirrhosis who suffered a hemopneumothorax [essentially, air and blood in the chest cavity] following a stab wound to the chest'.

While the Coroner investigated the strange nature of his death, there was no inquest. Colleen has no idea why.

It is chilling to read the contemporaneous twenty pages of handwritten notes provided to Blake under Freedom of Information about the police investigation into his father's death. And not, mind you, because they reveal much about what went on. Quite the opposite. It is chilling because virtually all twenty pages are blanked out with redactions marked 'not relevant'. Not relevant, the FOI people at Victoria Police have determined, to the son of a man who is trying to work out what happened to his dad when he died twelve years ago and what the detectives who were investigating knew. Surely, given this was in policing terms ancient history, Blake had the right to know.

There are other reasons to be concerned about the paucity of information in the Curran file presented by Victoria Police to Blake and why Blake decided to get the file in the first place. They concern Pell. Because well before he died, Curran had told a number of people that Pell was aware of his abuse by Ridsdale. Blake had grown up with the story about Pell. And Blake wanted to know what police knew about that.

One of the people Curran told was Rob Walsh. 'George Pell always said it was a spur of the moment thing that he walked into court with Gerald Ridsdale,' Walsh says of the famous pictures of Pell by Ridsdale's side as he walked into court in 1993 for his first tranche of convictions for abusing children. 'If Peter Curran was alive today, it would be totally different. We would all know that it was not.'

Walsh suspects there was a lot more to the relationship between Ridsdale and Pell than Pell has ever been willing to fess up to. Walsh was a friend of Curran's from St Alipius and had, like the other survivors, admired Curran's early willingness to go public with what had happened to him and other children at the school at a time when most survivors still felt too scarred or too shameful to come forward. Walsh was devastated when Curran died in 2004. 'He hated George Pell's guts,' Walsh says of his friend. 'He hated him from that incident at St Alipius.'

That incident, Walsh says, was described to him by Curran only shortly before his death. Walsh says Curran told him that on one occasion when he was being sexually abused at St Alipius by Ridsdale, 'George Pell was present'—that is, that Pell came in and interrupted them.

Stephen Woods knew Curran from St Alipius. Like Curran, Woods was also a survivor of Best and Ridsdale. Woods and Curran were pretty much the first survivors to really go public in Ballarat, back when people like Andrew Collins and Peter Blenkiron were still running successful businesses and suppressing the very thought of what they had been through. Woods says that Curran told him on 'multiple' occasions that when he was being raped by Ridsdale in the presbytery at St Alipius, Pell had seen it, but did nothing about it. 'The thing that really upset him about Pell was that he felt that Pell had put his ambition before protecting kids.' Woods says Curran told him the story on many occasions and it was always the same.

Curran went much further than just telling survivor mates. Before his death, Curran did an interview with the Channel Nine current affairs program *60 Minutes.* In the interview, which was filmed in shadow, Curran was called 'Derek' to protect his family's identity. In that interview, Curran again said that in the aftermath of a rape by Ridsdale, Pell had walked past the open doorway of the presbytery and had seen what was going on.

The segment was eventually pulled for legal reasons—at the time, there was far less information about Pell in the public domain and the allegations contained in the interview were risky. The program did not have the same access to documents that I have been able to gather and the fact that the complainant was speaking anonymously was problematic.

Colleen says that her husband told her on several occasions that Pell knew about the abuse. 'He said, "Pell's not innocent in this",' Colleen tells me. He was particularly angry when Pell accompanied Ridsdale into court in Warrnambool. 'He said he knew, he definitely knew, and I believed him,' she says.

Colleen is committed to the truth being exposed and would have been very willing to speak to detectives from Operation Plangere. The detective I spoke to from Operation Plangere confirmed that he and his colleagues had been given a policy from above that they were not to contact any family of the deceased, 'because there was so much emotion involved in it all'. 'Many of the people had passed away a long time ago and it was thought the families wouldn't be receptive to police coming to drag it all out. We did not want to drag these families through the mud again and that's the reason why we didn't contact any of the families,' the former detective says.

On face value, it makes sense. But upon closer analysis, aren't those the sort of conversations that police have to have all the time? It is no doubt a difficult thing to broach, but in the case of child sexual abuse, if you don't speak to the families—the people most likely to have had the conversation with a person who may not have reported to police for very compelling reasons—how can you find out the truth? I haven't spoken to a single relative or spouse of a suicide victim who wouldn't have spoken to the police.

On Carson's original investigation, the Plangere detective says that there were 'not too many suicides that we could attribute wholly and solely to the fact that these people had been abused'.

'A lot of them went off the rails and turned to alcohol and drugs, as people who are abused do ... Most of these kids were certainly abused. It's like a sliding doors moment—once it happens, you go off on a path they would not have gone on. I reckon a hundred per cent of them, it was a contributing factor. But we could not say that the abuse contributed a hundred per cent. Hardly any of them left suicide notes and those that did, didn't mention their abuse.'

It seems a strange and high bar to require the child sexual abuse to have been 100 per cent to blame for an adult suicide when there is decades of research to show that as the detective himself noted, the abuse often sets a person off on a dysfunctional trajectory which culminates, tragically, in suicide.

He said the widely held view at the time was that 'Kevin Carson had gone off half-cocked and said too much about it to the press'. 'It caused a lot of angst in the police force. Kevin Carson opened a can of worms,' the detective says. 'Kevin Carson was a great investigator of child sexual assaults in Ballarat, he just bit off more than he could chew. My impression is that he said something he shouldn't have said.

'Management got sick and tired of the whole thing—they told him to just leave it to others,' the detective said. 'I don't think that was done well.'

I ask him if he thinks that there was some other conspiracy at play there—some collusion by members of the Ballarat policing hierarchy with the Church, as is believed by many survivors in the Ballarat community.

'It's hard to say,' the detective replies, acknowledging that sort of thing had happened with Detective Denis Ryan, who investigated Monsignor Day in Mildura and was thwarted by corrupt Catholic police. 'I think they [Victoria Police management] just wanted it to go away. They knew they would have to put a lot of resources into it and I don't think they wanted to.'

He says that he and the other detectives on Operation Plangere were 'banned from talking to [Carson] in the end'. 'We would go up there to Ballarat to speak to him and his supervisors would tell us "he's gone home"—we went up many times and they would always say we couldn't speak to him. You can read into that what you want.

We just couldn't get to him. I think they just wanted it to go away, they wanted it to disappear.' Carson was wounded at hearing of this treatment.

Two months after a redacted form of the report quietly appeared on the Royal Commission website, it was discovered by *The Australian.* Badged 'EXCLUSIVE', the story was splashed across page one of the newspaper. 'Police in false claim on child-abuse suicides', it said. The article was critical of Victoria Police and of Carson's work.

'Despite knowing for more than two years that the figure was grossly wrong,' *The Australian* wrote of the number of suicides listed in Carson's report, 'the force has never publicly corrected it, regardless of the enormous damage it has caused the church.'

'Rather than scores of people committing suicide due to church-related sex abuse, Operation Plangere could substantiate only one firm case,' *The Australian* wrote. 'There were several suicides of people who might have suffered sexual abuse, but these could not be verified by police reports and several cases where the suicides were not abuse-related,' the story said.

'The police operation into Sergeant Carson's claims found that 16 people on his list of 43 could be confirmed as committing suicide ... The analysis of Sergeant Carson's work ... was damning ... There are significant limitations to the data supplied by Detective Sergeant Carson.' An editorial in the same newspaper accused the force, via Carson, of 'shameful distortions' and 'incompetence'.

Carson was gutted. 'Unfortunately, it is far too easy for people to sit in offices such as *The Australian* newspaper office ... and question my integrity alleging I had fabricated a number of suicides,' he wrote in a later submission to the Royal Commission.

'From behind a computer you don't see the mother's tears. You don't see the partners devastated, raising children as a single parent without their father. You don't see men crying because they can't hold their children, unable to hug them, unable to bathe their own children. You don't make it up!!!'

To be fair to *The Australian,* it was just reporting an internal data report which slammed the initial work of Victoria Police and appeared to point to incompetence. The redacted report on the Royal Commission website didn't have the names of the suicides, and therefore the clues that the picture was far, far more complicated than Plangere would have it. The journalist would have trusted that it was a competent piece of policing.

But Carson took it, unsurprisingly, as a personal affront after the years of painful and emotionally exhausting work he had done on behalf of his community. Carson was also livid when Francis Sullivan, lay CEO of the Catholic Church's Truth, Justice and Healing Council, wrote on the group's website: 'The Royal Commission processes and all that surrounds it are traumatic enough for survivors without false and misleading claims dressed up as official reports inaccurately amplifying the horrors,' wrote Sullivan, who wondered if this was a sort of 'get the Catholics' exercise.

Carson responded in his submission to the Royal Commission:

> Above all the most disappointing part is Mr Sullivan has sat before this Royal Commission and listened to victim after victim tell their horrific stories, talk about suicides and premature deaths, and hear stories recanted of half a class of students now being deceased. To suggest that the premature deaths which I initially sought to be referred to the Coroner for investigation were fabricated, is extremely disappointing.

Carson wrote an impassioned letter to Sullivan and the pair met. Sullivan realised that the story was not as it initially had seemed.

I have never met Carson nor had I spoken to him before his correspondence fell into my hands from another source. The point about all of it is that the 'false story' of the suicides has been used by many to champion the view that the abuse crisis in the Catholic Church, particularly in Ballarat and Melbourne, was overstated.

It has been used by the defenders of Pell, even when he later faced allegations himself that were aired in my story on the ABC *7.30* program. Shortly before he took the top job, Victoria Police Commissioner Graham Ashton had gone in to bat for Carson in the Victorian parliamentary inquiry in 2014. He also made the claim that not a single victim had been referred to Victoria Police by Pell's Melbourne Response. The Melbourne Response Special Commissioner Peter O'Callaghan, QC, gave detailed evidence saying that was not true—and citing the number of people that had been referred.

So when the Plangere report leaked out, the Pell defenders sprung into action. News Limited columnist Miranda Devine, a friend of Pell's, said Ashton had 'form when it comes to Pell, for whom he has barely concealed antipathy. His force has been slammed for failing to investigate complaints of child sexual abuse and for telling untruths to a parliamentary inquiry, including a wildly exaggerated claim about suicides, in an effort to offload blame on to the church.'

Andrew Bolt, who exclusively interviewed Pell in Rome, described Carson's report as 'vastly overstating the suicides', and the story of it in *The Age* as a 'stunning slander by the police'. Both Bolt and Devine argued that if the police could get it so wrong on suicides, they could easily get it wrong on allegations against Pell.

Now, all of that would be true were it not for the fact that Operation Plangere presented as a complete whitewash. What, in reality, Victoria Police tells me it was, was an attempt to not upset families of a bunch of guys who died a long time ago when it would be very difficult to establish on any measure exactly what caused them to take their lives. It seemed like a pointless and unnecessarily distressing exercise. But in the process, the report unwittingly undermined the force's new commissioner and the police case against Pell.

18

DOVETON

Cold-blooded old times. Cold-blooded old times. Cold-blooded old, times. The type of memories that turn your bones to glass. Turn your bones to glass.

Lyrics by Bill Callahan of Smog, 'Cold Blooded Old Times'

However many times it's said he turned a blind eye in Ballarat, however many child abuse problems it's alleged he mopped up after, George Pell remained at that time a reasonably junior priest. But the questions about his conduct in relation to the handling of child abuse in Melbourne happened when he was an auxiliary bishop. Talk to people in the know in the Church and they will tell you Melbourne is Pell's real problem. The Melbourne problem was forensically prosecuted on the third day of Cardinal Pell's evidence beamed back from Rome to Sydney in February 2016. If you boil day three down to its core, it's a story of Auxiliary Bishop Pell and a schoolgirl. A schoolgirl who was now all grown up and had flown from her home in Cairns to be in that courtroom, in the hope, however faint, that she would get some admissions about what the Auxiliary Bishop had really known.

The schoolgirl was Julie Stewart. A slip of a thing with tawny hair, crinkled from plaits and tumbling all the way down her back. Julie was from the hardscrabble parish of Holy Family, Doveton. Doveton was in the southern region of the city, which the Auxiliary Bishop oversaw. It neighboured Father Noel Brady's parish in Dandenong and coincidentally, Julie later went to the school there. She'd just made her First Holy Communion, and her photograph from 1984 floods the brain with memory, recalling mine from two years before. Same veil with scalloped edges. Same scratchy-stiff crown of artificial white flowers. Same high-necked dress, its hem threaded through with silk ribbon. Julie sits propped up against a pine-clad wall. Her frilly socks are pulled up to the knee, her feet shod with patent leather white shoes with little decorative holes punched out. They're dangling from the stool because she's so small. Her little hands are clasped as she beams at someone to the right of the camera.

'We went to church every Sunday,' Julie says. 'And we used to say our prayers before we went to bed.'

In 1984, along with her First Holy Communion (always in capitals, if you please) Julie also made her First Confession. The Church was modernising—masses, once Latin, were filled with the jangly guitar tunes of 'This Is the Day That the Lord has Made', walls were adorned with macramé owls and godseyes, priests were donning open-necked shirts and chunky brown wooden crosses hung from their necks. So at that time, they began to call confession 'reconciliation'.

The year of Julie's introduction to the blessed sacraments was the year that Peter Searson came to Holy Family, Doveton. Searson was a shocking piece of work, which of course little Julie didn't realise at first. A vain and shallow creature, his hair was slicked down like a shiny Brylcreem helmet. He brandished a gun, hung around the kids' toilets, was cruel to animals, dismissive to staff and preyed upon children. He was, by all accounts, dreadfully fond of himself and disdainful of pretty much everyone else. The very antithesis of what a priest ought to be. But like so many paedophile priests, he was very good at appearing to the kids when they first met him like a lovely guy.

The memory of Searson, wandering through a sea of students at Holy Family, is etched into Stewart's mind. 'I used to see him on the playground, cuddling. He was very affectionate with children and always had a smile on his face. And I remember, on the playground, he used to like playing with my hair. That's another thing, I don't like anyone touching my hair now...' Stewart trails off. But back then, she was initially delighted at the attention. 'I was like, "Wait till I tell my nana", because a priest was someone very important in our family.'

Also etched in Stewart's mind is reconciliation. Because it was reconciliation, and not stiff old confession in a tiny wooden box, the young confessor had the choice of sitting either behind a wall or in a moulded plastic seat next to Father. There was much discussion among the Holy Family youngsters about where they might sit.

But when Julie took her turn, Searson didn't give her the option to sit behind the wall. She was to sit on his side of the partition.

'I went to sit on the chair next to him and he said, "Come and sit on my knee".' She breathes in deeply. 'So that's, um, that's how it started.'

'It' was the grooming. 'I remember he placed his hand there,' she says, pointing to her leg, 'and his other hand was between my, uh, thighs,' Julie told me.

'He asked, you know, "Do you love Father?" And I said, "Oh, of course", I'm thinking The Lord, "I love Father, I love The Lord". And he giggled and I giggled. And he said, "No, no, no, do you love me?" And I said, "Of course I love you". And he said, "Give Father a kiss". So I gave him a kiss on the cheek, and he said, "No, no, no, give

Father a kiss on the lips". So I gave him a kiss on the lips. And that was just the beginning. That's sort of how it started.'

Paedophiles seem to possess a peculiar knack of being able to pick vulnerability in a child's eyes. And Julie had been abused before by a family member between the ages of five and eight. She'd become a bedwetter, beset with constant nightmares. She clung on to her mother like a little limpet. So when things got strange with Searson, little Julie knew what was going on. The first three occasions it was just the kissing. But from the fourth, the touching began.

Julie's police statement was handwritten in bubbly teenage script some years later, when she was fifteen.

> I sat on the very end of his knee, because I didn't want to get to [sic] close to him, but he dragged me right up his lap and sat me on his lap. When he sat me on his lap, he sat me on his penis. I know this because when I sat down I could feel that it was erect ... I knew something was wrong

because priests don't normally act this way and I became very scared.

In November 2015, ahead of her evidence to the Royal Commission, I meet Stewart at her hotel room. She is still a petite woman, with the same long shiny hair snaking down her back. She looks younger than she is and she's plucky as anything.

Stewart tells me that the initial touching led to Searson placing his hand on his 'private parts', 'and him trying to get his hands inside my, um, my underwear. But I used to brush his hand away. And I think I know I did that because I knew that that was wrong because of my previous abuse.' He began to flick and tickle her genitals over her underwear. His penis would always be erect.

'To be honest, I thought I must be a very, very bad girl for this to be happening to me again. And I just did not want to tell anybody because I thought I was such a problem to my family in the beginning because of family abuse—the family member that abused me. I didn't want to tell anybody. So I didn't. I just thought there must be something wrong with me and I'm really bad.'

'So you never told anybody?'

'I never told anybody ... The priest in your family is somebody that is very, very important in a Catholic family ... And you know, my nana, she had so much faith, she was the most beautiful...' she trails off at the memory. 'I was born on my nana's birthday, I was very close to my nana ... I just did not want to let her down. I didn't want to cause a problem. So I never said anything.'

And so, of course, the abuse continued.

'His face would always light up when I'd walk into the room, you know, you know, light up, straight away. And I was just *sickened* by it.'

She remembers vividly the last occasion, some time in the second term of Grade 4 the following year. She was willing herself to sit on the other side of the partition. It angered Searson that she didn't go over to him immediately. He grabbed her and pushed her backside down against his erect penis very hard. 'He whispered in my ear,

"You are a good girl. The Lord forgives you." And I just snapped ... I remember putting my hands on his knees and pushing myself off and I just turned around and looked at him and he was sort of shocked that I'd done it and I just bolted out.'

Braids flying in the wind, the little girl raced out of the church, sobbing and hyperventilating, into the arms of her teacher Shirley Barrett, who had the other children lined up for reconciliation. She was taken directly to her principal, Graeme Sleeman. 'They tried everything to calm me down and they couldn't. And I remember Mr Sleeman, Graeme, tried to console me by touching my plaits, and I wouldn't let him touch me. I can remember him saying, trying to ask me what happened, "What did he do to you?" And I recall saying, "it was horrible, it was horrible".'

It is hard to imagine such an incident taking place in a modern school, and if it did, it could only end with the priest being marched off the premises posthaste. But that's not what happened to Searson. He stayed at Holy

Family for another twelve years. Twelve. It tore apart the school community. And it wasn't like Sleeman turned a blind eye to what was going on with Searson. He fought the archdiocese for years. Sleeman lost his job and ultimately his career trying to expose the priest. Stewart told a series of other adults in the Catholic education system who did not act, or did not effectively act, or were nobbled by those above them.

Unable to stay at Holy Family while Searson was still there, Julie told a teacher at her next school about the abuse. Then, when she attended high school at St John's in Dandenong, also run by the archdiocese, she told a nun. The nun referred her to the school principal, Michael Quin. She had a meeting with him and the nun, Sister Colleen. She had by this time been to see a detective, Ben Condon. She gave Quin a manila folder containing her statement and Condon's business card.

'And [Quin] said he was going to get advice on what to do about it,' Stewart says.

'I got called in a week or a couple of weeks, later. I'm not too sure. And

[Quin] said "Um, well, there's not much we can do about it, I think it's best if you just keep seeing Sister Colleen and talking about it and trying to get on with your life" ... I–I never read that statement ever again ... I never saw it again. And I never got back the manila folder, I never got back the business card with Detective Condon's details,' Stewart says. At the time, she says didn't feel that she could ask her principal for the materials. But now?

'Well now, as a 40-year-old woman, it makes me question how big a cover-up this really has become,' she says with a sour half-laugh. 'They've all spoken to somebody. Who did they speak to? Who, who, above all of them is trying to shut it down?'

The type of memories that turn your bones to glass. 'I was alone in this whole journey, and that's how I felt. Totally. And broken. Totally broken, [I felt] that nothing is ever going to get done about this.'

Julie was fifteen. Her decision to go to police took place after she'd had her stomach pumped in hospital of the sixty Panadeine, twenty-four Panadol and some zinc tablets she'd taken to try to kill herself.

The police report, too, went nowhere. In fact, the Victoria Police investigation, or lack thereof, was a dog's breakfast. Julie had been interviewed by a single, junior police officer, Ben Condon. It is now accepted practice that two officers attend these sorts of interviews and, given it was a teenage girl making the statement, having a female officer present is always encouraged. It's unclear why that did not happen. When Julie told Condon that another family member had abused her, she says he made a curiously insensitive reply. 'He said, "Oh my god, what were you wearing, a neon sign above your head, that said, 'Come get me'?",' Stewart remembers. 'And from then, I'd shut down.' The police statement is, accordingly, less detailed about the abuse than the one she later gave to the Royal Commission.

Despite this insensitivity, Stewart does say Condon turned to her father as he was leaving the Stewart home and said, 'We'll get him'. 'Bewdy', was Mr Stewart's reply. But she says Condon rang her some time later to tell her there wasn't enough evidence. Condon gave evidence to the Royal Commission that he can't remember taking the statement. The statement was taken in the days before Victoria Police had formed its groundbreaking Child Exploitation Squad and was still under the auspices of the Child Exploitation Unit (CEU). The unit wasn't staffed by proper detectives and had no real expertise in the area. Children were still seen as chattels in the eyes of the law. Still, in 1994—weirdly, four years after Stewart first made her complaint—CEU officers wrote up a report, which concluded, 'CEU have investigated the complaint and find no allegations of a sexual nature'. Searson was never interviewed. Assistant Commissioner Steve Fontana, who was interviewed by the Royal Commission last year, seemed stumped as to the reasons for that.

'It appears that investigating officers erroneously did not characterise Julie Stewart to be a complainant who had made "allegations of a sexual nature". The reason for this is not clear to me.'

Stewart wonders whether Condon or someone else was nobbled. Certainly, when further complaints were made to Victoria Police about Searson, a Sergeant Caulfield recorded the following note on the file:

THERE IS HIGH LEVEL RESISTANCE TO ANY ENQUIRIES BEING MADE ABOUT SEARSON, WITHIN THE CATHOLIC CHURCH/PARISH.

In October 1995, Sergeant Caulfield closed his file and wrote that 'the enquiry [can] be taken no further by this office'. As Counsel Assisting Gail Furness, SC, and Counsel Assisting Stephen Free wrote in their final submission to the Royal Commission in October 2016, 'given an offence was disclosed, this was a failure by Victoria Police'.

An understatement, to say the least, but for Stewart, the biggest slap in the face was in 2013, seeing the most senior Catholic in the country up on television in a Victorian parliamentary inquiry acting like he didn't know about her situation. That is what jolted Stewart into action. That's what brought her to Sydney one sunny day in March 2016.

And the story of Julie Stewart is why, despite questions about his years as a consultor in the Ballarat Diocese, it is his stint as Auxiliary Bishop in Melbourne and how he handled the Doveton situation that commentators have privately and publicly said is Pell's stickiest when it comes to alleged knowledge of paedophile priests. Until the allegations were made about Pell's own offending, it was assumed it was the years as Auxiliary Bishop, and the Royal Commission's laser gaze on his action and inaction, that might bring the Cardinal undone.

The 2013 exchange that really got Stewart's goat was while Pell was giving evidence about Searson to the Victorian Parliamentary Inquiry into the Handling of Child Abuse by Religious and Other Organisations. Deputy Chair Frank McGuire interrogated Pell about his handling of teachers who had tried to complain about Searson. The Cardinal's performance in that chair was vintage Pell, pointing out that Searson had 'never been convicted of a sex crime.

He was convicted for an act of cruelty.' The pugnacious McGuire was undeterred. 'Just from your evidence, can you understand how victims regard what happened during this period was really "hear no evil, see no evil, say nothing about evil" from the Church?'

Cardinal Pell responded, 'I think that is an objectionable suggestion, with no foundation in the truth. No conviction was recorded for Searson on sexual misbehaviour. There *might* be victims...'

Stewart sat bolt upright in her living room at home. There was no 'might'. She had a letter from Pell, dated 26 August 1998, and there was no 'might' in that letter:

> I understand that, based on findings made by the Independent Commissioner, your claims have been considered by the Compensation Panel. The Panel has provided me with a recommendation, which I accept, and this letter is accompanied by a formal offer made on my behalf...
>
> Unfortunately we cannot change what has happened in the past. You may never be rid of the memories

or the hurt. Services such as those provided through Carelink can assist you in your recovery. The payment of compensation raises difficult and complex issues. It is my hope that my offer, based on the Panel's recommendation, will be accepted by you as a preferable alternative to legal proceedings and that it too will assist you with your future.

On behalf of the Catholic Church and personally, I apologise to you and to those around you for the wrongs and hurt you have suffered at the hands of Father Searson. Whether or not you choose to accept the enclosed offer, I offer you my prayers.

The letter was signed 'Yours sincerely in Christ, George Pell' with the little cross that Pell always pens with a flourish next to his name. The 'enclosed offer' had been generated through Stewart's involvement in the Melbourne Response. The process had been for Stewart 'the most horrible experience of my life', where she says she was made to sit across a small room from her abuser, Searson. 'I was just *sickened,*' she remembers. 'I couldn't believe it.' The enclosed offer was for $25 000. A very small fraction of what Stewart would have received had she successfully sued in a court of law. Note the Cardinal's hope that the $25 000 would be 'a preferable alternative to legal proceedings'. She was asked to sign a confidentiality agreement and she now believes the money was just to buy her silence. She couldn't bring herself to spend it for years. 'I think I bought my mum and dad a washing machine and put some gas in my brother's car and then I just put it away.'

But for Stewart, despite the paltry attempt at reparation and the manifest shortcomings of both the Melbourne Response and the letter, that letter simply proved that Pell knew when he went to the parliamentary inquiry in 2013 that there *was* a victim. That she was that victim. That she had, in Pell's own words, suffered 'wrongs and hurt ... at the hands of Father Searson'. And that the precise nature of those wrongs and hurts had been relayed by her to Pell's Independent Commissioner Peter

O'Callaghan. If she was not a victim, then why had this happened?

'Why did Peter O'Callaghan come to my house?' Julie asks me with clenched jaw in November 2015, reflecting with anger on Pell's evidence to the parliamentary inquiry. 'Why did we go through all of that? Why did I then get rung up from Peter O'Callaghan and he told me that they believed me 100 per cent? Why did I go before a compensation panel? Why did I get $25 000?'

'What do you think about George Pell?' I ask her.

'Not. Very. Much,' she replies, acidly.

'Do you think he tells the truth?'

'No. He doesn't. He does not tell the truth.'

Sitting in Victoria's parliamentary library, the shadow of St Patrick's Cathedral over his shoulder through the large windowpane, Frank McGuire, MP, is a little more circumspect when I ask him the same question, but he is acutely aware of the inconsistency. He chooses his words carefully and deliberately. 'I was shocked to find out about the letter and disappointed,'

McGuire says. 'Cardinal Pell may have misled the Victorian Parliament in his testimony or downplayed his knowledge.' I ask him if there is any alternative explanation. He looks to the side, sighs and half smiles. 'I'll leave that to Cardinal Pell to respond to.' Unfortunately, because of issues around separation of powers between parliament and the judiciary, Pell was never asked that question in the Royal Commission because Counsel Assisting was not permitted to do so.

But it had the effect of spurring Stewart from her home in Cairns into decisive and unbending action. Until the inquiry, Stewart's name had never been made public because she wanted a quiet life. But now, she knew that she needed to be heard and the Royal Commission was the forum for that hearing. It would cost Stewart her anonymity, but she figured it was worth it. 'There *might* be victims' kept ringing in her ears. 'That pissed me off, oh,' she says, shaking her head slowly and deliberately, 'I was *so* angry ... That was a trigger point for me. And I thought, "Let's get 'em".'

And hence, in November 2015, Stewart gave her evidence to the Royal Commission, along with her old principal, Graeme Sleeman. Filming a story for *7.30,* our crew watched them embrace in a Melbourne hotel room before their evidence—it was the first time they had clapped eyes on each other in thirty years. 'G'day Jules!' boomed Sleeman. 'How are you? Long time no see, eh?' Julie buried her head in the shoulder of the big bear of a man and wept. 'You alright?' Sleeman asked her. She shook her head and sobbed.

It was impossible not to be transported back to the little school shoes thwacking on the playground asphalt, the long braids flying in the wind, the principal trying to get the tiny, inconsolable kid to tell him what on earth had happened. Now, after three decades of anxiety, self-doubt and depression for one; and for the other, a trashed career and banging his head against a brick wall, someone was finally going to listen to them both.

19

THE BIRD

Counsel Assisting the Royal Commission, Gail Furness, SC: There is a reference in that paragraph to Father Searson stabbing to death a bird in front of the children Cardinal George Pell: I don't know whether the bird was already dead...

Royal Commission, March 2016

There were many, many attempts to get someone to listen to the fact that Father Peter Searson was dangerous, decades before Julie Stewart and Graeme Sleeman ever came to the Royal Commission. Infamously now, one of those attempts was by a delegation in November 1989 of Doveton parent and teacher representatives who went to see the Auxiliary Bishop responsible for the region, George Pell. A list of grievances which had been prepared included 'harassment of children', and a range of unsettling issues like hanging around the kids' toilets, showing children a dead body in a coffin, forcing children to attend confession on demand, harassing staff and parents, and cruelty to animals. The priest was known to wear army fatigues on school grounds and teachers from time to time found bullet shells on the playground. Pell was also given a briefing from a representative of the Catholic Education Office (CEO), Norm Lalor. Lalor is now in a nursing home and was unable to give evidence to the Royal Commission.

But Pell made the argument that while he was told about this in general terms, the real truth was shielded from him. That is, the real truth that Searson was a sex offender. According to the Cardinal, he was deceived by Lalor, the CEO, the delegation from Doveton and the then archbishop, Frank Little.

'I was a new boy on the block. I was known to be capable of being outspoken. They might have been fearful of just what line I—I would take when confronted with all the information,' Pell told the Royal Commission during his evidence on day three. Further, the CEO was, according to the Cardinal, 'fearful' and 'very keen to keep the lid on the situation'. Even further, he added that the CEO was trying to protect Archbishop Little, 'because they might have come to the conclusion that he had chosen a certain path and felt it was their duty to support him in that'.

According to the Pell thesis, there was a history of people deceiving him because they did not know how he might deal with the information. The consultors of the Ballarat Diocese, Monsignor Fiscalini, Bishop Mulkearns, his friend Brian Finnigan and even his first cousin Henry Nolan, by this interpretation, had also deceived him too.

'It's an extraordinary position, Cardinal,' Counsel Assisting Gail Furness, SC, said to Pell during his Rome evidence.

'Counsel, this was an extraordinary world, a world of crimes and cover-ups, and people did not want the status quo to be disturbed,' he replied.

'And you put yourself in this world as being the person who would disturb the status quo, do you?' Furness continued, archly.

'I not only disturbed the status quo, but when I became archbishop, I turned the situation right around so that the Melbourne Response procedures were light years ahead of all this obfuscation and prevarication and deception.'

At the time when all of this obfuscation and conspiring to deceive the intrepid truth-seeker, Pell, was allegedly happening—both in Ballarat and in Melbourne—there was no evidence at all to suggest that he was a fearless advocate of children, against child abuse, someone who rocked the boat. In fact, all of the evidence would suggest quite the opposite. He did nothing with the rumours he knew about Monsignor John Day abusing children in Mildura. And when a 'brave and honest lad' told him about abuse at the hands of Dowlan at St Patrick's, again he did not act. 'He wasn't asking me to do anything,' the Cardinal famously said.

There was also evidence that the Searson incident with Julie Stewart went further than just Pell. A memorandum on the letterhead of the Vicar-General, Hilton Deakin, talked about 'sexual interference' of a girl in the confessional by Searson. 'This could go to court', it said.

Parents set up a sustained letter-writing campaign—to Deakin and to Little. Strangely, Searson remained in the job for years after those letters were written, stamped and sent to the archdiocese. Deakin says Little told them they were not to be discussed. The one I find most difficult to read is written by the hand of a 10-year-old, complete with spelling mistakes. It recounts what happened to Julie Stewart and also says Searson 'pulled a gun out of his pants' when asking little boys to go and turn off the sprinklers.

> None of the teachers will let us go and see him alone there has to be three or four of us. Some children from our class went to see our princaple but it did nothing. He threatneds us you can't walk past him with out being scared. Our princaple is leaving because of Father you see, Mr Sleeman our princaple can't get on with Father

so he has to leave. If I was to say who should leave I would say Father as he sexuly assaulted my friend and it's not going to happen again.

Furness brought the Cardinal's attention to one particular 1991 letter from an irate parent who had written to Deakin to complain. At this point, one of the most truly surreal moments of the Pell evidence took place.

'There is a reference in that paragraph to Father Searson stabbing to death a bird in front of the children?' Furness asked the Cardinal.

'Y–es,' the Cardinal replied, appearing distracted.

'Did that come to your attention?'

'At some stage, I think. I don't know whether the bird was already dead, but at some stage I certainly was informed of this bizarre happening,' Pell replied.

Guffaws echoed around the courtroom. The tone had moved to high farce. On the one hand, it was something of a comic relief. People started tweeting madly. Stewart put her head in her hand and shook it. The collective feeling was that, however amusing, the bird was a tell. That a person could make such an absurd answer to such a question said something about the person answering. Ballarat survivor Andrew Collins, watching in the room in Rome, said the first word that came into his mind was 'empathy'. 'To me it showed that he struggled to show any,' Collins says. 'We didn't see it as a blunder, as he thinks carefully before he speaks and is very intelligent and articulate. This is just how his mind works. If it's not about him, involving him or of benefit to him, then it hardly registers.'

Furness did not miss it either. 'Does it matter whether the bird was dead, or it was stabbed when it was dead?' she asked the Cardinal.

'Not—not really,' said Pell, sounding bored and distracted. 'Not really.'

On 1 October 1992, there was a meeting of the Curia, of which Pell was a member, along with the other bishops and senior clergy of the archdiocese. The minutes of that meeting are an insight into how these matters were covered up in those days—the euphemistic way of referring to scandalous content in order to keep it off the written record. While the minutes go into a reasonable amount of detail about matters such as, for instance, sale of land, Catholic homes for the elderly and restoration of the cathedral, discussion of the ever-hastening crisis at Doveton is deliberately vague. The item is headed 'A CERTAIN PP'. PP stands for parish priest. 'The Archbishop referred to some material which had been provided to Bishop O'Connell by the Catholic Education Office.'

That's all it says. No more, no less. The material was the chilling typed accounts of children, bashed out on an old typewriter, talking about their dealings with Searson. It's shocking to read in a contemporary context, knowing how little was done.

> 'I think he is gay ... I think that something is rong about him. I think father needs medical help ... He makes me feel scared. He makes me uncof terbel. HE IS MAD.'

'Father has been hitting people in the gut, head, neck, stomach. He hits you as hard as he can. He says if you don't want to serve (as an altar boy) ... you are bad ... You are being bad to god.'

'Father gives me the no feeling when he touches me. Once I went serving and father hit me in the neck. And once father felt me. I think father is gay. I recon his will start to feel us all over.'

'...He hits us he digs his hands in your side he grabs you around the neck. Soon he will be feeling us all over ... I want to go talk to him and say FATHER YOU DO ANYTHING TO ME AGAIN AND YOU'LL BE SORRY ... I think that we should replace him. I HATE FATHER PETER.'

'When I was serving father Peter used to hit the severs on the back, on the side of the ribs, in the cheast, on your head.'

'We are all very scared because we don't know where he is going to touch us next. Father could sexually abuse us. He is dangerous...'

Even with these accounts floating around the Catholic education system and parked with the most senior people in the archdiocese, Searson did not leave Doveton for another five years. But Pell's ignorance of them can be explained, according to Pell: yet again, he was having the wool pulled over his eyes. When asked by Furness about this meeting of the Curia, Pell did not disagree that the minute was referring to the children's statements.

It is important to point out that while the then Bishop Pell was a member of the Curia, he was overseas at the time of this meeting. But of course, it wasn't just Archbishop Frank Little that knew of these matters. So too did Monsignors Deakin and O'Connell. So neither of them, Furness probed, thought to tell Pell about those accounts in *any* forum?

'Not in a way that led me to think that they thought further action should be taken against Searson or that he should be removed,' the Cardinal replied.

Counsel Assisting reminded Pell of another incident, in March 1993, where Searson held a knife to the chest of a young girl in the Holy Family church, saying to her 'if you move, this will go through you'. That incident, still a good four years before Searson was removed, was referred to the then Vicar-General, Monsignor Gerry Cudmore. That incident was referred to police and discussed by the Curia, whose minutes said:

> The matter has been discussed several times with the Vicar General and by Curia. The decision was taken that in the absence of action by the Police and the unwillingness of the parents to pursue the matter, nothing could be done about this incident.

The Cardinal could not, this time, say he was not informed, because there it was in writing. 'It is outrageous, I suggest to you, Cardinal, that the Curia could be given information of this sort and do nothing?' Furness put to him.

'The police had been informed, they'd investigated, and they couldn't proceed ... The recommendation was that nothing could be done,' Pell replied.

Furness pressed on, 'But it's irrelevant, isn't it, Cardinal, to the obligation of the Church to take action to prevent its parishioners and children from being harmed, whether or not the police act?'

'That—that is correct. Obviously, of course, if the police are unable to proceed for lack of evidence, that is a significant factor in colouring what the Church authorities might decide to do,' Pell responded.

Here, the Chair, Justice Peter McClellan, pointed out that though the parents were unwilling to go to the police, that didn't relieve the Church of the responsibility to act on the priest.

Pell replied that while it did not 'relieve the Church of such an obligation', it was 'a factor in how you can go forward effectively'.

'And given what you knew then about Searson, is it not the position that the Curia should have said, "This man has to go"?' McClellan asked Pell, who replied that it was 'a possible conclusion, for sure'.

'And in not giving that advice, the Curia would not have been doing its job properly, would it?'

'I—I think you would have to say that,' Pell conceded. Pell's lawyers made the point in their final submissions that the police knew far more about Searson than he did. Again, like Operation Plangere, the reasons behind what went on there are a mystery. There is another book in Victoria Police's handling of these matters at the time.

Furness drew the Cardinal's attention to the statement by current Archbishop of Melbourne, Denis Hart, that there was a 'complete failure of process' in the archdiocese when it came to Searson. She asked Pell if he agreed that he had participated in that.

'Tangentially, marginally ... because as an Auxiliary you're not part of the official procedures. I regret that even at this stage I wasn't a bit more vigorous in my questioning or commenting.'

During the years that Graeme Sleeman and the teachers and parishioners of Doveton were trying, in vain, to get rid of a dangerous paedophile in their midst, the parishioners of my own parish in a mortgage-belt area of outer Melbourne had a situation with a 'PP' too. His name was Father John van Suylen. He was a gentle and decent priest, but not particularly financially savvy. My father was on the parish finance committee and they had overseen the building of a school and now a church. The priest was insisting on employing four paid pastoral workers at a time when budgets were extremely tight because of the building program. Van Suylen's position was 'God will provide', but the finance committee knew it would put considerable pressure on the young families already supporting the parish. Van Suylen was implacable. The situation became untenable and, with heavy hearts, my father and the other members of the committee wrote to Archbishop Little to inform him of the problems they were having with the priest. Little supported the finance committee and van Suylen was fairly quickly removed. He was gutted, felt unfairly maligned, and it caused great division as many good parishioners simply wanted to support their priest.

The point is, the Archbishop supported the finance committee's concerns. The process was over relatively quickly and the matter was excised. Over a financial dispute. The message of the time? Don't mess around with the money if you are a priest. Harm children, on the other hand, and you get to stay in the job for twelve years.

The head of the CEO during the period that Searson was harming children was Monsignor Tom Doyle, who had, coincidentally, the same name as the American canon lawyer who is an expert on mental reservation. I went to see Doyle at his home in inner Melbourne after Pell's evidence from Rome. Doyle answered the door, but told me he was on the way to the doctor's. I told him I could meet him when he got back. But he said with a nervy halflaugh that that wouldn't be necessary. I said to him it appeared that Pell had thrown him under the bus during his evidence by saying his office and others had conspired to deceive him about what Searson had done. Didn't he want to correct the record? He fixed his gaze at me and smiled, two parts world-weary, one part wry, and told me he didn't want to comment. I repeated that this was his opportunity to correct the public record. This was a matter of some importance. He told me he needed to go to the doctor's. 'I don't mean to be rude, dear, but I really must go.'

My initial impression from this brief exchange was that Doyle had given up on worrying about such things. But the Royal Commission recalled Doyle some weeks later and his evidence suggested there were some burning embers in the old belly yet. He took his opportunity to set the record straight. Like a number of his fellow officials from the CEO, he took that opportunity to toss the Cardinal back under the same bus that the Cardinal had shoved him under. Of Lalor, now in the nursing home, he said, 'I do not believe he would have deceived Bishop Pell in respect of any matter'. He did not agree that the CEO deceived the Cardinal.

I do not understand the basis for Cardinal Pell's evidence that representatives of the CEO were reluctant to be frank with him because they were keen to 'keep the lid on the situation', and were fearful of any decisive action he might take. I was not aware of any person at the CEO having a reluctance to be frank with Bishop Pell.

In 1989, CEO personnel (including me) had for a number of years been trying to get Archbishop Little to take decisive action in respect of Father Searson and he would not do so. It does not make sense to me that the CEO would be reluctant to be frank with Bishop Pell because he would take the decisive action we had been trying to get Archbishop Little to take.

Contrary to the Pell thesis that Doyle was trying to 'protect' Little and lying to Pell, Doyle said quite the opposite. 'We would have welcomed "decisive action" and in Cardinal Pell's terms we wanted to "take the lid off" the situation and have it addressed.'

Another CEO official, Alan Dooley, gave similar evidence: he was never instructed to withhold evidence from Pell, was not aware of anyone else doing so nor of 'anyone being under any instruction to "keep a lid" on the situation at Doveton'.

A third official, Peter Annett, said the same:

> I do not believe any member of the CEO staff would have deliberately withheld information from Bishop Pell in a briefing.
>
> I also do not believe CEO staff would have had any reason to want to deceive Bishop Pell. I find it difficult to believe that staff were not frank because they were fearful that Bishop Pell might take decisive action against Searson, when CEO staff had long wanted decisive action to be taken.

Annett said his immediate reaction to reading the transcript of Pell's evidence was 'some shock'. 'I was disappointed, and perhaps angry, but certainly very disappointed,' he said.

One of the teachers who was involved in the Doveton delegation to

Auxiliary Bishop Pell, Simon Stack, remembered that they were received by a 'professional and polite' Pell. But the tone changed when Stack brought up the fact that Searson was not 'a well man and he is in your care'.

'Bishop Pell frowned and said words to the effect of "you don't need to tell me how to do my job. I know what my responsibilities are,"' Stack told the Royal Commission. At the end of the meeting, he recalled Pell saying, 'I will look into the matter and I will deal with it'.

Another teacher, Dorothea Stack, said she remembered talking about the 'coffin incident', a matter of cruelty against a cat, and 'Father Searson entering the boys' toilets'. 'It is possible that I mentioned my concern was a sexual one in relation to the toilet incident, but my personal concerns were primarily about Father Searson's mental stability and the safety of the children,' Dorothea Stack said.

There is certainly a sense that there was a bit of beating around the bush that went on in that delegation, as was the way of the time. Having read many letters written to bishops from parishioners in the seventies and eighties, I have noticed that there is a frequent simpering, somewhat cowed, tone. These are letters that are written to warn a bishop that a priest is or might be a predator. Even when people have very grave concerns and are trying to make it clear that children are in danger, it's clear that discussing these matters was not easy and that they defer to the bishop. They speak euphemistically of, for instance, 'the difficult situation', 'the nasty business', 'the trouble'. A union representative who was present at the Doveton delegation meeting, Gerard Palmer, gave evidence that he was disappointed the teachers did not push their concerns effectively enough.

Pell's lawyers' final submissions to the Royal Commission about the Searson matter pick up on this beating about the bush and run with it. 'This was not a meeting called to discuss the sexual abuse of children by Searson. This was a meeting called by teachers because they were exasperated about having to deal with a difficult man in a workplace setting,' the submissions point out.

The Pell submission makes much of the fact that, of the sixteen items on the list of grievances, the first items on the list raise 'such mundane issues as: lights removed from sockets in classrooms, windows secured closed, gas heaters not working/serviced ... Children were the last category mentioned.' You want to grab those teachers by the retrospective metaphoric shoulders and give them a vigorous shake. According to the Pell camp, the thing reads like a workplace health and safety document. However, name the person in any workplace in Australia, no matter how timid the complainants are against him, who 'harasses children', unnecessarily frequents children's toilets, shows kids a dead body for kicks, is deliberately cruel to animals in front of primary school students. Pell's legal team might argue that there was 'an ambiguity' to the sexual misconduct alleged, that it wasn't serious sexual abuse alleged. But this was a dangerous man. And most notably, dangerous to children.

It's a matter taken up by Pell's own good friend and successor, Archbishop Denis Hart, who clearly didn't toe the party line the day he gave evidence and declared, undoubtedly much to the aghast chagrin of the Cardinal in Rome, that the written list of grievances were sufficient to remove Searson from the parish. When asked what he would have done in Pell's position that day, being presented with this list of grievances, Hart said he would have 'gone to the Archbishop also and asked to say that "you've got to get him out of the place straight away".' If he was frustrated at the Archbishop's response, he agreed that he would have 'certainly, certainly' taken it to the Curia. And goodness, yes, he would have insisted that the matter be minuted—'yes. These are serious matters.'

Did Pell do all of this? No. He did not. And that, among other reasons, is what led Counsel Assisting Furness to conclude in her final submissions to the Royal Commission in November 2016 that both Pell and other archdiocesan officials 'failed to exercise proper care for the children of Doveton'. Notably, in his lawyers' final submissions, the Cardinal said that Hart had the benefit of hindsight and, because he was not involved in the delegation, it was 'necessarily speculative'. It says that the focus on the delegation to Pell was 'extraordinary and unwarranted', the connection with Searson and Doveton 'no more than peripheral', Pell's involvement in the Searson affair 'relatively minor'.

But the information of the CEO has to be coupled with those dreadful letters from the children that were available to the Curia when it was discussing the 'PP', not to mention the young girl making an allegation about Searson holding a knife to her chest.

In her final submissions to the Commission, Furness gave short shrift to Pell's claim that he was the victim of a vast and deceptive conspiracy by the CEO, the Archbishop and at least two members of the Curia of the Archdiocese: Deakin and O'Connell. She submitted that the evidence of members of the CEO that they had 'no interest in deceiving Cardinal Pell or in trying to protect Searson ... should be accepted'. Here, Furness is a model of understatement. The 'deception' theory completely flies in the face of the fact that those same officers were sending those harrowing accounts of children who were terrified of Searson to anyone in the archdiocese who might listen. It presents a slightly bizarre argument to suggest that they were so Machiavellian as to send those accounts to people they knew would not act, instead of to the brave and fearless truthteller, George Pell. And even if that theory held any water whatsoever, is there even a scintilla, to use the Pell defence's own language, of evidence that he did anything to halt the cover-up of clergy child abuse before that time? To call out the priests whom he believed to be offenders? From where did he get this intimidating reputation as truth-teller? The point is, he didn't have one at all.

Interestingly, in Pell's legal team's final submissions, they backed right away from the assertion of deliberate deception or elaborate cover-up: 'Ultimately, it is most probable that Bishop Pell was not told about historical allegations of sexual misconduct by the CEO because it was the view of its officers that Bishop Pell was not part of the decision-making process, and there was no point in providing that information to him.'

Furness concluded in her final submissions, 'The matters known to Cardinal Pell on his own evidence ... were sufficient that he ought reasonably have concluded that more serious action needed to be taken in relation to Searson.'

> One option was for Searson to be removed or suspended as parish priest. At the very least a thorough investigation needed to be undertaken as to the veracity of the complaints, in particular the allegation of sexual misconduct...
>
> It was within his power to investigate the matters further and it was also within his power to urge the Archbishop to take action against Searson ... Cardinal Pell should also have taken direct action of his own to investigate the veracity of the complaints, in

particular the allegation of sexual misconduct.

His failure to take any such action meant that Cardinal Pell, like other senior officials in the Archdiocese before and after him, missed an important opportunity to recognise and deal with the serious risks posed by Searson. Cardinal Pell and other senior Archdiocesan officials failed to exercise proper care for the children of Doveton.

As the complaints about Searson kept piling up during the 1990s, he was eventually placed on 'administrative leave' by the archdiocese in 1997. Searson was seventy-four. He was finally convicted of physical assault, rather than sexual, in December that year. He pleaded guilty to assaulting a 12-year-old altar boy. The Dandenong Magistrates Court was told he whacked two altar boys over the ears at Doveton because they were giggling in mass. When one of the boys' mothers complained to the school and to police, Searson initially denied the allegation, saying he merely 'touched' the boy on the head. But the boy and his mother stuck to their guns and eventually Searson caved. He was placed on a 6-month good behaviour bond. Searson retired as a Catholic priest the following year.

As Julie Stewart watched the Pell evidence that day in Sydney, her plucky demeanour vanished. After the hearing, we bundled her and Graeme Sleeman into a taxi back to the ABC. Julie marched into the building and would not listen to a victim's advocate who was warning her about the risks of going on television. She was furious. 'I'm talking, I'm talking, I'm doing it, get me away from that woman,' she kept saying, gripping on to my arm.

She sat down in a chair across from me in the darkened studio. I asked her what she made of the Cardinal's defensive attitude.

'I wasn't at all surprised because I guess I've come to the understanding and the...,' she trailed off, as if slapped in the face by that understanding. And that's when she kind of fell apart. Her lip began to tremble. Her brow furrowed and she became, once again, the little kid that was so hurt, so let down, so ignored. She looked down, choking back little sobs.

'Sorry,' she croaked out. '...Acknowledgment for all of us victims I speak on behalf of, that he will never acknowledge any knowledge.'

'[Pell] played a significant role in my past, along with Searson and many others who have failed in the Church's name. But for my future he is nothing. He is insignificant.'

Julie wrote to me some months after the Pell evidence. She said she'd had a big emotional crash after Sydney. She had reached her lowest ebb. But she felt she had bounced back. 'As usual, I picked myself up and got on with it, as I do.'

When I hear the term 'survivor', Julie Stewart is always the first person I think of. Julie Stewart is pretty much the definition of a survivor.

Graeme Sleeman was forced to leave Doveton, his career in tatters, when the Church supported Searson instead of him. Pupils and parents at Holy Family were gutted and commenced a letter-writing campaign to try to save him. It didn't work. He was unemployable as a teacher in the Catholic system. Pell now says he feels terribly for him. But Sleeman tells me that when, in the 1990s, after applying for fifteen jobs in schools after leaving Doveton, he asked Pell to publicly support him, he was rebuffed.

'He hung up. No more communication,' Sleeman says. Oddly, Sleeman was given money for many years, totalling about $90 000, by the Melbourne Response's Independent Commissioner Peter O'Callaghan, because, O'Callaghan told Sleeman, he felt sorry for him. This money came out of O'Callaghan's own pocket. He then received $150 000 in an ex gratia payment from the archdiocese—although O'Callaghan told him the archdiocese had done nothing wrong. It's a curious final detail in the saga, even more so when it's considered that Julie Stewart wasn't afforded the same pity—she got $25 000, on the books. Sleeman now manages a cattle property on the Gold Coast. He is still trying to find a way to sue the Catholic Church for the losses he suffered.

Peter Searson died in June 2009. He was eighty-six. Like Nazareno Fasciale before him, he was given a full requiem mass at Sacred Heart Church in Carlton. According to Hart, a decree of removal as parish priest had been issued, but there had not yet been a reply from Rome. That being the case, Searson remained 'in orders' and 'therefore he was still entitled to be buried a priest'. Photographs show a stream of priests filing into the church. His mass booklet shows a stern Searson. He is not smiling.

The procession walked in to the stirring hymn 'Be Not Afraid', which is, of course, Pell's motto:

> If you pass through raging waters
> In the sea, you shall not drown,
> If you walk amid the burning flames
> You shall not be harmed.

There was no mention in the booklet of Searson's 'past'. But the readings were thoughtfully chosen. And sort of chilling. The second reading came from the Romans: 'Could anyone accuse those that God has chosen? When God acquits, could anyone condemn? Could Christ Jesus? No!'

The mourners piled out of Sacred Heart and trundled down the road to the cemetery where Searson was laid to rest.

'God is good,' Julie Stewart once told me. 'It's man that fails.'

20

THE LAST DAYS OF ROME

The night is almost gone, and the day is near. Therefore, let us lay aside the deeds of darkness and put on the armour of light.

Paul's Letter to the Romans

For an almost 75-year-old man, George Pell's forensic nineteen-and-a-half hours of evidence to the Royal Commission, slogged out over four nights into the small hours of four Roman mornings, was no small feat. Particularly for a man whose Vatican doctor said was in such perilous health.

He was exhausted by it, and referred to his herculean effort in his interview with Sky's Andrew Bolt. After two days of the Cardinal's evidence, Bolt wrote a column in the News Limited tabloids criticising Pell for his 'sad story that wasn't of much interest' gaffe. Pell had, in Bolt's view, 'uttered words that will stain his reputation forever' and the Commission was 'rightly aggressive'. But Bolt then performed a spectacular backflip, and took back the criticism. 'I joined [the] attack on George Pell,' Bolt said. 'And I think for the first time in my life I'm trending positive on Twitter as a result. I think I owe an apology and I'll go back to being hated on Twitter.' Instead of implying that Pell had been, in effect, wilfully blind, Bolt now took the view that Pell was simply 'not plugged into the community' and was 'incurious'. The pair mended fences, and they sat down for a 1-hour interview in which Pell repeatedly appealed for a 'fair go' for him and the Catholic Church. It was, however, a nuanced and at times fascinating interview and Bolt did not flinch from asking some tough questions of Pell. For reasons known only to Bolt, the nuance of his interview with Pell has not been repeated in his columns since then. From that day onwards, Bolt has remained steadfast in his defence of the Cardinal and his assumption that any allegations about Pell are simply part of an attack by progressives and secularists.

Before he met with Bolt, Pell had also had a much-anticipated meeting with the survivors who had come to Rome to bear witness to his evidence. Although not all of them were interested in going. Paul Levey couldn't bring himself to listen to another utterance from the Cardinal's mouth. Chrissie and Anthony Foster also did not go. Anthony had been planning to meet with Pell, but only if the Cardinal would speak about the Melbourne Response—which the Fosters have always been passionately committed to reforming. The last time they had met with the Cardinal, in 2014 in Australia, Anthony says he had told Pell, 'I know you are not part of the Catholic Church in Australia, but you have the power and influence to make this happen', to which, Foster says, Pell replied, 'I'll talk to Denis [Hart]'. But this time, Anthony met Pell after he came out of the lift at the Quirinale following the Cardinal's evidence. He decided to approach him and remind the Cardinal of their earlier conversations about changing the

Melbourne Response. Anthony says to his surprise, the Cardinal replied that he would be 'unable to advance' the matter. Anthony was absolutely gutted. 'I then opened my heart to him and let him see the extreme sadness inside me by saying the words, "I am a broken man",' Anthony later wrote to Pell's private secretary. 'Words that truly express the suffering of a father who has lost a child to the scourge of clergy sexual abuse and another who is severely disabled for the same reason. 'I allowed him to see my suffering in a way that I have allowed no other person.'

Anthony says that Pell then placed his hand on top of his own and 'left it there for some time'. As they parted, Anthony says he told Pell, 'you have the influence to make things change'. But as Pell walked away, he says the Cardinal replied, 'If only it would be', and walked out to his waiting car, surrounded by a media pack. Anthony was reeling. He went straight out to the reporters who had finished trying to get a news grab from Pell and he told them about the conversation. He was highly emotional. After that, Anthony received an email from Pell's private secretary, Father Mark Withoos. The tone of that email was essentially that Anthony had blown it because his comments to the media 'significantly misrepresent the way the conversation went'. 'I am sorry to say that, despite the clear words of concern, sadness and support from the Cardinal, it seems the meeting was instead used by you as a platform for further unfounded criticism of Cardinal Pell,' Withoos wrote. There would be no meeting. When Anthony wrote back trying to make Withoos understand what he had actually said, Withoos did not reply, later blaming his tardiness on a 'bad cold'.

The survivors and supporters who did go went single file into a small chamber of the Hotel Quirinale to wait their turn. They were offered coffee and hard candies. 'Pell got himself a glass of water and I got one for everyone else,' says Peter Blenkiron.

Mark Harrison had originally not intended to go to the meeting, but after speaking to his family, he decided it was best to go—for their sake and his.

Harrison was one of the twins whose sister Donna Cushing had spoken to me—the family of little kids brought away for a week of horrible abuse by Ridsdale to Edenhope.

Chairs were arranged in a circle. Harrison watched as all of the others shook Pell's hand. 'I took a step back, I did not shake his hand,' Harrison remembers. 'How could you shake a hand like that, to be honest?'

'I told him I was really disgusted and let down by himself and the Catholic Church. And how it had affected my family and my life,' Harrison says. 'And how my brother had committed suicide. I said they needed to do much more to restore my faith. Then I read Donna's letter.

'I was emotional and crying a little bit. I had to say what I felt. Pell was looking down at the floor most of the time, looking very sombre and like he was feeling sorry for himself. He said something like, "Thank you for sharing that".' Harrison says another priest who was there came up to him afterwards and said, 'Well done, Pell needed to hear that. There are a lot of people that don't like him in the Church and he needs to hear that and hopefully he can change.' And then he said, 'pat your sister on the back for writing that, I'm really proud of her for that'.

Vanessa Beetham, who was there as a support person for the survivors, says they discussed the toll of suicide in their communities and how many people in that room had been affected by friends or family taking their lives. Andrew Collins and Peter Blenkiron believed that Pell's evidence had been simply the 'performance of a politician'. 'I don't think that what we heard there was the truth—it was a politician's answers,' Collins says. But they were focused on the big picture—trying to move on from the decades of dysfunction caused by the abuse in Ballarat and getting Pell's commitment to get the Catholic Church to contribute to that.

During the conversation, Collins says Pell remained a bit removed. Towards the end, the Cardinal indicated that he needed to go away and prepare a statement for the media, who were waiting outside. 'So I decided,' Collins says, 'to do something, off the cuff. I decided to hug him.

'And so, I went over and hugged him. And he just changed. He became a bit teary. I mean, who would hug a Cardinal? Anyone?'

Collins says that after that moment, Pell went back to being Ballarat George. His stiff, lofty demeanour dissolved, he became the bloke they had known and gone to in times of need. For a brief moment, all the pain and division and anger dissolved. The Cardinal was just a guy like the rest of them.

Pell went away to write the statement, walked out into the daylight and said words to the gathered reporters that Collins describes as 'groundbreaking, because it was the first time anyone from the Vatican had linked suicide to the abuse'.

> One suicide is too many, and there have been many such tragic suicides: I commit myself to working to try and stop this so that suicide is not seen as an option for those who are suffering.
>
> I too, despite separation of distance, want to make Ballarat a

model and better place of healing and for peace ... I support the work to feasibility of research centre to advance healing and improve protection ... I owe a lot to the people and community of Ballarat; I acknowledge that with deep gratitude. It would be marvellous if our city became well-known as an effective centre and the example of practical help for all those wounded by the scourge of sexual abuse.

After evidence that had been a public relations disaster, he managed, briefly, to turn the ship around.

Bolt later reflected that Pell seemed to have a euphoric sense of relief when he emerged from the meeting. Pell actually choked up when it came to that part of their interview. It was when he was speaking of David Ridsdale, the nephew of Gerald Ridsdale. The charismatic and media-savvy David Ridsdale had been fronting the media and organising logistics as one of the leaders of the survivor group who went to Rome.

David had, famously, accused Pell of trying to 'bribe' him when, in 1993,

David disclosed his uncle's abuse during a telephone conversation to Pell at the then Auxiliary Bishop of Melbourne's presbytery at Mentone. David says Pell asked him, 'I want to know what it will take to keep you quiet'. To which David says he replied, 'Fuck you, George, and everything you stand for'. The Cardinal, while agreeing that the phone call took place, has always denied that this was said and insisted he would have remembered this if it had.

The public slanging match between the pair had been going on since David first appeared on *60 Minutes* in 2002. David gave moving evidence to the Royal Commission about his abuse when it was sitting in Ballarat in May 2015. During that evidence, David also repeated his allegation against Pell.

Seven months after David's evidence, when the Royal Commission was sitting in Melbourne, Pell's legal team set about trying to discredit David's story. A priest came forward as a character witness for Pell—his name was John Walshe. Walshe had been living with Pell at the parish of Mentone in 1993.

Walshe told the Royal Commission that he was in the house with Pell when Pell took the phone call in his office. When Pell came out, he said Pell told him, 'David is a mess' and that he felt terribly for him. 'To my observation, his demeanour was not that of a person that had been in a rude or angry conversation. He did not describe the call to me in that way,' Walshe said.

Walshe has always been a very close friend of Pell's. He has been associated with a group of younger, conservative clerics whom Pell championed during his time in the archdiocese, sometimes referred to in the media (including by BA Santamaria's daughter Mary Helen Woods) as 'The Spice Girls'. Walshe seemed, prima facie, like a great witness for Pell on that day. Except he wasn't. It later transpired that when he was asked by Pell's lawyers to make a statement, a file note said of Walshe's recollection: 'In house when call made? Think I was.' But his sworn statement made it look like he definitely was in the house and he definitely spoke to Pell immediately after the conversation with David. Walshe ultimately agreed with the Royal Commission that it was 'difficult' to reconcile his definitive recollection that Pell had spoken to him immediately with the file note.

'It is likely that parts of Father Walshe's statement evidence were a reconstruction of what he thought might have occurred rather than his actual recollection of events,' Furness ultimately submitted. 'Therefore, it is submitted that Father Walshe was not a credible witness.'

Walshe's credibility was also given a beating when a witness, John Roach, came forward on ABC TV to say that Walshe had sexually abused him when he was an 18-year-old seminarian. The Catholic Church's Melbourne Response had paid Roach $75 000 in compensation—the maximum amount available under the scheme at that time. In the eyes of the Church at least, Roach was clearly a deserving recipient of compensation. The accusations against Walshe led to him being banned from ministering in Ireland while he was there on sabbatical, but for some time Archbishop Denis Hart allowed him to continue to be parish priest for two primary schools, describing the Roach matter as simply a 'breach of his vow of celibacy'. How that accorded with the $75 000 compensation payout is inexplicable and, according to the outraged parents and parishioners of St Patrick's Mentone, unforgivable. They campaigned furiously to have the priest removed. Finally, in November 2016, almost a year after he gave evidence for Pell and the abuse payout was revealed, Walshe resigned.

The parishioners also campaigned to have a portrait of George Pell, who lived there while Auxiliary Bishop, removed from their school hall after the ABC *7.30* program aired my story about allegations against Pell of child abuse. Parent Claire Bilos told *The Age* it sent the 'wrong message' to children that Cardinal Pell should be 'revered' and was 'above question'. The Catholic Education Office refused to intervene and the painting remained.

The parishioners of Mentone would not have known they had an abuser in their midst had it not been for David Ridsdale's evidence. I had interviewed David on two earlier occasions and found him thoroughly charming. He would sweep in to the ABC studios and kiss you on the cheek, and call you 'darls'. What had happened to him as a child was unspeakable and he found a way to express that which cut through. Increasingly, there was a sense though that he was thriving on the media attention. When we chatted off-camera, he spoke repeatedly of how he was being offered money for interviews and how it was expensive to go back and forth from Australia to London, where he had lived for many years. As time went on, something began to sit slightly uncomfortably with me. I wrote it off as the behaviour of someone who had had a ghastly childhood and was understandably severely psychologically affected by it—becoming, in his case, something of an attention-seeker. Still, he was fronting a survivor group and he did an excellent job of spreading the group's message and at the time they were all enormously grateful to him.

David had also disclosed that he had a skeleton in his closet. He had volunteered that he had had a police conviction as a very young man for something like 'flashing'. He seemed genuinely contrite about it and said it was his victim's story to tell, not his. At the time, we reasoned that given what had happened to him as a child, a flashing incident was something that could be understood, if not condoned.

But it turned out that David had seriously minimised that conviction and his victim, Corey Artz, had watched David fronting the cameras in Rome in disgust. Our program received contact from a victim's advocacy group, Bravehearts, who put the show in contact with Artz. It turns out that the abuse of Artz was far more serious than David had told me. He had also minimised it to other people as well—including the people he went to Rome with. Since then, there has been a major split in the survivor community of Ballarat. Collins says as survivors, they spend their lives fighting the—overwhelmingly false—presumption that they, too, will become offenders because they were victims, and here was David who seemed to prove the theory right. Others say compassion ought to be extended for David's dreadful childhood. *The Australian* and *7.30* simultaneously ran stories which featured Artz's account. From that moment on, David has disappeared from public view.

When Furness wrote her final submissions to the Royal Commission, David's was one of a handful of stories which Furness found, ultimately, did not really check out. Furness submitted that David was an honest witness, but that it was possible that he had misinterpreted Pell's offer of assistance as a bribe. She found that there was not sufficient evidence to establish that Pell had sought to bribe David. This has been seized upon by the defenders of Pell to plant a seed of doubt about any claims that Pell knew about abuse and covered it up.

But whatever the sentiment of Pell and his supporters now, it wasn't like that in Rome when the survivors had their meeting with him. Of all the survivors, Pell singled out his special relationship with David. 'If there's one thing in all of these terrible muck-ups I regret, it's the misunderstanding with him and the way it's been fought out publicly,' Pell told Bolt. 'I mean, I knew the family. I knew his dad. There's an added grief when you are in a public controversy with somebody whom you in fact like. And whose family you like. So, the reconciliation between us...' the Cardinal's voice went quiet and then choked a little, 'it was deeply moving.'

During that meeting, there was a woman standing in the room who had travelled to Rome with the survivors. Her name was Ingrid Irwin. Irwin is a Ballarat lawyer and, incidentally, a survivor of child sexual abuse herself. She has provided legal advice and friendship to Andrew Collins. But as she stood there, watching the reconciliation that Pell described, Irwin was holding on to information about Pell to which no-one else in the room was privy. Because of that information, she told me, 'I knew anything he said would be disingenuous ... I entered that room with a heavy heart.' Irwin had a client back in Ballarat. The client had made a statement to Victoria Police about a growing investigation by its Taskforce SANO. That investigation concerned accusations that Pell himself was an abuser of children. And Irwin knew the client was not alone.

21

EUREKA

If you continue in my Word ... you will know the Truth, and the Truth will set you free.

John 8:31, given on St Alipius parish school website, 2016

In 1974, in Ballarat East, a little boy was packed off to start school. His name was Lyndon Mark Monument. Lyndon was following his older brother and big sister to St Alipius primary school just down the road. The Monument children were attending a school and a church with an illustrious Catholic goldfields history. St Alipius sprang from a community of 1850s mining parents who camped on the land and wanted to see their children taught in the Catholic tradition. It was the thirteenth non-government school opened in the Victorian colony.

In the 1880s, the Sisters of Mercy and the Christian Brothers arrived in

Ballarat East, to teach, respectively, the little girls and boys. The religious orders were to stay at St Alipius for the better part of a century. The Brothers in particular will not be forgotten easily. On the drive into Ballarat from Melbourne, St Alipius is the first church and school you clap eyes on. And fluttering on the iron fence posts are hundreds of coloured ribbons. The ribbons, now somewhat weathered by fierce Ballarat winters, are there for the children. The children betrayed by those Catholic clergy. And anyone who arrives in Ballarat cannot fail to be confronted with the memory of that suffering.

So little Lyndon Monument, a good kid, was to grow up in the eye of a child sexual abuse storm. Lyndon Monument is one of George Pell's accusers. But you need to know a bit about Lyndon Monument to understand where he is coming from when he accuses Pell. By the time Monument went to St Alipius, literally dozens of children at the boys' school there had been abused by the Christian Brothers—Ted Dowlan, Gerald Leo Fitzgerald, Stephen Farrell and Robert

Best—and a priest, Gerald Ridsdale. They left behind them a generation of kids who grew up, in many cases, to lives of dysfunction, alcoholism, underachievement, suicide.

As of February 2015, two data analyses by the Royal Commission put the number of successful or substantiated child abuse claimants against Ridsdale and the four Christian Brothers stationed at St Alipius at fifty-two. But of course, they were the ones who had it in them to complain or to seek compensation. And they were the ones that were still alive. Along with them, there are many who couldn't bear to think of it, the many who took it to their graves; not to mention those who took their lives but have never been included in the abuse suicide stats, such as they are, because they never spoke up but, on reflection, all the signs point to abuse—in the wrong class, with the wrong teacher, at the wrong time. As is pointed out by Rob Walsh—who was abused by Ridsdale and Best and lost two of his brothers and his cousin, all St Alipius alumni, to suicides—there was barely a child at St Alipius at that time who escaped abuse in some form. Walsh knows of twelve suicides of people who went through with him.

One of the St Alipius suicides that flew under the radar was Lyndon's brother Craig. Two years older than Lyndon, he was at the boys' school during the danger period. Craig Monument never breathed a word about abuse to his family. Craig was in Fitzgerald's class. You were pretty lucky in old Fitzy's class if he didn't get at you. At bare minimum, he forced all the boys to kiss him on the lips.

'I can remember Craig crying every night, like he didn't want to go to school,' Lyndon says. 'You'd never seen someone who didn't want to go to school like that … He'd just find anything not to go to school.'

Craig Monument's classmate, Darren Mooney, brought a compensation case against the Christian Brothers in July 2016 for what he was subjected to by the now-deceased Fitzgerald. Mooney tells me the Christian Brothers' insurance company now refuses to indemnify the order for claims by Fitzgerald because it is clearly documented that he abused children—it was known by the order's hierarchy. 'In my grade alone, between now and March,' Mooney says, speaking to me in December 2016, 'there's about ten settlements due from Fitzy alone.

'It was just hell there,' Mooney tells me. 'There's no other way to describe it. I still deal with the anxiety from being a child in that place on a daily basis—it was beaten into you. You did not know if you were going to be loved one minute, or beaten the next.' He said it was also impossible to learn as a child when you were so hypervigilant to beltings and sexual abuse. 'We didn't learn anything—not a thing.'

'I remember thinking,' he says of Fitzgerald, 'all I wanted is for this prick to open the window so the world would see what was going on.' But the frosted windows remained jammed shut on all but the most stinking hot summer days. 'So we couldn't see out. It was just cruel. Thirty kids in a tiny room in an autocratic, brutal environment.'

Father George Pell lived at St Alipius in the presbytery. He was there in the seventies when the Christian Brothers were doing their worst work at the boys' school just a stone's throw away, and for one of his years there, he lived with Ridsdale. There were so many whispers about not just Ridsdale, but the four Brothers, and all of the kids at the school knew who was dodgy. Pell was a man who fancied himself as connected and a player. He is known to have at times walked the playground, to give confession to the children in the Church, to say a confirmation mass. Of the dozens of St Alipius people I have spoken to in my research, only one can't remember Pell being involved in their school or parish lives at some point or other.

Lyndon Monument had another teacher who was, he says, his abuser at St Alipius. To understand Lyndon and his friend and coaccuser Damian Dignan, and the impact of what they say happened with Pell, you have to understand the context of their treatment by this teacher. Even the barest mention of the teacher's name to anyone who went to St Alipius in the seventies brings with it a shudder. In fact, when I rang many people to ask what they knew about Pell, they volunteered, unprompted, stories of that teacher. At this point, I am not able to name the teacher for legal reasons. 'Cruel' and 'sadistic' are just two of the descriptions offered.

The teacher taught Lyndon and his group of mates. The tight little group comprised Lyndon's best mate Damian, and two sets of twins: the Murphys and the Anwyls.

The teacher had a sadistic streak, and would use metre rulers to discipline and humiliate students in front of others, Monument told police. Physical punishment was used to control the students—the teacher would 'belt you as soon as look at you', says Dignan, who describes the teacher as 'an animal'.

Monument's school friend Lauren Rowbotham says she in particular was targeted for beltings—something that others in the class have mentioned too. Rowbotham is currently receiving legal advice about it. She would come home with terrible bruising from being whacked. She says things got so bad, her parents, who are now both dead, went up to the school and complained about the violence. And she also remembers that Monument and Dignan were singled out for beatings too.

One incident etched on Monument's mind concerns a meat pie he'd been given for lunch, which he didn't finish. He threw the remains of it in the bin. Years later, he told police the teacher made him fish the cold pie out of the bin and eat it in front of the class. 'I ate the rest of the pie and I was extremely embarrassed and disgusted,' he says. 'I remember crying in front of the class.' But these stories pale into insignificance when compared with what Monument says he subsequently fell victim to.

It is a difficult story for Monument to tell—he squirms in his seat as he remembers. It started, Monument recalls, when he was in Grade 6. The class had gone on an excursion and as they were walking back to the school, he says the teacher approached him and started up a conversation about masturbation.

He then began to be kept in at playtime. 'At playtime and lunchtime, I wasn't allowed to join the other kids—I had to go and sit in [the teacher's] office,' Monument says, drawing breath and looking to the side. It was supposedly to do 'special work' by himself and he was instructed it must be kept a secret, he told police. The principal and another member of staff alerted Monument's parents and asked if Lyndon had explained why he was being kept in.

Meanwhile, the 11-year-old Lyndon was being subjected to, he says, strange and perverted behaviour. He was given a notepad, for 'homework'. 'Like, go home and wait for my brother and sister to go to bed and then crawl up to my parents' bedroom and then listen to noises to see if they were having sex and go back the next day and report what I'd heard ... I used to just make stuff up because I didn't want to get into trouble.'

The creepiness turned into full-scale abuse. Masturbation, oral sex—he was forced to give it and receive it. The teacher continued to ask him 'sex questions about my mum and dad', he says. 'I didn't know what was happening to me or what she was doing ... These incidents have had a big effect on my life. There is not a time in my life that I don't think about what happened to me.'

The case is being handled by Victoria Police. There is so much more to this story and the teacher's identity is about the most shocking part of it. When you combine what Monument says happened with this teacher and what happened with Pell, Monument's life trajectory starts to make an awful lot of sense.

Monument's abuse claims about Pell centre on Ballarat's Eureka Stockade Pool. Known locally as just the Eureka Pool, it's also in Ballarat East and was the place where children in the inland town flocked during the hot, dry summers. The Eureka Pool on Stawell Street was managed for nearly forty years by local Graeme McKenzie and his wife Loyola, or 'Roly' to everyone she knew. The McKenzies lived close to the Monuments. They ran a tight ship and were loved by their community. Graeme was king of the kids.

Like every other mother in that part of town during that era, Lyndon's mum would send her kids down to the pool every day during summer. From when the youngest, Lyndon, was eight, the three children were allowed to go on their own. This was the 1970s, and children had free rein.

I met Roly McKenzie in her home in Ballarat East in May 2016 to ask her about those days. Graeme had died a few months before and Roly blinked back tears as she recalled what were for her and her family golden times. Roly remembered in the late seventies that a priest used to come most days to the pool. He'd arrive alone about 4p.m. wearing his black priestly attire, pay his admission fee, go to the change room and come out wearing his Speedos. The priest's name was George Pell.

Lyndon's sister also remembers Pell at the pool. As she'd be lying on the grass on the side of the pool with her girlfriends, the intelligent and observant 12-year-old would watch the passing parade. She noticed that Father Pell had a routine. Once he'd changed, Pell would enter the water and swim some laps, and then he'd begin to talk to some boys, sometimes including Lyndon, in the shallow end of the pool. Then he'd bring them to the deeper water and he'd play the game. The game seemed like an awful lot of fun. But Pell never invited any girls to play.

Darren Mooney, who is now principal at a tiny primary school north of Ballarat, was allowed to play. 'It was always boys, there was never any girls flying off his shoulders or playing with him in the pool,' Mooney remembers.

I remember when myself and various producers discussed this decision not to play with girls at the pool, there were several possible interpretations canvassed. One was that it was not appropriate for a priest to play with young girls at the pool and Pell was according the girls the modesty they deserved. The second was that, well, he just liked boys better. The third is the sinister motive. The third is the motive that several of the kids who played there have now sworn to tell about in police statements. The third will see them crossexamined by an expensive criminal Queen's Counsel. The third, if they survive it, if they are all telling the truth, could see the end of the career of Cardinal Pell.

There were variations to Pell's game, but most commonly, as told to me by many children who were there at the time and adults such as Roly McKenzie, involved Pell clasping his hands under the water, then lifting the boys into the air and 'bombing' them. Sometimes they'd stand on his shoulders too and dive in. The laughing of the little boys echoed around the 2-acre lot.

'He would grab you, have his hands on your backside, then push you off. Hold your hand and then he'd be doing backflips. And it seemed to go on, you know, all day. He just seemed to be there every day. So, in a sense, as a kid, a 7-, 8-, 9-year-old kid, it was fun,' Mooney remembers.

Monument played the game. 'We all sort of knew who George Pell was,' Monument remembers. 'And looked up to him in a way I s'pose. And he was always like the godly figure we all had to look up to, like we'd all get told in class, "George Pell is coming today, so, you know, brush your hair and tuck yourself in".'

Monument's memories of Pell from that time at St Alipius are positive. 'He'd come in and everyone would sort of gravitate to him because he was an enormous figure and all us little kids, of course, we'd just run up to him and idolise him, basically.'

His mate Damian Dignan also remembers Pell, although his memories are less sanguine. Dignan was a very small kid, the youngest of six siblings brought up in their parents' milk bar. I first went to Dignan's house to meet him—on the suggestion of Monument, who had been told by police that Dignan had spoken to them. The pair hadn't seen or spoken to each other for a couple of years—too much water under the bridge, too much temptation to blot out all their sadness on mad benders. But they still had an abiding affection for one another. When I left Monument, he gave me directions to Dignan's house and told me, 'Tell him I said, "I love you, mate".'

I told Dignan that I was there to talk about Pell, that Monument had sent me, and that Monument said to say he loved him. I didn't say anything else. Dignan, by then a shell of a man who had destroyed his life and his health with substance abuse, just stared at me for a few seconds. As he did, a fat tear welled in his right eye, and rolled slowly and noiselessly down his cheek, plopping into his instant coffee. 'Yeah, I'll help ya,' he said. 'I'll talk to ya. I love him too.' As he said the word 'love', his voice did this barking thing I later came to recognise when Dignan is choked up. I explained that I didn't want to tell him about what I knew as I didn't want to pollute his account. He got that. So he told me about what happened to him.

Dignan remembers Pell saying mass and taking his confession at St Alipius. 'Father Pell was a big man with a strong and intimidating voice,' Dignan says. 'Father Pell scared the shit out of me. He was big. Solid man. Had eyes that'd stare right through ya. It'd pierce your heart.' I remember Pell's comments about his 'fiery' temper that almost never came out. I ask Dignan what he remembers of St Alipius. 'I remember best times I ever got was when a storm would come over the school and you'd feel the wind, you felt free as a bird,' he remembers. I picture this little kid with his bowl haircut, pants a bit too short for his little legs, running around, holding his little face up to the wind.

'But on the other hand, [I was] a very scared young child ... I was a free little kid, but I wasn't. I was in a jail of hell as an education system and the Catholic system.'

Dignan also told me and police that he remembers girls running, crying, from Pell's confessional. Lauren Rowbotham was one of those girls. She's speaking for the first time on the record about what she knows. Rowbotham estimates she had confession with Pell 'a good ten times' and she says on a couple of occasions, things got 'a bit boisterous'. I ask her what that means. She says that Pell would 'yell at you for sinning'. 'Sometimes he would hit you—push you around—you know, "Get out of here, you're a horrible child, you have sinned". I was not the most well-behaved child,' says Rowbotham, who is a bit of a rough diamond. Several of the other girls could not be found. But one in particular regularly phones my producer Andy Burns out of the blue, to ask her what is going on with the Pell investigation. We suspect she knows something, but we can't get it out of her.

But Father Pell clearly had magnetic qualities, albeit intimidating ones too, to Dignan at least. And that's why, in the summer of 1978–79, when Pell was playing the game, Dignan, like Monument, thought he might like to join in. The boys were eight or nine at the time. Monument wore footy shorts with his undies underneath to the pool. Dignan wore board shorts. Pell, both remember, always wore dark-coloured Speedos and goggles. Monument says that Pell would wade out to the middle of the pool where the boys were playing. 'I remember that he would call us over and then offer to throw us into the air. We would then dive back into the water.' The priest would use his hands as stirrups for the boys 'and you'd put your foot in his hand and "one, two, three!" he'd throw you out of the water', Monument remembers.

For Lyndon Monument and Damian Dignan, they say the game began to get weird.

'As we played the game, I remember that we seemed to drift slowly into the deep end of the pool,' Monument remembers. 'When we were in the deep end, I noticed that the way I was being thrown in the pool was different. He still offered both of [his] linked hands under the water and I would put both of my feet into his hands.'

According to Monument and Dignan, Pell's free hand under the water began to wander. At first in the sort of way that you might think was a mistake. But then you realised that it wasn't a mistake; that it was deliberate. That a 30-something-year-old priest in Speedos had a grip on your private parts in a public swimming pool and you were eight and you were damned if you knew what to do.

'Father Pell would let one hand go and I felt his other hand reach up and hold my crotch area,' Monument told police. 'The hand on my crotch would cover my penis and testicles and would also cover my anus area. Father Pell would throw me into the air and I would dive into the water.' Monument says the priest would have an open hand cupped around his crotch during this. He later explains to me at one point that he distinctly remembers Pell's fingers being at the entrance to his anus, but as to whether the priest digitally penetrated him, he could not comfortably remember. While the behaviour was repeated, Monument remembers it as furtive and fleeting.

'When Father Pell first started throwing in this way it felt uncomfortable and I didn't like it. I didn't say anything to Father Pell at the time, because I looked up to him.' Monument estimates that Pell would hold him on the crotch for about half of the throws. He also recalls that Pell would put his hands under the shorts and underpants that Monument was wearing, touching his genitals before rocking him up and down.

As for Dignan, he shifts uncomfortably in his seat as I ask about it. He says 'things got a bit rough around the testes, around the anus'.

'What would he do?' I ask.

'Grab you,' he replies, pursing his lips awkwardly. He swallows. '[I felt] scared. Scared but hurt. Very forceful around the anus.'

He told police it was a 'firm grip' when Pell grabbed him by the penis and testicles, and that as time went on, it became firmer. 'Towards the end, Father Pell began to hurt me when he threw me up in the air. I didn't like it and I knew it was wrong.'

It wasn't until much later, when I had listened back to Dignan and Monument's evidence and carefully re-read their police statements, that something about what they described suddenly seemed deeply familiar. I went back and read the Southwell Report. Phil Scott had in 2002 described Pell at the 1961 camp putting his hand's down his pants and getting 'a good handful of his penis and testicles'. On one of the occasions this had happened, said Scott, when they were 'in the water, jumping in the waves'. What Dignan and Monument were describing was not identical to the abuse alleged by Scott, but it was very similar, it showed a very distinct pattern, a certain modus operandi. What the lawyers describe as similar fact evidence.

Officials in the Catholic Church who were involved with the Southwell Inquiry did not miss it when the *7.30* program broadcast our story. They were aghast at the parallels in the stories. 'I was very, very aware of that when I watched the TV set,' one official, who had compared notes with other officials involved with the Southwell case who had watched, told me much later. 'It seemed to be exactly the same ... They were talking about the same kind of offence and here is the evidence mounting up. I believed them,' the official said. 'How could you not? I was aware of the earlier story [of Phil Scott] and I thought these ones were so similar—absolutely no grooming, just straight out grabbing.'

But as I am talking with Dignan that day in Ballarat, I'm simply scrutinising what Dignan tells me on its own merits. 'Could there ever be an interpretation,' I venture, 'that it just so happened that his hands slipped down there, you know, by mistake?' This was something that Dignan himself told police he thought the first time it happened. But it kept happening.

'Fair enough, one time,' he replies. 'But it got to a stage where every time he picked you up it was there. And ah,' he grimaces, 'not much fun, no.' He told police that the touching happened about four of the ten times that Pell threw him up into the air. He says among the kids the word about Pell began to be that he was 'a poofter', 'a very scary one'. I asked him why he thought Pell was scary.

'He'd snap your arm or snap your leg as soon as look at ya,' Dignan replies. 'Very strong and powerful.' A fiery temper. Dignan says he stopped going to the Eureka Pool soon after. There is no evidence from Dignan, nor does he allege, that Pell was ever violent with him, but he simply says he was left with the impression that something violent could happen at any moment.

Paul Auchettl, another St Alipius alumnus who was abused by the

Christian Brothers, is twelve years older than Dignan and Monument. But he too remembers seeing this 'scary' side of Pell—who knew his family—in the early seventies, when Auchettl was a teenager. Pell would offer to drive him to the pool and he too played the game. Auchettl tells me during one conversation that he always had a strange feeling that Pell was somehow 'keeping an eye' on him. But it was just his gut. He says when one of his friends stole the strap that the Brothers used to punish the kids and gave Pell a whack on the hand as a joke, Auchettl says Pell threw the boy up against the wall with a violent force that shocked them all. 'He was a sort of fearful figure,' Auchettl says. 'He was very large, very imposing, and he could raise his voice suddenly. So you stood there and listened, you didn't take him on.'

One of the other boys who was at the pool with Monument and Dignan was Gerard Murphy, who would go along with his brother David. The Murphy twins were big boys, much bigger than Dignan, and their father was a journalist on the local paper who had gone to school with Pell. Gerard Murphy knew in much later years what happened to Dignan and Monument, and he and his brother certainly played the game with Pell, but he says he believes the reason he and his brother were not targeted was because they were bigger, tougher kids who 'did not take any shit' and would have kicked up a fuss if they were touched in public. And he also thinks his dad's job made it risky for Pell. 'I was lucky,' he says. 'But Digs,' he says, using the nickname they all had for Dignan, 'was a lot smaller and he used to get launched from the front, where it would have been easier to touch him—whereas we were at the back, doing horsey rides'. So for Murphy and his brother, it remained an innocent game. 'It was cool fun, it was great fun. He never laid a hand on me,' Murphy says. But he doesn't disbelieve Monument and Dignan when they make the accusation.

The other set of twins in Monument and Dignan's circle, the Anwyls, both say that they have some memory of the game at the pool. But they did not spend anywhere near as much time there because they would go away every year for summer to Queensland.

But Lauren Rowbotham remembers feeling strange about what she witnessed at the pool. Rowbotham has decided, for the first time, to allow me to publish her corroborative account of Dignan's and Monument's story. We knew about Lauren before my story for *7.30* went to air, and she helped us in the background where she could. But she was very reluctant, as many people are, to be named or appear on television.

Rowbotham, too, is scarred by her childhood at St Alipius and she now feels that it is important to put on the public record what she says she saw. She would sit on the side of the pool and agrees that Pell would only ever play with boys. She tells me it has stuck in her mind for a particular reason: the way he would throw the boys into the air and catch them. 'He used to get them by their genitals,' Rowbotham says. 'He would grab them by the arse and the legs and the crotch. He'd never grab them by the arm or the leg. I remember thinking,

"I'm glad he's not catching me, because I've got a bikini on and it would come off",' she says. Rowbotham also remembers that her parents, who have both died, warned her about Pell. 'My parents told me to keep away from him,' she says. 'George Pell has managed so far to keep it very, very quiet. I don't know why. I know who he is. We all knew what Father Pell was like. How he has not been charged yet is absolutely beyond me.' Rowbotham believes that some of the people who have been approached by police about this issue are not telling everything they know. But then Rowbotham herself was angered by the way that the SANO detectives handled her—she feels they weren't interested in her own complaints about the teacher who abused her because they were of a violent nature, not sexual; she found their approach insensitive to the severe childhood trauma she says she suffered. She has refused to have anything to do with the taskforce since.

Roly McKenzie did not remember ever seeing anything untoward happening between Pell and the boys playing the game. She remembered Pell throwing the boys into the air, sometimes playing with a tennis ball. She found it difficult to believe anything of that sort could have occurred because she and her husband were such responsible managers of the pool and so passionate about children's welfare. Although she did say in her police statement she did not know how Pell threw the boys into the air, because she didn't 'pay that much attention to him'. She told Taskforce SANO detectives in a statement that no-one ever complained about Pell and, in fact, the children would ask her and Graeme when he was coming.

Roly had just lost Graeme when I went to see her. She was frequently teary and said for that reason, she wasn't comfortable going on camera, but gladly gave me her police statement and wished me well. Sadly, two weeks later she died. After my story went to air some months later, Andrew Bolt accused me of bias against Pell, partially because I didn't interview Roly McKenzie. I expect that at the time,

Bolt had no idea that Roly McKenzie was dead.

It wasn't just in the McKenzies' pool that some children had decidedly strange encounters with Pell. It was also in the change rooms. After swimming, Monument says Pell would frequently invite him into the Eureka change rooms. And in the change rooms, he says, things would get weird again. 'Father Pell then took off his bathers and was completely naked. Father Pell then began to dry himself and said to us, "Come on boys, dry yourselves off". I then pulled my bathers off and quickly dried myself between my legs. Father Pell would watch us when we did this.

'I don't know why Father Pell insisted that my mates and I go to the change rooms with him after he finished playing with us in the pool,' Monument says in his police statement. He points out that after this stripping off and drying episode, where Pell would warn him of the perils of chafing, he would then put his wet undies and bathers back on and jump into the pool. So the whole exercise was pointless from a chafing point of view. There was no need for him to get 'changed' at all—he had nothing to change out of, nothing to change into. If the priest had merely an innocent motive, why did he, as Monument alleges, invite Lyndon into the change room at all? Why did he insist they get changed when they were only going to run back into the pool again? Monument told police the only theory he was left with: 'I look back now and think that he only wanted to perve on us when he was naked.'

 Monument tells me that he struggled to make sense of it in his young mind. 'I don't really know what went through my mind,' Monument remembers. 'Like, I didn't like it, but because it was the Church and he was just, he was George Pell, you just weren't game to ever say anything, you know what I mean? So,' he says, raising his eyebrows and shrugging fatalistically, 'I just tried not to think about it.'

 Some weeks before I met Darren Mooney, I spoke to Darren's older brother, Peter. Peter is now also a teacher. Each brother was not aware that I had spoken to the other until after our interviews. Again, I took care not to pollute conversations with accounts of what others had told me. I'm not even sure how Peter's name came up—he was just one of those on the Ballarat grapevine. Peter remembers Pell turning up to the pool frequently in summer too, from the time when Peter was about twelve. That would make it approximately 1974.

Peter was another victim of St Alipius—the notorious Best and Dowlan got at him too—it started when he was just eight. He spent the better part of a decade 'being called a liar by QCs' who were representing the Brothers in criminal cases. Peter and the other victims prevailed, but it came at a cost. 'A lot of my mates are dead now,' he tells me softly.

Peter remembers Pell playing the game, but he also remembers Pell in the change rooms. 'Everyone used to say, "Pell's in there again",' Peter remembers. 'He used to give me the creeps.' Peter says that in the change rooms during his time, which was before Lyndon Monument's, Pell would sit on a bench across from the urinals and stare at the boys. 'I did not like him,'

Peter says. 'You just got a sense about him.' As we speak on the phone, Peter describes the layout of the pool change rooms, where Pell would sit, where the urinals were, where the showers were. He has no doubt in his mind what the priest was up to.

As for the other, younger, Mooney brother, Darren—he too was very wary of Pell in the change rooms. He said the priest would parade around, naked and unabashed, in front of the boys. 'Since the Royal Commission came to Ballarat, there's been a fairly high level of talks about, or allegations about George and his misconduct and paedophilia-type activity,' Darren says. 'Of course, it's allegations at this point.' But he says within his own little friendship circle, the St Alipius boys who went to the pool, the discussion about the weirdness in the change rooms, the inappropriate vibe around the pool, came long before the Royal Commission. 'Look, it's something that we've talked about for years,' Darren says. 'Well before any abuse allegations came up. We have a reunion every year and it's one of the first things that's ever mentioned—you know, how could someone like that put themselves in that position? In a change room, it just seemed odd.'

The odd bit, according to Darren, was that Pell would just be standing there, naked, for longer than he needed to be, on a regular basis. 'And he'd be towelling himself off,' Darren says, motioning as if he has a towel diagonally across his shoulder and back. The motion is distinctive and identical to another demonstration of Pell towelling himself off that I had been shown by someone who had never met nor heard of Darren Mooney and was talking about another inappropriate incident in change rooms that took place a good seven years after the time at the Eureka Pool. The person demonstrating it lived 110 kilometres from Ballarat and knew nothing about what had happened there. I will get back to the account of that incident by that person—named Les Tyack—later. Suffice to say that when Darren motioned with the imaginary towel in precisely the same manner, the hairs on the back of my neck stood on end.

Being a teacher himself, Darren lives in a time of working-with-children checks, male teachers being cautioned not to even give the kids a hug, stringent child protection policies, mandatory reporting. But he insists that he is not just imbuing Pell's behaviour in the change rooms with the societal norms of today. He says that even in his teens, he began to feel that this was inappropriate and weird.

'Going through adolescence and what I'd experienced at St Alip's, I think I came to the realisation, probably for the first time when I was about fifteen, sixteen, that what I saw in the pool [and the change room] was probably not what should have happened ... It just didn't seem quite right that a person in that position would be undressed in a public place, amongst young kids.

'And I daresay that a man in his position should know better than to, you know, be undressing in front of kids,' he says. 'Fair enough to go and swim and play with kids and do what you've got to do. But at the end of the day, to put yourself in a position where you're naked in front of young children, I just think it's unacceptable.'

Young Lyndon didn't speak up about what happened. This was an era where children were seen and not heard and, at St Alipius, he knew of kids who had been severely punished for making accusations about the Christian Brothers. 'They'd come to school with bruises and that from telling their parents and stuff, so a lot of people just kind of kept everything to themselves,' he says.

Pell never said a word about this behaviour either, Monument says. 'No, he just made like it was normal.'

'Now you've got kids,' I continue, 'how would you feel about a priest doing those things?'

His eyes glisten and he gets a hard look about him. 'I probably shouldn't say how I'd feel, because I would be very angry and yeah, I'd never let anyone touch my children like that.'

When Monument sees the Cardinal on television now, he feels a violent surge pulse through his body. 'I hate George Pell for everything he's done,' he says. And that's not just what he says the Cardinal did to him all those years ago—it's Pell's front seat in the institution which condoned and brushed under the carpet rampant abuse that went on in Ballarat, and Monument's belief, like every Ballarat survivor I have spoken to, that Pell must have known.

Monument says he saw Pell play the game with other boys for many summers after 1978–79, well into Monument's teens. And indeed, Pell only left Ballarat in 1984. 'I'd see him at the swimming pool and he knew who we were,' he says, giving a knowing nod. 'He'd just look because, we'd look, and then he'd look away. We'd look, because by then, we'd be talking about him, you know? He'd just walk along and look like that,' he says, demonstrating a furtive, sideways glance, 'and then he'd just walk away.

'But I can tell you today, if he came back, he'd know exactly who I am. And he wouldn't be able to look me in the eye.'

'What would you do if you were face to face with him?' I ask.

'I'd just ask him to admit and be honest,' he replies. 'And I'd say to him, you know, "Look, we've all stuffed up, we've all made mistakes, like, be honest about it. Let's fix what's happened." This town has been fucken ruined. Ruined. It really has. And you'll only hear about one third about what happened. Because there's so many more that just don't come out.' He takes a swig of his glass of water. 'And there's a lot of people that don't come out because their parents were very high in the Church. They were easier for the priests to get than people like us. You know what I mean? So there's a lot of people whose parents were very, very close to the Church who probably copped it worse than us.'

Indeed, when I ring some of the people that Monument suggested I call to possibly corroborate what happened with Pell, they say they can't remember, but mention by the way that Pell helped their brother out of legal scrapes, that Pell was very close to their father, that Pell put in a good word for someone in their family. These stories are legend in Ballarat. Pell the fixer. Or, as Paul Auchettl calls him, 'back door George'. He made himself indispensible. And perhaps that's part of the reason why these types of allegations have taken so long to come out. That and the fact that child abuse allegations always take a long time to come out—thirty-three years on average, said the Royal Commission. Thirty-three years before, as Peter Blenkiron says, the 'pimple pops'.

Damian Dignan stopped going to the Eureka Pool after 'the game' became so rough that, he says, Pell was really hurting him. But he says he continued to have confession with Pell. And in the confessional, he believed the priest to be playing mind games with him, goading him into admitting what had happened. Testing him. 'It's sort of hard to explain, just sitting in the confession box, with a very, very strong, scary man sitting on the other side,' Dignan says.

'You might have knocked off your sister's play lunch, or something like that, and it wasn't good enough. [He'd say] "Tell me what you've really done wrong",' he says. 'And you couldn't think of what you've done wrong. And I know what he meant.'

'What do you think he meant?' I ask him.

'[For me to] tell me what he'd done. As in, the way he groped ... held [me]. The way he threw me in the air,' he replies.

'Do you think that he was implying that you had done something wrong by allowing it to happen? Is that what you're getting at?' I ask further.

'Yes.'

But Dignan says he couldn't confess it. 'As an 8-year-old boy, what have I done wrong? I had done nothing wrong ... I think he was trying to tell me in his way, "if he thinks that I'm doing something wrong to him, I might have to shut him up".' There is, of course, no evidence that Pell was ever violent to Dignan, but as the likes of Auchettl and Rowbotham attest, Dignan was not the only one who felt scared of the priest.

I ask him how he has felt, watching Pell's ascendancy, first through the Church in Ballarat, then through the Australian Church, and to Rome. 'Absolute joke,' he mutters, darkly. 'Don't get me wrong, I believe in the

Catholic Church. I do. I believe in Jesus, I believe in God. But that man is evil. And he should not be there. Should not be there, where he is. He's got a sickness. And probably, today, if I looked at him, I'd be a scared little boy again.'

Two months after I first interviewed Dignan, the *7.30* story was due to go to air. It was a Friday night in July and we had already emailed a list of questions off to Pell in Rome through his lawyers. I left the office and went straight to a school disco for my 6-yearold daughter. It was a chaotic sensory overload of flashing lights, thumping Taylor Swift music and little kids with glowing bracelets and lollipops in their mouths. I was exhausted and trying to pretend to my excited daughter that my mind wasn't elsewhere. I saw a friend of mine who is a mother in the neighbourhood and, like me, had grown up in a Catholic family. 'What's wrong? You look so pale,' she asked me. I told her I had a very big story and I could think of little else. She asked me what it was. I figured, given the questions had gone out, I could allude briefly to the secret I'd been keeping all those months. 'Pell,' I replied, raising my eyebrows meaningfully. My friend's smile disappeared. All of the colour drained out of her face. 'Allegations about him as perpetrator?' she asked. I nodded. My friend took one look at me and said this, without stopping:

'Catholic World Youth Day, Canada, 2002. I was working for the Church. And I remember we were staying at this hotel and there was this swimming pool. And I remember seeing George Pell with these young boys.' My mouth dropped open. 'And he was throwing them up into the air and piggybacking them and I don't know, there was something about the way he was doing it, I couldn't put my finger on it, but something was just not right. I couldn't tell you for certain that he was abusing those boys, no way, I didn't see anything specific, but I just felt sick about it. And I've never forgotten it.' She shook her head slowly.

I had said nothing to my friend about the nature of the allegations, no detail about anything at all. Just his name and a nod in agreement that it was about allegations against him directly. My ears started ringing. I told her that she needed to speak to Victoria Police. I told her that some of the allegations concerned a swimming pool where exactly that sort of behaviour was going on, in the 1970s. She looked at me and kind of nodded and didn't say much more, and walked away to fetch her kid from the dance floor. I just stood there, numb, among the bobbing heads, and the disco lights and Pharrell Williams blaring from the speakers. 'Mum, Mum, Mummmyyyy!!!' I turned to see my 6-year-old daughter, who had been pulling on my leg, trying to get my attention. 'Let's dance to "Happy"!'

22

AFTER 'THE GAME'

The truth is rarely pure and never simple.

Oscar Wilde

Some time after the Pell business at the pool, Lyndon Monument says his brother Craig got wind of what the priest had been up to. It was Damian Dignan who let Craig know. Monument says his brother cautioned him it was best not to speak up about it. 'With the George Pell thing, we just kept that quiet and kept it all amongst us. Because you feel like a dickhead,' Monument says. 'No-one wanted to be called a gay-bo. And, you know what I mean, when your friends, when you are young, you just don't want that shit getting out.'

The fear of being a 'gay-bo' was a chilling one in 1970s Ballarat. Paul Tatchell is a survivor of rape by Brother Dowlan in the dormitory at St Patrick's

College in 1974. He's a representative on the local shire council and, unlike many other survivors whose lives have gone pear-shaped, he's done very nicely for himself in business—he refuses to let the abuse beat him, he says, because then, 'he wins'. But Tatchell remembers the utter social isolation of being a kid targeted by a paedophile and the mortification of the gay connotation. 'The greatest insult ever in Ballarat was to be called a poofter,' Tatchell tells me. 'If you were called a poofter, your life was over.' So, the boys who were targeted by the Christian Brothers or the priests kept absolutely shtum.

In some perverse way, perhaps because of the silence caused by this rampant homophobia, if you were a member of the clergy and sexually interested in boys, you could quite comfortably escape the same ignominy. You could rely on your victims not wanting to be seen as 'gay-bos'. You could easily fly under the radar. If things got a bit heated, you might be moved to another parish or to another school. You wouldn't lose your job. You wouldn't lose your prestige. And you wouldn't lose your constant access to children. As Ridsdale did for a good two decades after one of his superiors first found out about his secret life and Dowlan managed to do despite decimating St Alipius and St Patrick's with his sadistic abuse.

Whatever Craig Monument kept to himself, beyond his brother's secrets about Pell (and the teacher who abused Lyndon) will never be known. Lyndon lost his brother to suicide in 2007. It followed the earlier suicide of Lyndon's wife, Kim, in 2003, before she even made her thirty-second birthday. She left behind Lyndon and their two children. Craig was forty and left behind a young son. He is named in a report delivered by Ballarat detective Kevin Carson to the Royal Commission.

'So abuse in the Catholic Church has had a big impact on your family?' I ask him. His eyes well, his lip trembles. 'Yeah,' he spits the word out like a sour lolly. 'On my family and on a lot of other families. I worry so much about my mum and there's so many other old people out there—they've ruined their lives. Because it's horrible living with someone suiciding in your life. It's horrible having to live with that. And I know a lot of people that have to live with that. And for people to realise that they've stuck up for the Church all their lives and then their children are dead...' he shakes his head as a tear falls messily down his face. 'It's just wrong.'

I ask him how many people in Ballarat he knows who have been abused by clergy. He sniffs and stares at me. 'Fifty or more.'

'And how many people do you know who have died [by suicide]?'

He puts his head in his hand and rubs his face vigorously. 'Upwards of fifteen.'

'That's an enormous cross for a community to bear,' I continue.

He nods slowly. 'All from one school,' he says.

'St Alipius?'

He sighs and nods. 'That's where it all started. There's still places in this town where we drive past every day and you see the gouges out of the telegraph pole where you know that friends have run into it to kill themselves,' he says exhaling forcibly and bitterly. 'They put a rail up around it, but like, it still doesn't stop every time you've got to drive past it, thinking about, you know,' his lip trembles, 'your mates and they fucken … sorry…' he says raising his hand to apologise to me for swearing. 'They lived a horrible life and couldn't cope with it. And he just wipes his hands,' Monument says, referring to Pell. 'He doesn't have to drive past that pole every day. He doesn't have to look at people, kids that haven't got their fathers, because they fucken killed themselves because of what they had done to them.

'They don't have to deal with it,' he says, referring to the Church hierarchy. 'We have to deal with it.'

Damian Dignan also kept it close to his chest. He had good reason. Because, like Monument, Dignan has made a complaint to Victoria Police about another abuser at St Alipius. And his childish attempt to blow the whistle on that abuse went horribly wrong. The woman, he says, was a student teacher and he says her name was Miss Karen. He believed she worked as an understudy of sorts for a time to their Grade 4 teacher. To date Victoria Police have not been able to find who Miss Karen was and where she came from. St Alipius' records from the time are scant.

Dignan says she had shoulder-length dark hair, and if she were in a line-up today, he'd pick her straight away. Lauren Rowbotham also remembers Miss Karen being there—she believes she was a student teacher from Aquinas College, where, incidentally, Pell taught—and when I ask her for a description, she says she had longish brown hair, and, she thinks, a somewhat squeaky voice. But she says they had many student teachers come through and beyond that, she can't remember much more about Miss Karen. Dignan says that on several occasions in class, he asked to go to the toilet and the teacher said Miss Karen could accompany him. There, he says, she would sit on a toilet in the cubicle, stroke his penis to arouse him, and place his penis in her vagina. Afterwards, she would wipe him dry and walk him back to class.

'Miss Karen suddenly vanished from class,' he says in his police statement. 'I don't know where she went or why she left.' He never saw her again. Damian Dignan only ever told two people about what happened with Miss Karen. One was his little mate Lyndon. 'You got off lightly,' young Lyndon told him. The other person he told, he says, was his mother. 'She took her shoe off and hit me in the face about six or seven times and said I was dirty.'

'So that can't have given you much confidence to go and tell her about George Pell?' I venture.

'No.'

'Why do you think your mum did that?'

'I wish I had the answers,' he says, his voice faltering a little. 'Catholic system, I think. I–I don't ... I can't answer you that one,' he says, blinking. 'I don't hate her for it ... Parents back then were very misled.'

So Dignan decided that, apart from the odd occasion when he and Monument would vent together after a few beers when they were older, he would keep the whole business with Miss Karen and Pell under his hat.

'I never spoke of it. Sometimes, it would go away for two years, then six months of your life it would haunt ya,' he says. 'Then it'd go away, then it'd haunt ya. And I never, ever dealt with it,' he says, shaking his head. 'Never spoke of it. My partner of a lot of years—two children—knew something was wrong. I gave her a bit of a hint a couple of times, but never spoke of it. And just wanted to move on.'

But while he seemed functional, it had a devastating effect on his family life. '[I was] very distant. Didn't show emotion. Didn't know how to show love.' His eyes start welling with tears again. 'Took to alcohol. To not have … feelings. My way of never speaking of it. I lost everything I had.' Dignan swallows, really trying to keep it together. Something clicks in the back of his throat and he has to force out the words. 'My partner, beautiful children, a home…' He looks skyward and his eyes well. '…Freedom. Yeah.' He is a man who has made horrible mistakes and hurt people he loved. A man who finds himself, at the age of forty-six, living alone in a granny flat because of the mistakes he has made. A man with substanceabuse problems. Dignan is only a few years older than me, but he shuffles around like an elderly invalid.

Much later I speak to another Ballarat local, Pat Moran, who knew Dignan when he was younger. He is absolutely shocked when he sees the *7.30* story and barely recognises Dignan. He tells me that Dignan was a great young guy. A decent guy. When Darren Mooney sees Dignan on our program, he also can't believe it's the same bloke he hasn't seen in years. He tells me Dignan was an excellent footy player.

I ask Dignan the question I have to ask, the question I always hate asking survivors because I know it offends them terribly. So I tell him how I hate to ask it. 'Has it ever occurred to you to ever harm a child in that way?' He is blunt and immediate in his answer. 'No. No. Never. Never.' He pauses for a few seconds. 'I'll tell you the honest truth, I've never had much to do with children,' he admits.

'Too painful?'

'Mmm ... Um, they used to think I was a bit cold,' he looks off into the middle distance. 'Yeah,' he barks, trying not to cry again. '[I was] very distant. Didn't show emotion. Didn't know how to love. Took to alcohol. To not have feelings. My way of never speaking of it ... That's the problem with males,' he adds, wiping away his tears. 'We don't know how to talk enough.

'For years, I was very angry,' he says. 'I grew up a very angry young bloke. I took a lot of my anger out on myself. Self-destruction. And other people who cared about me and loved me.' After he split with the mother of his children, he took up with another woman, who was also a survivor. When the relationship soured he pursued her from Ballarat to Adelaide. He was aggressive to her and would explode into anger. Her children were very fearful of his temper, although they say he never actually harmed them. He was, by all accounts, pretty awful during that period. He is ashamed of himself and her family can't stand him. He was arrested for assault of that woman, but never convicted. It's fair to say he probably got a lucky break there. He was convicted of another assault, of drink-driving offences, of drug possession. There is no sugar-coating the fact that during that time, Dignan was not a nice man to be around.

In my company, years down the track, he is always just gentle, courteous, but beaten by life. He shuffles around his granny flat in a baggy old t-shirt, tracksuit pants and thongs. His large brown eyes are bloodshot. He sighs a lot. He takes responsibility for his own actions—doesn't resile from who he has been—but sometimes struggles to form the sentences to express his feelings. Monument believes Dignan is drinking himself to death.

Dignan got to Victoria Police's Taskforce SANO before Monument. In May 2015, Dignan had been watching the Royal Commission in Ballarat and reading the survivors' accounts in the newspapers with an elderly woman who owned the house in front of his granny flat. She was a dear friend to him. He spilled his guts to her about Pell and Miss Karen. She convinced him that he should go to the Royal Commission and say his piece. She drove him down to the Ballarat Courthouse, where the Commission was sitting, and deposited him on the doorstep.

'I went in and stated my name and said I was at St Alipius in the seventies and they wanted to talk to me in an interview room,' Dignan says. '[I was there] about two hours.' The Royal Commission staff contacted Taskforce SANO and that's how the investigation began. I spoke to someone who works around the Royal Commission, whom I discovered had met Dignan that day. I didn't ask the staff member anything about what Dignan said or any details of the case—by that stage I had already interviewed Dignan and didn't want to compromise the person. But I asked them what they thought of Dignan. Did they believe him?

'Yes,' the person replied. 'I did. We get a lot of people who walk through these doors and one of the first things they bring up is compensation. That's always a red flag for me. He didn't want anything. He just came in here, quietly said his piece and walked out. He had nothing to gain by telling it.'

Dignan made his statement to Taskforce SANO's Detective Senior Constable David Rae in July 2015. He told Rae a list of names of people he went to school with who had also attended the Eureka Pool. At the top of the list was Lyndon Monument. Dignan at that point had not seen Monument for a couple of years and certainly long before either of them thought of speaking to police. While they both say they will hold a lifelong brotherly love for each other forged in the trauma they suffered, they are simply too bad an influence on each other to stay in touch. Monument later tells me that if they were still hanging out, still going on the wild benders they always ended up on, he'd probably be in jail or dead.

When the cops went to see Monument, he did not welcome them at first. 'Taskforce SANO made phone calls to me and I didn't want to be involved and that, so I kept throwing them off,' he says. 'Eventually, they asked me if I'd give them five minutes of my time, which I did.' Monument says he just didn't want to open up the wound of the abuse. 'Because it was a lot of pain for not only me, but for a lot of other people and I had learned to deal with things by just keeping them close to me, I s'pose. So I didn't want to create...' he trails off, '...for my Mum and stuff like that—you know what I mean? Problems, I s'pose. Or worry. I'd rather worry myself.'

It is hardly the picture of a man who, as some have tried to paint him and Dignan since I broadcast their accusations on *7.30,* was a vexatious, delusional complainant. Monument approached neither Victoria Police, nor me. I found him through his lawyer, Ingrid Irwin. When I approached him through Irwin, Monument was simply ready. He had been waiting for almost a year for the Pell investigation to come to a head, and after Pell declined to come back to Australia 'on doctor's orders', Monument feared he would never come back.

Monument appeared on every occasion I spoke to him as lucid and coherent. Sometimes his memory for dates is not great—he shares that with almost every survivor of childhood sexual assault I have ever met, particularly those who have had substance-abuse problems. And he is unabashed about the battering he has given his brain cells over the years with drugs and alcohol. He presents as far more clean-cut than Dignan. His closely cropped hair is clean and steely grey. His silvery goatee is neatly managed. His eyes are small and sharp and somehow birdlike. He wears his heart and his foibles on his sleeve. He has a jocular, friendly manner. He's likeable.

He struck me as a man who has had a tragic life for a number of reasons and has made some pretty rotten mistakes, which left him hurtling down a serious criminal trajectory. He has let down everyone he loves. But despite some of his weaknesses, in all the conversations I had with him, nothing he said made me think he was on a delusional vendetta. Quite the opposite. Monument strikes me as the kind of guy who really couldn't be bothered with that kind of caper. He can't be bothered with survivors' groups or Facebook forums or compensation schemes. He would rather just talk to a mate at the pub.

I ask Irwin for her take on the theory that he has some sort of maniacal vendetta—proffered by Pell supporters who have never met Monument and know nothing about him beyond a news cut on his assault charge and what they've seen on *7.30* in my story. Has it ever occurred to her that Monument is simply engaging in a very high-stakes and poisonous campaign against an innocent man because of what he perceives Pell represents?

She rolls her eyes. 'No, absolutely not,' Irwin says. 'His experience with George Pell, and his response and his position on George Pell now, [are] based on what George Pell did to him. He's not like that. He's not a complicated person ... He's a survivor and he doesn't need to embellish anything, he doesn't need to add to anything. He's very honest. He's a humble man.

'I don't think Lyndon has an agenda about anything. I think he's just trying to find a way to survive, albeit poorly at times. I think [that's] totally to be expected. It's amazing that he's survived, really.'

In fact, Monument had more motivation to keep his head down and never go public. He had, after all, a chequered history with Victoria Police. The combined effect of deaths of his wife and his brother and the abuse he says he suffered had an awful impact on Monument, who had once run a successful business with his brother and comes from a decent family. 'That's why I took to drugs,' Monument tells me, tearfully. 'Just to blank it all out. And then, to this day, I know it sounds horrible and I would never hurt myself because I love my family and me kids, but I really don't like living. Like, I don't care if I get hit by a bus. I miss my wife, but I'd never do anything to hurt my kids either, so I just keep battling.'

Despite the embarrassment of speaking about his criminal past, Monument understands that it's necessary for me to know it all and to publish it so it does not look like he has anything to hide. He understands this because since he made his complaint to Victoria Police, he now knows loosely what happened to Phil Scott after he made his complaint in the Southwell case.

As Irwin puts it, 'I don't doubt that people will look for anything and we've seen Pell's lawyers do it before and they'll do it again.

'So many victims have trouble,' says Irwin, who, as a survivor of childhood sexual abuse herself, has that same air of vulnerability they all have. 'They have trouble with drugs, they have trouble with crime, start with, maybe, petty crime. They're angry, they're frustrated, they've been disrespected. You're changed as a person. It changes who you are, childhood sexual abuse. So to cope with it, you will turn to drugs, you will turn to alcohol.

'I'm no different to someone that's hanged themselves. We're all the same. We all have a common experience and it's horrible. It's like people hold up a picture of themselves as a child—you're stuck there. Whatever your issues are, you're there. You go there in a split second. You never forget it. People say, "Are these people making it up?" And you know you could test them a hundred times and they will say the same thing. You never forget what happens to you. You never forget.'

Lyndon Monument did not forget and his life derailed spectacularly. After the death of his wife and later his brother, Monument got into what he calls a 'very toxic relationship'. 'Mum and my sister basically looked after the kids and I would just drink non-stop, stay awake for three and four days at a time and the partner I was with, she was on drugs too. Our life just spun out of control—there was violence, there was assaults, there was everything. And in the end it just came crashing down. I was jailed.'

While Monument's tragic history perhaps contextualises his actions at that time, he is at pains not to use it as an excuse. He made very poor choices. His family, too, do not want him to be painted in that way. 'I deserved jail for what I did,' he says.

'And I don't blame that on nothing.' What he did, in 2010, was go on a drug-fuelled, sleepless bender and, over a dispute about drugs, went to the house of a man who was with his partner. 'I walked in the door and I assaulted him and I assaulted my partner,' Monument says.

'It was pretty reckless, I took to him with, I think it was, a cricket stump. And I punched her in the side of the head and I'm pretty sure I knocked her out at the time.' He then headed out bush for three or four days, still not sleeping, still up to his eyeballs on methamphetamines and booze. Eventually a couple of his mates came and got him and he was admitted to psychiatric services in Ballarat for twenty-one days. After he was released, Monument was arrested. He was convicted and jailed for eleven months.

This was, of course, mortifying for his mother and the rest of his family—with such a distinctive name in a relatively small part of a relatively small town. And Mrs Monument had already had her share of terrible heartache.

While all the Monuments were supportive of Lyndon going to the police and firmly believe he is absolutely telling the truth about Pell and the teacher, they felt very anxious about him going public on the ABC and the impact that it would have on the family. Monument relies on their support. There was little for him to gain from speaking out, from inventing a story about a very powerful man.

When I heard some of his criminal history before I met Monument, I had, I am ashamed to say, pictured someone altogether different. I too was worried that he might not be 'credible'. I had, frankly, a low socio-economic stereotype in my head and Lyndon Monument is not that stereotype. I did not expect to warm to him—I loathe domestic violence and this was, after all, a man who had violently assaulted his partner. But he makes no excuses for that. He is clearly genuinely sorry, for what that is worth. He says he feels 'shit' about himself for it. He is likeable, polite, funny, with an Aussie larrikin quality. After years of substance abuse and self-destruction, he now finally holds down a steady job, he has good friends and family who clearly love him and care about him. 'Lyndon's a good person,' his old school friend Lauren Rowbotham says. 'He's got a good heart. He's fried and marinated his brain, but he's got a good heart. He'd do anything for you.' Monument's kids feel like they have a dad back for the first time in years. He leads a quiet life. On the whole, he is managing.

While Monument was brought up a staunch Catholic, he doesn't think he'll be buried a Catholic. Too much water has passed under that bridge. 'I've lost hope in the Catholic Church. And I lose more hope every day, because they just keep covering up. Like, now is the perfect opportunity to just come out and get the whole lot out, over and done with, once and for all, but I feel like it's going to just keep dragging on and on because the truth's never going to come out. Like, just fucken tell the truth once, because it's happened.

'We can't change what's happened. We can't bring back those who have died and those who are alcoholics and drug addicts, but at least we can fix it, you know? And make sure that our grandchildren, or your children—you know, it never ever happens again. Because,' he says, inhaling sharply and staring at me steadily, 'it's fucking horrible. And if there's one kid that it didn't happen to, then that's a win. A massive win.'

He makes it clear that he's not after compensation—it couldn't change his life, couldn't undo what's been done. 'Money or nothing won't make no difference to me, so they can take their money and shove it. I'd just rather see George Pell come back and be honest. That's all I want ... You sit there and you have to listen to him talking about honesty and you'll go to hell if you don't tell the truth. Well, where is he going?'

Irwin believes that the dam in Lyndon Monument has burst. 'When he made his statement, I believe that he thought, "that's the big thing". Over the period of time where there hasn't been anything,' she says, referring to waiting for the police to act, 'Lyndon's been frustrated, because he's strong and ready for something to happen, and then when it doesn't, it's a difficult space to operate in ... It's like, "once I've told, something's going to happen and now the weight's off me and people will do their jobs".'

But of course, as hard as people try to do their jobs, a prosecution of this nature is about as difficult as it gets. A member of, effectively, a foreign government, with prima facie diplomatic immunity, commits alleged crimes with multiple victims decades ago, some of the complainants have substance-abuse problems and criminal convictions, alleged perpetrator lives overseas and could easily move into a jurisdiction which has no extradition treaty with Australia. It doesn't get much trickier, for detectives hoping to get a result.

Years of seeing these cases has made Irwin extraordinarily cynical about the system: 'To actually go to the police, it's at crosspurposes, really, with your mental health.'

'That's a pretty appalling indictment,' I counter, 'on the system.'

'Well it is,' she admits. 'If someone could show me different statistics, to what I know, if someone could introduce me to clients that have been respected by the process [I might feel differently] … I feel victims are on their last legs.'

Monument hopes that by coming forward, he will encourage others who are like him, who have held it all in, to also decide to tell their truth. 'We shouldn't feel ashamed of what happened to us … it's not our fault and we weren't wrong, you know what I mean? I just want people to realise that, like, we didn't do it, and hope that they can talk to someone and just try to live a better life instead of hating their life … I don't care about my life any more, I can't wait to see my wife again,' he says, looking to the heavens.

That's the thing about all this: it's not a good news story. It's the story of a guy that really struggles with life, who says he hopes that by telling the truth, the burden of hiding for so long will be lifted. But even then, he'll probably still, as he would put it, get on the piss after he does it. Indeed, after my interview with him, I watch him down in quick succession three schooners of some sort of whisky and ginger ale concoction.

'I work, I've got a great mate who looks after me and tries to keep me working, which makes my life better,' he says, the tears springing in those PTSD eyes again. 'And when I'm not doing that,' he says, 'I just try to go to sleep as quick as I can. Because I hate being awake.'

As for Dignan, after all of the sadness and disappointment, he says he too just wants to start telling the truth. To give those around him some understanding of why his life went so pear-shaped. How a very small boy who was abused tried to tell his mum, only to be slapped around the head and told he was dirty. How a little boy who grew up in an epicentre of pain, turned out for a time to be a man he wasn't proud of being. No-one else is to blame for his crappy choices. But maybe other people, particularly those he loves, might understand them a bit more.

Before the story went to air, he told his kids about the abuse, and he says they 'respect' him. 'But I did the wrong thing by never seeking help,' he says. He says the sexual abuse and corporal punishment he received at St

Alipius—the 'beltings'—left him 'like a dog that's been beaten too much'. 'You've got no confidence. You can't talk, and you'll never talk. You feel ashamed. And yeah, you asked me how it affected me, mentally? It ruined my life. Ruined it.' He breathes out quickly. 'But I ruined it too by not getting the right help. And a lot of self-destruction. Around the people that loved me.'

'I've got to the stage in my mind where,' he says, wiping tears away, 'I don't really want an apology. I want to tell my kids why they haven't got a father. Why they lost their dad.'

Dignan got back to me later. He told me that his kids had told him off for saying that on our show. 'We do have a dad,' he said they tearfully told him. He said he'd been spending every other day with them and he'd just bought a present for his son's twenty-first.

23

THE SURF CLUB

And so I decided to report it, so that those collating all the evidence could put it aside there, and it might help form a dossier on Pell's activities.

Les Tyack

Months before I even knew Damian Dignan and Lyndon Monument existed, I met a guy called Les Tyack. Tyack is a family man who lives on a sprawling property at Torquay on Victoria's Bellarine Peninsula. Tyack has three adult kids, is a retired owner of a manufacturing business and is an open-faced, easygoing man who has had, by his own estimation, a fortunate life.

A week or so before I met Tyack, a story had been broken in the *Herald Sun* about a Victoria Police investigation into Pell himself. The story named some of the locations of alleged abuse—the Eureka Pool, St Patrick's Cathedral,

Phillip Island. But it was completely unsourced and the journalist involved had not spoken to any of the complainants who are part of the brief. It was a bold move by the paper and, undeniably, what's known in the business as 'a good get'. But when I first read the article on 20 February 2016, I was sceptical. I had been preparing for Pell's evidence from Rome in ten days' time and had already done some filming. The bureau chief for *7.30*, Sarah Curnow, and myself spent that Saturday making calls. People we trusted from the law and police had nothing for us. Even a victims' group representative told me he thought it was a beat-up—it would detract from the real work of the Royal Commission in determining what Pell covered up, he just didn't believe it.

Pell responded swiftly that morning with a statement:

> The allegations are without foundation and utterly false. It is outrageous that these allegations have been brought to the Cardinal's attention through a media leak. These undetailed allegations have

not been raised with the Cardinal by the police and the false claims investigated by Justice Southwell have been ignored by the police for over 15 years, despite the very transparent way they were dealt with by the Cardinal and the Catholic Church.

The Cardinal has called for a public inquiry into the leaking of these spurious claims by elements in the Victorian Police in a manner clearly designed to embarrass the Cardinal, in a case study where the historical failures of the Victorian Police have been the subject of substantial evidence. These types of unfair attacks diminish the work of those good officers of the police who are diligently working to bring justice to victims.

The Phillip Island allegations have been on the public record for nearly 15 years. The Southwell Report which exonerated Cardinal Pell has been in the public domain since 2002.

The Victorian Police have taken no steps in all of that time to pursue the false allegations made, however the Cardinal certainly has no objection to them reviewing the materials that led Justice Southwell to exonerate him. The Cardinal is certain that the police will quickly reach the conclusion that the allegations are false.

The Victorian Police have never sought to interview him in relation to any allegations of child sexual abuse and apart from the false allegations investigated by Justice Southwell, the Cardinal knows of no claims or incidents which relate to him.

Victoria Police responded to the Cardinal's statement by immediately referring the leak allegation to the Independent Broad-Based Anti-Corruption Commission (IBAC). That morning, I was given a number for an inspector at Taskforce SANO. Still suspicious of the story's veracity, I gave him a call. I was sitting at our local pool watching my little daughter doing swimming lessons. By this stage, the IBAC referral was already on foot. The cop nearly had kittens.

The inspector told me I would need to call Police Media—the force's liaison unit for journalists. I told him that through years of experience, in a situation like this, that was pointless. I wanted an absolutely off-the-record conversation about whether this story was a crock. I didn't want information, per se. I didn't want to compromise him. I simply wanted an indication of whether I should just get back to enjoying my weekend. He apologised, but repeated stiffly that I should call Police Media.

Within minutes, I got a phone call from a very earnest Police Media operative. She wanted to know how I got the inspector's number. I laughed at that. I said I got it from a source. She wanted to know what I knew. I said I wouldn't last long in this business if I started talking about that. But I did tell her that I knew next to nothing, had only rung the inspector to see if there were any legs at all in this story, to see if he thought it was a beat-up. The Police Media person tried to make out I had done something inappropriate. I said I would be a pretty terrible investigative journalist if I were to rely on Police Media for stories. She sort of gasp-laughed. I went back to watching the swimming. I felt in my bones that this story would go nowhere. My bones lied to me.

Sarah Curnow also made a call to another well-placed contact we thought ought to have known if there was an investigation. But that person told her they knew nothing about the investigation. Thought it had probably gone nowhere. Suffice to say that at the end of that day, we were still very sceptical about whether this whole Pell thing was a real story or not. Repeatedly going through my mind was: 'How can it not have come out? He is so high profile, we've got a child abuse Royal Commission, and all of these other people have come forward and yet this hasn't come out? Come on.'

But then, out of the blue, Les Tyack came along. Tyack came to us through Andy Burns, my producer at *7.30* in Melbourne. Andy is a terrier of a journo and a Ballarat girl. As she puts it, she speaks 'fluent Ballarat'. Andy had a call from a contact in the advocacy community who said she had this guy who had this surf club allegation against Pell. The woman knew that we were looking for Pell leads. Andy and I got on speakerphone to Tyack. He said he'd have a think about it. When I called him back, he said other journalists had contacted him in the past—*60 Minutes* had been after him. But he hadn't felt comfortable about coming forward. He now felt that the time was right and trusted us to handle his information properly. I arranged to go and visit him.

Tyack meets me on the circular driveway at his property and gives me a solid handshake. He wears rectangle wire-framed glasses, short grey hair and a neatly clipped grey moustache. I don't know what it is about Tyack, but he seems like the guy at the family barbecue, the bloke you'd trust on a school committee—you'd be pretty happy if he was your kid's footy coach. He was actually a senior office bearer at the Geelong Football Club for many years as its assistant secretary. Since his retirement, he has been a dedicated volunteer. He worked in sports management for many years and also became active in surf lifesaving at Torquay and his kids were competitive members.

It was at Torquay that Tyack first clapped eyes on Pell. It was, he estimates, the summer of 1986–87—he says that because he was still driving his son to the surf club and after that he began not to drive him any more. Tyack, who was at that time a member of the club, noticed the new bloke around the traps. He knew most of the adults at the club and asked one of the other members who this man was. 'He told me it was George Pell. I didn't know who George Pell was and had never met him before. I didn't think much further of it,' Tyack says. Tyack is not a Catholic and so is not plugged into those social networks. 'It wasn't until much later that I found out who George Pell was,' he says.

Pell was, as it happens, a frequenter and member of the Torquay Surf Life Saving Club for many years. In 2002, Pell said in a statement included in an ABC story: 'Until late January 1993 I was on holiday at Torquay, as was my practice for nearly thirty years.' Surf club annuals from the time also show Pell's name.

Tyack remembers that the priest was quite a bit taller than him and had a 'solid' build.

'So there's absolutely no doubt in your mind that this was the same George Pell?' I ask him.

'Absolutely no doubt whatsoever,' Tyack says.

A few weeks after that first fleeting sighting of Pell, Tyack had been swimming and bodysurfing at Torquay and he made his way back up the beach to the club change rooms to have a shower. 'As I walked into the club rooms I noticed a fellow in there who had been previously pointed out to me as George Pell,' Tyack remembers. 'I said, "Hi George".' Tyack drew a diagram of the change rooms for me with a black marker on my notebook. I still have it. Tyack said he had walked in from an entrance at the far right bottom corner of the room. He walked towards the top left corner, where he says Pell was standing. 'And at that time he was towelling, had the towel going across his shoulders, drying his back.' At this point Tyack does a diagonal towelling motion across his shoulders. It's the precise same towelling motion I later see St Alipius old boy Darren Mooney demonstrate for me to show how Pell would stand and towel himself off, naked, at the Eureka Pool in Ballarat in the seventies.

As Pell towelled himself off, Tyack noticed the priest had company. 'He was facing three young boys standing about three or four metres across from him,' Tyack says. He indicated in his diagram where he put his bag down behind Pell towards the top left side of the room—Pell has his back angled towards the boys who are across from him in that top left corner. He says that when he said hello to Pell, Pell angled his body around more, towards the boys and away from him. He describes the boys as 'surf grommets', none he knew in particular, but typical of the little tanned, blond, salty pre-teens that hung out at the club every day. He estimates they were aged, like Monument and Dignan, between eight and ten. 'The boys were also naked and getting changed themselves,' he says. 'I thought it was a little strange, but I put my gear down on the bench and walked into the showers.' The showers were behind a screen on the far right of the room. To walk to them, Tyack says, he did not go past Pell and the boys, but away from them.

When he came out, five to ten minutes later, to his surprise, Pell and the boys were still there. 'The boys were dressed, but Pell just had the towel over his right shoulder still facing the boys,' Tyack says. Pell was, he says, still naked. 'There was no communication between them, but Pell was looking at the boys, they were looking at him. I immediately thought, "this is not right, there is something amiss here".' In a statement he had made to the Royal Commission, he says, 'Pell did not appear as though he was going to get dressed. He was just standing there, naked, in full view of the three boys and just staring at the boys.'

I ask him what it was that made him think this was not right. 'Well, I have been around sports organisations, swimming clubs, surf lifesaving, football, most of my life,' Tyack says. 'I'd always noticed that people when they are getting changed will normally face the wall, giving them a bit of privacy. But in this situation, Pell was actually full-frontal to the three young boys,' he says. 'And I thought that was not on—very strange situation for an adult to be full frontal to three young boys.' He says he was very concerned at what he saw.

When he first got out of the shower to be confronted with this scene, Tyack says he doesn't think Pell initially realised he was there because he 'did not react and look at me'. So Tyack says he immediately spoke up. 'I said to the three young boys, ah, you know, "get dressed, finish doing what you're doing, off you go",' he says, motioning with his thumb. 'When they left, I said to George Pell, "I know what you're up to, piss off, get out of here, if I see you back in this club again, I'll call the police".'

'I was fairly strong about it,' Tyack remembers. 'Because having seen that situation, it was not right and my immediate reaction was that the boys had to go and he had to be made well aware of what he was up to.' The boys packed their things and skedaddled. When Tyack spoke up, he says Pell turned his body around to face the wall. 'He made sure at no time was I given the opportunity to see the front of him,' Tyack says. 'He had no privacy in facing the three young boys. And yet, as an adult, when I fronted, he made sure that he kept his back to me at all times ... It makes me very suspicious that he was exposing himself to those three young boys.' His concern was heightened by Pell's other reaction. 'Very suspicious ... When I challenged him, he made no response. At all. Which I thought quite odd. You know? I'm certain that if I'd been challenged in such a manner, I would have fired up with questioning—"What do you mean, what are you talking about?" But no, Pell went very silent. Didn't say a word. Which made me very, very suspicious of his activities.'

'Is there any doubt in your mind,' I ask Tyack, 'that he was up to no good?'

'Absolutely no doubt,' he returns. 'Absolutely no doubt that Pell was exposing himself to those three boys.'

Tyack says he got his things and walked outside the change rooms, where he chatted to three other members. He didn't see Pell leave. When he went to check the change rooms again about ten minutes later, the priest was gone. For reasons he now regrets, Tyack did not mention the incident to other members when he emerged from the change rooms. He felt that he had made enough of a point to Pell to stay away and that the priest would have taken his threat to go to the police seriously. With the benefit of hindsight, he dearly wishes he had done more. 'I always regret that I did not tell the other club members so that they were aware of what was going on,' Tyack years later wrote in a statement to the Royal Commission. 'At the time, I was not aware of the bigger picture and the problem that was going on with priests and teachers within the Church and schools. I thought initially that it was a once-off of Pell exposing himself. The more I have heard over the years of the incidents involving the victims of the Catholic Church, the more this incident has played on my mind.'

As it happened, Tyack never saw Pell at the surf club again. As his boys got older, he was there less often. By then an auxiliary bishop of Melbourne, Pell did in fact continue to holiday at Torquay and attend the club. By 1990–91 and in subsequent years, Pell is listed as an associate member in the club's annual report. Since the 7.30 story went to air, one of the frequent criticisms from doubters on Catholic forums has been that Pell was not stationed at Torquay, was not a parish priest at Torquay. But in Pell's own words, he holidayed there every year for three decades. He was no stranger to the surf club and there were senior members there, Catholics, who knew him well.

Some time during that year, Tyack says he mentioned the incident to two close friends, whom he says 'were obviously disgusted with the information' but, as they thought it was an isolated incident, laughed it off as simply creepy. As it happens, one of those friends is the father-in-law of an ABC journalist and the journalist has confirmed to me that Tyack's friend had discussed it with her and her husband. Like me, in the absence of other allegations, she knew there wasn't much that could be done with the information.

Tyack felt the same. But he never forgot that incident, and was bemused as he watched Pell's ascendancy. 'Every time you'd see the Pell name, the memories of that day would come flooding back, and I kept thinking, "How the heck does this man keep rising within the Catholic Church?"' Gradually, over the years, the clergy abuse scandal in the Church became a major topic of public conversation and Pell was at the centre of that discussion. 'I started to take an interest in the progress of what was happening, seeing him rise in the Church, and yet seeing more and more people coming out with accusations on the priests, on other priests' activities, and then with Pell,' he said, 'my experience with him was that he wasn't the cleanskin that he was making out in the press.'

In 2012, Tyack saw an article in the local *Geelong Advertiser* reporting a meeting of local victims of clergy sexual abuse in the area. At the end of the article was a number to ring to report any abuse. Tyack decided that it was time to put the incident on the record. 'Well, I thought that, not being a victim, there may have been other instances—as I'd caught Pell—there may have been other instances out there in the public domain that people had seen or witnessed,' Tyack says. 'And so I decided to report it, so that those collating all the evidence could put it aside there, and it might help form a dossier on Pell's activities. I saw it as being perhaps very supportive of the victims of paedophilia.' For three years, there the statement sat. This was long before any of the Pell complainants I know of came forward to Taskforce SANO. In December 2015, Tyack also made a statement to the Royal Commission. But it was not made public because the report sat outside the Commission's terms of reference, as it did not amount to an institutional response or cover-up.

A couple of months after he delivered his written statement to the Royal Commission, Tyack got a call out of the blue from a detective from Taskforce SANO. That was only a few days before I interviewed Tyack at his Torquay home. 'The information that was given to me was that police were following up a lot of inquiries and that I wasn't the only one,' Tyack says. 'But that the information I had given was very, very important to them and would certainly be followed up at some stage.' It heartened Tyack that perhaps his information could help some victims of child sexual abuse.

I ask him the obvious question that I ask all of the people who make accusations against Pell: 'There will be the allegation that there is some sort of vendetta against Cardinal Pell, that you have an underlying agenda. Do you have any sort of agenda?'

'Absolutely not, absolutely not,' Tyack says without hesitation, shaking his head deliberately and slowly. 'I've got nothing against the Catholic Church.' Tyack says he's had no other dealings with Pell, nor indeed the Church. 'It was information that I had, on an activity that was not right, and it was decided after a period of time to make that report to the relevant authorities in the hope that my information can be added to others, which will form some basis as to what Pell was all about.'

After we film some sequences with Tyack that day at his home and the surf club, I hop in the car with my cameraman and sound recordist. As is often my practice, I ask them what they thought of him. News crews meet a lot of people in their travels. In my experience, they are excellent judges of character. 'Straight as anything,' the sound recordist says. 'Absolutely,' the cameraman says. Tyack had no skin in this game, no barrows to push, he was a straight-up family man who just saw something he didn't like and thought, upon years of reflection, that he'd better tell someone about it.

From that moment onwards, I begin to feel that there might be something in this Pell business after all. I know that the Tyack allegations, on their own, would be very hard to broadcast, that the rightfully careful ABC legal team will baulk at using them, but, like Tyack said, they could form part of a larger dossier.

On the drive back to Melbourne, I take a call from a private number. On the line is a 'deep throat' I have never met, but who is clearly a senior member of the Melbourne legal fraternity and had given me very strong tips about another story which had stacked up.

Somehow or other, he gets to talking about Pell. I say it is funny he should mention him, as I had just been to interview a man who knew some pretty concerning information about Pell. The deep throat then tells me that the *Herald Sun* story was right on the money. He says that a number of people at Victoria Police and the law were extremely frustrated when Pell had cancelled his trip to Australia in December 2015 (two months before) to give evidence to the Royal Commission. He tells me he believed, as did anyone who had knowledge of this, that His Eminence had been tipped off about the Taskforce SANO investigation. That's why he didn't fly, and that's why his heart problems suddenly became so problematic that a cross-continental plane journey would be simply impossible. He has some ideas as to who he felt might have done the leaking to Pell. He urges me in the strongest possible terms to keep investigating the Pell allegations. He gives me a number of lines of inquiry—not, incidentally, to the complainants themselves, as he does not have any knowledge of who they were or who was representing them. We speak for at least an hour. Many of the things he mentions subsequently stack up.

I have never spoken to the deep throat again. He went completely to ground.

My conversation with him and my day with Tyack made me determined to keep going with the Pell investigation. When I got back to the office, my producers were still sceptical. They thought that Tyack's allegations didn't amount to much without further proof. I could see their point. But I pressed, 'Let's keep the tape—it could be useful. I want to keep going with this.'

The following week, I flew to Sydney for Pell's evidence, which was videolinked from Rome. During an adjournment on one of those three days, a contact ushered me into a meeting room. We had spoken to the contact a couple of weeks earlier to inquire whether the *Herald Sun* story was a crock. Their reply at the time was they knew nothing and it would probably go nowhere. But that, the contact said, was no longer true. This contact now had firm knowledge that there was an investigation. That there were complainants. And that Taskforce SANO was 'waiting for all this to end' (that is, Pell's Rome evidence) to march on with their inquiries. Later, I discovered that this person—who did not divulge this—had direct knowledge of the details of one of the complainants' case. 'I didn't want you to think that I was leading you up the garden path,' the contact said. 'Keep on it, keep going.' I stared at the contact, open-mouthed, and the person left the room.'

I did keep on it. And because of that, five months later, Les Tyack became a household name.

24

ON CREDIBILITY

There needs to be just a huge amount of awareness that children who are troubled are troubled for a reason.

Associate Professor Carolyn Quadrio, psychiatrist, in her evidence to the Royal Commission

One of the things that has always bugged me a little by the response to the *7.30* story on Pell was that Tyack was the clincher. The part of the story that made people convinced that the Pell allegations were true. If I had a dollar for every time I heard someone say, 'That guy at the surf club was so *credible*', 'He's got *no reason* to lie', 'That surf club man is what made me *believe* your story', then I would have been able to buy myself a pretty fancy frock.

The reason it stuck in my craw was that the corollary of what was said about Tyack was that Lyndon

Monument, Damian Dignan and Phil Scott were not, prima facie, credible. And that was because of their criminal convictions and their histories of substance abuse. People certainly pitied them and ultimately we had far more positive responses to them than negative—their community, for instance, embraced them after the story went to air. That was a great comfort to us, that they were not pilloried, given the leap of faith they took to go on our program. But the overarching response was that without Tyack (and also another deeply 'credible' witness, another 'good man', Darren Mooney), it would have been more difficult to get the public to believe them.

At the other end of the spectrum, *Herald Sun* columnist Andrew Bolt tried to use the perceived lack of credibility as part of an argument which accused the ABC of bias against Pell. He pointed to Monument's criminal record and 'history of psychiatric illness' as evidence of why Monument's claims were dubious. It was the same approach adopted by his newspaper during the Southwell Inquiry in 2002, after the private investigators acting for the Pell camp did their best work in exposing Scott with their 'Altar Boy's Life of Crime' headline. But before anyone jumps to a conspiracy theory, it was also the same newspaper that broke the story that there was a police investigation at all.

Of course, I never sought to pretend that Monument didn't have a chequered past—I declared it up front and urged him in our interview to go through the humiliation of telling me just how badly he had behaved. He did it willingly—didn't give it a second thought. He professed he had nothing to hide. But as I wish to explore in this chapter, the fact that someone has had a criminal history tied to drug abuse and depression can in fact suggest probable childhood sexual abuse, rather than rule it out.

The fact that it is often used by criminal defence barristers as a way of trying to discredit complainants is all too convenient for their clients, the paedophiles, who have destroyed children's trust and self-esteem. Child abusers who have condemned those kids to a life of trauma can tip their hats to silks who then exploit the effects of that trauma to devastating effect under cross-examination. Ballarat is full of people who have endured horrendous cross-examination. And that's the people who have survived and haven't become part of the suicide or premature death toll. The ones that the likes of Kevin Carson hasn't had to scrape out of baths or cut down from nooses strung up in their rafters.

In May 2015, a psychiatrist called Associate Professor Carolyn Quadrio from the University of New South Wales gave evidence to the Royal Commission. Quadrio is perhaps the country's most experienced practitioner on the impact of childhood sexual abuse throughout a victim's life. The Commission had such confidence in Quadrio's expertise, it devoted an entire day to her evidence. Quadrio was particularly well-qualified to explore what happens to a child's mind and behaviour when the perpetrator is a member of the clergy. As far back as the 1980s, when clergy abuse was only first becoming a topic of discussion, she conducted a landmark study on a group of thirty-two men abused by the Christian Brothers at Bindoon in Western Australia.

I flew to Sydney to interview Quadrio in her Randwick office for the *7.30* Pell story and before I did, I read the transcript of her day of evidence. I read it open-mouthed. The trajectory she described could have been written about Lyndon Monument. It made me understand Monument and Dignan so much better. And remember that both men always allege that they were twice abused, by two adults they had trusted. Not to mention the beltings and humiliation they and their classmates have told me they routinely received at St Alipius too. It made me realise how utterly convenient it is for clergy abusers that their victims' minds become so scrambled. It made me sad and angry for all the survivors that I know.

Quadrio says that when a member of the clergy abuses a child, it can be more profoundly unsettling for the victim than when it is an ordinary member of the community. She tells me that the trauma of betrayal itself can be more traumatic than the memory of the physical act of sexual abuse. 'Little children obviously grow up seeing adults as being powerful and knowing right and wrong,' Quadrio says. 'They look up to them and that's where children get their values and ideas from. That's true of all children, but when the people you are looking up to are people in the Church, it gets another dimension again.' In the case of someone like Pell, who was held up as a sort of princely figure in the town, that sense of awe and wonderment is compounded.

She explained to the Royal Commission that it's the idea of clergy, to young and unsophisticated minds, as 'god-like' creatures. 'Especially young children see a priest or a member of the clergy as someone who is close to God, really, and so, the sense of betrayal is particularly shattering because it's kind of like, not just one bad person, but it feels like, well, maybe God's bad. The loss of faith and shattering of the belief is really very damaging to a child. If a child grows up feeling, well, you can't trust anybody and everybody's bad, and even God's bad, that's what I mean about the profound characterological damage that can have.

'So abuse by members of the clergy is very profound betrayal trauma,' Quadrio says. 'You can imagine that if perhaps one parent is abusing you, there is a lot of betrayal trauma involved in that, but you can console yourself that you're just unlucky to have a bad parent and all the other people in the world are okay.

'But if it's a member of the Church, then that becomes something that's even more profound because there's a sense of "these are good people, these are the people who know right from wrong" ... The child's idea of right and wrong and trust and their world view, if you like, is completely shattered and that's a really important part of your psychology—it's like knowing that the sun will come up in the morning and go down in the evening.

'When an infant cries and a parent appears and picks them up and cuddles them and feeds them and comforts them, they learn their sense of trust and that "there are people in the world who will take care of me, the world is a good place".' She says that the idea of 'I'm okay, you're okay',—the trust in the goodness of the people responsible for a person, is 'a very fundamental level of psychology'. 'It's the basic building blocks of the personality,' Quadrio says. 'If you don't have that basic sense of trust in the world, then it's really hard to build on that foundation.'

Quadrio makes the point that if a child's family, or entire community—as in the case of Catholic Ballarat—is strongly affiliated with a religion and the clergy that represent it, often when they make disclosures they get a 'bad reception' and are 'told they are lying, it can't be true'. Such was the case with Dignan's mother beating him around the face with the shoe. Monument saw children at St Alipius who were given savage beltings by their parents for disclosing rape. As he told me, some of those people are not here today. Wayne Brennan, beaten senseless by his father and not believed by his mother after he said Pell told them he was lying about sexual abuse, took it to his untimely grave. 'The negative response from family and community can really compound the damage enormously,' Quadrio says.

'The child's sense of the world becomes damaged,' she says. 'It becomes completely destroyed in an environment like that. It's like, everyone's living a lie. What's true? What's real? What's reliable? What's good? What's bad? If everyone's living a lie, a child's view of the world is terribly distorted.'

I keep coming back to Monument's overarching feeling that all he wants is for Pell to look him in the eye and admit what Monument says he did. To admit that like Monument, he's made some mistakes, but just to own up to what Monument says are his lies. Or for Scott not being interested in a criminal prosecution, but just wanting Pell in the room, and man to man, to say 'Sorry, I did this'. And then there is The Kid, who told me he had 'trust issues' and couldn't bear to not know how I found him. The idea that someone had broken his trust was all too much for him because at a fundamental time in his development, his trust in the world was shattered.

Through her many years of practice and through coming to grips with the local and international research, Quadrio has discovered that there is a distinct difference between the way that little boys respond to abuse, compared with that of little girls. Little boys, she says, tend to 'act out' as a way of dealing with the trauma they are suffering, becoming 'rebellious, naughty or defiant', whereas, on the whole, little girls tend to cope by 'being sad, upset, withdrawing'.

'A little boy whose trust has been destroyed, who has learned to feel, well, "maybe I'm not such a good person and maybe I can't trust the world and maybe the world is bad and maybe the world sucks",' she explains. The rebellion and defiance, often not linked with child sexual abuse because they have not disclosed it, is 'very quickly labelled as "bad behaviour"'. 'And you get this really unfortunate characterisation that little boys will suffer from, that they're "bad". Once the boy acquires that label, it becomes a snowball effect—the more he's treated as bad, the angrier he gets.' She says by the time these boys finish primary school, typically, their teachers, their parents, their community is pretty sick of them. Everyone has started to give up on them and they are just seen as naughty boys.

'By the time a boy is about eleven and if he's gotten big and angry, it's very just for people to see him as bad and he gets propelled down that track and it's really hard to turn it around…' She says often the children are labelled as having, for instance, Attention Deficit Hyperactivity Disorder, or Oppositional Defiance Disorder. 'And by teenage years, boys like this are seen as delinquents.' She says the juvenile justice system is full of boys like this.

Quadrio believes part of the cause of this is the 'macho' culture, which demands that boys be 'tough' and cope with their problems and not show that they are upset—lest they be seen as 'sissies' or 'sooks'. 'And so, more and more, boys will be propelled along the path of being tough and maybe being aggressive and being violent. The older they get, the less sympathy they get, until you get to the prison situation, where you see huge numbers of men who have been seriously abused during their childhood but are now simply labelled as "bad".'

Quadrio, who worked in prisons for many years, says the research and her own experience shows '60 to 80 per cent' of men in prisons have been abused as children—whether it be physical or sexual abuse. 'There needs to be just a huge amount of awareness that children who are troubled are troubled for a reason. There's so much gobbledygook going on about this disorder or that disorder, or this allergy or that allergy or whatever, and sometimes it is, but an awful lot of child distress gets ignored or covered up.'

The common trajectory for little girls is different but also painful. On the whole, Quadrio says, little girls tend to internalise the abuse. And so in later years, they can become beset with, for instance, eating disorders, they will self-harm, they may make poor choices in life partners—often choosing dominant or abusive men—or may be drawn to prostitution; they will become oversexed or sexually insecure, they will develop borderline personality and anxiety disorders, and, like male survivors, they often have issues with substance abuse.

'In our culture where, I'm afraid, substance abuse is seen as a way that we cope ... it soon becomes a pattern,' Quadrio says. While, she says, 20 to 40 per cent of survivors of childhood sexual abuse are, somehow, resilient and manage to keep their lives together—the Darren Mooneys of this world, for instance—60 to 80 per cent do not have this resilience. And for them, the big problems are depression, substance abuse and dysfunctional relationships. 'And you see this very sad trajectory that people get on of getting into trouble because of substance abuse, dropping out of school because of substance abuse, not succeeding in employment, having dysfunctional relationships, having relationship breakdowns, having a trajectory which is downward, really.'

Mooney says to me that while he appears extraordinarily resilient and together, his survival is a day-by-day issue. 'My wife says it's something that's there in my mind all the time,' Mooney says. His particular way of coping with it is exercise—triathlons, for instance, and throwing himself into his work as a school principal.

Mooney and his friends from Brother Gerald Fitzgerald's class at St Alipius in Grade 3 have a reunion every year. Many are struggling. The Grade 3 reunion often goes a bit pear-shaped as they drown their sorrows in alcohol. 'It will never leave us,' he says. He has friends who are not as resilient as him—some have turned to alcohol and drugs, and have had trouble with the law. Some of them, he says, are 'train wrecks'. Some, like Craig Monument, are dead. But, Mooney says, inside, he feels just the same as them. It's an eternal struggle.

Chris O'Connor is a retired policeman who was formerly detective senior sergeant in charge of the Victoria Police Child Exploitation Squad. He was at the vanguard of prosecuting clergy abusers after it first became apparent in the

1980s and 1990s that there was a huge systemic problem in the Catholic Church.

He says it was not uncommon for many of the people he came across who were involved in crimes related to prostitution, alcohol abuse and drug-taking to be survivors of childhood abuse. O'Connor says, 'In my experience, all victims of this type of crime as children will have some aspect of their development adversely affected. It will obviously vary in degrees, but if nothing else, childhood innocence or developing concepts of trust are severely distorted.' He would often encounter young people who either became abusive, challenging police to a verbal or physical confrontation, or disengaged completely and maintained a contemptuous silence.

The general assumption was that they reflected poor social skills and upbringings. But significantly, he says, it often transpired that many of these angry youngsters were victims of child sexual exploitation. 'Remove the behaviour and layer of bravado and what you have got is this scared little child. But the bravado often introduces them to violence.' While he says that sexual assault is often the initial catalyst for anti-social behaviour, as you age, you must also accept that you do enter 'the realm of adult choice'.

'What happened to these people is not something in isolation—what they are doing now can be relevant to what happened to them as children. In fact, it may be the cause. But they are still two separate issues,' he says, arguing that alleged lack of 'credibility' cannot be imputed just because a child exploitation survivor has a history of drugs and crime.

However understanding O'Connor may be about the foibles of the child victims turned adult substance abusers he met in his work, they rarely receive the same compassion when it comes to finding themselves up against a seasoned silk in a courtroom. And the Catholic Church likes to stump up for a classy sort of barrister.

For example, Robert Richter, QC, who, it's reported, has been engaged by His Eminence to defend the child sexual allegations against him. Richter pulled off the legal defence of the century by getting an acquittal for one Mick Gatto for the murder of Andrew Veniamin, during the underworld wars of the early 2000s. He is precisely what you want when you are accused of a very serious crime.

I remember speaking to a lawyer involved in Royal Commission proceedings, who said that he felt a sense of frustration when he saw complainants come into the Commission, because, he said, it 'lulls them into a false sense of security'. 'They think [if they have not already been through a court process] that this is what they are going to encounter, when in reality it is nothing like that. I feel like we're throwing them to the wolves.'

'When powerful people prolong legal processes,' Quadrio says, 'you can exhaust the victim. You exhaust them in terms of their resources, you exhaust them psychologically. Over time, their support systems break down. Everyone begins to suffer from fatigue and their resources are being drained and so people begin to give up.'

That's precisely what happened to Phil Scott, the complainant in the

Southwell Inquiry. When I went to see him at his home in inner Melbourne in May 2015, Scott answered the door politely. He smiled and asked me what I wanted. Even when I said I was a journalist, he did not seem bothered—which surprised me. But then it seemed to dawn on him. As the realisation skated across his face, it darkened, visibly. 'Is this about Pell? I've got nothing to say about him. Or that. Nothing. Ever. You're lucky my wife didn't answer, you'd have a piece of her mind.' Father Bob Maguire told me that reopening the wound of the public humiliation Scott suffered is just too painful. He vowed never to open it again. At Scott's home, I scrambled and tried to explain to him that the other complainants had come forward, that I understood him, that he was not alone this time. But he glowered. The trauma of the Southwell Inquiry, the private investigators, the silks, the leaking to the *Herald Sun* had, as Maguire said, retraumatised him. As his solicitor Peter Ward, told me, 'I think he built himself up, suffered the unfair disclosures in the media, went through that process, felt he had a moral victory [because Southwell said he believed both Pell *and* Scott] and does not want to go through any of it again.'

For Pell's legal team, the rough and tumble was all part of the game. They won. I know some of them honestly believed Scott was making it up. They thought that because people do. They thought it for the same reasons that everyone thought Les Tyack was the clincher. People think someone who went off the rails isn't credible. The Quadrio view, however well researched and however correct, is still not widespread and certainly was not in 2002.

Of course, through it all, Pell's solicitor is Richard Leder. In one of those strange twists of fate, Leder was my former solicitor when I was at Channel Seven, with whom I'd worked long and hard; he was a lawyer who went above and beyond—calls after hours, good advice about even non-legal matters. I liked him very much.

When I contacted Pell's media person in Sydney, Katrina Lee, to request an interview with the Cardinal for the *7.30* story, Leder became involved immediately. The media advisor initially came back to me, declining an interview. She wanted to know two things and two things only: when and where the incidents had taken place. She wanted exact dates. 'Cast your mind back to your childhood,' I said. 'Can you remember exact dates on which things happened?' She quipped that in the Royal Commission, some of the complainants had given exact dates. I answered that the complainants had only given Victoria Police approximate dates—the summer of 1978–79, for instance. I told Lee I would send her an email with a list of the dates. I did so. I heard nothing back by the deadline I had given, then suddenly a letter arrived from Leder, on behalf of the Cardinal, with a statement denying the allegations. This is what the statement said:

> Cardinal Pell will not be giving an interview to the ABC *7.30* Report. He emphatically and unequivocally rejects any allegations of sexual abuse against him.

The Cardinal's conduct has been repeatedly scrutinized over many years, including before the Royal Commission into Institutional Responses to Child Sexual Abuse, the Victorian Parliamentary Inquiry into the Handling of Child Abuse by Religious and Other Organisations and according to leaked reports, by Victorian Police's SANO Taskforce.

One of the claims dates back to the early 60s which was the subject of an exhaustive inquiry in 2002 by a former Supreme Court Judge Alec Southwell, who found the allegations were not substantiated.

The Cardinal does not wish to cause any distress to any victim of abuse. However, claims that he has sexually abused anyone, in any place, at any time are totally untrue and completely wrong.

He denies the allegations absolutely and says that they, and any acceptance of them by the ABC, are nothing more than a scandalous smear campaign which appears to be championed by the ABC. If there was any credibility in any of those claims, they would have been pursued by the Royal Commission by now.

Pause there for a moment. This last point is not true. As the Cardinal should have known, allegations about him—as an individual—offending, are outside the Royal Commission's terms of reference. The Commission has no power to investigate them and it passes any allegations of this sort on to the appropriate state police—in Victoria, Taskforce SANO. The Cardinal's statement continued:

> In February this year media outlets carried stories of purported allegations against the Cardinal which were being investigated by the SANO Taskforce.
>
> However, no request has been made to interview Cardinal Pell nor has he received any details of these claims from the police or anyone. In late May, the Cardinal was advised by the SANO Taskforce that there had been no change in the status of the investigation since the leaks were first reported.

When Victoria Police Chief Commissioner Graham Ashton was asked in June this year if there were any plans to speak with Cardinal Pell in Rome he replied '...it has not been put as necessary to me at this point in time'.

The Cardinal then returned to a tried and true formula—reminding the ABC of the fact that he was:

> ...the first Catholic Bishop to confront the evil of clerical child sexual abuse and implement the first program to assist victims when he introduced the Melbourne Response in 1996. He has apologised to victims of abuse on behalf of the Church many times and has met with many victims personally.
>
> [The Cardinal] expresses regret that the sensationalist attention given to these unfounded and untrue claims might cause distress to genuine victims and he encourages anyone with any legitimate complaint to pursue it through the correct channels.

If there is any genuine victim who was caused distress by the story, I am yet to meet them. Every single one of the dozens of survivors and family members I have spoken to since the story went to air has congratulated me on it and most said it did not surprise them at all. One of the most common things said was 'about time'. If Pell thinks he is at the vanguard of helping survivors of child sexual abuse, how come I can't find any who agree?

When I received the statement that day, three primary things occurred to me. The first was they didn't understand the Royal Commission's terms of reference. That was telling and a bit odd. The second was that the only things they were interested in were the dates and the places. The reason for this, I can only assume, is that the Cardinal had been successful on previous occasions at proving or suggesting that he was elsewhere on dates provided.

A classic example of that was a man known to the Royal Commission as 'BWE' who alleged that Pell said in 1983 'Gerry's rooting boys again' (a supposed reference to Gerald Ridsdale) to another priest, Frank Madden, in the sacristy of Ballarat's St Patrick's Cathedral when BWE said Pell was concelebrating a requiem mass for a lady from Bungaree. The Cardinal, who was particularly affronted at this evidence, was able to show diary notes which he says showed he wasn't there and there were no mass records saying the two priests had ever concelebrated mass. I have studied those diary notes carefully. There wasn't a lady from Bungaree buried a few days before a football final, as BWE had alleged. Madden was by then stationed 200 kilometres away in Horsham. Ridsdale was in Sydney. BWE, who is a jumpy sort of fellow and prone to colourful language, was demolished in the witness box.

Having said that, I have been able to establish that there was a lady who was buried the Wednesday after the football final. The lady's name was Gladys Pope. In her will, Gladys, a spinster, left a substantial estate to the administrator of St Patrick's Cathedral. The recently departed administrator of St Patrick's Cathedral was Madden. The administrator at the time was Father Hank Nolan—Pell's first cousin. The Church stood to inherit a tidy sum. The funeral, advertised in the Ballarat *Courier,* was a requiem mass. Members of the Arithmaea Society, a Church group designed to fill out funerals when people have nobody, were 'respectfully invited to attend', so whoever celebrated that mass wouldn't have had many witnesses to it. Gladys Pope's people were from Bungaree. Pell was at that time based at the Bungaree parish.

Dates are weird things—they trip you up. On the date of Gladys Pope's funeral, it says Pell had 'class' from 9 to 11. And there is an odd entry which says he was at a meeting in Melbourne and it has an arrow which indicates 2.30 to 4.30 pm. Except the 4.30 is crossed out. Why cross out the 4.30? Was it originally just 4.30? In the hypothetical event that it was 4.30 pm, Pell would have had time to get from the funeral to the meeting. The next day, it says 'Horsham dinner'. Horsham, being, of course, the parish of Father Frank Madden—was Madden returning there?

Of course, even if BWE got his dates wrong and he was at Gladys Pope's funeral, it doesn't mean Pell said 'Gerry's rooting boys again'. Pell's legal team argued forcefully that their client never spoke in such coarse terms. People who knew him in his Ballarat days beg to differ. But certainly, Counsel Assisting the Royal Commission, Gail Furness (who did not have all of the material at her disposal that I have just canvassed) submitted, essentially, that the story could not be stacked up. But it shows how easy it is to demolish someone in the witness box even if there is a possibility that they are right.

Getting back to the Cardinal's statement to me, when Leder responded, there was nothing about dates. It was just a blanket denial. It seemed clear he had no obvious date alibis (which I had already assiduously checked)—otherwise they would have been produced immediately.

The third thing that occurred to me was that I had never even asked the Cardinal any direct questions and had not provided very much detail of what was alleged in the story. I had a list of questions ready to send to Pell's media liaison. Perplexed, I rang Leder direct. It was a strange situation to find myself in with someone I had liked and respected. 'Well, Richard, here we are,' I said to him. We made friendly small talk, but then we got down to business. I told him I was confused—I'd been sent a statement and his client hadn't yet had the opportunity to know what the allegations were against him. I said I felt distinctly uncomfortable, as a journalist, because I would always give the subject of my story the opportunity to know what was being alleged about them. 'It doesn't matter, Louise,' Leder said. 'Because he hasn't done it. So he doesn't need to know what you have. Because he has never abused any child, anywhere.'

'Still, Richard,' I responded. 'I'd feel much more comfortable if he knew what I have. That's the sort of professional courtesy I give anyone.' Leder replied that he'd have 'to get instruction'. He promised to get back to me. He never did. One thing always stuck in my mind from that conversation. As we were dispensing with the niceties, having a dark chuckle at the situation we found ourselves in, Leder said, 'All's fair in love and war, Louise.' Of course, it was just a solicitor's black sense of humour—trying to get by in an awkward situation for both of us. But the fact remained that 'war' was the operative word. Love got left out of so many equations involving the Catholic Church and allegations of clergy abuse. 'Love one another, as I have loved you,' Jesus told us, that's what we used to chime back to our teachers in our Catholic primary school. Love one another, as I have loved you.

25

BREEN

I know in my heart, I know for a fact what he's done. And the police, they're barking up the right tree.

Michael Breen

On 27 July 2016, our story went to air. It was the first time in at least twenty years that the program had dedicated its entire slot to one story. The moments before we pressed send on the final cut are etched onto my brain like a lithograph. I felt like one of those people who dives with sharks in a nature documentary. You just step out, one flipper in front of the other, and plunge into the dark depths of icy water. The adrenaline courses through your veins like fizzy lemonade and you hope for the best.

If the sharks were circling, they were slow to pounce. The posse of Pell defenders was sluggish off the mark. The other media played a straight bat.

The fears I'd had that Lyndon Monument and Damian Dignan would be pilloried because of their pasts were never realised. And yet, for a couple of weeks, every time my email pinged, I wondered what it would bring. Every time I had a text message, I felt sick. I'm not quite sure what I thought would happen, but I was so nauseous I lost four kilograms. In a devastating development, I put them all back on.

The Cardinal's office published another statement. Naturally, he again denied the allegations.

> The ABC has no licence to destroy the reputation of innocent people and Cardinal Pell, like all those who have allegations against them that have not been tested by the Courts, is entitled to the presumption of innocence—not immediate condemnation. He is entitled to a fair go.

The statement then had a direct quote from Pell himself: 'I bear no ill will and have no desire to cause them harm, but what they say about me is not true.'

The 'fair go' line and the sensible decision not to vilify the complainants was repeated later when he made a brief doorstop for the cameras outside his residence in Rome. In that doorstop, he was measured, and appeared humble. Much more so than he had seemed in some previous appearances during the Victorian parliamentary inquiry and the Royal Commission. He said he was happy to cooperate with police, but would not participate in 'a trial by media'. That, I thought, was pretty good PR—that's the sort of thing I would have told him to say and do if I was doing his media. But the latter part of his statement? Maybe not so much.

Instead of going in for the kill against the complainants, he went in for the kill against Victoria Police and us. Just like he had with the *Herald Sun* when it published its first story on the investigation, he attempted to shoot the messenger. As so many priests and former colleagues have told me about Pell, he defends with attack. With the *Herald Sun,* it was to request that the leaks be investigated. Well, that went nowhere. So this time, it was to accuse Victoria Police and the ABC of collusion.

> It seems there has been leaking of information and allegations by elements of the Victorian Police to the ABC. This is consistent with previous patterns of improper and illegal disclosure of information from such sources to a variety of media outlets.
>
> Such information has in the past repeatedly been demonstrated to be inaccurate and unfounded.

How, Cardinal? Where? In what forum?

> In a context where police themselves have suggested, accurately or otherwise, that the making of charges is under review by relevant authorities, these disclosures and consequent publicity by the ABC clearly are apt and calculated deliberately to influence and compromise relevant judicial and prosecutorial processes.
>
> The Cardinal calls for an investigation to assess whether any actions of elements of the Victoria Police and the ABC program amount

to a conspiracy to pervert the course of justice.

This time, he didn't get his investigation.

'So that's all they've got', I thought, when it came through. 'Something that is completely untrue. Interesting.' If only I had been given leaks from Victoria Police. It wouldn't have taken me five months to get the story to air. I wouldn't have had to make dozens and dozens of phone calls to find people.

I have had, as an investigative journalist, at times, a rough-and-tumble relationship with Victoria Police when some of my stories have not pleased the organisation. I had tried to get Taskforce SANO to give me a background briefing on the status of the investigation. But those conversations were always one-sided. None of the complainants came to me via Victoria Police. I rang David Rae, the detective who had worked on the Eureka Pool allegations, perhaps three times during those months. I told him I wasn't after complainants as I'd met most of them. I just wanted to know the status of the investigation. He was always polite and decent. But he never gave me a single thing. He would always chuckle and say, 'You know I can't help you with that'. The only reason I had Rae's number was that I had obtained it from the complainants.

As it happens, police had never contacted many of the people we spoke to. We figured many of these people could have been potential witnesses because they stacked up, for instance, that Pell was at the pool, that the children knew Pell before they saw him at the pool—so there was no mistaking him, that he played the game, etc. We had a checklist for each person we called—have you spoken to Taskforce SANO? Have you spoken to other media? We wanted to know if there were others on the trail. In almost every single case, with the exception of a few key witnesses around the Eureka Pool allegations, the answer to the police question was 'no'. And not a single person had ever been contacted by any other media—so the cops weren't giving any of my colleagues the drop on that either.

The next time I spoke to Taskforce SANO was when the story was already cut and the questions had been sent to Pell. There was a person who had come forward at the last minute, who was unconnected to any of the other complainants, with some information that I felt was at that stage not appropriate for me to broadcast given that he had not made a police complaint. As myself and my producer Andy Burns were the first people to whom this man had made this disclosure, and we had some nagging questions about parts of his story, we felt that the appropriate thing to do, with the man's blessing, was simply tell Taskforce SANO what I knew. I telephoned the taskforce and gave them the man's details. Andy and I made very detailed attempts to fact-check his claims, but as we still had questions which had not been resolved, we did not broadcast his allegations. I'm not sure whether that man ever did make a formal statement to Victoria Police. At that point, I informed Taskforce SANO of my intention to broadcast the rest of the story in a couple of days. I volunteered the names of all the complainants I had spoken to and they confirmed it was still a live investigation and that those complainants I had independently discovered all formed part of the file. That was that.

There are two points to this anecdote. The first is that we did not publish the claims of anyone we felt could not be corroborated and fact-checked. The second is that if the relationship I've outlined with Taskforce SANO is what Pell and his advisors describe as a conspiracy to pervert the course of justice, then they have an interesting definition of such matters.

The Australian tried to discredit our story by publishing a piece online, the night of the broadcast, and in its newspaper the following morning, declaring that the Office of Public Prosecutions had sent the Pell brief back to Victoria Police saying there was nothing in it. But by first thing the next morning, it was clear *The Australian* had been given a dud tip. Victoria Police Chief Commissioner Graham Ashton, who had before the broadcast politely declined to be part of my story given the sensitivities therein, went on morning commercial radio with 3AW's titan of breakfast broadcasting Neil Mitchell. He immediately made it very clear to Mitchell that *The Australian's* story was a furphy.

'We haven't got that opinion, any opinion, back yet, it's still with them for assessment,' the Chief Commissioner said of the Office of Public Prosecutions.

'So does that mean,' Mitchell asked, 'the position we're in at the moment, charges are still a possibility?'

'Anything's a possibility at this stage,' the Commissioner returned.

When asked about the perverting the course of justice claim, Ashton also calmly batted it away. 'My response to that is that we haven't provided the ABC with materials,' Ashton said.

Ashton then said that he'd received a complaint letter back in February from the Cardinal about the *Herald Sun's* story and he 'sent that up to IBAC' (the Independent Broad-based Anti-corruption Commission) because he 'thought it warranted independent examination'. 'And IBAC had a look at that and wrote back to me saying they had examined that and dismissed the complaint,' he explained.

When Mitchell pushed him that perhaps this was a new leak that warranted another look, the Commissioner said it didn't. 'No, I absolutely don't think it—I'm sure it's not the police here, and I think anyone who saw that story last night can see it's the victims that are, you know, expressing a great deal of—well, you can see the emotions in their voices, and see it in them last night. They're, you know, highly traumatised from what they are saying happened to them and they're talking to the media about that.' The Commissioner also confirmed that, as we reported, there were other complainants and that the alleged crimes spanned several decades.

This was far more than I could have expected in a million years from Ashton. For a start, he appeared to really empathise with the complainants. He seemed quite moved by their stories. For another, he was completely dismissive, as he should be, of the suggestion of any collusion between his taskforce and myself.

Ashton's use of the word 'victims' instead of complainants incensed Pell's supporters. Within days, News Limited commentators, including The Sydney Institute's Gerard Henderson, pointed out that it showed that Ashton was prejudging the matter. To me, it seemed more like a case of poorly used language. If the matter was being prejudged, Victoria Police would have charged Pell long before now. It's clearly a case it has carefully agonised over. You only get one shot at this sort of thing and you don't want to mess it up.

In those few days after the story went to air, we got a number of tips from people who said they had Pell stories. Many of them were 'a friend who knew a friend'–type stories. Some were dead ends.

Then another man came forward, leaving a telephone message for me. His name was Michael Breen. Breen, as it turned out, was another Eureka Pool complainant. But he had kept what he says Pell did to him secret for his entire life. He had never breathed it to a soul. Breen is just not that type of fellow—he's a man of few words. Breen had neither met nor heard of Damian Dignan and Lyndon Monument. He hasn't lived in Ballarat for three decades and he only saw the back-end of our program, so he knew scant details of what was alleged. But his story is eerily similar to those that Monument and Dignan told.

Breen knew that the *7.30* program on Pell was coming on that night—he'd heard it advertised and he was interested to see what it was all about. He says he recorded it, but the recording hadn't worked. Breen was interested because five months before, when the *Herald Sun* story had broken, he'd seen it in the news, seen that it included a reference to the Eureka Pool, and had tried to contact a newspaper (he can't remember which one—he just saw it online) by sending an email through a 'contact us'–type link saying that he was at the pool and he had seen something. He'd never heard back. He has no record of that email now—possibly because it was automatically generated by the newspaper's site.

Michael Shane Graafmans was born in Ballarat on Anzac Day 1964, to a single mother and a father he never met. He later took the Breen surname after his mother married his stepfather, Terry Breen. Breen is five years older than Monument and Dignan. The family went to live in Melbourne for a few years, but returned to Ballarat when Breen was in his final year of primary school. They moved to Ballarat East, just around the corner from the Eureka Pool. During the hotter months, Breen would head to the pool usually about twice a week—once after school and once on the weekends. And that's where Breen says he met Pell. The maths put it at roughly 1976. Unlike the St Alipius kids who knew Pell from mass and confession, Breen was not brought up a Catholic. But he still knew who this towering fellow at the pool was.

'Everyone in Ballarat, let alone at the pool, knew George Pell,' Breen tells me during one of our phone conversations. 'He would arrive with his black suit and his white collar and he'd put his bag down and get changed in the change rooms.

'He was a friendly person, so whether you bumped into him, or otherwise, he would talk to you. There was just that contact—you felt comfortable with him.'

Breen remembers Pell playing with the kids—bouncing and splashing around with a rubber ball. And, just as he did two years later, Pell would play the throwing game. Breen thought it looked fun. He says that Pell would 'always come from behind us kids, placed both of his hands under my armpits and threw me, or whoever was there in front of him, up in the air. I was usually thrown a good three feet out of the water.'

But after a few throws, Breen says Pell changed his launching technique. 'His hands seemed to move around so that he was pushing or lifting me up from my bottom, my buttocks. As he did this, one of his hands moved around so that it would touch my groin area, my testicles and my penis.

'I was uncomfortable when his hands got down further,' Breen tells me, somewhat awkwardly, during that first phone call. 'He would fondle your backside and the front area and bounce you up and down on his knees.'

He says it was not exactly a firm grip. 'It was his palm on my skin, rubbing up and down. On the cheeks, on the entrance to the anal [canal].' I ask whether it was under the water or above. 'Oh, under the water, never above.

'Sometimes he slid one of his hands around the front of my groin. It was a gentle touch or caress of my penis and testicles from the front. Again, this was a gentle caress and all done in a way so that no-one could see what he was doing, always under the water.' There again was another version of that 'good handful' described by Phil Scott in the Southwell Inquiry. There again was the similar evidence. And as I later found out, Breen had never heard of Scott, had never heard of Southwell, and knew next to no detail about what Monument and Dignan had alleged.

'The other thing he did was pull me close to him when he was about to throw me in the air. I could feel his groin pressing or brushing against my bottom, but I cannot recall if his penis was erect or not.

'First couple of times I thought nothing of it at all,' Breen says. 'It was towards the end of having anything to do with him that I realised it was not right. You know, "this can't be an accident"? Yep.' He says for a while he ignored the 'wrong' feeling he had when the priest touched him because 'the thrill of being thrown into the air was so exciting that it made it all well worth the uncomfortable feeling of him touching me'.

He says it happened on many occasions, approximately once a week over the summer. Eventually, Breen decided not to play with Pell. The uncomfortable feelings usurped the thrill of the throw.

Like Monument a couple of years later, Breen also says he saw Pell naked in the change rooms at the Eureka Pool, but Breen did not make much of that fact.

In later years, he moved away from Ballarat and almost thirty years ago, he moved to Queensland. He's lived there ever since. He doesn't keep up with many Ballarat people and certainly before the *Herald Sun* story in February, had never heard anyone else discuss Pell behaving in this way.

Breen had until now never told a soul what he says happened to him. He says on a day-to-day basis, he rarely thinks about it and doesn't feel that it has had a permanently scarring impact on him. But he never forgot—it played like a super 8 film in his mind every time he saw Pell on television. 'It's always stuck in my memory—it never leaves. It never goes away. Never,' he tells me.

He decided to come forward, he says, to help the other complainants. 'I have been close to him. I know he's guilty. He can deny it all he wants.'

I spoke to Breen several times on the phone. He agreed to make a statement to Victoria Police and I put him in contact with Taskforce SANO. I told SANO I was the first person to whom he'd disclosed. A detective flew up to Queensland to take his statement. Being a heart-on-my-sleeve type of person, it was hard for me to understand how Breen could never have told anyone—especially given Pell's public profile. I felt I needed to go and meet him to better understand him.

When I meet him, Breen is fifty-two. He lives alone in a large brick-veneer 2-storey home on 7 acres of lush southern Queensland land, woven with orb spider webs, vibrating with cricket song. The property is littered with the truck parts he buys and sells at auctions.

Inside, his home is full of pictures of his children and grandchildren—he seems too young to be a grandfather. He has clipped grey hair, shining cornflower blue eyes, and is boyishly dressed in a cap and shorts. As he ushered me in, he apologised repeatedly for the mess—it wasn't messy—but he hastily swept up dust from the floor. 'You know what it's like—the old bachelor pad.' Michael split from his wife of twenty-five years about nine years ago.

Over a cup of tea at his kitchen table we plunged headlong into the awkward terrain one finds oneself in in my line of work—asking the most searingly personal questions of a deeply private person just minutes after clapping eyes on them for the first time. I often felt like I was ripping off bandaids. He frequently winced. But there was also a sense that he was speaking about things that perhaps he should have spoken to someone about before. I noticed to my surprise, because I did not detect the vulnerability in his voice on the phone, that he has those wounded eyes they all have. But he would never say that. He'd hate me to say that. I got the impression he would be mortified that anyone ever thought there was a reason to pity him.

But then he told me about his life—he had two brothers, one older and one younger, each to a different father. The last father on the scene was Terry Breen. 'Terry died two months ago. He was a complete idiot,' Breen said, early on. It was clear that 'complete idiot' was a euphemism. The first time I spoke to him on the phone, he mentioned that when he was a child, two other men had targeted him, two men other than Pell. Something in the way he spat out Terry's name told me

Terry was one of them. I asked him if that was the case. He sighed.

'Yep. Terry was a bit of a paedophile himself. He tried a few things with me. And there was one instance where a close friend felt uncomfortable.' Terry Breen had spent time in Pentridge prison for reasons his stepson was now unsure of. 'The worst time I remember was when I was naked, that was the worst thing...' He trailed off, then there was a long pause where he stared at the ground. I asked him about the proposition. He was so uncomfortable—he had never spoken about this to anyone.

'He basically asked about having some sort of sexual touching with him. I was, I don't know, twelve.' Breen shook his head. 'I remember being in the lounge room. Being confronted by him. I think he asked me to drop my pants. And that's as far as it went.'

Breen also said he was targeted by another paedophile when he was 'about six' and living in a block of flats in Melbourne's thenrough bayside suburb of St Kilda. Breen was selling newspapers and the man told him he had some odd jobs to do at his place for some extra cash. 'So I went. He had a massage table and he asked me to lie on it. I can't remember whether it was full body nudity or just my top off. He didn't sexually assault me as such—he was massaging. But of course, looking back now, it was definitely weird and he was definitely getting his rocks off. But I was a little kid. So at the time, I had no idea.'

Breen never told his family about either of these incidents—especially since one was with his stepfather.

Breen said while he loves his mum and brothers, they were never a family of talkers. They generally kept themselves to themselves. Breen thought, on reflection, that the experience of Terry, the lack of ever having a father in his life, made him warm to Pell when he first met him.

'As a person I found [Pell] very warm and comfortable and somebody I could look up to—I felt a lot of comfort with him,' Breen said. 'Being a priest, I thought he was somebody I could trust. What I seen in him, I never saw in my stepfather. I saw him as a little bit of a father figure.'

Breen said to me on the phone once that he couldn't understand why he was targeted by three paedophiles—it always made him feel strange. But he didn't see any point in telling his mother or anyone else. 'I could not see what I would achieve by telling. It was embarrassing. And you know, why the hell should we go through feeling embarrassed when [we kids] have not done anything wrong?'

While Breen repeatedly insisted he never suffered any depression from what happened to him, he did go through a distinctly nihilistic period in his adolescence. He spent nine months in juvenile detention when he was a teenager for car theft in Ballarat. It's not something anyone in his life these days knows about.

'I think I was at that age where I just did not care where I was going,' he said. 'I am telling you now, to be upfront, because I want you to know I have nothing to hide. But no-one knows about this.'

I agreed this was a good idea. Because of Southwell. He looked at me blankly. I asked if he had heard of the Southwell Inquiry. 'Southwell? No. What's that?' he asked, with no glimmer of recognition on his face.

I said it didn't matter. I asked him if he had ever heard about any earlier accusations against Pell and how they panned out. 'No. I know nothing about that,' he replied, shrugging. 'But I know that if this goes anywhere, they will dig up everything on me. So I want to be upfront. Even though I don't like talking about myself. And I trust you.'

Knowing what could happen if he went public, he also told me about a highly embarrassing episode in his life in the wake of his divorce six years ago when, for reasons he can't explain, the old nihilism came back. He was convicted for theft. Gulping, I asked him what he stole. 'Electrical tools,' he said, exhaling. 'It is so embarrassing for me. It is my worst regret in life.' I inwardly breathed a small sigh of relief at the mundanity of the crime.

'Look, I've always had a steady income, I always had plenty of money coming in,' he said. 'But at that stage, I had just left my job at RACQ [working as a tow truck operator] and it was after that—I–I don't know—slipped back into a bad part of me that does anything to get by.

'Look there's no excuse. I stole. I stole from a hardware shop.' Breen admitted he didn't handle it very well—he should have got a lawyer.

'But I didn't bother. It was just the frame of mind I was in. It was stupid. I asked the Magistrate to make sure that no conviction was recorded, but he refused. So that's that. It sticks to me for ten years. I got a fine and twenty hours community service work.' He sighed.

'So how much was the stuff worth?' I asked him.

'A hundred and fifty dollars. Yep.' He nodded sardonically at the stupidity of it all.

'Oh, Michael. A hundred and fifty bucks.'

'I know, I know. It's ridiculous.'

He sighed and looked out the window into the hinterland. He looked like he might cry. But he didn't. Michael Breen is not the crying kind.

I told him I didn't want to get all Psychology-101 on him, but maybe this was something to do with his split from his wife a couple of years before, the loss of his job. Maybe he had been depressed, after all?

'To be honest I don't know whether that had anything to do with it. I just don't know. I had never suffered from depression in my life. Maybe, I don't know, it just goes back to my early years, I would get into this frame of mind where I just don't care...'

Breen is a shy man and he's not interested at this point in going on television or in drawing attention to himself, but has agreed for me to name him and tell his story in this book.

'Look, Louise, I don't want to blow this out of proportion—I'm here if you need help,' he said. 'I'm a piece in the jigsaw puzzle. If we all come together, all of us who have truth in what we are saying, then you've got something.

'I know in my heart, I know for a fact what he's done,' he said, eyes shining. 'And the police, they're barking up the right tree.'

He said he felt fortunate that what he says Pell did has not left him terribly and permanently scarred.

'I'm only just supporting these other blokes. I've been through what they've been through. If nothing comes of it, I guess that's fine. But if it does and I have to be a witness, I've got no problem with that.

'I've got to a point in my life where I'm not going to run around telling people what happened, but if they find out, that's okay.'

Since making the disclosure to me about Pell and giving his statement to Victoria Police, Breen has started the process of telling his mother and brother about what he says Pell did.

'At my age, a lot of things just don't matter any more. Things that once mattered, they don't matter.' He smiled a bit bashfully, promised to keep in touch, gave me a hug and sent me off into the Queensland afternoon.

Five weeks after I left Breen's place, and two months after he'd made his police statement, three members of

Victoria Police flew to Rome quietly and by a circuitous route so as not to draw attention to what they were doing. The force took the job so seriously it sent a deputy commissioner. When they arrived in the Eternal City, the trio arranged to interview their suspect: Cardinal George Pell.

26

THE CHOIRBOYS

Truth is the child of time; erelong she shall appear to vindicate thee.

Immanuel Kant

One of the things that has helped George Pell and his defenders to bat off or gloss over the allegations of Lyndon Monument and Damian Dignan is what has been cast in some quarters as the ambiguity of the behaviour. It's the notion that this was simply 'horseplay' or 'a bit of rough and tumble' and that Monument and Dignan, damaged men, had simply misinterpreted what was going on. That is a highly questionable premise, but it remains in public discourse. Public discourse still so often weighted to protecting the accused and doubting the accuser.

Whatever the supposed ambiguity of these alleged actions, they were not actions befitting an archbishop or a cardinal. They are said to have happened when Pell was a relatively young priest. As Father Pell rose through the ranks of the Church, even at its most innocent interpretation, what happened at the Eureka Pool was too risky for a man of his stature to risk question marks over his reputation.

The story of The Kid and The Choirboy has no such ambiguity. For if what was told to Taskforce SANO at Victoria Police in a sworn statement and disclosed to a tiny circle of people is true, what it was alleged Pell did to those two 13-year-old boys at St Patrick's Cathedral in Melbourne is his biggest slip-up of all. If true, it is a horrible crime. And in its aftermath came heartbreaking consequences. Moreover, by the time it's said to have happened, Pell was Archbishop of Melbourne. By that time, Pell had set up the Melbourne Response to tackle the problem in his archdiocese of clergy child abuse. If these allegations are true, they point to utter, sinful, hypocrisy.

This is the story of two teenage boys sent on scholarships from what were then Melbourne's inner suburbs to a Catholic boys' school—St Kevin's College. St Kevin's is in Toorak, Melbourne's most exclusive precinct. The school is wedged between the Kooyong Tennis Club and the Yarra River and closed behind grand iron gates with gilded lettering. The boys wear boater hats and navy blazers, candy-striped with emerald and gold. While the area the boys came from has now gentrified, in the 1990s it might as well have been a different planet from Toorak.

I'm not at liberty to name the boys—complainants of sexual assault and their families have a legal right to anonymity and it has been requested here. I've called them The Kid and The Choirboy. The boys got their ticket to St Kevin's because they could sing. The choirmaster from St Patrick's Cathedral had sent scouts to the Catholic primary schools around Melbourne's suburbs to find boys on the cusp of puberty who had the voices of angels. In return for their vocal skills, the boys received choral scholarships to St Kevin's. When The Kid remembers it, he has tears in his eyes. 'It was a dream of my mum and I, that I could go to this incredible private school that we could never afford, she was so proud,' he says. The Choirboy's mum, whom I'll call Mary, had no idea her boy had this talent.

'But it was good, you know?' Mary says, smiling at the memory. 'A nice scholarship for a good education.'

It was to be a big commitment for the families but the boys were very enthusiastic. The working parents carpooled to help with the commute. The Choirboy threw himself into his new role as he did everything in life. 'Oh my god, everything had to be done yesterday,' Mary laughs. '[He] would disappear from sun up to sun down ... He was just gung-ho, you know?' Weekends were filled with song. The choristers were expected to sing from the first day of term one to Christmas Day. The boy loved it.

In 1997, the last year that The Choirboy and The Kid spent in the choir, the bluestone gothic pile known as The Cathedral Church and Minor Basilica of St Patrick, or simply, St Patrick's Cathedral, was celebrating a centenary since its consecration. Huge celebrations were planned and in its honour, the boys were to perform Handel's *Messiah*. The sounds of 'Hallelujah! Hallelujah! Hal-le-lu-jah!' echoed around the sacristies and the nave. His Grace, Archbishop George Pell was to say the mass.

Other boys, now men, who were in the choir at the time remember Archbishop Pell being a regular presence in their lives. During May 2016, I called as many of the fifty choristers from the time as I could muster. I think I got to about thirty-five. Of those left, the remainder were either adult or much older members, a couple of overseas visitors, a handful who could just not be found and one or two who chose not to answer my calls or messages. Several are now high-profile singers and musicians. The boys would practise four days a week, and two of those sessions would be at St Patrick's Cathedral. Pell would drop in to watch the singing from time to time. Some of the guys also remember him joining the annual camp they attended at Easter to prepare for the holy season's masses. He would say mass for the boys at the camp.

The Choirboy's older sister remembers he was a very amiable boy. 'He always liked company as well, he always had to have someone with him all the time and he was, he was a great kid. [He] was, as a child, just a normal child.'

But at some point between his thirteenth and fourteenth birthdays, The Choirboy's enthusiasm waned considerably. 'Little murmurs, you know? Like, he was tired, you know, of the commitment to getting up early in the morning to practise,' Mary says. The boys would start their rehearsals an hour before school two days a week and also on Sundays before mass. They'd also have evening sessions at the cathedral once a week. The lead-up to Holy Week at Easter was terribly busy. Mary's son began to grumble about getting up to go. Mary just put it down to his teenage years. Then, one day, he snapped. 'Yeah, just out of the blue, "I don't want to be in the choir any more",' she remembers. 'And we said, "Well you do realise we can't afford the school fees?"' And he said, "Yeah", and I said, "Well, think about it", I said, "We can't do anything till the end of the year and you can't really swap and change".'

Mary was not pleased. She says for her family, the St Kevin's school fees were 'astronomical', and it seemed a shame to miss out on the rest of the school experience just because her son was weary of choir. But the boy was immovable. The boy's father, John, also remembers a meeting with the choirmaster where the parents were told that their son was disruptive in choir practice—coughing during the singing. The choirmaster was also upset that the boy was bending the corners of the music sheets. He also wanted the boy to leave.

One of the other choristers volunteered to me that there was a boy who had that year become difficult at school. He couldn't remember the name at first. I listed a random selection of other names from the choir, with The Choirboy's buried in it. 'That's it!' his former classmate remembered. He told me The Choirboy became difficult at school—angry and a bit of a bully.

Certainly, while his photograph from the year before shows a cherubic young boy with a bowl haircut, in 1997 his face has hardened. He is frowning. His friend, The Kid, has a strange look on his face. In that photograph, The Kid doesn't look at all like the handsome young man I met at the RSL. The Choirboy's father, whom I will call John and who separated from his wife many years ago, said before his son was about fourteen, he had always been very well-behaved 'and all of a sudden to change from being well-behaved to that was a bit of a mystery'. The boy became disengaged and disruptive at school. His parents and school were so concerned that in September 1997 they brought him to see a psychiatrist at the Royal Children's Hospital in Melbourne. The assessment, which John has kept, found the boy was of average intelligence and had been a good student. But his grades had been slipping, and while a friendly enough boy, his answers now tended to the monosyllabic, his responses were 'under-elaborated' and his working memory was affected.

At the end of the year, The Choirboy was to be a chorister no more—he was moved out of St Kevin's to a more affordable local Catholic secondary. 'I just put it down to him being a teenager and deciding he'd had enough—that it was, you know, too tiring,' Mary says.

That very same year, his friend, The Kid, had also made the same firm decision to get out of the choir as soon as he possibly could. His behaviour at school also became a problem. His voice had broken and, no longer a soprano, his choir days were numbered. He too had gone to another Catholic school, and the families rarely saw each other. The boys drifted apart.

Mary's daughter noticed a marked difference in her little brother from that point. 'Looking back, yeah, his whole personality, well, he changed. He did. He wasn't the same person as what he was beforehand,' she says.

'His life spiralled,' Mary says. 'It really did spiral.' Her daughter nods and presses her lips together.

Mary and her daughter are sitting on a sofa in Mary's living room in her unit in a suburb of Melbourne. They are hospitable and decent women, unpretentious and plainly dressed. They have been searching for answers for what happened to their son and brother for years. Mary lives alone—her daughter is bringing up a young family. Mary works in a shop and tries to make sense of life. But her sparse little unit is a house of grief. While she is stoic and does not make a fuss about the raw deal that the past few years have dealt her, her mouth betrays her. It's permanently slightly drawn down at the corners. She's a woman who has had a full-time job keeping a son together and now he's gone. After it happened, she was left scratching her head, making meals for one and wondering how it all went so wrong. Until The Kid came along.

The year after he left the choir, The Choirboy got into drugs. In a big way. While at age thirteen he had sung Handel's *Messiah,* clad in a choirboy's crimson and white robes, eyes cast up to heaven, by his fourteenth year, he was already dabbling in heroin. 'It's devastating to watch your child spiral like that,' Mary says, shaking her head at the memory of anger, frustration, heartbreak that she dealt with in equal parts. The Choirboy became like one of the disengaged young men that Carolyn Quadrio charts in her research.

John had worked as an honorary probation officer for many years and he saw the same behaviour in his son as in the juvenile justice kids he worked with, who were often victims of abuse. 'I met a lot of young offenders of that age—and they are different. They behave differently, their mannerisms are different. That's the way [my son] was going and yet there was no reason for why he should be that way.'

His sister watched her brother completely withdraw. 'I think from my point of view, he changed to a point where you know, he was in his own world,' she says. The teenager changed friendship groups. He stopped talking. 'He just became very distant, very enclosed,' she says. 'It was embarrassing for me because, looking back, I didn't know why or what this stemmed from and how this was...' She trails off. 'It was embarrassing for me as a sister that I had a brother that was like this.'

For Mary, it was harrowing to watch her son constantly chasing heroin. Every now and then, he'd go to rehab and she'd have to drive him somewhere to help him score because you wouldn't get in to a program if too much time had lapsed since your last hit. It was mind-boggling for a decent woman who thought she'd brought up two great kids, given them the best education she could. From time to time, her son would report that he had bumped into The Kid somewhere when he was out socialising with his mates. He told his mum that The Kid was 'struggling a bit'. She asked her son was it drugs, too? But no, it wasn't drugs, he answered. He was just 'struggling'. Her son was a young man of few words, and at the time, The Kid's struggles had no meaning for her, and so she didn't inquire any further.

Her son's heroin chase went on for about fifteen years. The Choirboy never had a career, was never able to hold down much of a job. He was a devoted uncle to his small niece and nephew and Mary says he was, despite it all, a loving and good son. He lived with his mum and she was sometimes questioned about why she didn't kick him out. But Mary knew she was all her son had. 'I care about my son, I love my son, that's my son,' she says, speaking in the present tense of a mother who still struggles to come to terms with the fact that her youngest child is now a past-tense concept. 'If I don't care about him, no-one else is going to care about him—simple as that.'

The Choirboy died in 2014. He was thirty. Mary told almost everyone she knew that he died in a car crash. But it wasn't a car accident. It was a heroin overdose. She says she just didn't want the shame and the pity. All that's left of him now is a poorly tended Facebook page with a poorly taken profile picture. He's not smiling.

Mary's daughter kept her mum's secret too. 'I have never told anybody, only one of my closest friends ever knew,' she says. 'I told everybody it was because of a car accident because I don't want to have to explain to people that, you know, my brother lived half his life as a drug addict, and a heavy one at that.'

The funeral was on a Thursday in 2014. The sort of day when, all those years before, Mary would be packing her son off to St Pat's to sing his little heart out in the cathedral. Now she was preparing him to be buried. Although she had informed The Kid, she was still slightly surprised to see the young man respectfully take his place in a pew. In the following months, Mary would occasionally see The Kid when he came into the shop where she worked. They'd have a small chat. He was a well-brought-up boy, she thought. He'd always give her a hug and a kiss on the cheek.

Months later, Mary was serving customers at work when she received a telephone call from a detective from Victoria Police. Immediately she assumed they were trying to pin something on her son. 'I said, "You do realise [my son] passed away?"' And they said they did and they passed on their condolences. And the detective mentioned something about sexual assault. 'Well, I nearly fell over,' she says. 'And I said, "You can hang a lot of things on my son, but that's not one thing you can hang on my son".'

Of course, the detective wasn't referring to her son as a perpetrator. He wanted to know if her son had told her about anything that he'd borne witness to or experienced during his time at St Patrick's or St Kevin's. Mary was shocked. 'And I've gone, "Oh, I don't know anything about that one, you know, I have no knowledge",' she remembers. The Taskforce SANO detectives then came to take a statement from Mary. She was completely in the dark about what had happened. And in her confusion, a new trauma came flooding back.

'I was floored,' Mary says. 'I've buried a son, I've lost a son due to a drug overdose—which is not a nice way to lose a child. And then I get this into my life.' Scenes from the last fifteen years of her son's life began to flicker through her mind in fast motion. She was wracked with questions and struggled to sleep.

After the police went to see Mary, they also visited her ex-husband. 'Nothing shocks me; I've seen a lot of stuff,' John explains. 'But that did shock me. But then, when I mulled it over, in the back of my mind, I'm thinking, "that's making sense".' The visit, which police only expected to take an hour, took five. John gave the police the medical reports and other documentation about his son and signed a statement.

One evening, some time after the detectives took Mary's statement, The Kid happened to come by when Mary was on the late shift. The shop was empty. She decided to have the conversation with him that she suspected would upset her, but she needed to know. 'I just asked him if I could ask him what happened. If, you know, if it wasn't going to upset him. Because I didn't want to upset this person, um, because [my son's] passed away. I didn't want to bring back bad memories for him.' But The Kid understood immediately. 'He said, "No, no, ask me". I asked him if my son was a victim and he said, "Yes".' Her son was a victim, he was saying, of George Pell.

Mary was overcome with a hot rush of anger. Not at The Kid, but at her son, for not telling her. Because Mary had asked her son. Not just once. Something inside of her, some mother's intuition perhaps born in the shock after her boy went so quickly and spectacularly off the rails, had made her suspect that he had been a victim of abuse. 'I asked [him], I can't remember the words I used, whether he was touched up, or played with, and [he] told me "no".' The boy shrugged. She says shrugging was something her son would sometimes do when he didn't want to talk about things. She still had a niggling feeling something was up. 'I never said anything to anybody,' she says. 'And then, again, after a while, I asked him and again he told me "no". And then I get this. And I was just so angry with [him],' she says, closing her eyes at the memory of it, 'for not telling me. So angry. Sometimes I'm still very angry.'

The Kid gently told her what he says happened with the Archbishop. 'He told me that himself and [my son] used to play in the back of the Church in the closed-off rooms,' she says.

'In the cathedral?' I ask her.

'In the cathedral, yep. And um, they got sprung by Archbishop Pell and he locked the door and he made them perform oral sex.' The Kid still remembered the incident so clearly. Being picked up afterwards by his parents. Staring out the car window on the way home. Mary swallows and looks at me in disgust. Her daughter, who has tears in her eyes, keeps her gaze on her mother.

'What went through your mind, as a mother, when you heard that,' I venture quietly.

'Oh angry,' she says, sighing and stiffening her back. 'Angry, as I said, at [my son], for not telling me, but also angry at the Catholic Church. I sent my child there—I sent both of my children there—for an education, to be safe. You send your kids to school to be safe. Not to have this done.'

'It's devastating,' her daughter says, 'because it helps to explain a lot of incidents in his life. And yeah, it's devastating, it is, it's devastating...' The daughter says she believes that her brother never spoke up about it because he was a very private person. 'And he didn't like to share a lot of information and I think, as a young boy, you are embarrassed. You don't want to tell people that another man, let alone a priest, has touched you in any way. You might not think that people believe you. People might judge you, people might say things about you. There could be so many reasons as to why he didn't want to tell us.'

Mary shares this suspicion, but it breaks her heart. 'I would like to think that if [he] would have told me, I would have believed my son. I would have believed my son.'

Independently, The Choirboy's father also thought to ask his son whether he had been sexually abused. 'I wondered what the hell was going on,' the father said. 'Was he being molested? Had somebody got to him? I wondered about that.'

When The Choirboy went to live with his father for a time while he was in his late twenties, John finally decided to ask him. His son had been telling him about how he had got into heroin. It had started with 'chroming'—sniffing paint fumes—with another boy from school (not The Kid) and had moved on to smoking heroin, then to injecting. His father listened with a sick feeling in the pit of his stomach.

'And so I asked him. "Has anyone ever made advances to you or touched you?" He said "no". I found with my son that if you asked the wrong questions, he would be very guarded. For example, if I ever asked him "Are you using drugs?" he would never tell you straight (even though he clearly was using drugs). If you accused him, he would get very upset.

'So I did not believe him. Because knowing the person that he was before and knowing other boys in this situation through my work, I thought to myself, "this is not the end of it. There's more to it".'

The Kid told Mary that her son's funeral was the breaking point for him. It plunged him into despair and regret. His own mother was very concerned about his wellbeing. He had not been coping since his friend's death. He decided that he had to come forward, he had to say something. As The Kid told me at the RSL that night I met him, his jaw set, his eyes aflame, insisting that this was 'about me and it's about him'. The Kid, with the support of his mum and a victim's advocate, went to Taskforce SANO.

'He just couldn't live with it any more—he had to say something,' Mary says. She says she 'liked' that he did it for her son. But now she and her daughter are left with so many questions, so much fury. She believes The Kid. She can't think what he possibly has to gain by coming forward. Unlike Monument, Dignan, Scott and, yes, her son, The Kid has not led a chequered life. He's university-educated, he hasn't had trouble with the law. He has a lovely young girlfriend, lots of friends, he's a pillar of his community in a sort of understated, slightly ironic way, and in that part of his life, he is, he told me, very happy. He's managed, just, to keep it together. He's been able to compartmentalise. He's the sort of complainant you'd want as a Victoria Police detective alleging historic crime.

The Choirboy's father remembers The Kid well, although the only time he has seen him in recent years is at his son's funeral. The Kid actually stayed with The Choirboy's family for some weeks when the boys were at St Kevin's and John remembers a polite and honest young man. 'Basically, he was a really nice kid.'

The strain of all of this, the enormity of it, means The Kid hangs on by a thread at times—and the thread that held him together enough to make a statement was that Taskforce SANO would arrest George Pell. The Kid was never interested in going on television—he knows that as a sexual assault complainant, the law allows that he never needs to have his identity revealed. He complained because he just wanted justice. Like so many of the other complainants against Pell, The Kid had another run-in with a child abuser. Nazareno Fasciale exposed himself to The Kid when The Kid was still in primary school. The same Father Nazareno Fasciale whose funeral George

Pell attended three months before Pell became archbishop.

Mary's daughter believes The Kid had zero to gain from coming forward if he was not telling the truth. 'You would not put your family through that, you would not put a dead person's name through that, you would not put yourself through that,' she says. 'Because the emotional toll that would take on you for the rest of your life, knowing that people now know your circumstances, what's happened to you in your personal life—you wouldn't do it if it wasn't true. I believe 100 per cent in my heart what this young fella has come out and said, the allegations that he has made, I 100 per cent support and believe that they are true, because the effects of coming out, they are devastating.'

But The Kid has wrestled with the enormity of reporting to police. Talk to any survivor who has been through the mill with the Catholic Church after accusing a member of the clergy and they'll tell you she's right. Months, even years, of anxiety as you wait for the police to act. Legal teams delaying proceedings, demanding severing of trials. Arduous cross-examination where your every word is twisted, your every motivation in life scrutinised. Leaks to newspapers about your past. Your mental health questioned. Your sexuality probed. Your memory tested. And at the end of it all, if the charges are proven, a penalty you think nowhere near fits the crime. As Monument's lawyer Ingrid Irwin says, if victims knew what they were getting themselves into, many may not bother signing up.

'Growing up, we are told that clergy are closer to God,' Irwin's friend and survivor Andrew Collins says. 'Who would believe you? We must have been the one who did something wrong. We should just shut up and not speak about it, for the benefit of the Church and so as to not shame our family,' he says. But he says it's not just the Catholic guilt that gets you.

'For men there is the whole thing of not wanting people to know that you were sexually abused by a man, lest you be known as gay if you are straight. Then there are people who just assume that because you were abused that you probably will end up being an abuser yourself ... Then if you cope with all of this, and your victim is alive, you might be lucky enough to be able to see your abuser in court. This is an ordeal itself. People would think that clergy would plead guilty and would do all they could to minimise the stress and pain for the victim. But the Church will hire the best lawyers, barristers and even QCs to defend the abusers ... The victims are cross-examined as if they are on trial. The victims have to recount every detail of the abuse, and then are called liars.'

The entire thing is played out in public, and even if, Collins says, the victim is not named, they live in fear that they will be found out. He says the Church has traditionally met all the priest's legal expenses, taken years to defrock him, supported him financially for the rest of his life. By comparison, he says, the victim will face PTSD, depression, anxiety and the impact of the strain on their mental health. 'If you are eligible for compensation you will probably have received around twenty thousand as total settlement.

You will struggle, most likely be alone, and will die around ten years earlier than your peers. Your abuser will have his every need looked after. If we come forward, we are screwed. If we don't, we struggle to live with ourselves and will probably end up dead, so we are screwed anyway. It appears that it would be better to be the abuser than the victim.'

And lastly, there is the giant elephant in the room. Or the Cardinal, as the case may be. The fact that the allegations are being made about George Pell. The Prince of Ballarat. The denizen of Domus Australia. 'Imagine having Pell as your abuser,' Collins muses. 'A Cardinal. A man who advises the Pope.' Any accusation, Collins says, 'will be seen as a lie: You just want fame. Or money.' This failure to possibly countenance belief that Pell could be anything other than infallible, this prima facie dogged disbelief in the complainants, has already been well-ventilated by some Catholic commentators.

It's a bleak view but it is one I have heard many times. Mary's son was, in death, spared that; but like so many survivors, if indeed The Kid spoke the truth, The Choirboy's own short life became an ordeal of its own. Mary thinks it all falls into place—why her son so suddenly lost all interest in the singing he had loved. Why a cherubic choirboy turned into a taciturn drug user at the age of just fourteen. Why he never managed to kick the habit. 'These people,' she says, referring to abusive clergy, 'destroy lives.'

Her daughter nods in agreement. 'These people are supposedly someone you look up to. It's not right, not right at all,' the daughter says.

Andy Burns and I spent days and days tracking down as many of the choirboys as we could, then I spent a few more days ringing each one individually. None of the dozens of other choirboys I spoke to say that they were ever targeted by Pell. Several in particular were very helpful and said it would not surprise them altogether if he was an abuser. Others said there wasn't a scintilla of suspicion about him. Just like the Ballarat kids, some found him officious, some found him friendly enough, some were intimidated by his high rank and some don't remember much about him at all.

A couple suggested the real names of The Kid and The Choirboy as possible people to contact because they had left suddenly. And one noticed a marked change in the behaviour of Mary's son. But of all of the choirboys I contacted, none of them are at this stage willing to sign themselves up to the ranks of the Pell accusers. And granted, that could well be because, if true, the incident with The Kid and The Choirboy was Pell's last really spectacular slip-up.

Mary's daughter says she is overwhelmed by the courage The Kid showed in complaining about such a powerful member of the Church and society. 'It's not going to bring my brother back,' she says, emotionally, 'but it will help the many people that are out there suffering. Because it's so brave—it's a really brave thing to do.'

'And I like to think in my heart,' Mary says, 'this is what [my son] would say too: "This was a friend of mine".'

'Absolutely,' her daughter adds, 'he would absolutely want to help.'

The Choirboy's sister becomes tearful as she speaks of the impact that her brother's life and his loss has had on her three young children. 'My youngest will never meet his uncle. The two older ones remember their uncle and every night they tell me that they look out that window and they see his star.' Her mother swallows, her eyes filling, as the daughter continues. 'They should be able to hold him, and to hug him.'

'I shouldn't have lost my son like that,' Mary says, 'and nobody else should either. And it's wrong,' she says. Her lip quivers. 'This is something I live with now. This is something that kills me a little bit every day. And it kills me.'

'We can speak out, though,' her daughter says, staring at me levelly. 'Yes, we might not have known at the time, but looking back now, so many things just fit. And so if we can help them [the other complainants] to be sitting here and saying our story, I'm more than happy to be sitting here today and to be doing this. Because nobody should ever have to go through a struggle every day because of what someone did to them. When they were a child.'

'And even it it's only one person out of ten that believe us,' Mary says, 'well that's enough.'

Of Pell, they urge anyone else who can come forward to do so. Mary has no great confidence that Victoria Police will get him back to Australia. But she says that one way or the other, she will in some ways always hold the Catholic Church partially responsible for her son's death. 'They need to be responsible for that death.'

One of the most senior people in the Australian Catholic Church tells me that Pell has been in battle all his life—he is first and foremost an ideological warrior. 'It's life by battle,' the official says. 'That's just how he works psychologically. Division helps him define himself.' Apart from his battle with the outside world, was Pell also at battle with himself? Was he, like Mick Leahy said to me, 'actually a very vulnerable person'? I keep coming back to that telling moment he had with Andrew Bolt when Pell admitted to having that fiery temper he suppressed, ever so carefully, with the wooden demeanour. The Easter Island statue of a man gliding through the cathedral, papering over emotion, lest he snap. Lest he flatten someone, verbally or physically, like he did on the football field. If there is truth in what happened to Phil Scott, Lyndon Monument, Damian Dignan, Michael Breen, The Kid and The Choirboy (not to mention the other complainants to police I know of—in instances that are both alleged to have occurred in 1970s Ballarat—and, perhaps, those that I don't as I am not privy to the police file), were these snaps? If true, the picture of offending it paints is opportunistic, fleeting, transitory. There is none of the usual 'rock spider' grooming. No talk of 'our little secret', no carefully planned trips to the countryside, no creepily tender stroking of hair. It's just quick, aggressive; it has the victim second-guessing themselves as it came from nowhere. Did that really happen? Did he just do that? Maybe it's just me?

As has always been my journalistic practice, I sent a list of questions to the Cardinal in early 2017 about the key allegations against him contained in this book. It was sent through his longstanding media advisor, Katrina Lee. Ms Lee did not respond, and when I chased her up, she finally replied that the matter was being handled by the Cardinal's solicitors and I should expect to hear from them. A series of legal letters ensued in which Pell, through Corrs Chambers Westgarth, declined to answer any of the questions without having access to information including, but not limited to, full police statements, unedited recordings of interviews, full names of complainants, direct quotes from the book. In two decades in journalism, I have never had a single person, organisation or corporation make such onerous requests. Legal correspondence from my publisher, Melbourne University Publishing, said even heads of state and captains of industry had not had the same difficulties George Pell had with providing responses to a written list of questions.

So beyond the statements he released after the *7.30* story I have already flagged and his general assertion that he has never abused anyone, anywhere and he believes that publishing these allegations represents, to him, a grave injustice, it is unclear what George Pell's position is in relation to the allegations contained in this book as he declines to put it on the record. His solicitors say in one of the letters that 'previous allegations against the Cardinal ... have either been disproven, or are so vague that the benefit of the doubt may be given to Cardinal Pell'. It is unclear what this means. At the time of writing, the Royal Commission has still not delivered its final report into his evidence in the Ballarat and Melbourne case studies. Counsel Assisting, Gail Furness, SC, made a number of adverse recommendations about his evidence in her final submissions. In the Southwell Inquiry, Justice Southwell did not find against the Cardinal, but, crucially, believed his accuser, Phil Scott, as well as George Pell.

And of course, at the time of writing, the police investigation into the Cardinal continues.

If Victoria Police get their man, the process will be long and arduous. As, effectively, Treasurer for the Vatican, he is entitled to the presumption of diplomatic immunity. Australian law has an exemption to diplomatic immunity for personal injury and Pell does not actually live in the Vatican, but Italy—which does have an extradition treaty—but it's complicated. At the time of writing, he's seventy-six. How long before he reaches 'I don't recall' territory? Undoubtedly, even if he comes back, if a criminal trial proceeds, it will be delayed by whatever legal processes the finest silks can employ.

But regardless of whether the criminal justice system delivers the result that these men desperately want, the worm is turning for Pell and the Catholic Church. In February 2017, in the wake of the Royal Commission publishing its report on the astonishing extent of abuse in the Catholic Church, Greens senator Rachel Siewert put a motion to the Australian Senate acknowledging the numbers and calling on 'Cardinal George Pell to return to Australia to assist the Victorian Police and the Office of Public Prosecutions with their investigations into these matters'. Much to Pell's chagrin, the motion was passed by the Senate. At the time, a spokesperson for him called it a 'political stunt' and 'pathetic political point-scoring'. Six weeks later, the Cardinal wrote a letter, which was tabled in parliament, hitting back at the Senate:

> The use of parliamentary privilege to attack me on this basis is both extraordinary and unjust. Given that the investigation is ongoing, any calls from the Senate for my return to Australia can only be perceived as an interference on the part of the Senate in the due process of the Victoria Police investigation ... Any fairminded person would conclude that I have made every effort to be available to the Royal Commission and to Victoria Police to assist with their inquiries.

While the Senate motion may have had no real force and thus has the whiff of a stunt, it undoubtedly represents a wider zeitgeist against Pell. The tide of history is washing away from the Pell conception of the faith.

In the Australian Church, the winds of change are furiously blowing through. The staggering statistics heard in the Royal Commission, which brought the Church's Truth, Justice and Healing Council CEO Francis Sullivan to tears, have left the clergy and the flock smarting. There is a clear sense that many are moving away from Pell's rigid form of Catholicism. For those numbers show that it has failed them utterly. A staggering 7 per cent of priests, largely formed in the monastic seminaries that Pell wanted to return to, were accused of abusing children. 4444 people have alleged that they were victims. Certainly more than just poor Emma Foster. The fact that the tribe has protected itself, at the expense of little kids, is now exposed.

The language of Pell—'we object to being described as the "only cab on the rank"'; 'it's a sad story and it wasn't much interest to me'—has disappeared. The language is now bruised and contrite. 'These numbers are shocking, they are tragic and they are indefensible,' said Sullivan, struggling to form the words as he delivered an address to the Royal Commission.

'As Catholics, we hang our heads in shame,' the man who had been Pell's protégé, Archbishop Anthony Fisher of Sydney, said in a slightly more scripted YouTube message. Giving evidence to the Commission with archbishops from around the country in February 2017, he described the Church's response as a 'kind of criminal negligence to deal with the problems that were staring us in the face'. The public gallery applauded. His contemporaries used similarly damning language: Archbishop of Perth Timothy Costelloe described a 'catastrophic failure' in leadership, with the Holy See seeing itself as 'so special, so unique and so important' that it was untouchable. 'That's probably the way many bishops in their own dioceses might also think of themselves—as a law unto themselves, as not having to be answerable to anybody, as not having to consult with anybody as to being able to make decisions just out of their own wisdom.'

Survivors can only hope that the words aren't as hollow as all the holy lectures they received as children, all the while that they were being raped in presbyteries, touched up in confessionals. Eileen Piper, who met Denis Hart with a box full of 50 000 signatures asking him to finally give her an apology over how she was treated after her daughter Stephanie's death, certainly felt so. Rather than making any admissions or saying sorry, Hart offered to pray with Eileen. She declined that offer. As the lawyer representing many of the child abuse victims Viv Waller confirmed, at the same that these new apologies from Church officials were being conveyed, in Melbourne, some pretty extraordinary stuff was still carrying on. The Melbourne Response had increased the cap for compensation to $150 000; meaning that survivors could apply to get a top-up of their original payments, which were generally very low. The amount they had already received was being adjusted for inflation in favour of the Church. So for example, if the initial payment in 2009 was $75 000, in 2017 it would be treated as almost $90 000 and they would lose the increased value of their original payment.

'A few crocodile tears from Church officials—well I can tell you, it's not much different at the coalface,' Waller told ABC radio's Jon Faine. As Eileen's lawyer, Judy Courtin, wrote in *The Age:* 'whilst feigning compassion, this hierarchy is nervously propelling unknown millions of dollars at lawyers to help them defend the indefensible and to conceal the truth'. Courtin, like Waller, is weary. 'The inhumanity and utter ruthlessness of these hypocritical men of God makes me sick,' Courtin said.

Despite this, the most important bellwether comes in the form of a charismatic Argentinian octogenarian Jesuit, Jorge Mario Bergoglio. When Bergoglio was elected as the 266th Pontiff in 2013, he was the first Pope since the eighth century from outside of Europe. It is rumoured Pell was campaigning for another, conservative, cardinal—Angelo Scola of Milan—and a theologically rigid coterie of cardinals was most displeased with the choice of Francis.

The people who say they are Pell's victims had hoped that Pope Francis might admonish Pell, might support them, after the story first broke. That did not happen. The Pope wishes to wait until a court finds Pell guilty before he rushes to judgement.

But it is true to say that Pope Francis has set about quietly and deliberately sidelining Pell's faction of the Church. Archconservative Cardinal Raymond Burke has been particularly in the Pope's sights. Burke, who has called on Catholics to brace for martyrdom to defend the 'traditional' family, has been demoted from several senior posts. Pope Francis also ousted Pell, Burke and the conservative Canadian Cardinal Prelate Marc Ouellet from the Congregation for Divine Worship and the Discipline of the Sacraments. Four of the old guard, including Burke, sent a letter to Pope Francis known as a *dubia* questioning the papal exhortation *Amoris Laetitia,* The Joy of Love, which has in some quarters been interpreted as opening the door to divorced Catholics receiving communion. Pope Francis was unperturbed.

Pell, who was appointed by Pope Francis to the Secretariat for the Economy in the Vatican in 2014, had been making sweeping changes such as bringing in the accounting firm PricewaterhouseCoopers to overhaul Rome's books. But in 2016, the Pope cancelled the audit and removed a number of Pell's powers. There is much debate in Catholic journals about whether this is simply bloody-minded Italians resisting the forthright Australian Cardinal's changes, or whether it is that Pope Francis doesn't like Pell's take-no-prisoners style. Either way, the Cardinal's wings have been seriously clipped.

Pope Francis is an entirely different sort of leader to Pope Benedict XVI and Pope John Paul II before him. He frequently warns of the perils of theological rigidity in the Catholic Church. In a homily in October 2016, he said those who unbendingly followed the law of God were in need of God's help. 'The Law was not drawn up to enslave us but to set us free, to make us God's children,' he said. 'Behind an attitude of rigidity there is always something else in the life of a person. Rigidity is not a gift of God. Meekness is; goodness is; benevolence is; forgiveness is.' He even went so far as to say that rigidity concealed a 'double life' and a 'sickness'. 'They appear good because they follow the Law; but behind there is something that does not make them good. Either they're bad, hypocrites or they are sick. They suffer!' he said. Much of this is a direct challenge to Pell's faction in Rome.

Pope Francis will not heal some of the old wounds of the Church. He will not, for instance, bring back Bishop Bill Morris, sacked by Pope Benedict for daring to question the old, alienating ways. I say to Morris that he must feel extraordinarily cynical, especially in light of the many Catholic priests who had been protected after they abused children, or as bishops covered up that abuse and allowed it to keep flourishing.

'They call me a cockeyed optimist,' Morris says with a chuckle. 'But the thing is, Louise, out of the ashes comes new life. Something has to die for new life to come forward. People are just not going to take the garbage they did from us before. We bishops have let people down and we need to give people a voice. We have let our own people down.

'I can cry over that, but I am also enthusiastic about the fact that there is a whole new mission we are on about. It's about getting the relationships right. If you understand that we hold those beating hearts in our hands, the Church is going to change. We have been good at power, good at dictating the way people act. But we have not been good at relationships. We have protected our power and destroyed our relationships.'

Paul Connell, the theologian who Pell removed as Rector of Corpus Christi, tells me change takes time in Rome. It's fifty years since the Second Vatican Council and, Connell says, over centuries it has often taken longer than that for a council of the bishops to be fully accepted into the worldwide Church. After a half-century of divisions and revisions and resistance—a battle of whether to retreat, or to move forward into the light—along has come Pope Francis. 'Francis is an extraordinary phenomenon,' Connell says, 'and if you have faith, you have to believe the Holy Spirit is working here. Because Francis is what the Church needs.'

None of this will bring happiness, employment, mental health or sobriety to a small group of men who say that George Pell abused their bodies and their trust. They'll have to find their own ways to claw those back. It won't erase the story of their childhood that they say plays in their minds every day, like a rickety old super 8, spinning. There are no easy happy endings in this narrative, scant prospect of swift justice. The best they can hope for is that the truth can be known. As Peter Blenkiron always says to me, 'Truth is the child of time, Louise. Truth is the child of time.'

LIST OF PEOPLE

The Clergy and Religious

Jorge Mario Bergoglio, Pope Francis 266th Pope of the Roman Catholic Church

Brother Robert Best Christian Brother, principal of St Alipius Boys' School in Ballarat, serial paedophile

Father Noel Brady Parish priest of Resurrection Parish in King's Park, Melbourne, says Pell warned him off speaking about child abuse

Father Paul Connell Theologian, former rector of Corpus Christi seminary—managed out by Pell, parish priest of St Oliver Plunkett's in Pascoe Vale, Melbourne

Monsignor John Day Parish priest of Mildura in Ballarat Diocese, serial paedophile, deceased

Bishop Hilton Deakin Retired Auxiliary Bishop of Melbourne, former Vicar-General of the Melbourne Archdiocese

Brother Edward 'Ted' Dowlan Former Christian Brother of St Alipius and St Patrick's in Ballarat, serial paedophile

Archbishop Adrian Doyle Archbishop Emeritus of Hobart

Monsignor Tom Doyle Former CEO of the Catholic Education Office

Monsignor Tom Doyle (another one) American canon lawyer

Father Aidan Duggan Benedictine priest of the Sydney Archdiocese who abused John Ellis, deceased

Bishop Peter Elliott Auxiliary Bishop of Melbourne, friend of Pell

Father Nazareno Fasciale Priest of the Melbourne Archdiocese, serial paedophile, deceased

Bishop Brian Finnigan Retired Auxiliary Bishop of Brisbane, former secretary to Ballarat Bishop Ronald Mulkearns

Monsignor Leo Fiscalini Priest and consultor of the Ballarat Diocese, close to Pell's mother, deceased

Archbishop Anthony Fisher Archbishop of Sydney, 2014–

Brother Gerald Leo Fitzgerald Christian Brother of St Alipius in Ballarat, paedophile, died before was prosecuted

Archbishop Denis Hart Archbishop of Melbourne, 2001–, close ally of Pell

Father Eric Hodgens Retired priest of the Melbourne Archdiocese, theological adversary of Pell

Father Michael Kelly Jesuit priest, founding editor of progressive Catholic journal *Eureka Street*

Archbishop Frank Little Archbishop of Melbourne, 1974–96, deceased

Father Frank Madden Priest and consultor of the Ballarat Diocese

Father Bob Maguire Retired parish priest of South Melbourne, confidant of Phil Scott

Father Peter Matheson Theologian, parish priest of Our Lady of the Assumption in Cheltenham, Melbourne

Father Michael McGloin Dean at St Mary's Cathedral in Sydney, told by John Ellis about the abuse by Aidan Duggan, also accused of abuse

Sister Kate McGrath Former principal of St Colman's in Mortlake, whistleblower on Father Gerald Ridsdale

Father Bill Melican Priest and consultor of the Ballarat Diocese

Bishop Bill Morris Bishop Emeritus of Toowoomba in Queensland, removed by Pope Benedict XVI for questioning Church teachings such as the ban on women's ordination

Bishop Ronald Mulkearns Bishop of Ballarat, 1971–97, had knowledge of several paedophile priests including Father Gerald Ridsdale, whom he moved from parish to parish, deceased

Father Gerard Mulvale Former Pallottine priest of St Christopher's Parish in Syndale, Melbourne, convicted of abusing two boys, charged with raping Stephanie Piper

Monsignor Henry 'Hank' Nolan Priest of the Ballarat Diocese, Pell's cousin, deceased

Bishop James O'Collins Bishop of Ballarat preceding Ronald Mulkearns, Pell's champion, deceased

Father Kevin O'Donnell Parish priest of Oakleigh in Melbourne, serial paedophile, deceased

Father Lawrence O'Toole Priest and consultor of the Ballarat Diocese

George Cardinal Pell Australian Cardinal Prelate for the Catholic Church, Prefect for the Vatican's Secretariat for the Economy, former Archbishop of Melbourne, former Archbishop of Sydney

Father Terrence 'Terry' Pidoto Serial paedophile of the Melbourne Archdiocese, abused a boy at Corpus Christi seminary, deceased

Bishop Pat Power Bishop Emeritus of Canberra-Goulburn

Joseph Ratzinger, Pope Benedict XVI 265th Pope of the Catholic Church 2005–13, Francis' predecessor, theologically aligned to Pell

Father Gerald Ridsdale Former priest of the Ballarat Diocese, possibly Australia's most prolific paedophile

Bishop Geoffrey Robinson Former Auxiliary Bishop of Sydney, Chairman of National Committee for Professional Standards, architect of Towards Healing

Father Victor Rubeo Priest of the Melbourne Archdiocese, serial paedophile, abused two generations of boys in the one family, deceased

Sister Angela Ryan Former executive officer of the National Committee for Professional Standards, closely involved in Towards Healing and the Southwell Inquiry into alleged abuse of Phil Scott

Father John Salvano Worked at the Oakleigh parish with Father Kevin

O'Donnell, tried to raise the alarm with the hierarchy about his behaviour with boys

Father Peter Searson Former parish priest of Doveton in Melbourne, paedophile, deceased

Monsignor Kevin Toomey Monsignor of the Melbourne Archdiocese, brother of Eileen Piper

Father Dan Torpy Former priest and consultor of the Ballarat Diocese, psychological counsellor to whom paedophile priests were sent

Father Bill Uren Former Provincial of the Australian Jesuits, now rector at the University of Melbourne's Newman College

Sister Patricia Vagg Nun and former teacher at Mortlake, assigned with task of letting Bishop Ronald Mulkearns know about problems at the school with Father Gerald Ridsdale

Father John Walshe Friend of Pell, former parish priest at Mentone in Melbourne, accused of abusing a seminarian at Corpus Christi—seminarian paid compensation by the Catholic Church's Melbourne Response

Father Michael Whelan Parish priest of St Patrick's, Church Hill, in Sydney, and leader of Catalyst for Renewal—a progressive Catholic movement

Father Mark Withoos Pell's private secretary in the Vatican

Karol Wojtyla, Pope John Paul II 264th Pope of the Catholic Church, 1978–2005, deceased

The Children

Paul Auchettl Ballarat survivor of abuse at St Alipius, befriended by Pell when a child

Peter Blenkiron Ballarat survivor of abuse by Brother Ted Dowlan at St Patrick's College, leader of survivor movement who went to Rome for Pell's evidence

Michael Breen Former Ballarat local, not Catholic, alleges abuse by Pell at the Eureka Pool

Wayne Brennan Survivor of abuse by Brother Ted Dowlan and possibly Father Gerald Ridsdale in Ballarat, suicided, alleged Pell knew and covered it up

Neil Bourke School friend of Stephanie Piper, abused by Father Gerard Mulvale, deceased

BWE Altar boy who alleges he heard Pell say to another priest 'Gerry's rooting boys again' while in the sacristy of St Patrick's Cathedral in Ballarat—story hotly disputed

The Choirboy Former choirboy at St Patrick's Cathedral in Melbourne, whose friend, The Kid, alleges he too was abused by Pell at the cathedral, deceased

Andrew Collins Ballarat survivor of abuse by several perpetrators including religious brothers, a priest and a lay teacher, leader of survivor movement who went to Rome for Pell's evidence

Peter Curran Survivor of Father Gerald Ridsdale, Brother Ted Dowlan and Brother Robert Best, says Pell knew about Ridsdale, deceased

Donna Cushing, nee Harrison Survivor of abuse by Father Gerald Ridsdale on a holiday with her three brothers in Edenhope in the Ballarat Diocese

Damian Dignan Student of St Alipius in Ballarat, alleges abuse by Pell at the Eureka Pool

John Ellis Survivor of teenage and adult abuse by Benedictine priest Father Aidan Duggan in Sydney; his legal case against Pell and the Trustees of the Sydney Archdiocese created a legal precedent which makes it very difficult for victims to sue the Catholic Church for negligence

Emma and Katie Foster Daughters of campaigners Anthony and Chrissie Foster, Emma died of a drug overdose and Katie is permanently disabled after walking into a car when she was drunk, both victims of Melbourne priest Father Kevin O'Donnell

Tim Green Survivor of abuse by Brother Ted Dowlan at St Patrick's College, says he tried to warn Pell at the Eureka Pool, which Pell denies

Mark Harrison Donna Cushing's brother—abused by Father Gerald Ridsdale on the same holiday Donna attended

Paul Hersbach Abused by Melbourne priest Father Victor Rubeo who also abused Hersbach's father, Tony, his uncle and his brother

Richard Jabara Survivor of abuse by Melbourne priest Father Terence Pidoto, brought to Corpus Christi seminary for abuse

The Kid Former choirboy at St Patrick's Cathedral in Melbourne, alleges abuse by Pell at the cathedral

Paul Levey Survivor of abuse by Father Gerald Ridsdale at Mortlake in the Ballarat Diocese, lived in the presbytery at Mortlake with Ridsdale when he was a boy

Lyndon Monument Student of St Alipius in Ballarat, alleges abuse by Pell at the Eureka Pool

Darren Mooney School friend of Lyndon Monument's brother Craig (now deceased), survivor of abuse by Brother Gerald Fitzgerald at St Alipius in Ballarat

Peter Mooney Darren's brother, survivor of abuse in Ballarat

Gerard Murphy School friend of Lyndon Monument and Damian Dignan, was not a victim of abuse

Stephanie Piper Suicided in 1994 after police laid charges for her abuse by Pallottine priest Father Gerard Mulvale

David Ridsdale Ballarat survivor of protracted abuse by his uncle, Father Gerald Ridsdale, leader of survivor movement who went to Rome for Pell's evidence, convicted of abuse himself

Lauren Rowbotham School friend of Lyndon Monument and Damian Dignan, alleges she saw Pell touching them inappropriately at the Eureka Pool

Phil Scott Former altar boy, alleges abuse by Pell when Pell was a seminarian at a camp at Phillip Island in Victoria

Julie Stewart Survivor of abuse by Father Peter Searson at Doveton, Pell wrote to her to apologise

Paul Tatchell Survivor of abuse by Brother Ted Dowlan at St Patrick's in Ballarat, now a member of the local shire council

Rob Walsh Survivor of abuse at St Alipius in Ballarat, two brothers and a cousin also abused there and he is the only one surviving as the other three suicided

Stephen Woods Survivor of abuse by same perpetrators as Peter Curran, friend of Curran's, went to Rome for Pell's evidence

The Lawyers

David Begg Solicitor who represented John Ellis in his case against Pell and the Sydney Archdiocese

Dr Judy Courtin Solicitor specialising in representing child abuse victims at Angela Sdrinis Legal, wrote her PhD on the issue

John Dalzell Solicitor at Corrs Chambers Westgarth, represented Pell and the Sydney Archdiocese during the Ellis case

Stephen Free Counsel Assisting, Royal Commission into Institutional Responses to Child Sexual Abuse

Gail Furness, SC Counsel Assisting, Royal Commission into Institutional Responses to Child Sexual Abuse

Ingrid Irwin Ballarat solicitor representing child abuse complainants including Lyndon Monument and Damian Dignan

Richard Leder Solicitor at Corrs Chambers Westgarth, represents Pell and the Melbourne Archdiocese, one architect of the Melbourne Response

Justice Peter McClellan Chair of the Royal Commission into Institutional Responses to Child Sexual Abuse

Allan Myers, QC Barrister who represented Pell in the Royal Commission

Peter O'Callaghan, QC Victorian barrister, former Special Commissioner of the Melbourne Response

Robert Richter, QC Criminal barrister appointed to represent Pell to fight current allegations

Jeff Sher, QC Barrister who represented Pell in the Southwell Inquiry

Justice Alec Southwell Retired Justice of the Supreme Court of Victoria, conducted the Southwell Inquiry into allegations by Phil Scott against Pell of child abuse at Phillip Island in 1961

Angus Stewart, SC Counsel Assisting, Royal Commission into Institutional Responses to Child Sexual Abuse

Dr Vivian 'Viv' Waller Solicitor at Waller Legal specialising in representing child abuse victims

Peter Ward Solicitor at Galbally and O'Bryan, represented Phil Scott in the Southwell Inquiry

The Cops

Graham Ashton Chief Commissioner of Victoria Police

Kevin Carson Detective at Ballarat who investigated paedophile clergy including Father Gerald Ridsdale and Brother Robert Best

Peter Fox Former NSW Police detective whose interview on the ABC TV *Lateline* program sparked the Royal Commission into Institutional Responses to Child Sexual Abuse

Paul Murnane Former superintendent of Ballarat police, worked for Towards Healing after retirement

Chris O'Connor Retired policeman who was formerly detective senior sergeant in charge of the Victoria Police Child Exploitation Squad

David Rae Detective at Taskforce SANO, which investigates historic child sexual abuse claims that have arisen out of the Victorian Inquiry into the Handling of Child Sexual Abuse

Involving Religious and Other Organisations and the Royal Commission into Institutional Responses to Child Sexual Abuse

Others

Andy Burns Producer at ABC TV *7.30* program

Danny Casey Former business manager of the Sydney Archdiocese

Michael Casey Private secretary to Pell

Michael Costigan Corpus Christi seminarian and former priest, worked for the Australian Catholic Bishops Conference

Paul Costigan Corpus Christi seminarian and former priest

Blake Curran Son of deceased Ballarat victim, Peter Curran

Colleen Curran Wife of deceased Ballarat victim, Peter Curran

Chrissie and Anthony Foster Parents of Emma, who died of a drug overdose and Katie, who became permanently disabled after being hit by a car, both girls were victims of Father Kevin O'Donnell

Kevin Larkins Corpus Christi seminarian and former priest

Dr Michael Leahy Corpus Christi seminarian and former priest

Loyola 'Roly' McKenzie Wife of former manager of the Eureka Pool

Pat Moran Friend and colleague of Wayne Brennan, who Brennan confided in regarding his abuse

Phil O'Donnell Former priest of the Melbourne Archdiocese, worked with Father Peter Searson and tried to expose him, confidant of child sexual abuse victims

Francis Sullivan CEO of the Catholic Church's Truth, Justice and Healing Council

Eileen Piper Mother of Stephanie, who suicided after charges were brought against the priest she said abused her

Associate Professor Carolyn Quadrio Psychiatrist specialising in child sexual abuse

Dr Brian Scarlett Former seminarian of Corpus Christi

Graeme Sleeman Former principal of Holy Family, Doveton, lost his career trying to expose paedophile priest Father Peter Searson

Kieran Tapsell Former NSW District Court Judge, writer on canon law

ACKNOWLEDGEMENTS

I wish to thank all of the people whose childhoods were blighted by clergy abuse who agreed to speak to me for this book. I shall be eternally grateful to them. To the families who have lost sons and daughters before their time, for whom every single day is a struggle. To the families of the living, who continue to pick up the pieces. To the good people of Ballarat who have given me endless hours of your time—Andrew, Peter, Deb, to name but three. Your commitment to righting the wrongs constantly inspires me. To the good priests who have shown me what Christianity is all about. To the excellent CCC Guys. To the good lawyers and the good cops who are trying so hard to get justice. To the victims' advocates, who have been so helpful to me and have such tireless dedication. To all the staff at the Royal Commission. To Andy Burns for your tenacity and your kind heart. To Sarah Curnow, Jo Puccini and Bruce Belsham at ABC TV for believing in this one and for your utter professionalism. To the fantastic team at MUP. To Mum for your listening ear and your support, and Dad for all those hours you put in. To my darling Nick and my beautiful children for enduring this for the past year or so of our lives. I love you to pieces.

BACK COVER MATERIAL

George Pell is the most recognisable face of the Australian Catholic Church. He was the Ballarat boy with the film-star looks who studied at Oxford and rose through the ranks to become the Vatican's indispensable 'Treasurer'. As an outspoken defender of church orthodoxy, 'Big George's' ascendancy within the clergy was remarkable and seemingly unstoppable.

The Royal Commission into Institutional Responses to Child Abuse has brought to light horrific stories about sexual abuse of the most vulnerable and provoked public anger at the extent of the cover-up. George Pell has always portrayed himself as the first man in the Church to tackle the problem. But questions about what the Cardinal knew, and when, have persisted.

The nation's most prominent Catholic is now the subject of a police investigation into allegations spanning decades that he too abused children. Louise Milligan is the only Australian journalist who has been privy to the most intimate stories of complainants.

She pieces together a series of disturbing pictures of the Cardinal's knowledge and his actions, many of which are being told here for the first time.

Conspiracy or cover-up? *Cardinal* uncovers uncomfortable truths about a culture of sexual entitlement, abuse of trust and how ambition can silence evil.

Louise Milligan is an investigative reporter for ABC TV's *7.30* and Four Corners. She has covered the Royal Commission into Institutional Responses to Child Abuse. Her exclusive stories on the allegations against George Pell won her two Quill Awards from the Melbourne Press Club, including the Gold Quill for best story of the year, the highest honour in Victorian journalism. Milligan is Irish-born and was raised a devoted Catholic.

Index

A
Abbott, Tony, *71, 171, 196, 199, 256*
Alexander, Denis, *216*
Allen, Andy, *438*
Annett, Peter, *509*
Anwyl twins, *546, 564*
Archer, FB, *14*
Artz, Corey, *536*
Arundell, Father, *310*
Ashton, Graham, *468, 652, 668, 670*
Auchettl, Paul, *562, 576*
'BAI' (witness), *387*

B
Baillieu, Ted, *251*
Baker, Wilfred 'Billy', *27*
Bales, Ted,
   see Dowlan, Edward 'Ted',
Ball, Richard, *151, 154*
Barnes, Ricky, *442*
Barrett, Bernard, *181, 204, 206*
Barrett, Shirley, *478*
Bathersby, John, *169*
Beetham, Vanessa, *305, 359, 361, 528*
Begg, David, *229, 231, 234*
Benedict XVI, Pope, *54, 229, 234, 235, 267*
Bergoglio, Jorge Mario,
   see Francis, Pope,
Best, Robert, *436, 446, 451, 542*
Bilos, Claire, *534*
Blenkiron, Peter, *729*
   at meeting with Pell, *527, 528*
   memories of Pell, *40, 42*
   on catharsis, *414, 415, 418*

on 'mental reservation', *377*
on Pell's disassociation, *257*
on Pell's failure to attend Royal Commission, *270, 276*
sees Pell as 'deliberately provocative', *309, 310*
Bolt, Andrew,
accuses ABC of bias, *634*
accuses author of bias, *567*
interviews with Pell, *25, 76, 315, 538, 718*
on Carson report, *468*
on Minchin, *274*
on Nolan, *391, 392*
on Pell's meeting with abuse victims, *530*
on Pell's 'sad story' comment, *523, 525*

Pell discusses Mulkearns with, *378*
reports on Royal Commission, *305, 306*
Bongiorno, Anthony Salvatore, *30, 31, 178*
Bongiorno, Paul, *30, 31, 290*
Bourke, Neil, *94, 96, 98*
'BPI' (witness), *318, 321*
Brady, Noel, *76, 78, 80, 82, 84, 112, 471*
Brambilla, Franco, *73, 110*
Brazier, Paul, *169*
Breen, Michael, *660, 670*
Breen, Terry, *672, 678, 680, 682, 684, 685*
Brennan, Barry, *415, 418, 430*
Brennan, Frank, *82, 246, 247*
Brennan, Joy,
on Sue Brennan's statement, *419, 422*

on Wayne Brennan, *415, 430, 432*
school fees waived by Loreto Convent, *426*
suspects police conspiracy, *442*
Brennan, Paul, *430, 432*
Brennan, Sue, *414, 415, 418, 419, 422, 424, 430, 441, 442, 443*
Brennan, Wayne, *411, 414, 415, 418, 419, 422, 424, 426, 428, 640*
Brophy, Tom, *301*
Bryant, Eric, *190, 395, 396, 400, 405*
Burke, Margaret Lillian, *14, 17*
Burke, Raymond, *726*
Burnard, Don, *59*
Burns, Andy, *556, 613, 615, 667, 713*
'BWA' (witness), *301*
'BWE' (witness), *654, 656*

C

Callahan, Bill, *471*
Carson, Kevin,
  Age obtains leaked report by, *249, 251*
contact with Operation Plangere limited, *462, 464, 466, 468*
investigates suicides by St Alipius ex-students, *446, 447, 450, 451*
Moran approaches, *436, 438, 441*
report to Royal Commission, *583*
Casey, Danny, *223, 226, 228*
Casey, Michael, *223, 226, 228*
Caulfield, Sergeant, *482*
Chamley, Wayne, *347, 408, 409*
Chapman, Penny, *54*

Chaput, Charles, *246*
Charlesworth, Max, *38*
Chernov, Alex, *138*
'Choirboy', The, *8, 689, 692, 693, 695, 697*
Claffey, Bob, *30*
Clancy, Edward, *52*
Coghlan, Gorgi, *274*
Collins, Andrew,
   early memories of Pell, *40*
   family connections with Pell, *424*
   on being an abuse survivor, *536, 538*
   on 'cab on the rank' comment, *257*
   on fighting the Church, *710, 712*
   on 'mental reservation', *377*
   on Paul Levey, *359*
   on Pell's credibility, *284, 392, 528*
   on Pell's lack of empathy, *497*
Collins, Paul, *56, 61*
Condon, Ben, *478, 480, 482*
Connell, Desmond, *375*
Connell, Paul, *117, 118, 121, 123, 729*
Connors, Peter, *134, 339, 340*
Costelloe, Timothy, *724*
Costigan, Michael, *35, 49, 50, 171, 378*
Costigan, Paul, *17, 18, 31*
Courtin, Judy, *100, 726*
Crowley, John, *265*
Crozier, Georgie, *251*
Cudmore, Gerry, *94, 96, 103, 136, 500*
Cunneen, Margaret, *253*
Curnow, Sarah, *608, 613*
Curran, Blake, *451, 456, 458*

Curran, Colleen, *451, 460, 462*
Curran, Peter, *450, 451, 454, 456, 458, 460*
Cushing, Donna, *324, 326, 328, 330, 332, 335, 336, 339, 340, 343, 527*

D

Dalzell, John, *221, 226, 228*
Day, Daven, *69, 149*
Day, John, *288, 290, 318*
Deakin, Hilton, *49, 86, 88, 90, 136, 495*
Devine, Miranda, *175, 214, 468*
Dignan, Damian, abused at St Alipius, *546, 585, 588, 590, 591, 593*
  appears on broadcast, *606*
  contacts Monument family, *581*
  memories of Pell, *552, 555, 556, 559, 560, 562*
  views of Pell, *576, 578*
Dooley, Alan, *506, 509*
Dowlan, Edward 'Ted', *257, 292, 415, 418, 419, 542*
Doyle, Adrian, *49, 52, 54*
Doyle, Geraldine, *59*
Doyle, Tom (canon lawyer), *377*
Doyle, Tom (priest), *505, 506*
'Duck Butt', *18*
Duggan, Aidan, *216, 219, 221*

E

Elliott, Peter, *38*
Ellis, John Andrew, *216, 219, 221, 223, 226, 228, 229, 231, 234*
Ellis, Nicola, *221*
Exell, Ted, *147, 149, 226*

F

Faine, Jon, *722*
Farrell, Stephen, *542*
Farrow, Ronan, *183*

Fasciale, Nazareno, *132, 134, 708, 710*
Faulkner, Len, *169, 171*
Finnigan, Brian,
  appears before Royal Commission, *265*
  Brophy passes information on to, *301*
  on attitude to child abuse among priests, *370, 372*
  on 'gossip' among priests, *317*
  response to Ridsdale accusations, *380, 383, 385, 387, 398*
Fiscalini, Leo,
  approached about Mortlake, *383, 385*
  death of, *366*
  response to Ridsdale accusations, *301, 303, 310, 312*
  role in Pell's life, *14*
Fisher, Anthony, *724*
Fitzgerald, Gerald Leo, *450, 542*
Flynn, John, *94*
Foley, Michael, *181, 200, 202, 204*
Fontana, Steve, *482*
Foster, Chrissie and Anthony,
  Carelink service and, *151, 154, 155, 157, 159*
  dealings with Pell, *78*
  decline to attend meeting with Pell, *525, 527*
  make Salvano statement public, *88, 90*
  on the courage of whistleblowers, *261*
Foster, Emma and Katie, *78, 90, 154, 155*
Fowler, Andrew, *169*
Fox, Peter, *251, 253*

Fragonard, Jean-Honoré, *17*
Francis, Pope,
  accession of encourages recruitment, *125*
  chooses Pell to reform Vatican finances, *49*
  estimates, *4* per cent of priests paedophiles, *132*
  meets with Pell, *297*
  moves Vatican away from hard line, *726, 728, 729*
Fraser, Jane, *171, 173*
Free, Stephen, *482, 484*
Freeman, James, *52*
Furness, Gail,
  examines Finnigan, *372*
  on consultors' meeting, *406*
  on David Ridsdale, *536*
  on failure to report paedophilia, *310, 312, 315*
  on Father Walshe, *533*
  on Little's resignation, *110*
  on 'magic wand' comment, *346*
  on Paul Levey, *355, 357, 359, 361, 363, 366, 368*
  on Pell's alleged comment, *656*
  on Pell's failure to take responsibility, *513, 515*
  on Pell's role in administration, *278, 280, 282, 284, 286*
  on Ridsdale case, *301, 303, 321, 322, 387, 389, 391, 395, 396, 398*
  on 'sad story' comment, *306*
  on Searson case, *491, 493, 495, 497, 499, 500, 504*

on St Alipius case, *290, 292, 294*
submission to Royal Commission, *482, 484, 720*

G
Gatto, Mick, *646, 648*
Gillard, Julia, *249, 253, 256*
Gilroy, Norman, *52*
Gleeson, Jeff, *159*
Glennon, Michael, *27, 200*
Goldsmith, Paul, *30*
Graafmans, Michael,
  see Breen, Michael,
Grant, Genevieve, *103*
Green, Tim, *292, 415*
'H' (witness), *200, 202*

H
Harrison, Donna,
  see Cushing, Donna,
Harrison, Mark, *324, 335, 336, 339, 340, 527, 528*
Harrison, Sean, *335, 336*
Harrison, Simon, *335*
Hart, Denis,
contacts with Pell, *272*
cuts off funding for Pickering, *104*
early memories of Pell, *25, 27*
effect on Melbourne diocese, *125*
in Searson case, *504, 511, 513, 519*
in Walshe case, *534*
'manages' Maguire out of church, *183, 188*
on Eileen Piper, *100*
on 'lost' Catholics, *239*
petitioned for apology, *724*

Henderson, Gerard, *670*
Hersbach, Paul, *157, 159, 162*
Hersbach, Tony, *157*
Hinch, Derryn, *200, 357*
Hinchey, Margaret, *166*
Hodgens, Eric,
  debates Pell in The Swag, *239*
  on Little and Pell, *110*
  on O'Collins and Pell, *38*
  on Pell's political skills, *42*
  on Pell's promotion, *44*
  viewed as a liberal, *54*
Hoffman, Philip Seymour, *411*
Howard, John, *73, 171, 196, 199*

I
Irwin, Ingrid, *538, 593, 595, 598, 600, 602, 604, 606, 705*

J
Jabara, Richard, *30*
'John' (The Choirboy's father), *693, 695, 697, 702, 705, 708*
John Paul II, Pope,
  election of, *44, 47, 49*
  involved in Pell appointments, *110, 214*
  Pastores Dabo Vobis exhortation, *118*
  Statement of Conclusions, *169*
  Veritatis Splendor encyclical, *63*
John the Apostle, *540*
John XXIII, Pope, *35*
Jones, Tony, *251, 253*

K
Kant, Immanuel, *687*
Kelly, Michael, *66, 67*
Kelly, Paul, *256*

Kennett, Jeff, *128, 131*
'Kid', The, *2, 4, 6, 8, 629, 640, 687, 689, 692, 693, 695, 697, 700, 702, 704, 705, 708, 710, 712, 713, 716, 718*
Kiss, Vincent, *188*

L

Laidler, Terry, *40, 106*
Lalor, Norm, *491, 493*
Larkins, Kevin, *18, 21, 23, 25, 27, 31*
Latimore, Darren, *84*
Laurie, Meshel, *274*
Leahy, Michael,
  at Propaganda Fide university, *33, 35*
  on Pell as administrator, *123, 125*
  on Pell's vulnerability, *716*
  on seminary life, *18, 21, 23, 25, 190, 191*
Leder, Richard, *86, 154, 155, 650, 652, 654, 658*
Lee, Katrina, *650, 718*
Levey, Beverley, *357*
Levey, Paul,
  abused by Ridsdale, *353, 355, 357, 359*
  attempts suicide, *409*
  confronts Finnigan, *383*
  declines meeting with Pell, *525*
  Finnigan aware Ridsdale living with, *372*
  on meeting with Pell, *276*
  on Pell's credibility, *368*
Little, Frank,
  acts to remove van Suylen, *505*
  as Archbishop of Melbourne, *47, 49*
  aware of complaints against Fasciale, *136*
  favours Third Rite of Reconciliation, *169*

informed of O'Donnell case, *88, 90*

Pell's relations with, *109, 110, 493*

Livingstone, Tess, *14, 38, 47, 117*

Lockett, Tony, *171*

M

Madden, Frank, *310, 398, 654, 656*

Maguire, Bob, *183, 186, 188, 190, 191, 194, 199, 648*

Mahon, Peter, *117*

Mann, Colette, *56, 61*

Mannix, Daniel, *14*

Marr, David, *117*

'Mary' (The Choirboy's mother), *689, 692, 693, 695, 697, 700, 702, 704, 705, 708, 710, 712, 713, 716*

Matheson, Peter, *125*

McAleese, Mary, *241, 243*

McAteer, Phillip, *415, 450, 451*

McCann, Paul, *228*

McCarthy, Joanne, *253*

McClellan, Peter,
on church's definition of 'paedophilia', *400, 402*
on church's responsibility to protect, *504*
on 'gossip' among priests, *391*
on Pell's relations with Mulkearns, *321, 340*
on Ridsdale case, *312, 315, 317, 406, 408*
response to Myers application, *265, 267*

McGarvie, Richard, *131, 132*

McGauran, Peter, *59, 61*

McGloin, Michael, *221*

McGrath, Kathleen 'Kate', *321, 347, 350, 351, 389*

McGuire, Frank, *251, 484, 488*
McKenzie, Father, *310*
McKenzie, Graeme and Loyola, *550, 567*
McMillan, Kate, *199*
Melican, Bill, *288, 312, 317, 322*
Milligan, Louise (author), *114*
Minchin, Tim, *264, 272, 274*
'Miss Karen' (teacher), *583, 585*
Mitchell, Neil, *668*
Monument, Lyndon,
  abuse allegations at St Alipius, *540, 542, 544, 546, 548, 550, 552, 555, 556, 559, 560, 562, 564, 567, 568, 570, 572, 575*
  criminal record of, *634*
  friendship with Dignan, *588*
  informed of Pell's activities, *581*
  sees children beaten for making accusations, *638, 640*
  Taskforce SANO interviews, *593, 595, 598, 600, 602, 604*
Mooney, Col, *305*
Mooney, Darren,
  attends class reunions, *644*
  compensation case against Christian Brothers, *544*
  credibility of as witness, *631*
  on Dignan, *590*
  on Eureka Pool activities, *550, 570, 572*
Mooney, Peter, *568, 570*
Moran, Pat, *419, 432, 434, 436, 438, 441, 442, 590*
Morris, Bill,
  asked to resign by Papal representative, *246, 247*

on changing attitudes to church, *728, 729*
on Pell's ambition, *52*
on Pell's approach to administration, *71, 145, 147, 149*
Morrison, Andrew, *226*
'Mrs C' (witness), *204*
Mulkearns, Ronald,
  aware of paedophilia at St Patrick's, *294*
  becomes Bishop of Ballarat, *42*
  Costigan stands up for, *378, 380*
  Day praised by, *290*
  death of, *366*
  fails to report abuse at Mortlake, *350, 351, 353, 385, 387, 389*
  heads Special Issues Committee, *140*
  in Ridsdale case, *286, 288, 297, 299, 301, 303, 357, 392, 395*
  on consultors' committee, *310, 312*
  Pell claims he was deceived by, *317, 318, 321, 363, 370, 372*
  Pell writes to about his role, *282*
Mulvale, Gerard, *92, 94, 98, 100*
Murnane, Paul, *454, 456*
Murphy, Gerard and David, *546, 562, 564*
Murphy, Glynn, *359*
Myers, Allan, *265, 267*

N

Nangle, Paul, *294*
Naughtin, Patrick, *294*
Nolan, Henry 'Hank',

administers St Patrick's Cathedral, *656*
attends Corpus Christi, *25*
helps remove Paul Levey from Ridsdale, *357, 389*
Pell not informed of abuse by, *366, 391, 392, 495*

Noonan, Paul, *149*

O

O'Byrne, Xavier (pseudonym), *173*
O'Callaghan, Peter,
  at Melbourne Response launch, *138*
  investigates Piper case, *98, 100*
  refers abuse cases to police, *468*
  relations with abuse victims, *154, 157, 159, 161, 488, 519*
O'Collins, James, *17, 33, 38, 361*
O'Connor, Chris, *644, 646*
O'Donnell, Kevin, *78, 80, 82, 84, 86, 88, 90*
O'Donnell, Phil, *106, 109, 112*
O'Farrell, Barry, *251*
Olle, Andrew, *63, 66*
O'Neill, Sharon, *67, 69*
O'Toole, Lawrence, *292, 368*
Ouellet, Marc, *726*

P

Packer, Frank, *71*
Packer, Kerry, *71*
Palmer, Gerard, *511*
Paul the Apostle, *523*
Paul VI, Pope, *267*
Pell, David, *14*
Pell, George,
  alleged abuse by, *178, 179, 181, 183, 186, 188, 190, 191, 194, 196, 199, 550, 552, 555, 556, 559, 560, 562, 564, 567, 568, 570, 572, 575, 576, 578, 579, 581, 583, 585, 650, 652, 654, 670, 672, 674,*

676, 680, 682, 684, 702, 704, 705, 708, 710
alleged comment on Ridsdale, *654, 656, 658*
alleged indecent exposure by, *608, 610, 613, 615, 617, 619, 621, 623, 625, 627, 629, 631, 634, 636*
alleged obstruction of justice, *173, 175*
allegedly witnesses child abuse, *458, 460*
as Archbishop of Melbourne, *106, 109, 110, 114, 117, 118, 128, 131, 132*
as Auxiliary Bishop of Melbourne, *47, 49, 50, 52, 54, 82, 84*
as Metropolitan Archbishop of Sydney, *171, 173*
as rector for Corpus Christi, *44, 47*
at Fasciale funeral, *134, 136, 138, 710*
at Propaganda Fide university, *33, 35, 38*
attends Corpus Christi College, *17, 18, 21, 23*
attitude to homosexuality, *164, 166*
becomes Cardinal, *216*
Brady warned by, *80, 82*
Carson investigations and, *468*
Catholic Youth Day organised by, *234, 235*
charitable work, *49, 50*

Corpus Christi staff and, *117, 118, 121, 123*
directs Aquinas College, *42*
early life, *10, 13, 14, 17, 25*
edits Light magazine, *42*
eulogy for Santamaria, *73*
Eureka Pool attendances, *42*
evidence on Ridsdale case, *276, 278, 280, 282, 284, 286, 288, 290, 292, 294, 297, 299, 301, 303, 305, 306, 309, 310, 312, 315, 317, 318, 321, 322, 340, 343, 355, 359, 361, 363, 366, 368, 372, 383, 385, 387, 389, 391, 392, 395, 396, 398, 400, 402, 405, 406, 408, 530, 533, 534*
evidence on Searson case, *484, 487, 488, 491, 493, 495, 497, 499, 500, 504, 505, 506, 509, 511, 513, 515, 517, 519*
friendship with Bongiorno, *31*
heads Project Compassion, *49, 50*
ideological views, *235, 237, 239, 241, 243*
in Brennan case, *422, 424, 426, 428*
in Curran case, *451, 458, 460*
in Ellis case, *216, 219, 221, 223, 226, 228, 229, 231, 234*
in Foster case, *155, 157, 159*
in O'Donnell case, *78, 86, 88, 90, 92*
in Pickering case, *103, 104*
in Piper case, *92, 94, 96, 98, 100, 103*
in St Alipius case, *542, 544, 546, 548*
influence in Ballarat, *38, 40*
meets abuse survivors, *525, 527, 528, 530*

Melbourne Response to child abuse, *136, 138, 140, 142, 145, 147, 149, 151, 154*
on defining paedophilia, *400, 402, 405*
police investigations of, *270, 272*
Pope Francis's relations with, *726, 728*
reaction to Royal Commission, *256, 257, 260, 261*
relations with subordinates, *243, 246, 247*
response to allegations against, *660, 662, 664, 667, 713, 716, 718*
Ridsdale shares presbytery with, *40*
Scarlett photographs, *33, 69*
Southwell Inquiry clears, *199, 200, 202, 204, 206, 208, 210, 212, 214*
studies at Oxford, *38*
television and radio appearances, *54, 56, 59, 61, 63, 66, 67, 69, 76*
unable to attend Royal Commission hearings, *264, 265, 267, 270, 272, 274, 276*
Pell, George Senior, *14*
Pell, Margaret Lillian, *14, 17*
Pickering, Ronald, *103, 104*
Pidoto, Terrence, *27, 30*
Piper, Eileen, *92, 94, 96, 98, 100, 103, 724*
Piper, Stephanie, *92, 94, 96, 98*
Pius XI, Pope, *377, 378*
Polisca, Patrizio, *265, 267*
Pope, Gladys, *656*

Power, Pat, *52, 142, 164, 166*
Price, Steve, *274*

Q
Quadrio, Carolyn, *432, 634, 636, 638, 640, 642, 644, 697*
Quin, Michael, *478, 480*

R
Rae, David, *593, 664*
Ratzinger, Joseph Alois,
   see Benedict XVI, Pope,
Rayner, Brian, *231*
Richter, Robert, *646, 648*
Ridsdale, David, *173, 530, 533, 534, 538*
Ridsdale, Dominic 'Nick', *422*
Ridsdale, Gerald,
   abuses Rob Walsh, *542*
   at Corpus Christi College, *27*
   at Edenhope, *326, 328, 330, 332, 335, 336, 339, 340, 343*
   at Mortlake, *346, 347, 350, 351, 353, 355, 357, 359, 380, 383, 385*
   at St Alipius, *40, 290*
   Pell accompanies into court, *136*
   Pell's alleged reference to, *654, 656*
   public allegations against, *173, 299, 301, 303, 305, 306, 309, 310, 312, 315, 317, 318, 321, 322*
   sent for psychological treatment, *286, 288*
Ring, Brother, *434*
Roach, John, *533, 534*
Robinson, Geoffrey,
   in Scott case, *194*
   Pell's relations with, *175, 178, 235, 239, 241, 246*

runs Towards Healing scheme, *138, 140, 142, 145, 147, 149, 378*

Rowbotham, Lauren,
  corroborates Eureka Pool story, *564, 567*
  on Lyndon Monument, *602*
  on 'Miss Karen', *583, 585*
  on Pell's hearing confessions, *555, 556*
  targeted for school beltings, *546*

Rubeo, Victor, *157*

Rushton, Stephen, *221*

Ryan, Angela, *142, 175, 194, 206*

Ryan, Ann, *350, 454, 456*

Ryan, Denis, *464*

Ryan, Paul David, *103*

'S' (altar boy), *219, 221, 234*

S

Sallie, Richard, *267, 270*

Salvano, Father John, *86, 88, 90*

Santamaria, Bartholomew Augustine, *14, 38, 71, 73*

Scarlett, Brian, *17, 23, 31, 33, 69*

Scola, Angelo, *726*

Scott, Phil,
  Bob Maguire discusses, *183*
  claims abuse by Pell, *178, 179, 559, 560*
  meets author, *648, 650*
  seeks apology from Pell, *640*
  treatment of abuse claims by, *191, 194, 196, 199, 200, 202, 204, 206, 208, 210, 212*

Searson, Peter,
  allowed to stay in post, *112*

arrest, resignation and death, *517, 519, 520*

church's reaction to abuse claims against, *495, 497, 499, 500, 504, 505, 506, 509, 511, 513, 515, 517, 519, 520*

confronts Stewart at Doveton, *157, 487, 488*

list of grievances about from parents, *491*

Stewart abused by, *472, 474, 476, 478*

Sebastian, Guy, *235*
Sher, Jeff, *199, 202, 204*
Siewert, Rachel, *720*
'Sister Colleen', *478, 480*
Sleeman, Graeme, *478, 489, 504, 505, 517, 519*
Southwell, Alec J, *175, 200, 202, 204, 206, 208, 210, 212, 716*
Stack, Dorothea, *509*
Stack, Simon, *509*
Steinbeck, John, *17*
Stekelenburg, John, *418, 419*
Stewart, Angus, *155, 317, 322*
Stewart, Julie, abused by Searson, *157, 472, 474, 476, 478*

reaction to abuse, *478, 480, 482, 484, 487, 488, 489*

reaction to Pell's evidence, *305, 517, 519, 520*

Sullivan, Francis, *161, 162, 260, 466, 468, 722, 724*
Swan, Wayne, *256*
Swift, Jonathan, *216*

T

Tapsell, Kieran, *377*
Tatchell, Paul, *581*
'The Choirboy', *8, 689, 692, 693, 695, 697*
'The Kid', *2, 4, 6, 8, 640, 687, 689, 692, 693, 695, 697, 700, 702, 704, 705, 708, 710, 712*
Tomasi, Silvano, *402*

Toomey, Kevin, *92, 96, 98*
Torpy, Dan, *301, 303, 310*
Tovey, Michael, *210*
Tyack, Les, *572, 608, 613, 615, 617, 619, 621, 623, 625, 627, 629, 631*

U

Uren, Bill, *63, 69, 71, 147, 149*

V

Vagg, Patricia, *350, 351, 389*
van Suylen, John, *505*
Veniamin, Andrew, *648*

W

Waller, Vivian 'Viv', *251, 326, 339, 724, 726*
Walsh, Damien, *446*
Walsh, Martin, *446, 447*
Walsh, Noel, *446, 447*
Walsh, Rob, *446, 458, 542*
Walshe, John, *530, 533, 534*
Ward, Peter, *199, 210, 648*
Whelan, Michael, *241, 243, 246*
Wilde, Oscar, *581*
Williams, Sue, *186*
Withoos, Mark, *527*

www.ingramcontent.com/pod-product-compliance
Lightning Source LLC
Chambersburg PA
CBHW070902300426
44113CB00008B/920